THE LANGUAGE ARTS

A Pragmatic Approach

THE LANGUAGE ARTS

A Pragmatic Approach

Dewey Woods Chambers
University of the Pacific
and
Heath Ward Lowry
University of the Pacific

wcb

WM. C. BROWN COMPANY PUBLISHERS

Dubuque, Iowa

Photographs taken at Tully C. Knoles School, Stockton,
California by Leonard L. Eiger.

Copyright © 1975 by Wm. C. Brown Company Publishers

Library of Congress Catalog Card Number: 74–14443

ISBN 0–697–06005–5

Printed in the United States of America

CONTENTS

INTRODUCTION

Language is a phenomenon that is unique to the human species. It is one of the major variables that takes the human from the ranks of lower animals, denotes him as a rational creature, and places him on a pinnacle above all other animals. Ideas and languages are inseparable. Communication of ideas and the subsequent embellishment and improvement of those ideas demand the medium of language. Anthropologists and historians tell us that man's whole adventure on earth and his creation of successively higher civilizations have been largely a result of man's ability to generate ideas and to communicate them. Without question, language is, and has been, a major factor in the development of man as the supreme earthling.

As teachers of the young, we know the importance of language development in the children we strive to teach. We know that language is the very heart of the learning syndrome. Without effective language and language skills, learning is retarded at best. Most learning problems stem from the inability of the learner to cope with language. This is a reasonable assumption, since language is the major vehicle of learning.

Educators have long been concerned with the intricacies of language, and how to best utilize it for effective teaching and learning. The modern educator continues and enhances that tradition. He knows that acquisition of effective language skills is essential if the learner is to move successfully through his school experiences. He is convinced that the key to the lock of learning is mastery of the language.

Research in language (and it is a vast and an enormous field) is impressive if not staggering! Tomes and volumes exist, reporting research findings, theories, professional opinions, methodology, and all manner of knowledge concerning language. This body of knowledge is a healthy adolescent. It promises to grow into a mature adult capable of greatly enhancing man's instinct to improve his condition. It is a body of knowledge that is vital and essential to the classroom teacher who seeks to help the child's language grow, and thus his ability to learn. It needs to be understood, however, that this body of knowledge is still in adolescence and, as such, it will grow and change. The next few decades promise a near revolution in all curriculum areas, language-learning being its major thrust. The only constant in these decades may well be that of change.

Today's professional teacher and tomorrow's practitioner of that art need the skills, the controls, the understandings, and the knowledge of teaching more than any group of educators has ever needed them before. Modern education is making more demands of its students and teachers now than at anytime in history. The modern teacher needs to be a "professional" in its absolute sense! Becoming that professional teacher takes years of preparation and years of practice. The acquisition of the skills, controls, understandings, and knowledge that create a professional teacher is, and should be, a full-time occupation.

This book is designed to aid the student of teaching and the professional teacher to gain some needed insights into one aspect of the profession, the successful teaching of the skills of language to the young child. It seeks to synthesize theory and research into a workable theme to aid the teacher in the art of teaching language and the language skills.

The authors, both elementary teachers for many years and both professors of the language arts at the university level, have designed this book in a somewhat unique fashion. They have sought to be both theoretical and pragmatic. They have attempted to offer theory, then go beyond that theory to practical application in a classroom setting. Each segment of this book offers illustrative teaching strategies, sample lesson plans, and expanded activities that will carry the concepts of this book from the theoretical level to the level of active application.

The Language Arts: A Pragmatic Approach is based upon developmental language theory. The authors purport that language is learned in successive layers or steps. It is their contention that one level of language attainment is contingent upon another, that basic foundations must be built before the language structure will indeed stand. For this reason, the book is divided into four sections, each considering a basic language vocabulary while discussing the ramifications for teaching and building for the next successive vocabulary. Part I deals with the listening vocabulary as the basic vocabulary for all language skills. Part II is concerned with the next phase of language development, that of the speaking vocabulary. Building upon the listening and speaking vocabularies, Part III explores the intricacies of the third level of language-learning, the reading vocabulary. Part IV moves to the last, and most sophisticated of the language skills, the writing vocabulary. These sections are divided into the natural progression of language development.

The authors believe that in dealing with this holistic language approach, the teacher will appreciate not only a pragmatic point of view, but an eclectic philosophy as well. Too often, to the woe of the teacher, it "looks good on paper" only to fail in actual practice. The election of theory and method featured in this book has been submitted, as much as possible, to the ulimate test, actual empirical research in real classroom situations. Little is contained in this volume that has not been successfully utilized by teachers. Thus, in writing this book, the authors have placed theory and practical application in juxtaposition. This concept may not be a new idea, but it has been handled here in a different, and hopefully more effective, way.

Language growth is a natural part of the child's maturation. That fact is a major principle in this book. *The Language Arts: A Pragmatic Approach* is an effort to help the classroom teacher understand how to work effectively with the child's maturational patterns and to develop with him an effective language system.

THE DEVELOPMENT
OF LANGUAGE
THROUGH LISTENING

LISTENING,
THE FIRST VOCABULARY
THE THEORETICAL APPROACH

The entire, complicated, mulifaceted system of language-learning is based upon the human's ability to listen. A child's first contact with language is what he hears. He develops his whole system of language communication upon what his listening environment provides. All of his vocabularies—his speaking vocabulary, his reading vocabulary, and his writing vocabulary—are based upon this first vocabulary, his listening vocabulary. Without the basic, first listening vocabulary, the child's entire language development will be blighted.

The beginnings of language are imitative. The child in his crib hears sounds and learns to respond to them. He knows the sound of his mother's voice and his father's voice and is able to interpret from those sounds the amount of love and security that surround him. He can, in the same sense, interpret hostility and rejection from the world of sound around him. Among his first impressions of the world outside the womb is the world of sound.

As the infant matures, he too makes sounds. He expresses happiness, anger, contentment, joy, hunger, fear, alarm, and all the rest with nonlanguage sounds. He cries, laughs, gurgles, and coos. It is not at all unusual for a mother to interpret those nonlanguage sounds and to know what they mean. Mothers will often understand the hunger cry and differentiate it from the anger cry. The giggle and gurgle of the infant will be interpreted too and will receive a response. With each response, the child learns to sort out the vocal stimulus that causes it. He soon learns that sounds have meaning and he utilizes these sounds to meet certain basic needs.

As he gurgles, coos, cries, laughs, and in other ways practices vocal play, he is encouraged. The tending adult plays with him and talks to him, conversing in a way with his vocal play. He hears sounds coming from the adult, sounds in the form of language.

As he matures and his vocal play continues, helping his mouth and tongue muscles to develop, he attempts to imitate the sounds he hears. The first utterance or two are most likely accidental. The word "mama," due to its ease of articulation, is likely to be part of his vocal play. Its utterance may cause such a reaction from the mother that he learns the sound "mama" will get additional positive attention each time he uses it. He soon makes the connection that the sound "mama," and the tending adult who cares for him, feeds him, and loves him, are one and the same. An important step in language development has been made.[1]

Soon other vocal-object connections are made. He hears words that stand for items and objects he wants. "Daddy," "water," "Kitty," and other ideas or objects soon take on meaning. He imitates what he hears and relates what he hears to certain objects. He learns the names of objects by imitating the sounds that the adult uses to identify them.

As he continues to grow and mature, his needs and wants become more and more sophisticated and complex. One word utterances, often accompanied by physical movement as a way of communicating, give way to the need for a pattern of words to more clearly express his needs. He again depends upon imitation of the language sounds he hears in his language environment. If his language environment is rich, if language is used around him, and if he is given ample opportunity to attempt oral communication with guidance, he will soon compose simple sentences to express needs, to ask questions, or to relate his wants. He learns that language is a functioning life tool. He learns to use that tool by listening and by attempting to recreate what he hears to satisfy himself.

If, on the other hand, the language environment is a poor one, where language used by adult models is limited or the language used with the child is a series of one word commands, vocal nonlanguage utterances, or the like, his opportunity to develop a listening vocabulary and thus a speaking vocabulary is considerably lacking. The probability is high that subsequent attempts at reading and writing will meet with minimum success or even failure. It is essential to language growth that a youngster have a good listening vocabulary as a base for his further language development.[2]

PRESCHOOL EXPERIENCES WITH LANGUAGE

Language-learning, to be effective, must depend upon the development of subsequent vocabularies. From listening, vocabularies develop for speech, reading,

1. Dora V. Smith, "Developmental Language Patterns of Children," in *Elementary School Language Arts: Selected Readings*, ed. Paul C. Burns (Chicago, Ill.: Rand-McNally & Co., 1969), pp. 64–77.
2. Harry A. Greene and Walter T. Petty, *Developing Language Skills in the Elementary Schools*, 4th ed. (Boston: Allyn & Bacon, Inc., 1971), pp. 157–161.

and writing. One cannot effectively build toward language proficiency in one without the preceding vocabulary being firm.

The preschool or kindergarten teacher knows the importance of the child's language environment before he comes to school. She knows that the child is interacting with a new world and is attempting to cope with it. One of the tools he uses to understand and sort out aspects of that world is language.

The preschool teacher, be she in a nursery program, a Head Start project, or other preschool activity, knows that children often come to her with a limited language background. Some, in fact, come with what is apparently no background in that they often cannot or will not speak. They will make their needs known and felt with nonlanguage utterances, physical activity, or kinetics (body language) such as pointing, grasping, and pushing.

Others, of course, come into preschool with a well-developed language background and are able to cope quite well linguistically in their new environment. They are able to communicate easily with the teacher concerning all manner of needs, likes, dislikes, and wishes. They are capable and eager to share experiences with other children of like language proficiency. Language development for these youngsters in a preschool kindergarten situation is often rapid and most rewarding.

Why do children come into a preschool or kindergarten situation with so much variation in their ability to communicate? Why are some children able to "chatter like magpies" and move rapidly into reading readiness and beyond, while others sit, remain silent, and fall behind in school activities? The answers to these questions are not simple and cannot be adequately handled in a book of this nature. However, certain patterns seem to emerge when children come into a preschool or kindergarten experience and do not respond positively to its stimulus. Some children have been born with more native ability than others and are able to learn with greater ease. Some, because of various physiological circumstances, have not matured as rapidly as others and simply are not physically or emotionally "ready" for the experiences offered them. Others cannot cope effectively in a preschool or kindergarten experience because of a home environment that has not given them adequate preparation to meet the needs of an organized, group-learning situation. Most often that poor home environment manifests itself in language development. The child does not have the ability to speak and thus is hindered in most of his preschool activities. Most likely the youngster does not have an adequate listening vocabulary from which speech is a natural growth. His home environment did not provide him with sufficient and adequate models of language that could serve in the development of a listening vocabulary and provide the necessary background stimulation for imitation.[3]

---

3. Alvina Burrows et al., *New Horizons in the Language Arts* (New York: Harper & Row, 1972), pp. 4–5.

This is especially true of the so-called culturally deprived or disadvantaged youngster. Many times he comes into a preschool or kindergarten situation from an environment that has not provided a good language background, in that the language pattern at home has been one that consists of one word commands or nonspeech utterances. He has not had a language model to help him to develop a listening vocabulary. Therefore, he has a very limited speaking vocabulary, if indeed one exists at all. If, in his early school experiences, he is expected to respond to reading readiness or actual instruction in beginning reading, his inability to cope is understandable.

The teacher who finds a youngster in her preschool or kindergarten class with a limited listening vocabulary needs to develop a program that will improve or rectify that situation. She needs to plan a program that will develop the child's listening vocabulary so that his speaking and subsequent vocabularies can develop.[4]

What kind of activities can a preschool or kindergarten teacher plan that will aid in developing this all-important listening vocabulary? What kinds of experiences can be engineered in a classroom for very young children that will cause them to listen and attempt response? An experienced, successful, preschool teacher can list many individual exercises that offer children reasons to listen and speak. They seem to fall into the following categories.

A shared extraschool experience. This kind of activity provides a common experience for the entire group. It provides a time for the youngster to "intake"— to listen, to look, and to expand his experiences outside the classroom. Activities such as a walk through the school grounds, a walk through the neighborhood, or an excursion to the supermarket, the dairy farm, or other planned outings are examples of this kind of an experience. The teacher guides and talks to the group, identifies specifics, points out various areas and objects of interest, always providing children with opportunities to listen, to look, and to respond. New words, new ideas, and new concepts are pointedly emphasized. These extraschool experiences are then brought back into the classroom or wherever the group meets, and are discussed or retold by the teacher. Lots of language is used. Language that is meaningful, explicit, and pertinent to the experience shared. The teacher helps the youngsters to summarize, to attempt language that will recreate the shared experience.

A shared in-school experience. This activity, as is the case with extraschool experience discussed above, provides a common experience for the children from which language learning will generate. Such activities as the care and feeding of classroom pets (hamsters, mice, birds, turtles, etc.), growing a classroom

4. Paul M. Hollingsworth, "Teaching Listening in the Elementary School," in *Language Arts in the Elementary School: Readings,* ed. Hal D. Funk and DeWayne Triplett (Philadelphia, Penn.: J. B. Lippincott Co., 1972), pp. 267–268.

garden (can be done indoors in a "nursery flat"), preparing simple foods, and the like, exemplify this kind of experience. These projects require directions from the teacher to the students, opportunities to observe and discuss observations, and in-group sharing—all requiring the use of language. Models of language are evident to the child so that he can hear, understand, and recreate that language.

Opportunities for dramatic play. A youngster with a retarded listening vocabulary can develop and expand that vocabulary not only by teacher led experiences, but also by interacting in a rich language experience with his peer group. One of the best techniques for peer group language exchange is in play experiences. Dramatic play describes that activity in which children act out in an informal, unstructured way certain familiar, usually adult, roles. Playing "house" with toy dishes, dolls, and appropriate paraphernalia is a fine example of this kind of play activity. Children playing cars or trucks, airport, or with other mechanical toys are other examples of this kind of play. When children play at these activities, conversation is a necessary part of the action. An active language environment is created, and the vocabulary expands.

Experience with children's literature. One of the most familiar, "tried and true" ways of helping children develop a good listening vocabulary is by providing a continuing exposure to children's literature. With good children's literature read orally by the teacher, both familiar and new words are put into the context of a good story. Listening, of course, is the key to an experience of this kind. As the story unfolds, listening becomes, as it must, an active experience. Children will listen and listen again to favorite and familiar stories. Often, when these books are placed back on the library table or library shelves, children will "read" them again by telling the story to themselves as they turn the pages.

The picture book or picture-storybook (E. J. Keats' *The Snowy Day, Goggles, A Chair for Peter;* L. Ward's *The Biggest Bear;* Dr. Seuss's *To Think That I Saw it on Mulberry Street,* among many others are good examples of this kind of book) is probably the best kind of material to present to the preschool or kindergarten youngster. This kind of literary selection is valuable for this age group in that it is a twice-told tale, told once in text and once in illustration. As the teacher reads, she should show the pictures to the children to enhance their understanding of the story being offered. These pictures, of course, lend themselves well to the "rereading" that children will often do on their own. Few ways of helping children develop their listening vocabularies are more effective than rich listening experiences with children's literature.

Group oral sharing of experiences. Children will often listen to each other with more attention than they will listen to an adult. This is one of the major reasons that a good preschool or kindergarten teacher will provide many opportunities to "share-and-tell." So many times one hears an experienced teacher of the very young say "if we can just get them to open up and talk, the rest will follow." This is probably very true. By listening to each other's experiences, descriptions of toys and objects, and by attempting a like oral offering, beginning language will grow. An informal, individualized chance for children to listen to each other and talk to each other as a regular part of the day's program will many times pay handsome rewards to the child's listening vocabulary.

Needless to say, the creative teacher can develop many modifications from these five idea clusters. The major thrust should be, however, a rich language environment where children can, and are encouraged, to listen and to recreate what they hear in the form of speech. A good preschool or kindergarten classroom is not a quiet place. It is a place where language is used. Listening demands that something be heard. It is our job as teachers of the young to make what is heard valuable, immediate, exciting, and relevant to the young child's world.

DIALECT AND LANGUAGE PATTERNS

Children learn to speak by imitating what they hear. If what they hear when they are developing their listening vocabulary is a dialectic speech pattern from the Deep South, the Northeast, the Midwest, the Southeast, or the Far West, that is the dialect style they will probably adopt as their own. Family dialect and peer group dialect do affect the child's own style. Even after the child has developed a workable listening vocabulary and a speech pattern based on that first vocabulary, he often will change or modify his speech pattern by what is heard in a new listening environment. Children moving from one region of the United States to another frequently adopt the dialect of the new region, or modify greatly the dialect they learned earlier when they find themselves in a new dialectic region. This is not surprising when we consider that speech is made mainly from what is heard.

Speech authorities wondered if regional American dialects would become less pronounced with the advent of radio, television, and other mass media presenting a "Standard American Dialect." Speech experts in England had the same concern about the multitude of dialects spoken throughout the British Isles. Would the regional dialects disappear, and a standard dialect replace them? Their concern, at this time at least, seems unfounded. Regional dialects continue and flourish. Children still seem to learn language patterns, or at least dialect patterns, better from their immediate environment than from a secondary source such as mass media.

Most authorities in the field believe that a regional dialect is the right and privilege of the persons living within a region. It is a part of their self-concept, their individuality. A teacher working in a dialectic community different from her own is ill-advised to foist her dialect as preferable. One needs only to imagine one's own reaction to an Oxford-trained teacher telling us that our dialect is incorrect, that "Oxford Speech" is the correct one, and that we must work to attain it. A dialect pattern is best left alone.[5]

---

5. Walter Loban, "Teaching Children Who Speak Social Class Dialects," *Elementary English,* May 1968, pp. 592–599.

Language patterns other than dialects are another matter. Children imitate, along with dialects, the structure of the language they hear. They learn through listening to models the way words are strung together to make ideas and sentences. Grammar, correct and incorrect, also is learned by a young child as he imitates the language environment in which he finds himself. To a large extent, he learns syntax, structure, linguistic sets, and form and usage from his home and peer group language environment. These he uses as a part of his life tools. Many children come into a school situation with these well set and operating.

If the youngster comes from a rich, positive language environment, where superior American English is used as a model for his imitation, all is likely to be well and good. His language development can grow and flourish. With a good background, he can move easily into the higher levels of language, the levels of reading and writing.

If, on the other hand, the youngster comes from a language environment where nonstandard English is the model he hears in terms of structure, construction, grammar and syntax, his language pattern is likely to be the same. Unlike dialect, this language syndrome is likely to adversely affect his future language growth and stunt his whole learning career in school.

The child comes into a learning situation, be it at the nursery/preschool level or kindergarten, with a language pattern of some sort. He has learned that language by listening and reacting to the language environment in which he has lived. In

The child's first vocabulary is that of *listening*. The models that he finds when listening affect all future language learning.

most cases, if he does speak, a dialect and language pattern are evident. He has learned these by imitating models of language that were close at hand. His listening vocabulary has dictated what his second vocabulary, speech, will be.

LANGUAGE MODELS

As we have discussed, the child develops his basic language pattern, his listening vocabulary and his consequent speaking vocabulary, from that language environment in which he finds himself. If his preschool language environment is rich, and language is used in many and varied ways in a positive manner, he is likely to come to school with a well-developed language syndrome and is able to cope with the language demands of the average school curriculum. If, as we have noted, his language environment has been a poor one, he comes to a school situation lacking the skills and controls he needs to achieve in most curricular adventures.[6]

The language model provided to a young child is, therefore, of vital importance. That language model may very well set the stage for all subsequent language learning.

The teacher is an important language model. She probably provides the most important language environment the child has, after his family and peer group environments. He listens to her and communicates with her. He many times will modify his language pattern because of the new school environment in which he finds himself. His listening and his speaking vocabularies certainly grow and expand. It is most important at all levels of elementary education, but doubly important at the preschool/early elementary level, that the teacher be an excellent language model and provide a rich listening environment so that youngsters can learn from her.

BILINGUALISM AND ENGLISH AS A SECOND LANGUAGE

It is often a perplexing situation for a child, and for the teacher working with him, to find one language spoken at home and another language used at school. This bilingual situation is not at all uncommon when one considers the polyglot society in which we live. This phenomenon is easily seen in such areas as the American Southwest, where for many children Spanish is the native language at home; yet the children are taught in English at school. The same is true to a large extent of the Puerto Rican children in certain eastern areas. Chinese-American children in areas such as San Francisco's Chinatown speak a Chinese dialect at home while attending a school where the language environment is English. The American-Indian child who speaks his native language at home and goes to an

6. Jane B. Raph, "Language Development in Socially Disadvantaged Children," *Review of Educational Research,* December 1965, pp. 389–400.

English-speaking reservation school experiences the same problem. This kind of situation is repeated over and over again in various languages in various parts of the nation.

Some educators are telling us that certain nonstandard, dialectic English can be classified as very close to a "foreign language." The language that is spoken at home is quite another language from that spoken at school, even though they both may be called "English." Many times this is the language of the so-called "disadvantaged" or "deprived" youngster.

Certainly when the language model in the home and peer group environment provides the child with a listening vocabulary, and thus a beginning speaking vocabulary that stems from a language other than English, his reaction to an English-speaking learning environment is going to be affected. He is oftentimes going to be confused, unable to attend and understand, and is very likely going to fall behind in the other language skills of reading and writing. It seems evident that if his listening and speaking vocabularies are not in English, he will be hard pressed to learn the skills of reading and writing in English.

The listening environment that the bilingual child or the child for whom English is a second language finds himself involved with at school is a major factor in helping him cope with English. He must hear English and be allowed to develop an English listening vocabulary, and then attempt to reproduce what he hears in a speaking vocabulary before he can successfully continue with language education. The teacher needs to provide immediate, meaningful, English language models for the youngster. He needs to be induced into an English-speaking environment as quickly and as easily as possible.

Oftentimes regular "English" lessons are to be considered for this bilingual child. He needs to be talked to and involved in the language actively. He needs to be gently but firmly encouraged to develop an English vocabulary, correct pronunciation, standard syntax, and all the rest. He, of course, should not be forbidden to use his native language, and he should never be ridiculed or punished for using it! He should, however, be encouraged to use English and be provided with models of English at all times.[7]

Many times a youngster's cultural heritage is involved with his native language. It is a precious and ego-involved system of communication. As teachers, we need to know and understand this. We also need to remember that if the child is to succeed in school, and in life later outside the school, English is a linguistic necessity. The fact is that the official language of the United States is English, and that one prerequisite for success in the culture is the mastery of that language. Teachers of a child whose first language is other than English have a sensitive, difficult task to face. The cultural linguistic heritage of a child must not be de-

---

7. Doris C. Ching, "Methods for the Bilingual Child," *Elementary English,* January 1965, pp. 22–27.

stroyed by depriving him of his native language; but by the same token, we owe him the mastery of English so that he can compete in the real world in which he will find himself.

There is little question that this special child needs real help in developing an English listening vocabulary. He must be helped to understand this new language and must be encouraged to speak it before he can function effectively with the language at other levels.[8]

SELECTIVE LISTENING

Levels of Listening

Research concerning the phenomenon of listening as it relates to language growth is admittedly sparse. We do have some valuable threads with which we can attempt to weave a pattern of sorts. Much theory is available, but little actual empirical research. A recent trend initiated by certain linguistic scholars may, hopefully, modify this fact. As it stands now, however, theory far outweighs actual known truth.

As teachers concerned with language growth in elementary students, and listening being a part of that concern, it is necessary to know that listening occurs on two basic levels. The youngster listens in two ways, in a classroom situation and in the world outside. He will listen in an *active* way and in a *passive* way.

Active listening is specialized listening. It is listening to receive special, important information. This is listening with a definite purpose. The conductor listens actively as he rehearses his orchestra. The physician listens actively through his stethoscope. The athlete listens actively to directions from his coach. Active listening implies readiness, listening for a special purpose. Children listen actively to a spelling list being read by a teacher, since after they hear a word on the list, they are required to write it on paper.

Active listening does not comprise most of the child's listening efforts. Often he does not know how or when to listen actively. He will usually need clues so that he can listen in an active way. A good teacher will provide those clues. She many times will have a device that will bring children's attention to her, so that they will be able to participate in active listening. Such a device as calling for attention and waiting until all eyes are toward her and quiet prevails is a common one. Preschool and kindergarten teachers many times will strike a chord on the piano or ring a special bell to bring children to attention so they will listen in an active manner.

It is probably wise also to tell children that they will receive directions or other information that is important to them. It is good to simply tell them that

---

8. Ibid.

they need to listen carefully! What the teacher is actually doing is structuring their listening. They are told to listen carefully, and why they are to listen carefully (see figure 2.2, p. 28). Sometimes it is necessary to present the information and/or directions more than once. After they have been given, many teachers will ask a student to repeat what they have heard, so that additional reinforcement is provided. Active listening is specialized listening. Teachers must realize that some children will not know how to listen in this way and will need help in learning this skill.

Passive listening describes that level of listening that does not require the attention, the concern for detail, or any specific requirements of active listening. This kind of listening is largely an unconscious process and contrasts with active listening, which is largely a conscious process. Passive listening is the kind of listening that one does as he listens to the radio, aware of the sound, but not paying great attention to it. One responds to classroom "hum" in a passive way, aware that it is present, but not consciously concerned with it. The everyday sounds of the world are heard in a passive way. They occur and pass with little attention from the listener. Only when the listener is given a clue that what he is hearing is of importance to him will this unconscious, passive listening become active and conscious.

Most of the youngster's listening (and the adult's, for that matter) is of a passive nature. He is aware of sound activity and accepts it passively. His environment teaches him to be actively aware of certain sounds for his protection or to satisfy needs. Other sounds will go relatively unattended.

Teachers are often frustrated by the fact that passive listening seems to be the only kind of listening that some children are able to accomplish. This is especially true of very young children in the early grades. Certainly this phenomenon is not exclusive to primary children. Upper-grade youngsters and, indeed high school and college students, sometimes seem "not to listen," and fall into academic and social pits because of this inability. Teaching children to know about, and operate successfully with, these two general levels of listening is a major job of the classroom teacher.[9]

Modern World Sounds

We live in a world of sound! Some have gone so far as to say that the major pollutant of the air is the noise it contains. Our ears are accosted constantly with clangs, shrieks, bangs, clatters, demands, requests, directions, music, roars, hums, and a whole assortment of cacophonous hullabaloo. Silence has almost become a national treasure. We seek it and revel in it. The quiet place has nearly become the property of the privileged few.

9. Paul S. Anderson, *Language Skills in Elementary Education* (New York: The Macmillan Co., 1964), pp. 81–87.

There can be no question that this world of modern sounds has an immense effect on the youngster's learning to listen and finally coming to *aud*. He is surrounded by hearing stimuli and is forced, as a protective device, to ignore or "tune out" much of that which he hears. If he were to attempt to respond to that hullabaloo of modern sound that surrounds him, one might fear for his psychological well-being. To sort out that which is worthy of his conscious attention is a monumental task for a child. That he needs help in this accomplishment seems self-evident. The teacher who might complain that the youngsters in her class seem not to be able to listen may be well advised to ask why. The answer may be that in the modern world of sound they have been forced not to listen, simply because there is so much to hear.

Protective Reactions

Reacting to sound happens at several levels. The first level is that of simply hearing. The human is aware, through the auditory senses, that sound exists. He makes little or no attempt to sort out these sounds, except where possible instinct may intervene. The second level is that of listening. At this level the human sorts out those sound signals that require his attention. These can be signals of danger, security, and equally immediate stimuli that require action. The third level is that of auding. This is the act of hearing, comprising auditory acuity, perception, discrimination, and comprehension. The act of auding is the level teachers seek in children so that teaching and language growth can be evident. It is a lofty level for some children. It is a level that must be worked toward in all teaching-learning activities. Auding is, in effect, the foundation in the edifice of most good school learning.

The ability to aud is not developed in all young children. Many come into a school setting and seem to remain there without this ability to aud. If these children have a normal ability to hear and are not physically impaired in any way, the dilemma is apparent. What can we do to increase a youngster's ability to aud? Probably the first concern the classroom teacher needs to have is one of understanding why the child is having this problem. Once that is determined, the teacher can go about providing experiences for the problem's dissipation.

It seems the inability to aud well probably clusters around one major factor. The child is protecting himself from a world of sound with which he finds it most difficult to cope. When one considers the noise level that many children find as a regular part of their environment, one might understand the credibility of this idea. He simply is surrounded with so much auditory stimulation that in order to remain in a psychologically upright position, he learns to "tune out," to not hear, much of what is around him. He *learns* to do this as he learns other important life tools. He has not been given opportunities to sort out what is important and what is not important in that sea of noise that surrounds him. He will respond to dramatic sound stimulation, but by and large ignores the rest. It is simply a matter of survival that he "tunes out" much of the sound that is around him.

Some authorities have suggested that this is especially true of the disadvantaged child coming from a large family situation. Survival is the issue there too. Coming, as he does from an overcrowded environment with all that it entails, he learns not to listen. He learns to "tune out," to ignore, much of the auditory stimulation that is such a large part of his living environment. Scholars further suggest that this phenomenon occurs often in the disadvantaged child's second year of life. He learns early to "tune out" so that survival is more possible in his environment. Some feel that as early as age two, the child falls behind in his language development and is hard pressed to recover when he attends school.

The seeming inability to listen (aud) is a common occurrence in many children. As teachers we need to understand the causes for this. Certainly one valid reason is a protective reaction to a world of noise that surrounds him.

LISTENING AND THE SCHOOL SETTING

Since listening at its various levels is a skill process, it is necessary that the teacher plan for specific experiences in which practice in listening with a purpose is provided for her students. Not only do they need to be taught *to* listen, but also *how* to listen selectively and actively. They have come to their learning situations with various listening abilities already developed, their sensitiveness to sound signals already functioning. Three facets of listening as a process should be distinguished: (1) acuity—the ability to hear sound; (2) discrimination—the ability to note likeness and contrast in sounds; and (3) interpretation—the ability to comprehend, or get meaning from, speech or communication sounds.[10]

Difficulties or deficiencies in the first area (acuity) will be dealt with chiefly by the school nurse, the family doctor or specialist, or in severe cases by an otologist. Hearing loss cannot be remedied by the classroom teacher; however, she does need to be aware and concerned in order to make every opportunity for effective listening available to each student. Nearness to the center of various activities, positioning in such a way that the impaired hearer can view the speaker clearly, and providing an adequate level of sound energy are some of the preparations that any instructor can provide her listeners. These are basic, but they are vitally important and must not be ignored.

Deficiencies in the second area (discrimination) are more in the realm of classroom activities and experiences. Frequently teachers at the preschool, kindergarten, and primary levels have given more attention to the development of such

---

10. Sarah W. Lundsteen, "Teaching and Testing Critical Listening," in *Elementary School Language Arts: Selected Readings,* ed. Paul C. Burns (Chicago, Ill.: Rand-McNally & Co., 1969), pp. 155–162.

The listening skills continue to develop throughout the elementary grades. The modern school setting offers a variety of devices and/or media for enhancing this important language skill.

skills, while the intermediate- and upper-grade instructors, for a variety of reasons, may have failed to continue providing opportunities for the development of the more discreet abilities. The following chapter will include, at the lower levels particularly, suggested lessons and activities dealing with strategies specifically consistent with the development of discriminatory skills.

So much of learning is concerned with hearing and getting meaning from oral communication—words, sentences, summaries, lectures—that it becomes imperative for teachers at all levels to continue to include specific instruction for listening in the curriculum. In this third facet of the subject, the student will make use of the total abilities acquired and strengthened previously, but will now progress in understanding and interpreting what he hears and what he listens to. This third level of skill has more recently been referred to as auding, a neologism, expressing a high level of aural performance; listening with a fine focus of intent for learning.[11]

11. Gloria Horrworth, "Listening: A Facet of Oral Language," *Elementary English,* December 1966, pp. 856–864.

Preschool and Kindergarten Listening Experiences (See figures 2.2–2.4, pp. 28–33.)

In viewing the young child, it is almost impossible to consider listening without also including speaking, the two go hand in hand. Listening may be thought of as an intake skill which expands and enriches the self, while speaking is an expressive, communicative output.

When the child comes into his first experiences of school, be it nursery school, extended day care, Head Start, or the actual kindergarten itself, his developed listening skill may vary greatly from that of his peers. His ability to listen will depend on his experiential background, home environment, and family structure. These, likewise, will be influenced by his physical, social, and intellectual capacities. One important factor, not to be overlooked, is the child's *interest*. This factor will not only have affected the student's present level of listening skill, but will be of importance in guiding his teacher(s) in leading him into learnings and achievement. If he has come with an awakened interest, it will push him into new interests and expand his old ones with energy and zest. His aroused curiosity will be the catalyst for developing his listening abilities.

The teacher must also be aware that the level of a child's listening abilities is often dependent upon the way he has been listened to; thus, a give-and-take experience heightens the value in which the student will hold listening. *If you want him to listen to you, you must listen to him!*

One other factor in teaching listening to young children, or for that matter to students at any age, is the component sometimes referred to as "listenability." If it is important for reading material to be tested by certain criteria (e.g., clear type, format, vocabulary load, concept inclusion) why not consider certain elements which are essential to good listening? Perhaps the teacher could and should consider such qualities as an appropriate tone of voice; a pleasant level of volume; rhythmic flow of words, phrases, sentences, or paragraphs; variations of speed and pitch; clear, distinct pronunciation; and a choice of words to stimulate and activate interested listening. Perhaps this can be summarized by saying: When the teacher speaks, she has something to say, and she says it well.

Listening and Readiness

The very young child, as well as the older learner, needs to be *ready* for listening. Just as in any of the other areas of communication skills, the good teacher considers the readiness factor as very important. She must make allowances for the pupil's readiness for instruction in the learning skills of listening. The physical comfort and environment of the learner are important: a quiet, relaxed atmosphere; minimal distracting noises; comfortable chairs, cushions, or carpeted areas—all of these enhance the listening milieu.

A further word must be included in this context relative to preparation for listening. This is the introduction, or clue to listen, that catches the student's interest and attention, that provides a meaningful purpose for listening. This clue for listening leads to more thoughtful concentration during the listening or input time, and should result in an increased involvement of the child as he reacts and responds to the input materials. Remember, the child is adding to what he has already acquired; as he assimilates new information, experiences, and/or pleasurable input, he will react. He now *wants* to hear, to understand, and to interpret what he listens to. So he actively reaches out to gather auditory stimuli now that he has been given a clue to listen actively.[12]

Listening and the Young Child in Primary Grades (See figures 2.5–2.8, pp. 35–41.)

The very young child has normally grown easily into the habit pattern of listening when somebody speaks directly and solely to him. Likewise in the family setting—at the table for meals, during times of recreation, driving in the car, when friends or relatives visit, and in many other situations—he has learned to listen also to the interchange of conversations when it was within the scope of his understanding. However, unless he has frequently attended some sort of class—Sunday School, nursery school—he will not have become accustomed to listening in a group setting in the same expected manner as is often required at certain times during the school day. The beginning teacher, or the teacher new to the level of teaching the very young, will need to remind herself of this in teaching the listening skills.

It must also be remembered that an entirely new set of attention cues will need to be learned early in the school setting. The child has learned to respond to parental guidance and has followed certain aural signals: tone of voice, use of *his* name, choice of words, loudness or softness of speech. In short, he has learned when it is wise to ignore and when it is wise to give immediate attention to what is being said. In talking with and listening to his friends and playmates the child has learned a set of functional "rules." Incomplete sentences, even word fragments, gestures, and the whole gamut of nonspeech communication signals—these he has learned and used. Now he is in the more formal setting of the classroom, and it may be difficult for him to know when he is required to give full attention, listening with focus, and when he may give a sort of halfway, marginal listening response.

His listening difficulties may result from several new situations and will require understanding and guidance from the teacher. These new experiences include the following elements.

- The child is now part of a group and may not be spoken to directly as an individual.

---

12. Greene and Petty, *Developing Language Skills,* pp. 138–140.

- Frequently spoken words from the teacher involve specific instructions or detailed directions to be followed.
- The whole environment is new and there are many different situations to be understood "all at once."
- The teacher's way of speaking, her choice of words, her own particular way of expressing herself, everything about her speech may differ greatly from the accustomed voice to which the child is used to listening.
- The whole situation may seem impersonal, group oriented, and foreign to the child.

Indeed, the whole listening situation will require certain value judgments: "What is important? Do I need to listen to this? Does this include me?" It will take varying amounts of time for different children to learn what is required in each situation. They must also discover how to make the transitions necessary in moving from one level of listening to another.

At best, this is a plea for the teacher or teacher-to-be to have an awareness of the degrees of differences in the children involved, the differences in the tasks involved, and the differences in the teachers involved.

Listening in the Middle and Upper Grades (See figures 2.9–2.14, pp. 43–56.)

Teaching for good listening is certainly not the sole responsibility of the primary teacher. The teacher in the intermediate and upper grades has an important role in this all-important aspect of teaching as well. Helping children learn to listen effectively permeates all educational endeavors.

Certainly the points discussed in the section above concerning listening and the young child are pertinent to the upper grades as well. Probably the most important point being that children need clues as to when to listen, so that active listening will occur. Perhaps the teacher in the upper grades can simply inform students that they will need to listen carefully now, and that the directions, instructions, information, or necessary data are important for specific reasons. Many upper-grade teachers will repeat twice the material that needs to be heard and understood, allowing students to receive the information accurately and well.

Without question we need, as teachers, to make sure that what we ask children to listen to is really important to them. The cry of "wolf" too often in a listening situation will have obvious effects. Check carefully the lesson plans that follow this section. Note the strategies and applications. Analyze them for techniques.

The Listening Span

One important consideration for the teacher is the amount of time that young children can give full attention. Various terms have been used to describe this ability: "attention span," "'listening span," and "interest span." The last term seems most appropriate to the authors, for certainly the length of time that any person can profitably listen will be determined largely by the degree of interest he has in the topic. This is certainly true of children. They will be able to listen longer to discussions about a class Halloween party in the making than to directions on how to properly head papers or to prepare for a certain lesson. Attentive listening to a story that interests and excites them as they hear the teacher read will vary recognizably from that when hearing directions for writing spelling words. For the teacher to attempt to force listening is inadvisable. Any undue persistence may actually result in tensions which can undo or inhibit the positive attitude being sought toward listening.

SUMMARY

The listening vocabulary is the foundation for all language learning. Without a good listening vocabulary, the skills of speech, reading, and writing will develop feebly, if at all.

Children come to us in the classroom with a varied pattern of backgrounds and abilities. They come, as a result, with a variance of this all-important language foundation. We need to accept this variance as fact, along with the many individual differences that we know about and accept.

Learning to listen and the building of a listening vocabulary cannot be taken for granted. This aspect of language learning is too important to be left to chance. Regular, planned experiences for the enhancement of listening and development of this primary vocabulary need to be a regular part of our professional preparation as teachers. The following chapter will provide some ideas and plans that can start the teacher, and the student, on a meaningful road toward the goal of teaching for and the learning of this first vocabulary.

2

LISTENING INSTRUCTION
THE PRAGMATIC APPROACH

Teachers, as well as instructors at the preparation level in the college, have frequently voiced the complaint that most of the professional literature related to the teaching of the language arts has dealt chiefly with theory and/or research findings, but has consistently neglected the practical application of such material to classroom problems. The authors have attempted to create a balance in this text that will correct the exclusion of valuable material which has made "theory without application futile." In attempting to translate educational theory and psychological generalizations and principles into classroom practice, one is immediately aware that it is a difficult task. However, goals become meaningless and theories only empty words without developing organized teaching strategies. These strategies must demonstrate that theory and principle are sound; that objectives are reachable and measureable.

The authors have sought to bridge the gap between theory and practice by continuing where many others have left off—by developing with actual teachers and students lesson plans which have been used, revised, and developed for teaching specific skills in listening to all levels of elementary language instruction. The results of this work are tested, usable, and comprehensive learning experiences.

A WORD ABOUT LESSON PLANS

Various models for developing instructional plans have been used. It seems that a simple outline form, brief and concise, should suffice in most instances. The student/intern will usually follow a much more detailed and expanded plan than the experienced classroom teacher. However, the same form can be used with either shortened or more lengthy information being included in preparation. The model to be used in this text can be reproduced on a single sheet and used for almost any subject area. Note that it can be used by the student in the teacher education class, by the student interning in the classroom, or by the teacher pursuing her daily or weekly planning, preparation, and teaching. Note also that the model provides space for the (1) background data, (2) goals of the lesson, (3) assignment and materials, (4) procedures, (5) related activities, (6) evaluation, and (7) expanded enrichment activities and follow-up (see figure 2.1, p. 23).

Background data. This section of the plan merely identifies the teacher/intern, the date, subject area to be taught, and level of instruction planned. Thus if the plan is part of an assignment, the student provides this data as he would in any written task. If the plan is for actual teaching by the teacher/intern, it can be filed in order as an integral part of a series or unit of instruction. As such, it will serve not only as a guide and reminder at the time of teaching, but can be referred to later as a matter of record or for use as a model in developing other teaching materials and strategies.

Goals of the lesson. Much is being currently said about the importance of clearly stated purposes. These are called by various names: goals, aims, purposes, objectives. Simply they can be thought of as *targets*. With the recent emphasis on accountability, most educators have been increasingly aware of the necessity for concise, pointed objectives both for the TEACHER to follow in each lesson, as well as for STUDENT evaluation to see if the goals were reached in a measurable performance (VI). Under this heading of the lesson plan, then, there should be two related aims.

The first may be termed Teaching Goals, *Instructional Objectives*, Educational Aims. Currently the second term is preferred and will be used in the model (figure 2.1) as well as in the illustrative lesson plans throughout the book. These refer to the teacher's stated purpose for actually planning and teaching each lesson. It may identify the particular task, skill, or learning that the teacher wishes to focus on in the lesson. This objective will be stated in broad or more general terms and merely specify the instructor's purpose in teaching that particular lesson.

The second section includes the *Behavioral* or *Performance Objectives* expected from the student(s) receiving the instruction. These objectives will be couched in concise terms designating four facets: (1) a presented condition, (2) a specific performance, (3) a measure of evaluating the behavior, and (4) a stated level of acceptable performance. The term "behavior" although widely used by educationists seems more ambiguous than "performance." The latter referring more clearly to that which the student is able to do, or does, as a result of the teaching effort.

Assignment and materials. The third section of the lesson plan deals with the assigned materials and tasks, giving full information as to titles, amounts, page numbers, and any such relevant guidelines. This will not only be a reference source to the student/teacher, but in the event another teacher is designated to continue or teach, there will be clear data for their use as well.

Suggested Model for Preparing Lesson Plans

I.   Name: _____   Date: _____   Grade: _____   No.: _____

     Subject: _____   Text: _____

II.   Instructional Objective: _____

     _____

     Performance Objective: _____

     _____

III.   Assignment: _____

     _____

     Materials:

     _____

     _____

     _____

IV.   Procedures:

       1. _____

       2. _____

       3. _____

       4. _____

V.   Related Activities:

       1. _____

       2. _____

VI.   Evaluation: _____

     _____

     _____

VII.   Ongoing Activities: _____

     _____

     _____

     Comments:

Figure 2.1

Procedures. Under this heading, the planner will list the sequential steps by which he anticipates to proceed through his lesson. These are the teacher's notes, the order and method of presenting the various components of the lesson itself. This often takes the form of a simple phrase outline with the succeeding steps numbered in order.

Related activities. The activities, be they group or individual, that are planned for enriching and/or strengthening the teaching of a particular lesson, must be based on the specific performance objectives stated. Since these objectives are the desired pupil response, the whole lesson hinges on them, particularly the activities. Far too often activities have been included as part of a unit or lesson plan merely on some ambiguous relationship: geographical, historical, aesthetic. However, in the matter of teaching communication skills, each part of each lesson relates directly to reaching the stated goal(s). In many of the model lesson plans, the reader will note that certain activities have been included as part of each teaching situation. Then in part VII of the model, numerous other related activities have been suggested as ongoing, expanding activities.

Evaluation. Primarily this facet of the plan deals with assessing and measuring student performance and progress. With the lesson focused clearly on a realistic pacing and presentation of materials, the instructor will be able to provide some measurement—the specified tasks, observation with a checklist recording, a teacher-prepared test—that will quickly and accurately evaluate the desired performance of the learner and the degree of correctness deemed necessary as satisfactory learning results. If objectives have been clearly thought through and stated properly, they will provide the guide for evaluation, thus eliminating the "guesswork" from assessment of the amount of learning that has taken place.

Expanded enrichment activities and follow-up. In the instructional preparation and planning, the teacher will see single lessons as part of a unified whole. This larger unit of work will provide for many lessons and may cover days, weeks, or even months of continued exploration, practice, projects, skills, tasks, and some culmination in performance and assessment. However, there should be a certain weaving together of the segments and fragments to provide the holistic gestalt—the entire pattern—of the larger units of learning/instruction. It is in this attempt, that the planner will think through those linking activities that will expand the present task or skill as well as provide the continuity leading into the next sequence or learning area. These ongoing activities, projects, or learning experiences, then, will be included in this final section of the plan.

In the remainder of the chapter, the student/teacher will be presented with numerous teaching strategies, illustrative model lesson plans, and enrichment and developmental activities. These all center on the kinds of curricula a teacher may develop and include in teaching listening skills. These will serve chiefly as "seed" ideas for teaching and activities, models for lesson plans based on specific teaching objectives and performance objectives, and learning experiences which are theoretically sound as is indicated in each strategy rationale.

PRESCHOOL AND KINDERGARTEN LISTENING

Four actual models of lessons have been developed and presented here for the student's guidance in thinking through the kinds of learning lessons which need to be included in the curriculum sequence for this level of listening instruction. It can be noted that these cover skills arranged so that they progress from the most basic to more discrete tasks which lead toward formalized instruction in the other communication skills, particularly reading and writing. As the reader examines each of the following models, he will discover that many opportunities for listening instruction will actually be found embedded in areas of the curriculum other than language arts specifically. He will also become aware that the teacher makes use of many experiences and situations throughout the day to reinforce and strengthen previous teachings. New experiences and situations are introduced in a meaningful, natural context in classroom management, routine directions, arranging and providing pleasurable, enrichment activities; in short, in numerous incidental teaching situations. Since good listening is a skill, it must be practiced and thought about frequently.

In seeking to select model lessons, the authors chose four topics which, in their opinion, give as wide a range as possible of areas important at the beginning levels of schooling. They are teaching patterns for work in four basic listening skills: (1) Attention Cues Via Auditory Stimulus, (2) Following Directions and Instructions, (3) Auditory Discrimination and Basic Speech Sounds, and (4) Reproducing Sounds from Listening.

Teaching Listening for Attention Cues Via Auditory Stimulus

How important it is for the young student to learn to listen for particular cues to signal "listening time." These are those valuable words, tones of voice, topics of interest or value, or moments of absolute quiet when the hearer "gets the message" via the aural modality that he should *listen*. "S-s-shhhhh! Hist! Psst! Listen! Silence! Hark!" These, and numerous other heard signals, are decoded stimuli for paying attention, listening closely, ceasing to make disturbing noises; signals for preparing to aud. There are preparation signals aimed at stimulating interest in the hearer, in prompting concentration on sound symbols (the aural code), and in receiving a message of meaning and importance.

Teaching Strategies

The teacher will not assume that her younger students have either been naturally endowed with, or have already acquired, the necessary knowledge which makes for good listeners. Here, as in other areas of her teaching, she will need to constantly assess students' strengths, weaknesses, attainments, and/or deficiencies. On the basis of this continuing evaluation-diagnosis process, she will prescribe and plan her teaching strategies.

A successful lesson in listening requires the same careful planning on the part of the teacher as in any other area of the curriculum.

How, then, will one teach this important facet of language learning? It was previously inferred that there will be times when this type of actual instruction will take place as the result of direct planning and teaching; at other times it will be incidentally brought into the learning situations that occur throughout any school day; and at still other times instruction will be included as a part of the teaching in the other areas of the curriculum. The necessary practice times for strengthening learnings will likewise be provided in the three kinds of settings just described.

Below are some teaching strategies which may be used in attempting to break the barriers to good listening.

1. Informal discussion-type lessons when the teacher and group or individuals examine the value and importance of good listening abilities.
2. A group or individual exploring and identifying appropriate goals or objectives for listening improvement. The chalkboard or large chart paper may be used to record these stated aims and kept for review and reminder.
3. The instructor and students may cooperate and participate in planning and executing listening-learning activities consistent with their level and the instructional area being handled at a particular time.
4. The teacher may present, or various students may share, listening materials in a variety of media: familiar sounds, voice sounds, recorded sounds, environ-

mental noises, multimedia combinations (both live and recorded, demonstrating varieties of tone, pitch, or volume).

5. The lesson strategy may combine listening situations with response or reaction tasks; something to be said, done, or written down.

6. Numerous publishers have developed good materials which combine listening and doing. These may be used with an entire class, or with a group, or even at a listening station.

7. Frequently the listening instruction can be part of another learning situation: (1) a *listening* walk combined with a nature experience, (2) listening for directions to go to a particular place, (3) listening to instructions for doing a particular project in activities such as art or games.

8. Sometimes the teacher will use, with students at this early age, a variety of games or play situations to teach some of the listening skills desired. (Examples of some of these are included in the activities section of the lesson plan, figure 2.2., p. 28).

These are but a few of the kinds of actual attacks the teacher/intern will plan in providing consecutive opportunities for students to learn the (1) *whys* of listening, (2) *hows* of listening, (3) *whens* of listening, and the (4) *whats* for which to listen.

Teaching Listening for Following Directions and Instructions

Have you ever stopped to consider how many times during the school day that even the very young child is required to listen to instructions or directions? These at first may be just simple one-step procedures, but they rapidly change into directions of multidimensions—two, three, or four separate tasks to be performed in an exact fashion and particular sequence. Unless this is done as requested, the child fails to succeed in the required activity. Perhaps it is in just such simple areas of education as this that the student begins a chain of nonsuccess that carries over into many "higher" level challenges. This may be the beginning of many small failures that eventually gather themselves into a whole syndrome of attitudes that are responsible in part for many of our so-called *disabled, handicapped,* or *deficient* learners. Certainly in such a listening area as following clear, concise, uncomplicated instructions, it is imperative that the teacher do her best work in pacing the child's ability and in seeing that her demands are realistic in terms of the level of difficulty required, allowing the young child to accomplish the task successfully.

It is suggested that the teacher select instruction times and related activities in terms of the pupil's needs as she diagnoses them. Teaching listening skills will only be effective when they are closely related to student needs. We should, and actually do, listen best when we have some specific need or purpose. Therefore in preparation for following directions, the teacher and student(s) should establish

Model Lesson Plan
Teaching Auditory Cues

I. **Name:** Norma Jean King   **Date:** 2-17-72   **Grade:** K **No.** 1

   Subject: Language Arts (Listening)   **Text:** None

II. **Instructional Objective:** To introduce auditory cues for attention signals.

   Performance Objective: When presented with six attention cues, the student will identify the signal, stop what he is presently engaged in, and then respond with the appropriate behavior.

III. **Assignment:** Participation in the group activity of listening.

   Materials:

small table bell	chop sticks
piano	metal snapper
whistle	small metal triangle
buzzer	gong

IV. **Procedure:**
   1. Arrange group for Circle Time.
   2. Lead discussion on importance of signals in life situations: traffic lights, sirens, bells, alarms, clocks.
   3. Elicit from students kinds of signals which can be used in classroom for getting attention.
   4. Use various cues and decide on their meanings.
   5. Develop "Good Listeners Chart" for room.
   6. Practice using signals with group.

V. **Related Activities:**
   1. Film: "Sounds As Signals"
   2. Attention Cues in Pictures: Art Project
   3. Game: "I am Thinking of a Sound"

VI. **Evaluation:**
   1. At incidental times use each clue and record student(s) responses to signals.
   2. Use pictures of signals in chalk tray for selection at appropriate times.
   3. Check sheet with pictures of cue signals to be circled in orally dictated quiz.

VII. **Ongoing Activities:** At home and at play listen for signal sounds. Remember them and describe them in sharing time for tomorrow.

   Comments: None.

Figure 2.2

clear reasons for listening carefully; listening in some sort of general fashion is not an acceptable goal in today's language arts program.

Teaching Strategies

In planning specific teaching times for listening to follow directions, the teacher will capitalize on the fact that responding step-by-step in some simple sequence of tasks is listening with a purpose. Thus, focused listening becomes more efficient because it is necessary.

Again, not only will there be specific times for teaching direct lessons on this facet of listening, but many times throughout each day the skill will be used incidentally in carrying out simple routines of the classroom. At other times, the teacher will see opportunities to call attention to situations requiring careful listening as a prerequisite to further activities, tasks, or fun times.

Here, then is a list of meaningful situations which the teacher may make use of in planning her instructional strategies.

1. A lesson or lessons may center on procedures to be followed in taking a field trip: setting boundaries, recognizing priorities (what is most important, etc.), deciding the steps to be followed during the experience.
2. Many simple activities in the day require following procedures. Simple listening lessons can be planned which outline these directions and explanations for their use: getting ready for a new activity, putting materials in certain places, getting ready to share an experience with another class, participating in some program or presentation. These sorts of situations offer excellent opportunities for listening and then following instructions.
3. Perhaps a new game is to be played in the classroom or on the playground, or for a recreation period. Use this for a listening activity. As rules, purposes of the game, scoring, and technical points are discussed, the child will be given specific experience in mentally jotting down the steps of the game to be followed and the things to be done in participating in the exercise. This can prove to be an effective setting for teaching listening skills.
4. Often a lesson which has some sort of demonstration involved while the children listen to directions will provide a new meaning to the learning. Such an activity might be centered in an art lesson in *oragami*. For this level of student, choose a simple paper-folding task and proceed step-by-step with the children listening to the teacher's clear instructions.
5. The alert teacher may also take advantage of numerous situations in classroom activities each day: getting ready for snack-time—setting the tables in a particular order after directions have been given; cleaning up times—washing tools or hands, putting objects in a designated place; arranging furniture in proper spaces, cleaning up, after a specific order of doing the various tasks has been decided.

These suggested strategies are certainly not all-inclusive of the variety of situations which provide excellent opportunities for teaching students to listen to directions or instructions and then to respond correctly as an indication of their careful auding. At best, these are examples of the kinds of teaching strategies which may be used in planning both directed teaching times as well as the incidental instruction times. The model lesson plan which follows (figure 2.3) illustrates how one such lesson can be planned and prepared for teaching.

One further word to the teacher who instructs in listening. There may be times when it is necessary to repeat one's directions; however, in general practice, *once* should be the rule. If the practice is established of giving simple, clear, impressive rules without repetition, the students will learn the expectation of following directions with a single telling. If, on the other hand, instructions are repeated several times, some will learn *not* to listen at first realizing that they will have other opportunities to get directions. The same policy can be followed when the teacher is dictating simple response quizzes—each item is given only once.

Teaching Listening for Auditory Discrimination and Basic Speech Sounds

One of the important tasks of the teacher at the very low levels of elementary education is to develop auditory discrimination abilities in the child. These skills cover tasks requiring the child to not only hear a variety of sounds (environmental, human, musical, animal, etc.), but also to be able to identify them with the added dimension of whether they are (1) close or far away, (2) low or high in pitch, and (3) soft or loud in volume. The student will also learn to distinguish affective qualities in sounds as well as words—anger, sorrow, happiness, caution, and danger. These abilities are all requisite to successful interpretation and input via this important communication modality.

Teaching Strategies

Perhaps in this one facet of listening development, the teacher will be able to make use of more informal situations for learning experiences. At almost any time during the day, and during many of the activities used, there will be numerous opportunities to give brief times of emphasis on the sounds around us. In this area of listening instruction, too, the teacher will find many opportunities to use those materials which may be identified as being more recreational, aesthetic, and/or pleasurable: songs, rhymes, poetry, and music. From this more simple beginning of identifying and interpreting various sounds will begin the more formal learnings leading to the discrimination abilities necessary for hearing the initial, medial, or terminal letter sounds used in beginning reading.

As the teacher seeks for fresh, interesting channels for planning teaching approaches, her strategies may be based on, or embedded in, such activities as those suggested which follow. These have been chosen as merely examples of good

Model Lesson Plan
Teaching Listening to Follow Directions and Instructions

I. **Name:** Patricia Greene   **Date:** 2-21-72   **Grade:** K **No.** 2

   Subject: Language Arts (Listening)   **Text:** None

II. **Instructional Objective:** To provide a learning experience in listening to follow directions and instructions.

   Performance Objective: Given a sequence of oral instructions requiring three specific procedures for successfully performing a task, the student will be able to accomplish the three-step process in proper order.

III. **Assignment:** Preparation for listening to the teacher's instructions and then following them carefully.

   Materials:
   sheets of paper for each student
   crayons

IV. **Procedure:**
   1. Distribute crayons and paper to each student.
   2. Describe the listening lesson to follow.
   3. Give the directions in proper order.
      a. Make lengthwise fold.
      b. Make top-to-bottom fold.
      c. Select green crayon for circles.
      d. Select red crayon for X marks.
      e. Select black crayon for squares.
      f. Select orange crayon for names.

V. **Related Activities:**
   1. Groups (six each) for following directions game: "You Should" (Simon Says).
   2. Listening post activity: Listen and Then Do recording.

VI. **Evaluation:** Use the paper-folding, crayon-drawing exercise papers for evaluating the correctness of the responses of each child. Assess two (2) folds one pt. each; also four (4) colors one pt. each; and sixteen (16) figures one pt. each. Total 22 with 20 correct as acceptable level.

VII. **Ongoing Activities:** Good suggestions for expanding these skills will be found in many of the teachers' manuals accompanying your language arts materials. Also such published materials as Russell's Listening Aids Through the Grades and Listening Games, offer a wide variety of suggestions for expanding and enhancing the learnings attempted in this respect.

   Comments: None.

Figure 2.3

learning situations. They are meant only as stimulators and examples which may be modified, expanded, or substituted with others thought to be more relevant to a particular group or need. Some learning lessons for auditory discrimination may be included as part of the following activities.

1. Frequent sharing times when students are encouraged to repeat favorite rhymes or short verses they have learned. As they recite, others can listen for like sounds which form the sound pattern of the poetry. If mistakes are made in confusing *almost* like sounds, the alert teacher will base instruction on clarifying, reteaching, and new teaching of basic sounds.
2. The kindergarten teacher will take advantage of the interest value in storytime by often reading aloud or retelling a good story. Occasionally during the story-time a pause may afford opportunity to emphasize or teach a specific sound, or relate it to a recent lesson. Probably the end of the story is a better time to go back and recap several minor learnings included in the actual narrative. This is less disruptive to the pleasure and enjoyment of the activity.
3. Group recitations, simple choral "readings," or any oral situation for an audience can provide a valuable setting for impressing, reviewing, relating, or introducing listening learning for discrimination skills.
4. During the music time when songs are being sung or taught by rote, the aware-ness of like sounds will provide a useful mnemonic reinforcer as well as sharpen-ing the ability to differentiate between different sounds.
5. In the occasional "pause" time just before dismissal for recess, lunch, or going home, there is an opportunity to "listen and identify as many sounds" as possible.
6. Often auditory and visual abilities are linked in preparation for more formal reading readiness tasks. This is particularly true if the letters of the alphabet are being considered, names are being compared, pictures of objects whose names begin with the same sound, and other materials are used in instruction.

These illustrations of learning situations which will form the base for teaching strategies should suffice to alert teachers to a variety of experiences for effective teaching of auditory awareness. In the lesson plan following (figure 2.4, p. 33), one small segment of the total learning has been used to form the basis of one lesson in this area of listening ability at the preschool or kindergarten level.

Teaching Listening for Reproducing Sounds from Listening

In the steps of sequential development of the child's four vocabularies, though listening certainly comes first, it is followed closely by speaking. It is through hear-ing sounds that the child learns to sort out the particular ones used in his first language. Actually, he is able to make a much wider variety than he needs for a specific tongue, but learns to reproduce those which form the words used by his parents, siblings, and/or peers. Thus through a sort of discriminatory screening, he

I. Name: Phyllis Anne White   **Date:** 2-26-72   **Grade:** K   **No.** 3

Subject: Language Arts (Listening)   **Text:** None

II. Instructional Objective: To sharpen and strengthen auditory discrimination abilities.

    Performance Objective: Given a dictated list of ten pairs of words (some beginning with the same sound, and some not), the student shall be able to accurately identify likenesses and differences.

III. Assignment: Participation in a circle activity involving reciting favorite nursery rhymes.

    Materials:
    book of nursery rhymes

IV. Procedure:
1. Arrange children for circle activity.
2. Introduce lesson by briefly playing: "Do We Sound Alike?" (Coupled words.)
3. Let different people recite a favorite nursery rhyme, then choose another to identify the words sounding alike.
4. Can others think of words rhyming with the ones already suggested?
5. Give short oral quiz with written response.

V. Related Activities:
1. Small groups to build rhyming word lists.
2. Play "Blindman's Bluff"; "Animals."
3. Sing-a-Song-a-Rhyming-Word (music).
4. Draw pictures of objects whose names rhyme (art).

VI. Evaluation: To evaluate, use a simple auditory assessment. Ten sets of words, some alike, some not. Each youngster, on a numbered paper 1 to 10 makes an <u>X</u> for each rhyming set; or makes an <u>O</u> if they do not (9/10 satisfactory).

VII. Ongoing Activities: Ongoing experiences should be planned for strengthening and broadening learnings.
1. Additional listening games. <u>"What Is that Sound?"</u> an environmental sound to identify (footsteps, tapping, water running, etc.) with all heads down or <u>"What Kind of Animal Is It?"</u> where teacher or student makes animal sounds for others to identify.
2. "Help Me Tell the Story." Choose story with repetitive line and have children repeat it, listening for specific sounds; e.g., "There Was a Crooked Man" or "This is the House that Jack Built."

Figure 2.4

sorts out the usable sounds he is capable of making and through experimentation learns the linguistic sequence required in the formation of words, short sentences, and then more difficult, discrete arrangements.

The teacher in early childhood education will note that some of her students may not have learned to reproduce certain basic sounds, may have a very limited ability to use words in even simple communication, or may have had such sparse experiences with language that it is necessary to begin with very basic learnings. This must begin, then, with emphasis on good listening, for without hearing sound, it is difficult to make clear sound segments. The result is obvious. Without adequate listening skill, there will be deficient speech skills, and beginning reading will be affected because reading must be based on oral language. Thus listening becomes foundational to subsequent learning in speaking, in reading, and in writing.

It should be pointed out, too, that even if the child has developed some listening skills and has learned to speak at a normal level, he will still need work in auditory discrimination to be able to hear the fine distinctions between sounds which are formed and sound nearly the same. English has a number of basic sounds which may be difficult for the listener to differentiate from one another. The child's listening ability will, then, determine his enunciation, his pronunciation, his voice quality, his speaking patterns—in short, his whole language development.

Teaching Strategies

In planning for instruction to strengthen the child's abilities to hear the differences between basic sounds, the teacher will make use of many aural activities, both incidental and specially prepared. These varied approaches will afford the student numerous opportunities to use his listening skills in a relaxed, informal, and often recreational setting. The following will suggest situations which can be adapted for individual classrooms and classes for work in reproducing the heard sounds.

1. Frequent use of multimedia as a channel for intake. Recordings, the listening post, music, singing, speaking—all offer a wide spectrum of sound variations: high–low, near–far, loud–soft, beginning–ending, rhyming–nonrhyming.
2. Using poetry in many forms provides beautiful listening opportunities: alliteration, onomotapoeia, and matched sounds. These will give practice in hearing basic sounds of the language.
3. The familiar animal sounds which the young student has heard in natural settings, recorded form, through mimicry, and in song can be used by the alert teacher to give instruction and to strengthen abilities for hearing and then verbally encoding specific sounds.
4. The storytelling time, or the read-aloud time, affords children listening and then participation in role-playing, sociodrama, or acting out stories. As they hear, interpret, and then make the actual sounds, their own capacities are expanded.

Model Lesson Plan
Listening Instruction: Reproducing Sounds

I. **Name:** Zola Morton   **Date:** 2-28-72   **Grade:**   K   **No.** 4

   Subject: Language Arts (Listening)   **Text:** None

II. **Instructional Objective:** To provide a learning experience for strengthening listening to be able to reproduce animal sounds.

   Performance Objective: Presented with pictures of ten common animals, the student shall respond by naming the animal and making its particular sound.

III. **Assignment:** Listening to a read-aloud story, "Animals You and I Know," and playing the game, "Which Animal Am I?"

   Materials:
   read-aloud storybook—Animals Near and Far
   large colored pictures of familiar animals
   recording and record player

IV. **Procedure:**
   1. Read the story to the group.
   2. Play the game: "Which Animal Am I?"
   3. Listening time—recording and response.
   4. Use pictures for practicing appropriate sounds.

V. **Related Activities:**
   1. Game: "Pretend You Are an Animal."
   2. Music: "Old MacDonald Had a Farm."
   3. Read-aloud: "The Little Red Hen."

VI. **Evaluation:** The assessment for this lesson will be made by teacher observation and listening with pupil performance recorded on a simple checklist of animal sounds and space for student responses.

VII. **Ongoing Activities:** Several ongoing experiences could be planned for further listening development:
   1. A visit to the local zoo planned as a field trip.
   2. Share and Tell Activity: Pet Day at School.
   3. Planning a bulletin board: Favorite Animal Friends.

   Comments: None.

Figure 2.5

5. The child's delight in reciting after rote listening often makes an interesting lesson setting. The refrain-type poem, the repetitive story or verse, or a simple antiphonal response-type poem can be used as an opportunity for the young child to hear and then reproduce words, sentences, verses, or stanzas. And along with the repeating of these, certain amounts of interpretive voice inflection and emphasis can be used.

These few situations should serve to guide the planning of certain activities and actual lessons focused on listening to reproduce sounds. These activities will of necessity be partially listening and partially expressing. The lesson plan model figure 2.5 at the preschool/kindergarten level makes use of one activity situation as a lesson base.

LISTENING EXPERIENCES IN PRIMARY GRADES

Actually the listening instruction which continues into primary grades may vary only somewhat from that included in the earlier learning activities. In many instances, it will be a refinement and expansion of the same skills. If one can picture the curriculum in terms of an inverted pyramid, he can conceptualize the organization and inclusion of various basic skills as being built upon and broadened in each succeeding level of teaching. Note in figure 2.6 how the various abilities are arranged in the paradigm to indicate specific reteaching and emphasis.

As the teacher builds upon the previous learnings of the child, varying degrees of listening skills will be noted. Often as in any other area of the curriculum, it will be necessary to reemphasize certain experiences and provide the student with additional opportunities for further learning in a particular facet. You will note that four actual lessons have been included in this section. They are closely related to the four chosen for teaching listening skills at the beginning level of instruction, and one, Listening to Follow Oral Instructions, is a direct repeat of an earlier teaching. However, the teaching strategy chosen differs, and the level of expectancy for the child is more refined.

Listening to Identify

In a world of constant noise, the child is called upon to sort out various important sounds and to identify them as having specific meanings, or else to ignore them as unimportant. He can only learn these differences through direct experience and involvement in meaningful situations where he has opportunities for exploring to discover which sounds belong to the two broad categories. His teacher will have the responsibility to offer him the kinds of activities for such experimental learning. How can this be done?

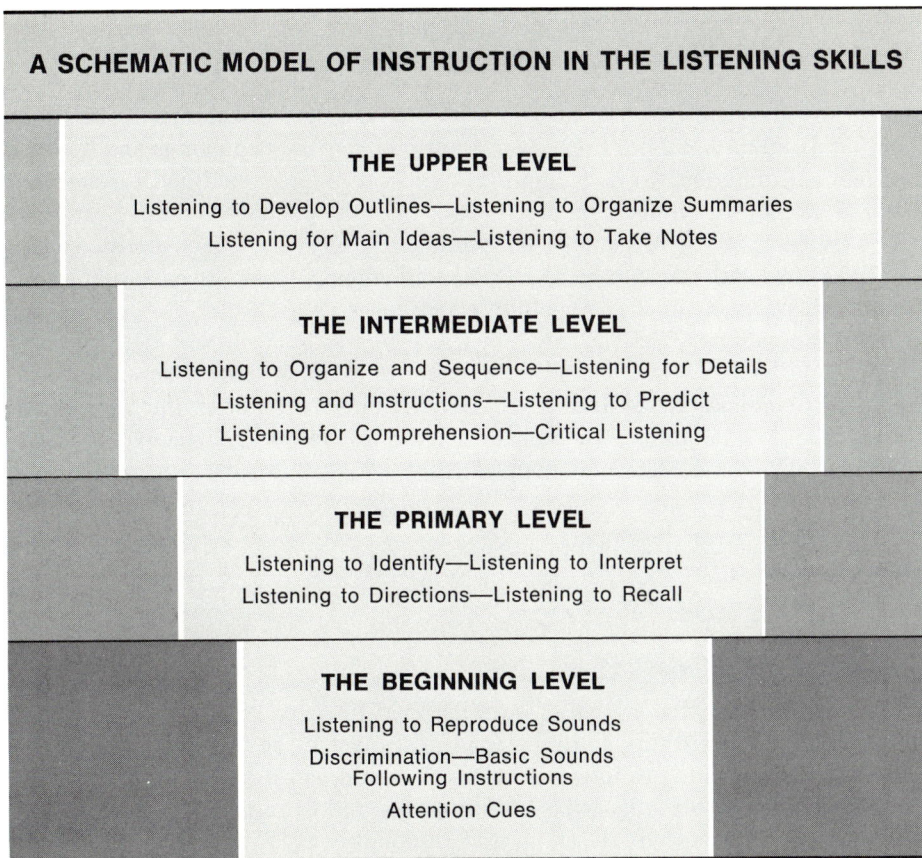

A SCHEMATIC MODEL OF INSTRUCTION IN THE LISTENING SKILLS

THE UPPER LEVEL

Listening to Develop Outlines—Listening to Organize Summaries
Listening for Main Ideas—Listening to Take Notes

THE INTERMEDIATE LEVEL

Listening to Organize and Sequence—Listening for Details
Listening and Instructions—Listening to Predict
Listening for Comprehension—Critical Listening

THE PRIMARY LEVEL

Listening to Identify—Listening to Interpret
Listening to Directions—Listening to Recall

THE BEGINNING LEVEL

Listening to Reproduce Sounds
Discrimination—Basic Sounds
Following Instructions
Attention Cues

Figure 2.6

Teaching Strategies

Numerous modes and media employed by the instructor at the preschool and kindergarten level will again be used as the child continues to progress from grade to grade, or from level to level. As outlined in considerable detail in the preceding section, the teacher will make use of a variety of games, exercises, incidental learning situations, activities closely concerned with oral speaking and listening, and direct times of instruction as in any other skill area.

At the primary level, many of the listening activities which are directed toward identification of sounds will be closely correlated to beginning reading instruction. These may be planned for total class teaching, small groups working on identified needs, or individuals using a listening station. In this context, the teacher will be concerned with specific auditory skills which may involve the pre-reading areas listed below.

1. Phoneme-grapheme relationships, or sound-letter associations; consonant sounds in initial and terminal positions. This ability to hear the beginnings and endings of like and different words is important and can be accomplished through the use of word lists, rhymes, jingles, tongue-twisters, poetry, or simple couplets.
2. The teaching of vowel sounds—long and short. Often teachers combine these oral lessons with written work; dictated language-experience stories, word games or puzzles, or simple spelling experiences.
3. The combinations of letter sounds heard in blends and clusters, digraphs and diphthongs. These will frequently be taught in learning stations set up for specific skill emphasis in the individual, self-contained classroom; the large, open area, flexible-scheduling situation; or a learning center arrangement for individual teacher or team-teaching approach.

The lesson plans developed for teaching primary level listening skills may make use of any of these varying situations and settings.

Listening and Interpreting

It is safe to say that probably no other area of listening instruction offers a wider variety of interesting activities for the student to be involved in than this important skill, listening to interpret. Here the child can use his inimitable sense of mimicry. Few children lack this ability or will fail to respond to using it. The born imitator will particularly shine and thoroughly enjoy his accomplishment. Provide him with opportunities to listen and then interpret by word or action—or a combination of these—and he will delight you, the teacher, his friends and peers, and himself as well. Teachers may fail to take advantage of this seemingly inherent talent as a means of establishing rapport, easing room tensions by a quick "shift" of gears into such an activity, building a foundation for friendships, and most of all, provide a pleasurable learning experience.

While it is true that children respond to acting out situations after having listened, it is equally true that the teacher will need to plan for experiences which allow each child to develop his listening and interpretive abilities. A variety of strategies will lend themselves to doing this effectively at the primary level.

Teaching Strategies

Frequently the classroom will provide opportunities for incidentally including situations from which listening and interpreting can be drawn. The teacher must not, though, rely on such happenings alone for strengthening students' com-

Model Lesson Plan
Teaching Listening to Identify Sounds

I. **Name:** Phyllis Anne White   **Date:** 3-4-72   **Grade:** 1 **No.** 1

   Subject: Language Arts (Listening)   **Text:** None

II. **Instructional Objective:** To provide a lesson on identifying basic speech sounds: Letter B.

   Performance Objective: Given a list of ten words pronounced orally, the student shall be able to identify those six which begin with the sound of B in the initial position and record them on a checklist.

III. **Assignment:** Participation in a group activity based on seeing-and-saying pictures and words beginning with the letter B.

   Materials: None

IV. **Procedure:**
   1. Tell the story of "Bobby Beaver Who Blew Bubbles."
   2. Introduce the "bubbling" sound of B.
   3. Use the Jingle "A Big Brown Bug Bit a Big Black Bear."
   4. Play the game "Bee Pictures and Sounds."
   5. Use short oral quiz on beginning B—students recording SAME (S) or DIFFERENT (D).

V. **Related Activities:**
   1. Scrambled sentences: listen and rearrange them. (Many B sounds.)
   2. Listen to the recording of "Bobby Beaver" at the listening post.
   3. Identifying pupil's names which begin with B: Bobby, Betty, Ben, Brenda, Billy, Bonnie, Bert, or Belle.

VI. **Evaluation:** Have the students number from 1 to 10 and listen as you pronounce the words:
1. big	5. sell	8. ball
2. yellow	6. boat	9. dough
3. bring	7. pond	10. bite
4. bad		

   If the sound is the same (S), different (D).

VII. **Ongoing Activities:**
   1. Arrange for several activity groups: Consonant Lotto; Webster Word Wheels: Initial B; Alphabet Scrap Books; and the game, "Whose School Box Are You In?"
   2. Plan a bulletin board (small) for the reading center. Children will bring attractive pictures of articles either beginning or ending in B.
   3. Learn a new tongue-twister: "Betty Botter Bought a Bit of Bitter Butter."

Figure 2.7

municative abilities. In the planning stages, numerous vehicles of instruction will be identified.

1. A group involved in a choral reading while others pantomime the actions suggested by the recitation. This offers an excellent opportunity to interpret by body motions the mood and tone of the chorused material. This use of kinesics has received recent emphasis as a valuable means of expression for the more nonverbal person.
2. The read-aloud situation, in which the teacher or aide shares trade books, stories, or poetry, offers the child listening experiences for acting out the story or incident. As he identifies with the situation or characters, the listener responds by interpreting the affective tone as well as the physical action. This depth of interpretation can be foundational to later skills of inferential comprehension from inherent or implied meanings.
3. The oral reading exercises which make up a good portion of primary instruction will afford certain children an opportunity for the voiced parts while others can role play the action of the stories or poems. The renewed emphasis on oral reading indicates an awareness on the part of educators to make use of listening and responding.
4. Many fine recordings of the listening and doing variety can be used as a setting for responding and interpreting suggested action.
5. Music, particularly the words of songs, can be used for imitation and dramatic play. The creative force in many children will find this a means of expression in many fresh and original interpretations.

These few suggested strategies will serve to guide the teacher or intern in discovering numerous other avenues to follow in planning interesting and meaningful activities for listening and interpreting. In the following model lesson plan (figure 2.8), the teacher will find an example of one such planned and used strategy.

Listening to Oral Directions

Teaching at the primary level necessitates giving oral directions frequently throughout the school day. These situations will offer the students many incidental lessons in listening to specific directions. The instructor will often channel learnings through preparation of lessons in content areas: math, science, social studies, health. In giving particular instructions for work in these subjects, the teacher can couch listening to follow instructions in those settings. Despite the many times that incidental teaching and learning may take place, the carefully planned lesson will still be necessary for emphasizing the need of listening to the sequential steps of a procedure as it is orally presented and outlined. Hence, the teacher will inter-

I. **Name:** Miss Mary Jones   **Date:** 3-7-72   **Grade:** 2 **No.** 2

Subject: Language Arts (Listening)   **Text:** None

II. **Instructional Objective:** To teach primary students to listen and interpret action and mood.

Performance Objective: After having listened to a story read aloud, the child shall remember action words from the story (running, sitting, playing) and shall interpret them with appropriate movements.

III. **Assignment:** To participate in listening group and do the written responses and actions.

Materials:
recording: "Winnie the Pooh"
record player
crayons
paper and pencils

IV. **Procedure:**
1. Arrange group at table by listening center.
2. Introduce lesson purpose and plan.
3. Play the record for preview.
4. Replay record for assigned tasks.
5. Elicit "action" word responses from students.
6. Volunteers to interpret actions suggested.
7. Play game: "Finding Picture Words."
8. Read further story incident: "The North End of Pooh" for listening and acting.

V. **Related Activities:**
1. Correlated art with picture words.
2. Read-aloud time for creative dramatics.

VI. **Evaluation:** Assess degree of learning by tabulating action word responses on children's papers, and by noting and recording (checklist) descriptive actions.

VII. **Ongoing Activities:**
1. Use recorded songs for listening and pantomiming action, mood.
2. During music period have one group sing while listening group interprets.

Comments: None.

Figure 2.8

mittently develop specific experiences for this phase of listening instruction. The following suggestions will help in planning and preparation.

Teaching Strategies

As indicated, valuable opportunities for strengthening listening skills will often be planned as one facet of the day's activities in teaching in areas other than the communication skills. In this context, the student can find meaning and purpose for attention and careful response to direct instructional steps. Teaching strategies making use of such settings are listed below.

1. The discussion of rules and directions for playing a game, sports event, drill, folk dance. Here there are sequences to be followed with a degree of precision, set boundaries to be observed, and/or specific procedures to be noted. These are usually given orally and must be listened to at the auding level if successful participation is to be assured.
2. In many small tasks, the student is requested to follow simple steps: heading papers correctly, getting ready for assignments, making corrections, recording progress, writing a simple report. Planning a lesson around such an activity results in a double reward: (1) a meaningful lesson setting, and (2) "oil" for lessening the friction that occurs in simple tasks not being done well.
3. Certain curriculum areas such as mathematics and science make use of rules and formulas to be carefully followed. In introducing a new concept, outlining a demonstration, or assigning particular work, the teacher can encourage careful listening for detailed directions. This oral outlining requires alert listeners and makes use of a teaching strategy in a practical instructional situation.
4. The classroom teacher, particularly in elementary grades, is often called upon to administer certain formalized tests: a battery of achievement tests covering numerous subject areas, specific diagnostic or progress tests (reading, math, or spelling), or to give teacher-developed evaluations. This requires giving clear directions to be followed throughout the evaluation period. Normally these instructions are given one at a time with sufficient intervals allowed for completing a particular task before the teacher moves on.

Listening to Recall

The primary student learns much via the auditory modality. Many of the songs, poems, stories, and cognitive skills are memorized as he hears them presented by teacher, parents, or peers. It is at this level of learning that many of the foundational skills which will ultimately result in critical listening and sustained auding will be developed. Naturally, the assigned tasks and the level of expectancy in respect to respondent performance must be consistent with the student's maturity and skill ability. However, as the teacher develops her instructional plans,

Model Lesson Plan
Teaching Listening to Follow Oral Instructions

I. Name: Harvey Peterson   **Date:** 5-14-73   **Grade:** 3   **No.** 3

   Subject: Language Arts (Listening)   **Text:** None

II. Instructional Objective Within a meaningful setting to present a lesson on listening
   to follow directions.

   Performance Objective: When presented with a paper-and-pencil situation, the student shall listen to a set of sequential oral directions and perform each
   step as outlined by the teacher, his response sheet to be the instrument
   of evaluation with no more than two errors.

III. Assignment: For each student to participate in an activity requiring
   step-by-step performance as requested by the teacher.

   Materials:

   sheets of unlined paper   rulers for each
   pencils   crayons
   scissors for each

IV. Procedure:
   1. Prepare for activity by distributing materials.
   2. Explain the general purpose and plan.
   3. Dictate clearly the following steps:
      a. Fold paper to form halves and then fourths lengthwise.
      b. Fold top to bottom, then from fold to bottom.
      c. Unfold paper and outline each fold mark using ruler and pencil to
         make sixteen squares.
      d. Number squares 1-4 across top, next row 5-8, third row down 9-12,
         and bottom row 13-16. Use pencil.
      e. Give variety of tasks to be followed in boxes by numbers, colors,
         and things to do; e.g., select a red crayon and make an X in box 7,
         use a green crayon and draw a circle in box 12, etc.
   4. Exchange papers and correct from teacher model.

V. Related Activities:
   1. Play the game, "Doing What Simon Says."
   2. Dictate simple procedure steps for playing P.E. game, "Grab the
      Bacon," and have children list them by number.

VI. Evaluation: The lesson procedure will be evaluated by examining the corrected
   papers of each student, tallying correct responses: folding, numbering,
   colors, and required task performance. Two errors acceptable.

VII. Ongoing Activities: Use the game described for P.E. period.
   1. Plan an art lesson and give specific directions for participants.
      Note response.
   2. Prepare a demonstration for a science experiment and use oral direc-
      tions for sequence in carrying it out.

Figure 2.9

the curriculum will include direct teaching of basic skills and provide scope for strengthening and developing him toward growth in auding abilities. One facet of this high level of active listening involves listening in order to be able to remember and recall significant details, facts, sequences in action or time, main ideas, and/or developing concepts. In order for such learnings to accrue, the teacher must plan carefully and assess progress frequently.

Teaching Strategies

An alert instructor will find opportunities to work on specific listening abilities in almost every school day where oral communication is being used; in the demonstrations, the explanations, the factual teaching times, the read-aloud experiences, the storytelling times, the discussions and reports given by students themselves, and in the use of audiovisual media. One of these vehicles can be used for carrying a valuable opportunity to instruct in listening for the purposes of remembering in order to recall needed information. The following situational strategies may be used, or suggest other means of including this facet of listening learnings in the busy school day.

1. Planning a listening to recall time when showing a film in your science, social studies, health, or physical education classes. It is a good practice when showing the film a first time that children have the freedom to watch and hear unhampered. During the second showing they can be asked to note details, facts, and information which you may want to use for recall purposes.
2. After a storytelling time, have the students recall such data as: the main characters, sequence of events, places described, or dates and times that were significant.
3. At the close of a lesson time, have a brief summary time by allowing various students to recapitulate the important parts of learnings included in the session.
4. After having given a set of instructions or directions, ask a student to stand and repeat them as closely as possible. Other students can be involved by supplying missing details or correcting the sequence.
5. Plan a "Quiz Program" after some oral report, discussion, or learning time. Discuss the procedure, prepare the question box, and have the participants draw a question related to material just orally presented. Audience listening can be encouraged for further responses to add to participants' recalling of materials.
6. After a read-aloud, or oral reading time, have a recall activity in which students may remember a particular kind of word, e.g., action words, describing words, new words, etc. Let students suggest substitute words for some of the suggested ones. Refer to these at a later time for recall and vocabulary enrichment.

Examining these kinds of learning experiences will give the teacher/intern other ideas of planning interesting instructional plans. The "Listening for Recall" lesson model which follows (figure 2.10, p. 46) provides a schema for developing these ideas into additional actual teaching materials.

TEACHING LISTENING IN THE INTERMEDIATE GRADES

It is frequently difficult to assign a particular listening skill to a teaching level, for who is to say that certain learnings should be introduced or emphasized within the graded structure of our schools? Actually, the time to introduce any instructional experience is when that skill or activity is needed by the student. However, for the sake of sequential organization and developing a continuum of skills, the authors have arranged various skills to fall within the different teaching levels. Hence, those skills included in the following section seemed to be the more discrete aural abilities requiring higher levels of maturation and cognition. Four such skill areas will be developed as models of teaching for both the preservice intern and the in-service professional. These are listening instructions to (1) organize or sequence, (2) recall details, (3) strengthen skills in following requests or instructions, and (4) be able to predict outcomes. The teacher will note that the use of listening at this middle-grade level begins to have useful purposes for the student in actual learning situations other than the language arts. Here the communication skills become utilitarian to the learner.

Listening to Organize or Sequence

At an earlier level, the young student has been introduced to the visual and psychomotor tasks of ordering, seriating, and classifying objects, pictures, or test articles to determine his ability to note progression, likenesses, differences, or some other such characteristics. Gradually as he progresses in his education and maturation, he will be able to listen and think through, solely from auditory stimuli, the patterns of information that he is receiving. Now he mentally categorizes facts, incidents, details, and arranges them in varying organizational schemas. This, of course, becomes a most useful input and output communication tool. Let us examine some of the techniques at the disposal of the alert teacher for arranging the environment of learning to provide interesting activities and valuable learning experiences for each student.

Teaching Strategies

What are some of the situations which the instructor may employ to give a setting for the development of these functional learnings? Here are some suggestions which may be helpful in the discovery of numerous ways to channel student involvement to a successful meeting of performance objectives.

1. Using any list of names, objects, places, the teacher can dictate or read them clearly and ask the students to categorize them according to a prearranged pattern: listing in order, grouping items, sorting and arranging from aural cues.
2. After listening to a report or discussion, the student can be asked to list in

Model Lesson Plan
Teaching a Lesson on Listening to Recall

I. **Name:** Jeffery Brigham   **Date:** 4-21-72   **Grade:** 3 **No.** 4

   Subject: Language Arts (Listening)   **Text:** None

II. **Instructional Objective:** To provide learning experience for developing listening skills necessary for remembering and recalling.

   Performance Objective: The students shall be able to listen to a four sentence incident read orally, and then recall four out of five facts asked for by the teacher. (See Evaluation.)

III. **Assignment:** Participation in a group discussion following couple-group reading of "Life in an Indian Village" in which basic facts are identified.

   Materials:
   social studies textbooks
   paper and pencils

IV. **Procedure:**
   1. Divide class into reading couples.
   2. Orally read the story in couple-groups.
   3. Put away books and arrange class in one group.
   4. Discuss the information by eliciting response with prompting questions by teacher or students.
   5. Return to seats for short dictated quiz based on data listened to and discussed orally.
   6. Exchange papers and correct.
   7. Return papers to owners and assess listenability.

V. **Related Activities:**
   1. Show film: "Indians of Early California," listening for details.
   2. Play the game: "True or Make Believe." Using first lines of nursery rhymes and real-life statements.

VI. **Evaluation:** Read the following lines: Johnny came running into the kitchen. "Mother, Mother," he cried, "See the book my teacher gave me today." "It is a beautiful picture book and is a fine reward for your hard work," said his mother. Johnny had spelled 100 words correctly.

   Ask: What was the boy's name?   What room did he enter?
         What was he carrying?   What kind of book was it?
         Who gave him the reward?   What had the boy done?

   The students' written papers will be the means of evaluation.

VII. **Ongoing Activities:**
   1. Use a cassette tape or disc recording of a description of a simple incident, and use it as a base for a listening-recalling exercise.
   2. Use "Can You Name the Story" activity for prompting listening for suitable information on which to base titles.

Figure 2.10

writing, or to orally state, events or data in a designated order: chronologically, in series, opposites.

3. Following an oral presentation: debate, round-table or panel discussion, dialogue. Students can respond by recalling significant details, points of interest, or specific information and by ordering or classifying it as per request.

4. Nonverbal activities—listening to rhythm patterns, musical movements, instrumental sounds—can be used for the listening activity and then from auditory memory the student can give the correct sequence in which they were presented.

5. Number sequences, letter arrangements, oral spelling activities can all be used to test auditory sequencing and memory. These can be used in small groups with written responses, or individually in oral situations.

These few suggested types of activities should serve to stimulate other productive kinds of learning experiences from the creative and imaginative intermediate instructor. Any type of listening situation which can be utilized to provide the use of oral input to later be arranged in some ordered fashion should provide the student with reinforcing opportunities to practice and make use of listening skills necessary to organize and sequence information or material for orderly presentation. The preservice intern as well as the in-service professional teacher will note that in the planned lessons which follow, such strategies have been used to provide a model for other related learnings at the intermediate level.

Recalling Main Ideas and Details from Listening

It has been determined that actually recalling main ideas is of a higher level of cognition than merely remembering detail information. So, for the middle-grade student it may be more difficult to listen and then remember a series of main ideas than to recall smaller bits of detail or fact. Certainly in most schools, the child is asked to listen and then to use the information which was offered in the oral part of the particular learning experience. This requires skill in retention, recall, and response. Although there are other factors involved—interest, concept load, vocabulary used, length of material given or read aloud, number of details or ideas to be handled—listening for the purpose of responding *does* require some practice and direct teaching just as most skills do. A certain learning by doing, and a certain strengthening of skills by practice, is obtained only by actual involvement.

Teaching Strategies

At this intermediate level of teaching, the alert instructor will not need to arrange artificial environment in order to teach the skills needed for recalling facts, details, or the larger main ideas, for these will be embedded in the very fabric of the teaching-learning act itself. In other words, the students will not

Model Lesson Plan
Providing Listening Learnings for Organizing and Sequencing Data

I. **Name:** Miss Julia Jones   **Date:** 1-28-74   **Grade:** 6   **No.** 1

   Subject: Language Arts (Listening)   **Text:** None

II. **Instructional Objective:** To teach the importance of listening in order to be able to organize materials or information in logical order or sequence.

   Performance Objective: The student shall be able, at the conclusion of a teacher read oral presentation, to list in correct sequence the five happenings preceding the outbreak of a riot. His written list shall be used to assess the listening skill.

III. **Assignment:** Each student in the group will listen to the oral reading of "The Newark Incident" and then respond by listing the events in order.

   Materials:
   teacher's copy of "Incident" for reading
   paper and pencils for students
   correction key

IV. **Procedure:**
   1. Introduce the listening lesson by discussing the importance and value of remembering information in clear detail and order.
   2. Discuss situations in which such ordering was important.
   3. Read the selection which outlines the steps leading up to the incident.
   4. Distribute materials and ask for written responses.
   5. Correct lists and evaluate in class.

V. **Related Activities:**
   1. Use short film without light for listening to sequence.
   2. Have group tape record a reading for listening post activity.

VI. **Evaluation:** The lesson will be assessed by checking the responses of the students, noting errors and successes. Also by checking oral responses by students.

VII. **Ongoing Activities:** Plan some art activity in which the students work in groups to illustrate the sequential happenings of a social studies event.

   Comments: None.

Figure 2.11

The joy of listening to evocative language often sends imaginations spinning into far and diverse worlds.

be merely "learning to listen," but they will actually be "listening to learn." In the teaching of the content areas—social studies, science, mathematics, or any other special topic area—a certain amount of the teaching will be done via the aural modality. Hence many opportunities will be afforded the student to *practice* his listening skills frequently. Lectures, reports, discussions, oral presentations of many varieties—all will require careful listening in order for the student to sort out important details or generalize with the broader concept of topics or main ideas. The recalling and sharing of the listening skills, either in written or oral form, will provide the teacher with evaluative guides for assessing the correctness of responses.

Inasmuch as listening at this level is so closely interrelated with content teaching, a model lesson plan hardly seems necessary to illustrate how one can strengthen this skill or nurture its development. However, a model (figure 2.12) is included as an example of the kinds of activities which one may make use of in specially planned lessons for teaching or strengthening particular skills. The reader will note that this planned exercise could be nicely integrated with a reading or literature lesson within which the analysis is set.

Other Listening Skills for Intermediates

The other two specific areas of listening abilities mentioned at this middle level are concerned with strengthening the child's skills in following directions

Model Lesson Plan
Listening for Details and/or the Main Topic of a Story

I. **Name:** Gloria Treadway   **Date:** 3-16-74   **Grade:** 8 **No.** 2

   Subject: Language Arts (Listening)   **Text:** Literature We Use

II. **Instructional Objective:** To provide a lesson for teaching listening for the main idea.

   Performance Objective: The student, after listening to a short story read aloud by the teacher, will be able to identify the main topic and state it in no more than two (2) written sentences.

III. **Assignment:** Participation in the listening activity.

   Materials:
   Pearl Buck, The Big Wave
   paper and pencils

IV. **Procedure:**
   1. Organize group in listening circle.
   2. Review generalization concepts.
   3. Read the story: Chapter 1.
   4. Small group discussions of details of narrative read.
   5. Individual work: thinking and writing.

V. **Related Activities:**
   1. Workbook exercise on writing topic sentences.
   2. Written "suggested" titles for the story.

VI. **Evaluation:** The teacher will collect and read the written work to determine correctness of identifying main ideas.

VII. **Ongoing Activities:** Discussion centered on the conciseness of "telegraphing" information: news items, editorials. Encourage students to select several written articles or stories for taping. These then to be listened to and "topic sentenced" for critiquing by others.

   Comments: None.

Figure 2.12

and a newer facet of aural input, that of listening to decide or predict what logical outcomes or results will occur. This presupposes that only partial input is given, and the student then uses the information, incomplete as it is, to conclude that certain happenings will result. This, it can be seen, requires a higher level of cognitive skill than recall, or even application as was used in the following of directions or instructions.

Since teaching strategies and plans for implementing those techniques were included at the primary level (see figure 2.3) another set will not be given for the intermediate teacher. Here again, much of the listening for instructions and directions now will be chiefly relevant as they occur as an integral part of the regular teaching-learning experiences. The teacher, however, must not fail to be aware of the importance of the skill and give it only incidental emphasis. Whenever listening is required in order for the student to respond to specific requests, orders, or tasks, the instructor has opportunity to reinforce and enhance the student's abilities with success. This can be accomplished by giving step-by-step procedures clearly, slowly, and with an emphasis on the necessity for careful listening to prevent error or omission in the student's performance of the required directive.

Teaching Strategies for Predictive Listening. Setting up conditions for working on this facet of listening skills may require thought and planning on the part of the teacher. Special materials and situations will normally be necessary in order to provide an interesting, relevant setting for eliciting student involvement and responsiveness. High interest, narrative materials as well as current informational articles can provide attention getting and maintaining readings for listening to predict outcomes. It seems logical that this step should follow that of identifying details, then important topics, and finally the main idea of an orally presented text or story.

Teaching Strategies

In order to keep this type of activity as viable and creative as possible, only enough should be presented to pique the imagination of the listener. Once this has been accomplished through aural input, he is on his own. Seek only to elicit originality, logical conclusions to the circumstances, or pure flights of fancy unless of course the material is informational. Then work to get realistic cause-and-effect relationships and outcomes. A variety of materials and situations can furnish settings for such learnings. The following should serve only as idea-starters.

1. The use of recorded portions of short stories from good youth literature can be used to provide adequate knowledge about a situation. These should be cut off at a strategic point so that the student listener can then proceed to make his "prophecies" on the basis of information given.
2. Teacher read-aloud selections (prose or poetry, fact or fiction) can activate thinking of possible outcomes to be discussed, written, or given solo to a group.

3. After listening to a complete account, let students think out loud and brainstorm about "what if" certain actions, conversations, incidents, had been changed. After discussing these alternatives, they may be stimulated and challenged to predict other endings or results for the situations explored.
4. Incidents from history, geographical information, science principles, can likewise furnish the alert teacher with possibilities for prompting students to see what will happen, or why it did happen, or even "What would happen if?"

These few brief suggestions may help the reader to think of numerous other situations to be used for listening experiences in which the student will get sufficient input to make "decisions, judgments, or prognoses."

TEACHING LISTENING IN THE UPPER GRADES

As the elementary student progresses into the junior high years, he will discover that listening skills increasingly become foundational to other important study skills. As he is involved in learning situations where auditory input is used, he will become keenly aware of the need to listen carefully in order to (1) take notes, (2) identify topics and main ideas, (3) develop outlines, and (4) organize summaries. Besides the amount of information he assimilates via reading, he will be constantly receiving valuable knowledge from peers as he interacts in discussions, dialogues, reporting, and debating issues. As he listens to instructors and/or aides, he will likewise be attending in order to (1) sort out ideas and concepts, (2) store information for future retrieval and use, (3) analyze and evaluate data, and (4) compress and organize the amount of aural materials coming to him via incidental remarks, lectures, explanations and demonstrations, and/or direct verbal involvement. Hence, the teaching person will recognize that listening activities at this higher level of work must be basically functional. By this the authors mean that they are chiefly utilitarian tools. They are useful not only for gaining information, but also for organizing and recording the facts, figures, and data for future useful purposes.

Let us consider the four previously mentioned, more discrete study skills which are often based on auditory input. These are examples of the relevant kinds of learning experiences the teacher may use in planning instructional activities or direct teaching lessons for advanced listening learning. As the student listens carefully, he records abbreviated ideas, concepts, or topics. From these notes, he identifies the important central learnings or main topics. These then become the divisions and subcategories for the organized, concise outline which serves as the skeleton form. From the three previous steps of utilizing aural input, the student is able to capsulize a large amount of material into a succinct, inclusive summary. All or each of the processes is based on listening ability coupled with the various study skills involved.

I. **Name:** Ron Jalisco   **Date:** 4-19-74   **Grade:** 6   **No.** 1

   Subject: Language Arts (Listening)   **Text:** None

II. **Instructional Objective:** To present a listening lesson for introducing a predictive situation.

   Performance Objective: When given an oral reading of a partial story or event, the student will be able to predict outcomes from the aural information. His stated result to be compared to the original author's.

III. **Assignment:** To listen to a prerecorded, incomplete short story; then, on the basis of information given, to write a predicted conclusion.

   Materials:
      recorder and listening post
      writing materials
      taped story

IV. **Procedure:**
   1. Introduce lesson by exploring ends-means, cause-effect components in happenings.
   2. Discuss purpose of lesson in listening.
   3. Read "brief" of "The Big Black" for a discussion and trial run of this lesson.
   4. Assign students to listening posts and after listening to do written work.
   5. Form group to read and critique each other's predictions.
   6. Collect papers for assessment.

V. **Related Activities:**
   1. Write endings to partial sentences on dittoed work sheet.
   2. Play the game: "Imaginary Monsters."

VI. **Evaluation:** In order to see if students succeeded in performance objective, read written responses to determine if additional work is indicated.

VII. **Ongoing Activities:** Suggest an activity (home) in which students bring "cut" news items for completion in news discussion period, or rewrite headlines for others to fill in details from predictions.

   Comments: None.

Figure 2.13

Listening for Taking Notes

The student soon discovers that if he listens, even with serious intent and concentration, retention is temporary, and he easily forgets many details and important facts. Later when he attempts to recall these, they have been extinguished. Without some means of refreshing his memory such as the use of his written notes, outlines, summaries, he is unable to function adequately. Naturally this ability of recall varies from student to student, but the majority soon discover the value of aiding memory by some sort of note-taking.

Teaching Strategies

The consideration of the various learning experiences that the teacher/intern may use and the instructional activities planned for strengthening listening abilities may serve for a whole spectrum of objectives at this level of learning. In other words, the following suggested strategies could serve not only to provide a setting for listening to take notes, but also to identify important ideas and main topics. The same learning experience would likewise be just as well used for teaching students to listen for outlining purposes or for developing good summaries. For this reason, the authors have grouped these strategies and sample lesson plans.

The following then can be considered as useful suggestions for the kind of double sequencing necessary for successful progression in content materials as well as skills development. As the teaching materials become more advanced, the student's powers are likewise enhanced. Lesson settings for developing these powers could well include some of the ideas listed.

1. The many times during each school day or week when upper-grade pupils are passively listening in a typical lecture or teacher presentation. Information is being considered and shared by the instructor for the benefit of the listening student. This becomes a relevant, purposeful means of interjecting some learnings about careful listening in order to record pertinent facts or data.
2. Another situation which may be used for listening instruction with a purpose is the less formal talk time or buzz session when students are encouraged to talk together in a sort of free-flowing, conversational climate. As they share their own ideas, comments, and reactions, the alert student will use listening for recording this type of peer teaching-learning.
3. Teachers may wish to think through the more formal situation of the round-table discussion, group discussion or panel discussion and its valuable contribution to the listening student's opportunities for input to be recorded in one of the previously mentioned aural objectives. This particularly lends itself to outlining and summarizing.
4. The debate, with its pros and cons, offers a listening lesson for students to sort out and evaluate, to organize and record, and to reject or retain from the audi-

tory input of the nonparticipant as well as the active debater involved in the oral presentation.

5. Any kind of oral reporting, live or recorded situations alike, provides a reason for the listeners to use their aural powers as a means of reinforcing and recording this information-getting situation. Be it note-taking, outlining, or summarizing from aural reception, the record can only be a good one if careful, thoughtful listening precedes it.

6. Frequently in the upper grades, students are involved in demonstrating how-to-do-it kinds of materials, social situations, or science experiences. A large part of their presentation is often the verbal explanations given. These, again, provide the teacher with a fine opportunity for reemphasizing the need for focused listening and active recording response.

These suggested individual and group activities exemplify the kinds of situations which aid the teacher in the planning of strategies for enhancing student listening skills. A single model plan should be sufficient to illustrate the use of such activities to help the student reach the behavioral objective in his performance.

The authors have sought to show that the upper-grade student will frequently need to "pare" down the bulk of aural material which is presented in the ordinary classroom via the lecture, report, demonstration, debate, and film. This recording, organizing, condensing process requires a high level of cognition combined with advanced listening abilities. These abilities should be utilized in learning situations so that they provide the student with a meaningful setting in actual classroom work. Whenever the teacher can make use of the learning situation for reinforcing any of the communication skills, it should prove to be a valuable asset in the reaching of the instructional as well as the performance objectives specified. This, then is an appeal for clear thinking and thorough planning on the part of the instructor. Thus the teacher/intern will take professional advantage of every opportunity for developing curricula that provide for the double sequencing progress in both content and power areas.

SUMMARY

The teaching of listening skills can hardly be overemphasized to teachers in the modern elementary school. The shortness of the school day, the fullness of the schedule, and the number of children assigned to each teacher often combine to make it difficult to find time and opportunity to include this important facet of language learning in the instructional planning and curriculum offerings. However, without this basic input modality, the student will be seriously handicapped for future learning success.

The levels of listening must be recognized and provided for. As the child progresses academically and maturationally, new demands are made of his growing abilities to aud. The student may well find himself unable to cope with edu-

Model Lesson Plan
Strengthening the Ability to Listen in Order to Record Information for Future Use

I. **Name:** Mr. Sam Jones   **Date:** 11-6-74   **Grade:** 8   **No.** 1

   Subject: Language Arts (Listening)   **Text:** None

II. **Instructional Objective:** To present a listening lesson which would form the basis for using the information input to instruct in taking notes, outlining, identifying main topics, or summarizing.

   Performance Objective: When presented with a fifteen-minute listening situation (lecture, demonstration, report, discussion), the student will be able to outline the four main points with at least two subpoints for each. The outline shall follow correct form as evaluated by the teacher model with a minimum of 15-20 possible points.

III. **Assignment:** Review correct outline form from English textbook, Ch. 7, pages 214-216.
   Participation in listening and note-taking for outline of presentation.

   Materials:
   English textbook and enlarged outline model
   prepared tape-recorded presentation—"Fossils"
   writing materials
   overhead projector and screen
   tape recorder

IV. **Procedure:**
   1. Five-minute review of outline model projected.
   2. Discussion of importance and need for outlines.
   3. Play recorded presentation for student listening and note-taking during aural session.
   4. Writing period: outlines from notes.
   5. Project preoutlined model for socialized correction of student work.
   6. Evaluate and check outlines.

V. **Related Activities:**
   1. Show and discuss the film: "Listening with a Purpose."
   2. Group activity: Demonstration and cooperative outlining of main ideas.

VI. **Evaluation:** Teacher will use, with the student group, the corrected outlines and note-taking sheets for determining needs for further listening sessions for the purpose of recording.

VII. **Ongoing Activities:**
   1. Use techniques in science lab session for recording experimental data.
   2. Plan to use listening skills to analyze film presentation with only sound track, no pictures.

   Comments: None.

Figure 2.14

cational and societal listening requirements unless instruction is given; activities and experiences provided for nurturing the growing skill; and time and attention given to needs, impairments, and/or deficiencies.

All beginning language development builds on the child's listening. The sequential skills have been considered in a continuum organization—one building upon the other in a growing hierarchy. Both theory and practice combine in the educational effort to assist the child in his growing development into a total being. His listening abilities enable him to listen creatively, selectively, functionally, and for aesthetic appreciation. Hence, the task of the teacher includes learning experiences and specific instructional objectives which will cultivate active successful listeners.

Selected Readings: The Listening Vocabulary

FUNK, HAL D., and TRIPLETT, DEWAYNE. *Language Arts in the Elementary School: Readings.* New York: J. B. Lippincott Company, 1972.

JACKSON, ANN E. "An Investigation of the Relationship Between Listening and Selected Variables in Grades 4, 5 and 6." Ph.D. dissertation, Arizona State University, 1966, in *Dissertation Abstracts* 27 (1) 53A, July 1966.

JACOBS, LELAND B. "Speaking and Listening." In *Skill Development in Social Studies,* edited by Helen McCracken Carpenter, National Council for Social Studies, NEA, Washington, D.C., 1963.

KELLEY, CHARLES E. "Mental Ability and Personality Factors in Listening." *Quarterly Journal of Speech* 49 (April 1963):152–156.

KRANER, ROBERT E. "A Comparison of Two Methods of Listening Instruction in an Eighth Grade Language Arts Program." Ph.D. dissertation, University of Texas, Austin, 1963.

LEWIS, THOMAS R., and NICOLS, RALPH. *Speaking and Listening.* Dubuque, Iowa: Wm. C. Brown Company Publishers, 1965.

LOGAN, LILLIAN M. *Teaching the Young Child.* Boston: Houghton Mifflin Company, 1960.

——— et al. *Creative Communication: Teaching the Language Arts.* Toronto: McGraw-Hill Ryerson, Limited, 1972.

NICOLS, RALPH G. "Do We Know How to Listen? Practical Helps in a Modern Age." *The Speech Teacher* 10 (March 1961):120–124.

ROSS, RAMON. "A Look at Listeners." *Elementary School Journal* 64 (April 1964):369–372.

RANKIN, PAUL T. "The Importance of Listening Ability." *English Journal* (College Edition) 17 (1928):623–630.

SMITH, E. BROOKS et al. *Language and Thinking in the Elementary School.* New York: Holt, Rinehart & Winston, Inc., 1970.

TRIVETTE, SUE E. "The Effect of Training in Listening for Specific Purposes." *Journal of Educational Research* 54 (March 1961):276–277.

WILT, MIRIAM. "A Study of Teacher Awareness of Listening as a Factor in Elementary Education." *Journal of Educational Research* 43 (April 1950):626–636.

WINTER, CLOTILDA. "Listening and Learning." *Elementary English* 43 (October 1966):
569–572.

WOODWARD, VIRGINIA A. "Young Children Initiate Their Own Listening Experiences."
Young Children, National Association for the Education of Young Children 31 (October 1965):10–11.

THE DEVELOPMENT
OF LANGUAGE
THROUGH SPEAKING

SPEAKING,
THE SECOND VOCABULARY
THE THEORETICAL APPROACH

SPEECH DEVELOPMENT IN THE HOME SETTING

The Second Vocabulary: Imitation

As pointed out earlier in Part One of this book, the child's second vocabulary, that of speech, develops directly as a result of his first vocabulary, listening. Without that first vocabulary, listening, speech cannot develop. Listening is an *intake* activity. Speech is an *output* activity, dependent upon the intake that has occurred. When the child speaks he is, by and large, imitating what he has heard. It is a new and effective tool for the child to bring attention to his continued and more sophisticated needs and wants.

As the child develops and grows, he is more and more able to sort out certain sounds in his listening environment and attach them to specific items, objects, wants, and desires. As maturation continues, he will attempt to imitate the sounds he hears in relation to his wants. When this occurs, speech is in the initial stage.

Communication starts, as we have noted in Chapter 1, through nonspeech communication. The child will gurgle, coo, and occupy himself generally with other vocal play. A parent will attempt (and often correctly) to understand what these utterances mean. Responses to these utterances are, of course, positive reinforcement. Children will often develop a whole system of nonspeech language that will assist him in meeting his basic needs. In the process of this kind of communication, the parent talks to the child, using words and phrases that soon become familiar to him. He is soon able to sort out such key words as "water," "bottle," "mommy," "daddy," and the like. Later, when these words become familiar enough and speech muscles have developed sufficiently, he will attempt to recreate those sounds that stand for items he wishes. When this happens the flurry of responses his utterances cause certainly are positive reinforcements. He is encouraged to repeat his new words for father, grandmother, grandfather, aunts, uncles, or anyone else within grasp of the proud parents. The commotion his imitative utterances has caused will likely manifest itself in attempts at other words and phrases. The phenomenon of speech has begun.

It is important to know that speech is *imitative*. It is developed directly from what the child hears. If his listening environment at home is a poor one, and he has not been encouraged to speak through vocal play, speech development is likely to be retarded at best. Speech is an attempt to recreate (output) what he hears (input). If the input is slight, the output will suffer as a result. The very young child needs an environment that is conducive to speech development.

Certainly the home environment is most important for early speech development. If the family "talks" to the child, if there is a rich use of language in the home, if the child is encouraged to respond verbally, then with the normal child, language will advance. If, on the other hand, language use is sparse in the home, the child is left to "fend for himself" in an environment that does not value verbal communication. Retardation is likely to occur in normal speech development.

Sibling and peer group oral language patterns also have a noticeable effect on the young child's mastery of speaking skills. Other young children in the home certainly will provide models for imitation and stimulus for acquisition of new vocabulary and speech patterns. Peer playmates, in an informal setting or in a more formal environment such as a nursery or a preschool setting, also can provide a situation from which oral language can grow. It is important that oral language surround the child, and it is equally important that he contribute to that oral language environment. "Silence is golden" may be a delightful folk expression, but it is certainly invalid as a way of developing the youngster's oral language skills. If he is to imitate speech, he must hear it. He also needs the opportunity to attempt to recreate what he hears. His home and his peer experiences provide the foundation for further growth.[1]

The good preschool or kindergarten teacher knows that in many children oral language is still in its initial stages. Knowing this, the teacher will plan carefully to provide the youngster with many and varied experiences that will aid, enhance, and encourage his ability to communicate with the spoken word. Her class is not likely to be a quiet place! The hum of activities is constant in this classroom. Children are encouraged to talk. Physical equipment is available to the children that is designed to stimulate conversation. There are valid reasons why the teacher of the very young will provide a playhouse for dramatic play, certain classroom pets, game areas, and the like. Each of these are reasons for children to talk! The walking trips that she takes with her youngsters provide more experiences for her children

---

1. Robert Ruddell, "Oral Language and the Development of Other Language Skills," *Elementary English,* May 1966, pp. 489–498.

to talk about. To the layman or the unknowing, preschool and kindergarten seem to be a time of "endless fun," and of little educational value. What nonsense! The informed know that the good preschool/kindergarten experience is laying the groundwork and setting the foundation for the learning that will continue as the child matures. Much of this groundwork and foundation is in the realm of oral language development. The kindergarten teacher knows that the other skills of language—reading and writing—depend heavily on a primary vocabulary, that of speech (see Chapter 4, pp. 77–107).

Dialect: Kinds of Speech

We Americans enjoy our regional dialects. We can often determine a person's origin in the United States by the dialect he uses. A person from Georgia uses a particular dialect that is uniquely his. So does the Bostonian and the "down east-erner" from Maine. The western twang of Texas is different still, as is the speech of the Midwest and the Far West. These dialectic differences have emerged from complicated social and ethnic forces, much too complex to discuss in a book of this nature. That the phenomenon exists is a fact and needs to be recognized as a fact.

What then, as teachers, should be our concern about regional dialects as youngsters learn the communication skills of speaking? What stance should we take concerning regional dialects in our classrooms?

Perhaps it would be good to accept the idea that dialect itself is part of what may be considered as standard American English. Many times the dialect of a region is involved with self-concept, family pride, historical ties, and ethnic involvement. Often more is involved than just "speaking differently." There can be a whole socioemotional syndrome connected with regional dialects.

Oral language is learned through imitation of what one hears. If the child's listening environment in the early years contained the element of dialect, then his imitative attempts to recreate what he has heard will certainly reflect that dialect.

In our very mobile society where families are likely to move from one region to another, these differences are likely to be very apparent. The teacher would be wise to accept these regional dialects as part of the cluster of individual traits she finds in all students. To "point up" a dialectic difference in a classroom situation would not, in any sense, be advisable. To embarrass a child for acceptable English in one geographical context while he resides in another is really more cruel than educational. Probably the best advice to the teacher concerning regional dialect might be: Leave it alone. Do not call attention to it or attempt conscious correction of it in the classroom. Regional dialects have emotional dimensions. To replace one with another is questionable. Time, and exposure to good oral language will diminish any problem in this area.[2]

---

2. Alvina Burrows et al., *New Horizons in the Language Arts* (New York: Harper & Row, 1972), pp. 196–197.

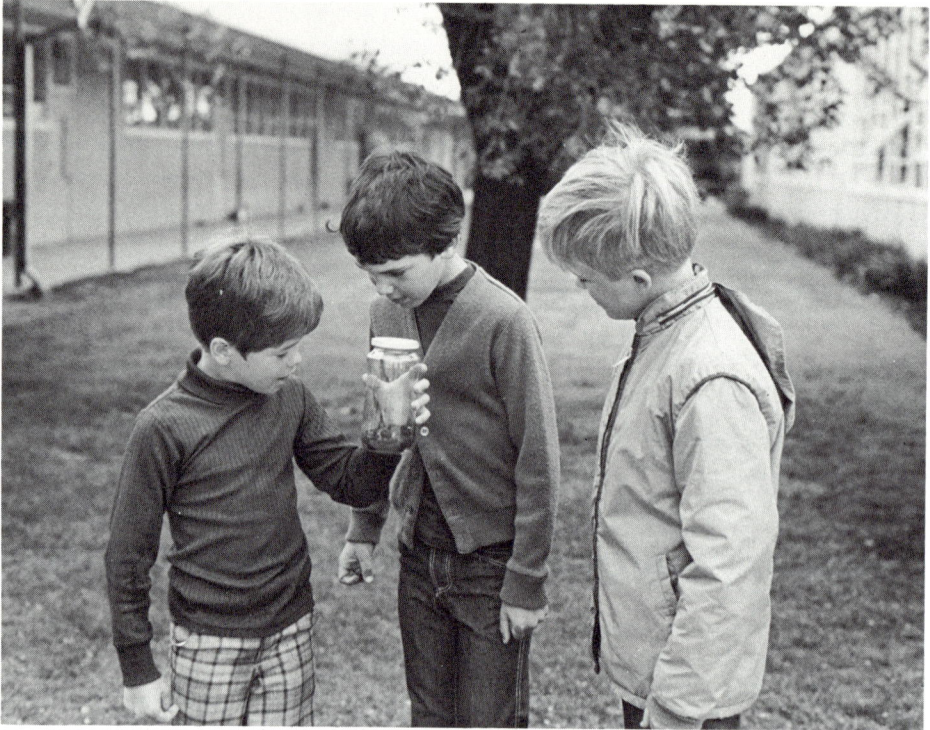

Opportunities for informal conversation are a major variable in helping to develop the child's speaking vocabulary. A school environment must provide such opportunities.

Problems of Nonstandard American English in Speaking

While we, as teachers, are wise to accept regional dialect as a form of standard American English, the issues of structure and syntax of the language are quite another matter. Some children come into our classrooms with a language pattern that is nonstandard. That is, they have learned through their adult models to string words together in a nongrammatical or incorrect fashion. They literally have "another language," a language that belongs to the home and peer environment. They can function well in these contexts, but when they attempt standard American English either in a spoken or written way, they find themselves at a disadvantage.

Unlike the syndrome of regional dialect, this form of oral language should cause us concern. The concern should stem from the fact that this form of nonstandard American English can be a hindrance in a child's social development as well as a major roadblock in the youngster's ability to learn the other language skills of reading and writing. We can consider, perhaps, the notion that he speaks a language of his own, and we as teachers are asking him to read and write in another.

It is not a simple matter to change a child's linguistic pattern. He has come to learn a language set and to use it as a functional life tool. When he comes to us in the early grades, or younger, the language syndrome that he functions with in that environment probably met his needs quite well. Now he is faced with the monumental task of changing or modifying that language pattern to meet the new needs of his school environment. This is coupled with the fact that his listening environment at home, the major force in developing his speech pattern, probably has not changed. The possibility of a language dichotomy is very real. He speaks one linguistic pattern at home and with his peers and is expected to work with another at school. Since his home and peer environment are primary, the task of the teacher to change the structure of his language in school, certainly not a primary environment, is not to be taken lightly!

What then are we, as teachers, to do to improve nonstandard American English when we find it as a functioning life tool of the youngsters we seek to teach? What teaching strategies can we prepare and perform that will aid in helping children develop a more acceptable standard of oral American English both in and out of the classroom? Probably the best we can do is to provide them with a good language model. In short, the language we use when we speak needs to be an excellent example of structure, grammar, and syntax. We need to augment the listening environment that has taught the substandard speech pattern from the beginning. What is heard from us, his teachers, needs to be correct American English in form and structure.[3]

Certainly we do not need to be pedantic about it! We do not need to consciously and pointedly correct him when he uses substandard speech in the classroom. This often causes embarrassment and will force the child to retreat from oral language in his contact with us. Perhaps a more realistic approach might be to simply rephrase what he has said in a correct form immediately after he has said it. This needs to be done in an easy, relaxed, friendly way, without a condescending, superior attitude. The authors remember well a situation in which this kind of rephrasing was shown to be a very effective teaching tool. The teacher was working with a class of Hawaiian kindergarten children in a rural agricultural community. The children came from an environment that fostered speaking a nonstandard form of American English that was highly dialectic. The teacher, an Oriental-American herself and a native of Hawaii, knew well the speech pattern her youngsters used. She, in fact, had spoken this form of "Pidgin English" herself when she was a child. Her dialect, or accent, still retained the distinctive Hawaiian flavor.

---

3. Hans Kurath, "Area Linguistics and the Teacher of English," *Language Learning*, March 1961, pp. 9–14.

The children gathered around their teacher, anxious to know the next phase of their activity, full of giggles and lots of talk. Miss Yamoto informed the children that next week they were going to visit a pineapple processing plant to see how the fruit was made ready for the canned product that sold around the world. The children were delighted at the prospect of going by bus to the large cannery nearby.

"Miss Yamoto, we going do that?" one bright-eyed lad demanded.
"Yes, Kimo, we are going to do that," Miss Yamoto answered.
"We going do that really?" another asked.
"*Are* we really going to do that?" Miss Yamoto replied.
"Are we really going to do that?" the girl smiled back.
"Yes, we really are going to do that," Miss Yamoto replied, and the conversation continued.

That small, seemingly insignificant conversation, wherein Miss Yamoto informally, but firmly, requested the child to rephrase the question using her phrase as the model, clearly began to establish a new pattern of spoken English. This kind of teaching, if consistent, can modify nonstandard American English in oral usage. Miss Yamoto gave no correction relating to dialect or accent—simply grammar and structure. No embarrassment was felt, no feelings injured. One pattern of speech was replaced with another, and acceptance of the correct form served as positive reinforcement.

It is important to recognize that many times a child will develop two kinds of oral language. He will learn to use a more correct form of American English in the classroom setting while retaining a cultural nonstandard form for other situations. The authors do not view this situation with any alarm. In fact they view it as a rather normal reaction. It is a simple matter of formal and informal speech. We all use different patterns of language for different situations. The important issue[4] is for the child to know the difference and to be able to switch from informal to formal speech when the occasion calls for it.

It is not unusual for a child to maintain his status in his family and peer group by using the language common to those settings, switching to a more accepted form when the situation demands. As said before, the ability to make that switch and to function in an acceptable form when required is the important issue. That is what our teaching should provide.

Publishers have provided a myriad of work sheets, workbooks, pamphlets, and the like to assist the teacher in helping students overcome the problem of non-standard American English. They offer exercises in grammar, programmed experiences with structure of the language, and endless blank spaces to be filled. If one were to read the propaganda accompanying these work sheets, one might actually believe that the panacea has been found. Actually, while these exercises probably

---

4. Paul C. Burns et al., "Oral Composition," in *The Language Arts in Childhood Education* (Chicago, Ill.: Rand-McNally & Co., 1971), pp. 100–144.

won't harm the student (other than to provide extreme boredom), they very likely will not aid the student in improving nonstandard oral speech in the context under discussion here. Despite the exciting claims made, there is little evidence to warrant their use in the classroom as a way of improving oral language.

We need to remember that the major factor in speech development for a normal child is the listening environment he has been immersed in, and the opportunity to imitate what he hears in the form of speech. It is an active *intake* and *output* activity that requires much more than hand and finger muscle use. "Does it sound right" will likely be the criterion he will use when he operates with these work sheets anyway. It is important that we give him the opportunity to know whether it "sounds right" or not. That can only be done through oral models.

SPEAKING VOCABULARY FOR THOSE WHOSE FIRST LANGUAGE IS OTHER THAN ENGLISH

Because we are a polyglot society made up of the many peoples that we are, the issue of one national language has always been a problem. Historical and sociological clusters have determined that English be the official language of the United States. Because of this fact, a proficiency in the English language is really a necessity if one is going to succeed in our society. Yet there are many thousands of Americans, both young and old, whose native language is other than English and have a marginal—if any—command of the official English language. Certainly our schools are familiar with this problem. Children coming into our classrooms speaking languages other than English, yet attempting to receive instruction in English, are not rare. One need only to examine the phenomena of the Spanish-speaking child of the Southwest or the East Coast and the child of the Far West and Hawaii whose native language may be Chinese, to understand the dilemma in which both the child, and the school attempting to aid the child, find themselves.

Some controversy has existed over whether or not the child should be required to learn English and function in the official language. Some have argued that the native language (other than English) is part of the child's cultural heritage, and he should not receive instruction in the official English. He should be instructed in his native language and should be judged, linguistically at least, on his ability with his native language.

The authors are not willing to agree with that point of view. The fact remains that English *is* the official language of the United States, and if one is to take his rightful place in the society, a proficiency in English is necessary. A child whose first language is other than English, and who does not receive instruction in English, is being shortchanged educationally. When one finds himself in a linguistic milieu, he needs to function in that milieu to assure his well-being. Retaining another language other than English as an auxiliary language, while developing proficiency in English is another matter. Bilingualism is often, and rightly so, encouraged. Bilingualism, however, is not the issue being considered here. We are concerned with the child whose first language is other than English, and our attempts to help him master English so that all his language growth can develop in the official language.[5]

First and foremost, the child should never be punished for using his own language in the classroom. To punish, to embarrass, to belittle a child for using a functional life tool as important as language in the classroom setting is not only cruel, but can often disturb the relationships we seek to establish with our students. We need to encourage his use of English and discourage his use of another language.

It is most likely that the child who prefers to communicate in a foreign language has had a listening environment that provided a foreign language model. He simply hasn't heard enough English to establish a listening vocabulary so that a speaking vocabulary can emerge. Our first job, then, is to provide that listening environment. We give the child an English-speaking environment so that he can learn to sort out words, phrases and sentences in English and can imitate these utterances to meet his needs. We give him linguistic patterns, oral-aural stimulation so that his listening and thus speaking vocabulary can grow.

It would, of course, be ideal if the teacher spoke the foreign language of the child so that she could assist him in his task of learning English by occasionally clearing up misconceptions for the youngster in his native tongue. Of course, with a teacher who speaks the foreign language, the danger exists that she might not restrict the use of that foreign language enough, and cause the child to rely more on his native language than on his new language, English. Regardless of this possibility, the scarcity of bilingual teachers makes this possibility less than probable.

The English language milieu with which we seek to surround the child then, increases his listening vocabulary and, as a result, his speaking vocabulary. Some teachers of foreign-speaking children label objects about the classroom so that not only will the child hear the name of the object but will see it in written form too. Such familiar classroom objects as *chair, sink, desk, blackboard, book* are labeled This is particularly valuable for middle- and upper-grade children.[6]

Teachers need to be aware then when we seek to teach children whose first language is other than English, confusion on the part of the learner is very apt to be a regular part of his learning. Not only is he confused socially, but many times his confusion extends to the object and the description of it. The authors are aware

5. Charlotte K. Brooks, "Some Approaches to Teaching Standard English As a Second Language," in *Elementary School Language Arts: Selected Readings*, ed. Burns and Schell (Chicago, Ill.: Rand-McNally & Co., 1969), pp. 398–405.
6. Hartford Board of Education, "Hints for Regular Classroom Teachers And Special Teachers Having Non-English Pupils," in *Effective Language Arts Practices in the Elementary School: Selected Readings*, ed. Harold Newman (New York: John C. Wiley & Sons, Inc., 1972), pp. 112–118.

of one situation in which this kind of confusion was manifest. The teacher, working with a group of Spanish-speaking children, was attempting to induce oral-aural learning by holding an article, pronouncing it, and asking children to repeat back the name of the object. The object she was holding was a blue book. She carefully enunciated "this is a book." The children repeated after her "this is a book." Several other items were held up to be viewed and identified in the same manner. Children repeated the phrases until the teacher felt that the items were recognizable in English. Soon after the lesson was completed, one of the girls in the group came proudly to the teacher and pointed to her blue dress and happily stated "this is a book." Obviously the child confused the description with the object. The book was blue. So was her dress. The meaning to her at least of "this is a book" meant the description of the book which was blue. The teacher then quickly gathered several books of various colors and held each one up to the child and repeated "this is a book." The confusion was cleared, and both teacher and the authors of this book learned a lot.

It needs to be understood that English is learned with greater or lesser ease, depending upon the foreign language the child speaks. If structure of the foreign language is similar to English, the new target, English, is learned with greater ease. If not similar in structure, greater problems must be faced. A German-speaking child, for instance, will have greater ease in learning English than will a Chinese-speaking youngster. The structure of the German language is more similar to English than is Chinese, thus an easier transition is possible.

Since developing an English speaking vocabulary is dependent upon a listening vocabulary, listening needs to be emphasized. With some language groups, certain sounds in English are completely alien. That is, some sounds are simply not heard and therefore cannot be reproduced. Real care in these cases as to aural acuity is important. A Spanish-speaking child, for instance, finds it very difficult to hear the difference between *sit* and *sat*. He hears *sēt* and will reproduce that sound. The Oriental child does not hear the "l" sound, because it does not exist in his native language. His attempts to reproduce words having an "l" involvement are very difficult for him. When these problems occur, an emphasis on these particular sounds needs to be pointed. He needs to listen, and listen again so that his acuity in hearing is sharpened to the point that he can reproduce sounds that are alien to his first language. In planning for children for whom English is a second language, this important phenomenon needs to be considered.

Children coming to us with the problem of having a language other than English as a first language need special consideration. Their growth in all the language levels will be blighted if they are not able to communicate in the official English language. The base of their problem is a listening-speaking environment. They have, through a listening, imitative syndrome, learned the symbols of speech in another language. That listening and speaking environment needs to be replaced, or at least augmented, with English. From the English speaking vocabularies, those of reading and writing are apt to proceed with more ease.

Problems of Bilingualism

Bilingualism implies that one speaks two or more languages with equal ease. It may be assumed that one of those languages is the official language of the culture in which one lives. Under this definition, bilingualism is to be envied, if not cherished. How fortunate one is to listen, speak, read, and write in more than one language! When possible this kind of situation needs to be encouraged.

Unfortunately in some cases, bilingualism leads to confusion in both languages. When this occurs, real problems of language development may result. This kind of confusion is best exemplified by the Spanish-American combination that has developed in certain Latin American communities of New York City and in the American Southwest. Living in a bilingual environment, the child's listening and thus his speaking vocabularies have been a combination of both Spanish and English. No attempt to help the child sort out the difference between the two languages has been apparent. The result has been "Spenglish," a term coined several years ago by linguists to describe this language as it exists.

This youngster coming into an English-speaking school as he does, and attempting to meet the linguistic needs of the school as he must to succeed, is at a distinct disadvantage. Some authorities indicate his plight, being for all practical purposes functionally disabled in both languages, is as serious as that of operating with English as a second language. Certainly his English vocabularies are slight, his syntax is often incorrect, and his patterning of the language is many times wanting. In a practical sense, he does speak a language that is other than English. If we are to help him succeed in school, he must have a command of English. One would hope that in helping this child cope with a new linguistic set, one would interact with him on a level that would be appropriate for a child speaking a foreign language. At least one would assume that the guidelines set in the section of this chapter called *Problems of Nonstandard American English in Speaking* would be utilized. His is a most serious problem. He needs help with the language. His future growth as a student very well may be at stake!

PROBLEMS WITH SPEAKING: DISABILITIES AND DEFICIENCIES FOR THE SPECIALIST

In all of our classrooms there are a number of children with speech problems that we as teachers have insufficient training to correct or even understand. These speech disabilities or deficiencies require the attention of a specialist. Rhythmic disabilities, or the flow of words; problems of articulation, or how words are formed; problems of phonation, dealing with such problems as chronic hoarseness; and language or symbolic problems, dealing with issues that cluster around the large area of language-deviant children, are part of this problem.

Our professional education that gave us the knowledge and skills necessary for teaching did not provide us with the specialized training that will allow us to deal with speech disorders of this nature. To treat problems of this magnitude requires intensive graduate study in the area of speech disorder and speech correction. Most school districts provide such specialists. Probably our major role in helping children with deviant speech is simply to call the attention of the specialist to the child who is experiencing difficulty. Once we have done that, we need to follow through with any and all recommendations that specialist may suggest.

For us to attempt speech therapy would be foolish and possibly dangerous. Perhaps we should think of speech disorders of the described magnitude in the same way we think of physical disabilities or psychological disturbances. It's best to leave these areas to the physician or the psychologist. We need to follow their suggestions and not attempt to diagnose and treat.[7]

ORAL LANGUAGE IN THE CLASSROOM: THE NEED TO SPEAK

The modern classroom is not a silent place. It is a place where language is used. It is a place to listen and a place to speak. It is a place where vocabularies are built, or at least enhanced. It is a place where language input and output occur.

The experienced teacher knows that a chaotic, disorganized, confused class-

A vital classroom setting allows for children's use of oral speech. Teachers often stress the courtesies of speech as being equally important in emphasis.

7. Evelyn Young Allen, "What the Classroom Teacher Can Do for the Child with Speech Defects," *NEA Journal,* November 1967, pp. 35–36.

room is one that is likely to hinder language development as effectively as one that is consistently silent. She knows that the classroom that encourages the development of a speaking vocabulary is well planned, well organized, creative, and always under the control of a professional teacher. She recognizes the need to speak on the part of the students. She, therefore, provides opportunities for children to speak. This opportunity for meaningful, oral language development is part and parcel of her professional planning for the educational well-being of the children she is charged to educate.

Apart from the normal flow of conversation that is inherent in a classroom that fosters language growth, what activities can a teacher provide that will enhance the speaking vocabulary? What can she do, within the confines of a classroom, that will motivate children to use oral language in a meaningful, developmental way? The following idea clusters may well provide many creative plans. These, plus the illustrative lesson plans that follow, should provide the genesis for an orally rich environment in the elementary classroom.

Share-and-tell. This often abused, and sometimes disliked, technique does have value in oral language development if handled correctly. Essentially this technique requires that a certain portion of the day (fifteen to twenty minutes, usually) be set aside for children to share experiences or to discuss a personal object with his peers in the classroom. It gives the student an opportunity to describe, to demonstrate with language, and to relate happenings to his peer group. In doing so, oral language is utilized as a workable, practical tool.

This technique, sometimes is thought of as an "old chestnut" by teachers, has been in the classroom for many years. It has openly been misused by too many teachers. What seems to have been missing in the use of this technique is the issue of structure and objectives on the part of the teacher. In too many cases, it has been allowed to fall into the category of a rambling kind of a waste of time while the teacher completes necessary book work and clerical duties. It is a sad state of affairs when a technique for language development becomes an activity to free the teacher.

Many teachers have structured, placed certain requirements, and have utilized this technique in a very effective way. Share-and-tell may only be employed several times a week, instead of the every morning syndrome with which it has become associated. Some have required that objects be brought from home to stimulate the discussion, rather than a last minute "oral ramble" that so many teachers dislike. The good teacher will also structure the opportunities for share-and-tell with the students. The shy, nonverbal child will be encouraged; while the child with excessive verbal potential will be urged to listen rather than monopolize this time period.

Variations on this idea are available for any creative teacher. They range from the "Magic Circle" of the kindergarten to the complicated oral discussions in the junior high school. The technique is a valid one. Its use sometimes needs to be questioned (see figure 4.3, p. 92).

Retell extraclass experiences. Many times students will have experiences that are directly related to class activity, but yet are removed from the confines of the regular classroom. Such experiences as a field or study trip, baseball games during the lunch recess, hobby shows, children's clubs and the like, all offer opportunity for speaking. These extraclass experiences, if seized upon by the teacher, can become meaningful speech exercises in that they offer valid and often exciting opportunities for retelling. Even the less verbal child will tell what his favorite part of the study trip was, and he will often relate it with relish! To retell how a team won the game in the last few minutes before the bell will offer a flood of language from a group of children. This kind of informal oral language, if allowed within the structured classroom, will pay handsome dividends in all aspects of language development for the elementary school pupil.

Oral planning for activities. All good, creative teachers know the value of planned activities as a regular part of classroom procedure. That activity can range from a short field trip or a construction project in the social studies, to a classroom party to celebrate a special occasion. Any activity requires planning if it is to be successful. A large part of that planning should be done by the students and the teacher working as a team. Much of that planning is done with oral language, in that the students and teacher need to talk over what the activity will be about.

Some teachers, and wisely so, will help children learn to organize for oral planning. Often they will structure the phases of planning for an activity by posting on the chalkboard (or other places) certain parameters needed for good oral planning. Many teachers seem to prefer the classic three-stage approach: (1) *What*—what is the activity we are about to plan? (2) *Why*—why is the activity important to us as students? and (3) *How*—how will we go about doing what we have proposed to do? This kind of structure helps children focus more clearly, and it facilitates the activity under consideration. Planning for activities offers a wealth of opportunity for helping children develop skills in oral language.

Prepare and deliver oral reports. Many areas of the elementary curriculum provide opportunities for oral reporting. These reports can range from the highly structured science activity reports or reports on projects in the social studies, to the informal oral book report in which children share with other children the delight they found between the pages of a trade book. These reports, of course, will vary in length and sophistication depending upon the age and ability of the youngsters involved. Oral reports offer children another way of using oral language as a functional life tool. Their value, if not used excessively, is great in helping children develop the skills of speaking (see pp. 100–101).

Class government and committee meetings. Many classrooms will elect officers periodically to manage certain student affairs within the structure of the usual class day. These officers (usually a president, vice-president, and secretary) have roles that vary depending upon the age and ability of the students. Some class governments are as simple as having the elected officers open the day with the flag salute, take the roll, and the milk and lunch count. Others are the very sophisticated class governments of some upper grades where actual constitutions are written to govern the class activities and where lengthy and complicated meetings are held adhering to elementary Robert's Rules of Order.

These class governments, and the meetings that are held as a result of them, are often excellent in ways of helping children develop greater facility with oral language. Children discuss, learn certain rudimentary rules for persuasive speech in an attempt to win a point, and learn that oral language is a potent force in a life-style. Oral language growth, coming partially as a result of a stimulating class government structure, can be dramatic (see p. 104).

Creative drama or dramatic play. Drama, in any form, is a stimulus for growth in oral language. Creative drama, that phenomenon that allows children to create a structured scene built from a storyteller's tale without script or theatrical property, is probably one of the finest techniques available to the teacher to encourage oral language growth. This technique has been employed by successful teachers for many years. The results, as reported by teachers, are most rewarding.

The somewhat involved techniques of providing for creative drama in the classroom have little place in a discussion of this type. It is recommended that the reader refer to one of the publications offered in the *Suggested Readings* at the conclusion of this chapter.

Courtesies and demonstrations. There are, of course, the structured lessons that employ strategies for speech development. These lessons deal with courtesies: how do you greet someone, what does one say upon parting, how does one thank another in a gracious way for a compliment or a gift? These important speech courtesies require planning on the part of the teacher and may take the form of a unit in the language block for a week or more.

Telephone manners are important also and demand facility with speech. Mock telephones are easily obtained and practice in answering and conversing on the telephone can be a delightfully interesting and informative class experience. Often youngsters are surprised to discover that when one simply says "Hello" upon answering the telephone, a limited amount of information is available to the caller, and the resulting conversation can be embarrassing and confusing. The very simple idea that youngsters identify themselves and the residence is often a revelation. When they are given an opportunity to practice in a classroom "mock telephone conversation," the need to speak clearly, distinctly, and with precision may likely become a part of a total speaking syndrome.

Demonstrations on the part of students are another way to encourage speaking in the classroom. When youngsters demonstrate a skill in sports, an art technique, a way of using a saw or hammer, a method of mixing paint or other materials, they have need to speak in order to make themselves and the demonstration clear to those watching and listening. It is always interesting to watch youngsters reach for word combinations that will make ideas clear. That, of course, is exactly what a lesson in developmental speech should do (see figure 4.5, p. 103).

The retelling of a learning experience in the content areas is another activity for the enhancement of speaking vocabulary.

SUMMARY

Learning to speak is a direct product of the listening skills. Without a good listening vocabulary, the speaking vocabulary will be blighted. Because of this fact, the good teacher continues to give the youngster many opportunities to listen so that his speech development will be satisfactory.

The speaking vocabulary does not develop by accident. An important part of its development is the classroom environment and its allowance for speech to take place. A planned, well-executed program for speech development is a regular part of any successful ongoing classroom.

Speech in the United States is often a dialectic phenomenon. With the variable of correct structure, dialect should be thought of as part of the child's individuality and should not be derided by the teacher. Incorrect structure, however, needs attention.

Bilingualism and the issue of English as a second language often causes confusion for youngsters as they strive to gain facility with the official English language. These problems require attention and often remedial efforts.

Speech correction for children with speech defects should not be attempted by the ordinary classroom teacher. Any attempt to provide speech therapy should be done under the guidance of a trained professional in the field.

Above and beyond all, the modern elementary classroom is not a silent place. It is a place for language input and output. If oral language is to develop it cannot be fostered in a silent atmosphere.

4

ORAL LANGUAGE INSTRUCTION
THE PRAGMATIC APPROACH

As the teacher faces the interesting but demanding task of teaching children to communicate adequately, she will often recognize that they have multiple difficulties in easy language usage. Certainly, many authorities have agreed that some of these deficiencies may well result from the fact that children have actually never learned to handle language well enough to really express their ideas with ease and fluency. This would indicate that they have probably never had sufficient opportunities for the development of adequate speech tools for effective oral communication. They are then expected to be able to cope with numerous writing and reading situations before they have actually learned their own spoken language. They must have many experiences which can help them recognize the basic function of their own tongue, its symbolic nature, and the facility of its use before they can be expected to succeed in the later, more discrete tasks. Children are often expected to read before they have even grasped the idea of, let alone the ability to cope with, abstract thought and concept forms. Further, they are expected to put in proper written form their ideas and thoughts, not yet having learned to *say* these same expressive impulses. Oral speech is certainly basic to, and necessary for, further successful language development.

Hence, in approaching this whole area of the curriculum, the teacher/intern must recognize that everyone is a teacher of speech throughout every day. This may be intentional or incidental, but the speech habits and the development of good speaking ability result from, and are continually affected by, the activities of the classroom. This is true whether it be in a ghetto school with children from language deficient backgrounds, or in schools of the inner city, the affluent suburbs, the small town schools, or the periphery schools of the metropolitan areas. Wherever there are children in the school setting, their experiences with their teachers and peers are constantly shaping their expressive abilities; and wherever there are teachers, they are teachers of speech. Whether students are termed "handicapped, retarded, dull, or disadvantaged" or "accelerated, bright, gifted, or average," they all have one thing in common—they need to learn to communicate effectively. The teacher's role in this development is most important and cannot be overemphasized. Each one has the ability to reach children, and each one *can* teach them creatively. Communication itself is a creative skill, and all humans have an innate possession—the ability to think, to create language to express that thought, and thereby to communicate with themselves and others. We have not always done well in this area of education for life, however.

It is important that all children be surrounded by a learning environment that emphasizes and provides for a holistic concept and process of language learning. The child who has been disadvantaged because of emotional stress, social impoverishment, or educational deprivation must have this total immersion in such a language-developing climate. To him, an educational program that gives a meaningful and rich involvement not only in the skills of language, but in numerous opportunities for oral self-expression can well mean the very crucial difference between his own success or failure in the school setting as well as in his later life.

Teachers must clearly understand that all phases of language learning should be a part of basic living, that words are the very threads interwoven throughout the fabric of daily experiences in life. From this stance, then, education in language becomes a carefully planned program which will allow for many spontaneous activities in oral speech. Recently educators in many areas have sought to clarify the thinking of teachers of the language arts by specifying the various skills thought to be important in communication development. They have further worked to arrange these basic abilities into a sequential hierarchy, each dependent on and building upon the other. These continuums, though differing in minor points, usually include the important areas of each of the strands of the language arts. One such illustrative continuum has been included by the authors as an example.

ORAL LANGUAGE SKILLS CONTINUUM

In facing the stimulating task of language development in children, the teacher may wish to base her instructional program on certain assumptions. These significant basic premises can form the foundation of a clear understanding of the importance of the language arts—in the curriculum, in the home, in life itself. Further, these understandings will guide the teacher in planning teaching strategies and in evaluating the total program of enhancing oral communication by children. Offered is a list of suggested posits.

1. Human beings have the unique ability to use language. It is the tool which

enables children to express answers to such questions as: "Who am I?" "Who are others?" "How does their life affect mine?" and "Why does their being affect me; why and how does my life and being affect them?" It is through the effective use of language that the child can come to see himself as a worthy member of his family, his community, or his school. Likewise, without adequate communication, he may come to assess himself as an unworthy, inadequate, or isolated individual. It is through the communicating process—adequate or deficient—that the world in which the child finds himself becomes a warm, friendly, accepting environment or a hostile, forbidding, cold community.

2. Whatever may be the climate fostered by the school in its language program, the child will learn some means of communicating. Before his school experience began he increased his language powers from the beginning of first sounds to his entering level of skills. If his early experiences were sufficient, it is likely that never again in such a short period of his life will his language powers develop at such an accelerated pace.

3. It becomes the task of the school, then, to build on these early communication acquisitions; to expand, to refine, to enrich, and to develop these primary language foundations. Heretofore he has learned largely through informal means; now the process of education uses a more formal, structured approach to skills learning that involves the use of more abstract symbolization. Such abilities generally require planned teaching.

4. Today's world is immersed and saturated by symbols. Such symbolization usage by the media of communication can play an important role in the shaping of the normative domain of the young citizen: his value orientation, his personal attitudes, his use of time, and his consuming of the products of his environment. Hence, the child's ability to cope adequately with the use of symbols in his society will result in the measure to which his own affective development matures.

5. Likewise, it is through such symbolization that the cultural heritage of a society is transmitted. This accumulated body of "public philosophy" is communicated from generation to generation largely through the educational institution which teaches its young to communicate via language. This infers, then, that adequacy in language ability is requisite to success in most areas of life endeavors as well as in achievement academically and educationally.

6. Total language development and instruction must begin the first day the child commences his schooling. It will not cease to be the responsibility of the instructor until the final day of formal education. It must be seen as a continuing process that is woven through all areas of the curriculum and classroom activities throughout the day. This is to say that there can be no mere "language period" each day sufficient to meet the need. The perceptive teacher will seek to develop within herself a sensitivity to opportunities for challenging the use and stimulation of good oral language throughout the entire school day.

Based on these primary assumptions, then, the teacher/intern can make use of a skills continuum in planning the curriculum for oral communication. This should be viewed only as a guide for including the requisite learnings, and a means for evaluating student growth in specific skills areas. A type of individualized diagnosis of pupil needs and strengths can then result in good prescriptive planning and teaching of oral communication skills.

Primary Level Teaching Concepts and Skills

Concepts

In approaching the teaching of oral language in the primary grades, the teacher/intern may wish to consider certain concept principles which can be stated in brief as follows:

1. The basic function of language is to communicate feelings as well as thought.
2. Listening is as important as speaking to effective conversation.
3. The development of adequate vocabulary is a prerequisite to effective expression.
4. Sequential order is important to asking good questions, as well as to reporting events clearly and accurately.
5. Meaning and feeling are reflected by intonation and pacing of language.
6. Dramatizing a story is an interesting and exciting means of communicating the narrative.
7. Audience communication with clear, correct diction indicates courtesy and respect.
8. The first responsibility of a speaker is to be heard.

These few basic concepts to be shared by the teacher with the student should serve to suggest others which may further enrich the oral language learnings. They are important only to the extent that they aid the learner in realizing the value of communicating clearly and effectively.

Skills

The following oral language abilities introduced or strengthened during the beginning years of school are expressed in behavioral or performance terms so that the instructor may well use them in writing both instructional and performance objectives.

During the time that the student is working in the grades (K–3) or by the time he has completed them, he should be able to:

A rich classroom environment will provide ample opportunities for students to exchange ideas in an informal setting.

1. Speak clearly and audibly.
2. Pronounce words distinctly.
3. Participate in conversation with one or two others.
4. Speak in turn by waiting for proper time.
5. Follow acceptable speech patterns.
6. Relate an event or story in ordered sequence.
7. Use the linguistic dynamic: juncture, stress, and pitch.
8. Develop an expanding oral vocabulary.
9. Express himself in correctly constructed sentences.
10. Relate a personal happening or experience.
11. Develop speaking poise commensurate to level of development.
12. Repeat from memory simple rhymes and/or poems.
13. Present orally a brief explanation, demonstration, description, or report.
14. Participate in a choral activity: unison speaking, refrain response, antiphonal choir, solo.
15. Give one-, two-, three-, or more step directions orally.

16. Participate in varied speech situations: individual conversations, telephoned activity, in small groups, in total class, and/or on stage for an audience.
17. Make proper use of kinesics in enhancing oral speech: facial expressions, gestures, body movements—nonverbal, kinesic language usage.
18. Follow an ordered pattern in storytelling:
    a. Use an interesting beginning.
    b. Proceed in logical order.
    c. Make use of dialogue and/or dialect.
    d. Indicate mood by variations of voice: pitch, stress, tempo, and intonation.
    e. Interpret characterization by appropriate stance.
19. Participate in role-playing and/or creative dramatics.
20. Take part in simple monologues, dialogues, skits, plays, or drama activities.

Evaluating performance

These suggested oral activity skills for the primary level could well be used by the teacher for developing a simple checklist, observational instrument for informally assessing student progress and attainment. Some sort of graded continuum such as a five-point rating scale should adequately interpret performance.

Check the appropriate level: ____1 ____2 ____3 ____4 ____5
1: Superior   2: Good   3: Fair   4: Needs Improving
5: Unable to do

Or, the teacher might wish to simply indicate on a dated form the successful performance of a child on an Oral Development Profile (see figures 4.1 and 4.2 for partial models of such informal inventories).

PERFORMANCE RECORD: ORAL SPEAKING

Name _____ Grade _____ Date _____

SKILL	LEVEL: (Circle one)
1. Pronunciation of words	1 2 3 4 5
2. Enunciation	1 2 3 4 5
3. Speech patterns	1 2 3 4 5

Figure 4.1

If the instructor wishes to keep a profile report on each student (this is an excellent means of charting for individualized planning), the simple form of figure 4.2 could be modified or followed as is for recording skill development at a satisfactory level.

ORAL SKILLS DEVELOPMENT PROFILE

Student _____ School _____

has demonstrated a satisfactory level of performance in the following marked areas of oral speaking:

SKILL ASSESSED	DATE	GRADE
1. Pronounces words clearly		
2. Enunciates correctly		
3. Relates event in proper sequence		

Figure 4.2

The brief, partial model of figure 4.2 should serve to illustrate the way in which the suggested skills continuum of primary level oral skills could be assessed and recorded. If either of these suggested checklists is devised, or another form is used, the record should be included in the student progress file for a means of charting performance and indicating areas of deficiency for further teaching and strengthening.

Intermediate Level Teaching Concepts and Skills

Concepts

Suggested continuing skills as the child progresses from year to year might include the following more discrete abilities and conceptual learnings. The listed concept principles offer a reasonable rationale for specific oral skill activities.

1. Good oral speech is the result of clear thinking and careful planning.
2. Successful communication results from using basic essential speech patterns.
3. Adequate oral communication is dependent on distinct expression, voice clarity, and audible speaking.
4. Valuable information can be shared via oral speaking.

5. A growing, usable vocabulary lends variety and interest in oral speech.
6. Carefully worded directions or instructions are the result of clear thinking and articulation.
7. Societal mores govern courtesies to be used in conversations, telephoning, greetings, and introductions.
8. Oral speaking skills are not inherent; they are learned abilities.
9. The concise, correct use of words in accepted speech patterns enhances activities in the class, group, club, or home.
10. Dramatization and choral speaking provide enjoyable and satisfying experiences in oral expression.
11. Effective language usage is developed and strengthened by consistent, daily use and conscious effort.
12. Clear knowledge of the linguistic structure of a language is an aid to effective speech performance.
13. Acceptable levels and standards of speaking should be established and maintained for effective language usage.
14. Simple parliamentary procedures and presentation techniques should be agreed on prior to performances.
15. Oral interpretation is enhanced by dramatization, well-used gestures, and/or stance.

This suggested list of basic principles is by no means complete. If it serves to stimulate thinking on the part of the teacher/intern, or helps to clarify instructional goals, or provides a reasonable rationale for instructional planning, it will have justified its inclusion in the text. In the present emphasis on relevance and accountability in educational practices and endeavors, it may happily aid the busy educator in stating clear instructional objectives. These, then, may be translated into proper behavioral terms and become performance guides in lesson planning and evaluation of instruction. The following list of oral skills at the intermediate teaching level provides further steps in the skills continuum in the elementary school setting.

Skills

During the student's work at the intermediate level (grades 4 through 6), or by the completion of these grades, he should be able to:

1. Plan and present short oral reports.
2. Make brief introductions or presentations.
3. Give clear oral announcements, directions, demonstrations, and descriptions.
4. Demonstrate correct use of the telephone in formal and informal situations.
5. Correctly use an expanded and enriched vocabulary.
6. Introduce a guest, a parent, or a speaker to a group.
7. Narrate for a "radio" or "TV" presentation.

8. Enunciate clearly and correctly at the appropriate level.
9. Use effective techniques in storytelling.
10. Apply persuasion techniques and logical reasoning to convince.
11. Participate actively in group discussions.
12. Perform in an audience situation: solo, unison, group.
13. Observe common courtesies in conversational involvement.
14. Apply voice techniques (pacing, pitch, volume, stress, inflection, etc.) in effective speaking.
15. Participate in a variety of discussion situations: panel, round table, debate.

Again, it is suggested that the teacher/intern use these suggestive progressive skills as a measurement of student progress and development, as a guide in planning and executing directed teaching activities for speech improvement, or in developing a simple form of recording from observation.

Other skills activities which may be considered for inclusion at this middle-grade level include:

- Reading, poetry, or being involved in choral reading.
- Demonstrating correct use of the tape recorder, microphone, or public address equipment.
- Participating in volunteer activities for assemblies, parent programs, or special occasions.
- Taking responsibility for keeping conversation, discussion, or debate flowing without teacher prompting.
- Using oral speaking to demonstrate a clear understanding of its varied purposes: entertaining, stimulating, informing, convincing, and activating.

Evaluating performance

In seeking to evaluate these learned skills, the instructor should first state each desired performance in proper behavioral terms. This will include a clear thinking through of the means of measurement for specific skills. Some may well be best observed and results recorded on a rating scale or checklist. Others may be assessed through the use of teacher prepared tests or by comparison with a group-designed model. In some activities the use of recording devices for self-evaluation may prove the most beneficial technique. "Live performances" as well as recorded demonstrations may also lend themselves for evaluation and critiquing by a group or the entire class.

Concepts and Skills for the Upper-Grade Students

Concepts

As one considers the continuing skills to be taught and strengthened as the learner progresses into the junior high years, he may feel that much is a reteaching of earlier learnings. However, consider the following widening concepts and abilities which are especially appropriate at the upper levels of teaching.

1. The ability to speak well is an important asset to each individual in his social, intellectual, cultural, and economic developments.
2. Effective oral presentations require correct pronunciation and enunciation, clear articulation, adequate voice control and appropriate intonation, as well as expressive kinesics (body language).
3. Oral communication involves speaker *and* listener responsibility—participation in discussions, courtesy and consideration of listeners, and a fair give-and-take of time and conversation.

There are many opportunities in informal environments that allow for and nurture peer communication. This informal speech development needs encouragement.

Skills

To important concepts, the teacher/intern will add the following skills for inclusion in the curriculum. During the years of learning at the upper-grade levels, the student should be able to:

1. Logically organize thoughts and ideas and present them orally with clarity and fluency.
2. Use appropriate language (standard English) for a variety of formal and informal situations.
3. Get and hold the attention and interest of his listeners—peers as well as adults.
4. Participate in questioning situations or discussions and give pertinent, correct answers in concise, clear language.
5. Give an oral presentation making use of the acceptable speech principles and delivery: enthusiasm, poise, correct posture, controlled voice, and responsive eye contact.
6. Involve himself and effectively participate in varied speaking activities: conversations, dramatizing, reports, audience reading, interviews, introductions, presentations, demonstrations, and a variety of forms of debates and discussions.
7. Organize, prepare, and deliver a speech including the following: introduction, main topic, illustrative material, and conclusion.
8. Make an oral presentation and demonstrate the following abilities and competencies while speaking: proper breathing, correct pronunciation and enunciation, suitable volume and voice pitch, and effective stance and gestures.
9. To use a basic plan for preparation of an oral presentation: suitable topic choice, selection of interesting main ideas in terms of situation and audience, collecting usable materials for developing the speech, outlining and organizing the speech materials, and practice the presentation making use of outline, notes, chalkboard, and/or visual aid materials.
10. Create and present simulated television and/or radio talks, programs, or dramatizations.
11. Become involved and participate in informal, impromptu class activities which require oral speaking or extemporaneous responses.

As the instructor examines many of these speech skills, she will immediately realize that written communication skills are closely related to the preparation of a number of the speaking activities suggested in the continuum. These are particularly interrelated with the more advanced skills required to effectively participate in the upper grades.

TEACHING STRATEGIES AND IMPLEMENTATION

The development of a sequential step-by-step skills framework, important as it is, provides merely a guide for the teacher's planning. It should insure that there will be orderly progress without gaps and deficiencies because of careless instruction. However, the actual teaching for proficiency will require careful, thorough preparation centered in an accepting, relaxed classroom climate. Certain learnings will require specific instruction and emphasis, while other skills may be handled as an incidental inclusion as the actual work in other areas of the curriculum provides a suitable setting for making use of the skills being learned or strengthened. In either situation, the teacher will be constantly alert to opportunities for meaningful oral speaking.

Sources from Which to Build Vocabulary

Whatever the format of instruction may be, the teacher will continually remind herself that *words* are the important vehicle of communication for children in the school setting. A sensitivity for words, good words, expressive words, vibrant words, wonderful words—all kinds of words—is a must for oral speech at any level. The classroom becomes a developing laboratory for creating a child's sensitiveness to the beauty of words to be used in vivid expression. In order for this to happen, the teacher herself must be intrigued with words, must have a certain sense of the power and beauty of words. Too often, because of years of association with and trying to "talk on the level" of children, the teacher's own speech may become sterile and sparse, a sort of tepid, unimaginative vocalizing. Children will only become excited by language when they are exposed often to good speech filled with a wide variety of well-chosen, expressive words and terms. Many of today's teachers pass along to the new generation this prized legacy inherited from the teachers of the preceding generation who were able to relate their own enjoyment of beautiful language. Others were not so fortunate and must work to acquire this excitement about words; their origins, their shades of meaning, their relationships to other words or word families, their rhythm and cadence in oral use.

The alert teacher will make use of those words: "tasted, smelled, heard, felt, seen, and put into action." These are valuable clues to finding the clear, vivid word for describing the feelings and sensory experiences with which the child is so familiar. A variety of activities can be planned to help the student "discover" other descriptive words or phrases to provide freshness and flavor to the young speaker's oral expression. These sensory words are often very personalized by the child and add the facet of individuality to his own speaking. Since his own sense inputs are especially keen, he is making use of acute responses to help him describe or differentiate in order to clearly express a thought, feeling, or concept.

Another category of expressive tools is the "impact" words—those that have an emotional tone, those descriptive words which can arouse, stimulate, or affect the hearer. These are those strong words which relate to our emotive nature—expressing our likes or dislikes, prejudices or biases, our positive or negative feelings. In short they are our tools for persuasion, propaganda, selling an idea, or causing someone to reject or change an opinion. A list of such words can be found from the advertiser, the politician, the editor, and the enthusiast.

The common, environmental happenings around all of us provide another source of important, expressive words for the child's vocabulary enrichment. These are the ordinary societal events, the phenomena of nature itself, the day-by-day milieu which is life itself—the sights, sounds, happenings, reactions, and interchanges occurring continually. The words which describe such events enhance the relating of common occurrences and make them something vital and special. They are the descriptive specifics which lift the ordinary to another level so that it becomes an item of interest rather than a drab incident. An awareness of the extraordinary within the commonplace is a rare quality for the speaker and writer. It is this ability to express clearly that lends a fascination to the speaker's narrative, and this awareness and wonder will find its expression in words, wonderful words.

A further wealth of descriptive words comes from one of the most common sources of all—the people around us. People with whom we live, play, work, and study. We may like them, dislike them, be amused by them, admire them, or scorn them. Whatever our feelings about them, they afford a rich store from which to expand and enhance our vocabularies whenever we try to describe them, explain them, or picture them. The intricacies of their personalities, the complexities of their lives, and the diversities of their behaviors—these afford the speaker a tremendous challenge and a need for varied language if he would do the task well. Children frequently amaze us with their awareness of human differences and their abilities to describe playmates, friends, relatives, or even strangers with clarity and insight. However, this can only be accomplished if the young speaker has a rich store of words and terms from which to draw with ease and surety. This then results in the fluency and variety that make speaking and listening delightful. This end result comes from careful planning and enthusiastic performance on the part of the teacher who herself needs not only an adequate, but an enriched, expanded, vivid vocabulary.

Activities for Vocabulary Enrichment

Several broad areas of speech activities were suggested in the previous chapter. These included (1) sharing experiences, (2) retelling a happening, (3) activity planning, (4) oral reporting, (5) class meetings, (6) creative dramatics, and (7) demonstrations. These can be divided into numerous specific classroom games, activities, and exercises that will allow the students a wide variety of experiences for speech development. A quick review of the skills continuum will suggest to the teacher many differing oral situations that can be useful for involving both reluctant as well as avid speakers in valuable learnings. Actually the reader may refer to Chapter 2 in which a number of teaching strategies for listening activities were suggested. Listening presupposes oral presenting. Hence, the experiences listed there can be useful in planning for speaking situations.

Content fields, other than the language arts, provide the impetus for using oral language and speech development. Good discussion can center around group projects such as the one shown above.

Preschool Instruction

With the current emphasis on early childhood education, the teacher at this beginning level will be aware of the many opportunities for developing language with the young child. The following list of techniques should serve as "primers" for stimulating many other creative ideas.

1. Using rhymes and poetry for chants, unison speaking, or antiphonal responses. The use of simple, rhyming poetry is especially effective with the preschooler. Most children seem to *have* poetry within them and are able to interact with teacher and peers without reservation. Finger-plays and acting out the poem delight them. Use of pictures to illustrate the verses, or use of the flannel board to build the narrative can further enhance the magic of the words themselves. The repetitive, refrain-type of poem lends itself easily to young speakers. They enjoy the chorus-type lines which are easily remembered. Children have

often been described as *being* poets and readily respond with rhyming words to complete jingles, couplets, quatrains. With gentle guidance they will often surprise the teacher with their sensitivity and feeling in developing their own poems. Poetry, too, provides an interesting setting for simple solo or group pantomiming.

2. Developing speaking activities correlated with holidays, special events, special people. The teacher of the preschool child can make valuable use of the annual calendar to stimulate oral response in the setting of special occasions: simple role-playing situations, creative dramatic experiences, recitations, plays, and/or sharing of information about the holiday or festival. These are fertile soils for nurturing speech activities appropriate to the child's level and the interest in the occasion.

3. Using social situations for stimulating extemporaneous, free language. What child does not respond to "let's play . . . ," or "pretend we . . . ," or "make believe . . ."? From these beginnings, simulated telephoning, conversing, buying and selling, introducing, presenting, demonstrating, and play parties evolve naturally and easily. Further, they aid the young student to learn in a warm, fun climate so that words and sentences, requests and commands, reactions and responses come with fluency and pleasure.

4. Using sensory stimulating objects to promote descriptive language. All types of sound boxes, smelling bottles, and touching bags can be easily assembled and will provide the learners with new reasons for "sensing" and describing those sounds which are alike and different and telling how various odors are similar or dissimilar, or for touching and telling what textures are or what shapes and sizes one discovers inside the bag. Let your imagination go, and there will be no end to the novel and useful devices you will find which will aid in the child's language of inquiry and discovery.

5. Bringing the young child and good picture-storybooks together. With today's supply of excellent trade books, the teacher will have innumerable opportunities and occasions to use the beautiful and fascinating books for young children. Sharing these, discussing the pictures and situations, retelling them, making up new endings, supplying other words to describe, or playing the story are but a few of the many ways these books can be used effectively in the speech learnings of young children.

6. Using all types of audiovisual media for stimulating children's speech. These will cover the whole spectrum of materials from sounds to be identified and reproduced to various types of readings to be modelled. Or these may be more abstract sounds to be described.

The teacher/intern will note that the suggested strategies make use of learning situations which are centered in the feelings and understandings of young children. Indeed any program that is to succeed must be interwoven continually through the everyday experiences. Since language is a basic part of living itself,

I. Name: Miss Pat O'Niel   **Date:** 3-17-73   **Grade:** K   **No.** 1

Subject: Language Arts (Oral Speech)   **Text:** None

II. Instructional Objective: To provide a high-interest experience to stimulate description.

Performance Objective: When presented with a familiar object, the child will be able to isolate and orally describe a minimum of three characteristics using complete sentences so that other members of the group will be able to identify the said object.

III. Assignment: Group participation in oral speaking exercise.

Materials:
familiar objects: globe, glove, ball, purse
Touch Bag with several like articles

IV. Procedure:
1. Arrange group for circle activity.
2. Discuss details and characteristics of one of the articles.
3. Using Touch Bag, ask for volunteer to describe the contents.
4. Elicit "guesses" from the other members of the group.
5. Use other Bags for further participation.

V. Related Activities:
1. Divide class into groups and provide a tasting object to the leader. Pass it around and let each group think of descriptive words to describe the taste of the object. Then form sentences to make a "riddle" for the rest of the other groups to guess what was tasted.
2. Play "I Spy" with objects in the room being described as clues for guessing the article.

VI. Evaluation: During the responses by individual students, the teacher will use a checklist to record numbers of descriptive words, correct sentences, clarity.

VII. Ongoing Activities:
1. Use "Heads Down—Eyes Closed" game for identifying and describing sounds around us.
2. Play "Word Tag Game," each child giving correct response to be "it" for his turn.

Comments: None.

Figure 4.3

the school setting must provide a rich, meaningful exposure to the many relationships and involvements that are an integral part of the daily scene.

In planning for specific learnings, the teacher will find it necessary to develop clear objectives and then base particular lessons and activities on her stated goals. An example of such a teaching plan is included here. See figure 4.3 for details of such learnings.

Oral Language at the Primary Level

As the young student enters the more formal situations presented in the early grades, the need for oral language and opportunities to use it will continue. Many of the preschool activities and skills will be carried on at a more sophisticated level. The games and exercises will require certain oral abilities which build on the earlier strengths. These will make use of enriched vocabulary, discrete skills in pronunciation and articulation, and functional uses of oral language. It is during these important years of school, too, that the student develops a certain independence and freedom to be himself and express himself in verbal situations. His creative impulses can result in rewarding experiences of shared communications.

However, children cannot create in an empty environment, nor can they talk and express themselves orally unless they have something to talk about. Creative communication can flourish on many actual as well as vicarious experiences: visits from resource people, field trips, visits to points of interest, seeing natural phenomena; viewing films, film strips, transparencies; being involved with recordings, tapes, and record players; sharing books, magazines, news items; seeing dramatic productions, attending musicals, listening to poetry and good books—all of these experiences will increase the child's awareness and interest in his world. Likewise, an alive, attractive classroom can do much to stimulate interest and engender conversation, comments, and discussions. Bulletin boards, interest centers, varied displays, social studies realia, and science charts and materials can all add to the flavor of the learning situation. This rich classroom environment coupled with an enthusiastic teacher who has a varied and interesting instructional program will do much to foster a full participation in the verbal aspects of learning and exchange.

The following suggested use of creative materials should suffice to stimulate other imaginative and original ideas on the part of the teacher of oral language. They are meant to serve in this capacity and are not considered to be all inclusive or necessarily the best.

- Simple costumes do much to stimulate and "change" ordinary children into marvelous other beings. Articles of clothing, or pupil-prepared costumes from paper, cloth, or crepe paper can make the difference between a sparse, sterile response and an animated, delightful acting out of expressive experience.
- Using simple props for setting the stage is a valuable adjunct to any creative

endeavor. Even crude drawings, backdrops, murals, or painted signs signifying a person or object can be the magic that transforms the ordinary into the realm of extraordinary reality.

- Try using a variety of hats to suddenly envelope the child with a new personality and feeling. He immediately becomes the characterization of a person from storybook land or the long ago. With this new personality, conversation and words seem to come more easily. Gestures and voice quality miraculously assume a new dimension. The role-playing experience, or creative drama, or monologue come alive and the sparkle of reality can be noted.

- Many teachers have discovered the reward of using a variety of puppets for oral situations. The assumed role and the ability to become the puppet has freed many otherwise inarticulate children. Simple paper bag or sock puppets, stick puppets, hand puppets, papier-mâché puppets, and marionettes can be used effectively. The materials for such need not be elaborate, and the very act of making the characters enhances the performance.

- The use of music to set moods, to "say something" to the listener which he can describe or communicate is another valuable aid. At first the primary child may be shy or reticent in oral expression; however, through the media of rhythm and sound, he may begin to pantomime what he feels and hears. There is no "right" or "wrong" response, hence he soon begins to feel confidence and security and gradually is able to begin to articulate in words what he is feeling, sensing, and interpreting.

Perhaps a word about the value of pantomime should be included here. It has been defined as a language of movement by means of which an individual signifies who he is, what he is doing, where he is, and how he is feeling. It seems to intrinsically convey imagery and express a certain communication inexpressible with words. Thoughts, emotions, and feelings find an outlet in motion patterns. Children generally will respond to this form of body language. The so-called normal child, the inhibited introvert, or even the emotionally troubled and disturbed child can find a means of communication in response to poetry, music, song, or story. This becomes a sort of spontaneous dialogue between the teacher and the child as he responds. Initially the focus is upon movement; but movements inspire words, and words stimulate a free verbalization. Thus the teacher's objective is realized as children are able to express themselves with fluency and ease.

As indicated, many of the learning situations for promoting oral communication may come almost unplanned or as part of another learning. However, the teacher/intern will need to plan her curriculum and select those learnings which she will emphasize at particular times and in specific "set" situations. From the continuum of skills she will arrange a definite pattern of procedure for speech development at her level. Then, not relying on chance and incidental learnings, she will prepare for actual instruction in the various aspects of oral speaking. This will require a framework of her own teaching goals and the desired behavioral outcomes to be performed by the learners. One such lesson plan, which may serve as a model, is included in figure 4.4, p. 96. Note the detail with which this lesson period was planned, and the care and thought which resulted in a unified period of learning and reinforcing activities.

Poetry is one of the media for use with children of all ages. At the primary level it can be sheer magic. The teacher who wants to help her students enjoy encounters with poetry should choose the poems wisely. At this age level, children particularly enjoy verses which have (1) a humorous touch, (2) swinging rhythm, (3) some inherent suspense or secrecy, (4) poetic construct—definite alliteration, distinctive sounds, repetitive refrains, and definite rhyming patterns, and (5) sensory content.

In Part Five of this text, the reader will be introduced to many more ideas for using good literature in teaching the entire gamut of language arts experiences. Good literature can strongly support the teaching of oral skills, not only for the primary student but for all age groups.

Oral Language at the Intermediate Level

With the experiences of the middle grades, the student increasingly becomes aware that speech usage is valuable not only in personal and informal situations, but that it is used more and more for formal presentations: discussions, debates, reports, demonstrations. Likewise the instructional program becomes somewhat more concerned with rhetoric, the discrete speech skills, organization of thought and concept, delivery, speech patterns, and excellence in vocabulary. These increasing emphases were clearly indicated in the Skills Continuum included in this chapter. Since many of these activities are of necessity more structured than earlier grade involvements, the instructor will need to plan carefully in order to maintain an element of interest and freshness.

Many of the speech activities at this middle level will concern themselves with classroom discussions and reporting. The listening and reading done at this level frequently focuses on information input, and the speaking and writing exercises are often combined with sharing data and reporting on material researched by small groups or individuals. Hence organization, sequence, chronology, and the like are important considerations in preparing for oral participation. This functional aspect of communication in the intermediate grades, however, is not to be exclusive of the recreational and creative facets of the speech arts. Students at this level find a great deal of enjoyment in participating in skits and short plays as well as in various forms of choral speaking and responses. Several general ideas of "sparking" their speaking learnings are included here.

- Creative writing and dramatization often go hand-in-hand with middle-grade youngsters. They can do a particularly fine job of rewriting favorite stories into play format and then producing and presenting them. The conversation

Model Lesson Plan
Choral Speaking Activity

I. **Name:** Fred Cassels   **Date:** 4-12-74   **Grade:** 2   **No.** 1

   Subject: Language Arts (Oral Speech)   **Text:** Ferris, <u>Favorite Poems</u>

II. **Instructional Objective:** To teach a directed experience in choral reading—solos and chorus.

   Performance Objective: After practice and instruction, the students will be able to participate in a choral reading. Their performance to be assessed by the following criteria and rated on a check-scale: distinct pronunciation, rhythmic phrasing, expressive rendering.

III. **Assignment:** Listening to and then participating in a choral reading of "Poor Jonathon Bing."

   Materials:
     Ferris' <u>Favorite Poems Old and New</u>
     record player and recording—"Choral Readings"
     ditto copies—"Poor Jonathon Bing"

IV. **Procedure:**
    1. Play the recording of "Bing."
    2. Practice pronunciation by reading poem in unison.
    3. Assign parts to be performed.
    4. Discuss expression and rhythm of poem.
    5. Do the choral reading in parts.

V. **Related Activities:**
    1. Plan an audience situation program for recitations and readings.
    2. Play other recordings of children's chorus.
    3. Let children select favorite poems and suggest arrangements for choral speaking.

VI. **Evaluation:** During the performances, use the rating checklist to record individual and group behaviors.

VII. **Ongoing Activities:** Plan for the TV "Show" to be presented to primary department and then to P.T.A. parents.

   Comments: None.

Figure 4.4

and dialogue are frequently hilariously funny and show keen insights into and interpretation of characterization when students are given opportunity to use them.

- The teacher will find informal discussion an excellent means of assessing learnings as well as providing peers within the group a chance to share and learn from one another. Her role is often that of leader and must be done carefully and with a certain delicate finesse lest it dominate the activity. Discussion must be more than a question and answer session. Rather, it can develop into an analytical, probing, evaluative exercise. (Further word on conducting discussions is included below.)

- The use of visual aids by the middle grader often strengthens his report. The overhead projector, interesting charts or graphs, or large pictures can enhance his presentation and lend a certain security and authority to his oral presentation. The preparation of a good report puts definite responsibility on the participant. Unlike being one of several discussants, he is now on his own. It is his show and he can either succeed or dismally fail to produce at an adequate level. There must be a certain significance and appropriateness in the topic chosen as well as in the manner in which it is handled. Its value lies in that the reporter is seeking to inform, to answer certain questions, to expand concepts, and to help solve problems. (Further information regarding a good report follows the section on Discussions.)

Discussions

The good classroom discussion is actually a "talking it over" time. In planning such an activity, the teacher/intern should keep several facts in mind.

1. The topic or problem for discussion must be appropriate to the level of maturity of the students.
2. There must be a certain personal, social, or educational significance inherent in the subject.
3. A good discussion will result in a good level of attendance and participation on the part of the students involved.
4. The discussants should be challenged by the situation to think, rationalize, make judgments, probe, test, and/or be critical.
5. There must be planned direction by the leader of the group, who actually becomes a "facilitator," to see that the activity moves logically and with purpose toward a clear conclusion.
6. Good discussion should move from participant to participant in an easy flow of reactions, contributions, and deliberations.
7. Once the teacher-leader has established an easy, favorable climate, she becomes a member of the group, not dominating or forcing issues, but contributing to the effective patterning of the discussion.

8. Materials and information important to the discussion activity should be made readily available to all members.

9. Specific standards of procedure should be set by the group prior to the actual activity.

10. A mimeographed copy of the outline of the topic may be prepared, or copied on the chalkboard where all can see it.

11. A planned list of open-ended questions may be used as a guide in the actual discussion period. These can aid in stimulating movement and participation.

12. Discussion can be a very effective means of developing problem-solving behavior as the students are encouraged to make evaluative judgments and critical analyses.

13. Discussion should lead naturally and steadily toward a rational summarization and conclusion.

14. This systematic oral process should facilitate clear, logical expression leading toward a unified, cohesive presentation.

15. The well-planned and executed discussion should also provide scope for further research, gathering of more data, and an opportunity for later thought and examination.

Throughout the entire process, good speech abilities should be developing. These can result from some of the following practices.

1. Developing speech habits for effective communication.

2. Development of careful listening for the purpose of responding.

3. Strengthening of poise when handling problem situations.

4. Becoming aware of and making use of social skills in the give-and-take of group processes.

5. Improvement in clear, orderly thinking and speaking.

6. Development in organizing, evaluating, and summarizing.

7. Realization that problems are complex in nature, and that solutions may be reached by group decision.

8. Concluding that objective evaluation can be made by a group as well or better than by an individual.

9. Strengthening of vocabulary through usage and hearing others use new words.

10. Improving of human relations through exercising the group process.

Conducting a successful discussion requires a cooperative effort on the part of the teacher as well as the students involved. Otherwise, boredom, disinterested behavior, extraneous responses, reticence, and lack of response can occur. Over-contribution and domination of the discussion time can also result from the loquacious student. Thorough study and preparation on the part of the students is necessary if there is to be adequate knowledge for responding intelligently. This requires reading and research ability and use.

Perhaps one of the finest accruals from this type of oral activity is that children learn to talk with each other. Far too often they have been accustomed to answering the teacher's questions and talking to her. Discussing provides many opportunities to interact with and talk to peers. This can be a most rewarding experience to intermediate age children.

As a preliminary learning experience, the teacher may wish to work with a demonstration group who actually show how a discussion is carried on. After the demonstration, allow for the class to discuss the performance, analyze it, and evaluate it and the participants. Some means of recording interactions between discussants can be developed. An interaction analysis grid, flow chart, or observer-recorder check is useful in discovering who contributed, how often he spoke, to whom he responded. This makes for easy evaluation of speaking habits, contributions, types of responses, and the like.

A wide variety of discussion forms can be used by the group. These will provide a wide range of speaking experiences and add a certain freshness to the program. The teacher may wish to include some of the following opportunities.

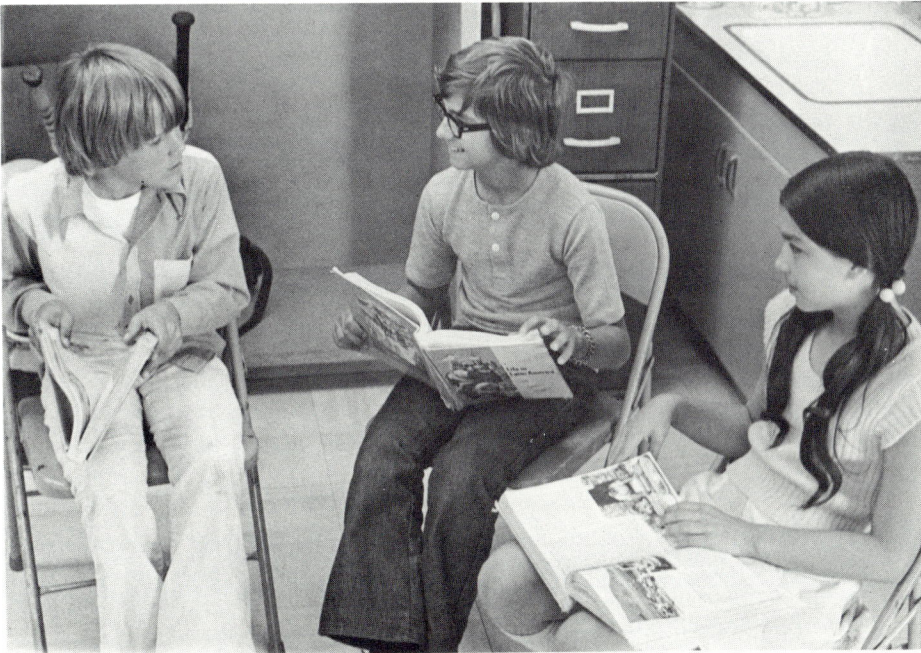

The formal discussion group stimulates yet another means of using oral language and thus insure its growth.

Buzz groups. These are small groups of not more than six members who are assigned or select a specific topic for short, intensive examination in order to arrive at a consensus, conclusion, or summary.

Brainstorming groups. A stimulating type of group dynamic in which the group releases many ideas on a particular subject or problem. It is a nonjudgmental process (no criticism allowed), all suggested ideas are acceptable, and the number of suggested responses is important. It is thought by many to be one of the most "creativity releasing" kinds of group discussions.

Panel groups. A rather audience-oriented, formalized type of discussion group in which panel members carry the responsibility for information at an authoritative level. Usually a question and answer time is included in the activity.

Role-playing groups. An informal group situation in which participants seek to discover the point of view and feelings of the problem person(s). It is perhaps a more spontaneous, creative form of involvement in which solutions are sought with the realization that there are two sides to most questions.

Round table groups. This moderator-led-type of group usually involves from six to eight students in an informal examination of a problem or topic. It may involve an audience who can share and participate when the moderator indicates such is in order. He plays an important leadership, guiding role.

These different forms of discussion groups are chiefly valuable in that they add a certain element of interest and variety, increase activation of students, and may be useful in handling specific problem situations. In the small group dynamic, there is a certain "uncovering" and bringing into "the action" the reticent member. It often helps to develop an amount of confidence and skill which aids the participant to function better in the total class experience. The audience situation also serves as an observation learning in which the nonparticipants can watch, listen, evaluate, and learn the process, procedure, and purpose of the entire function.

Reporting

This important speech activity, much used in the middle-grade years, is rather closely related to discussion, and most of the guidelines suggested for pre-planning are applicable here. The most significant difference between reporting and discussion is that whereas the group situation can carry a few ineffectual members, the reporter is solo. Nobody else can help him out. He either does well or falters and fails to function adequately. This fact poses certain responsibilities both on the student involved and the teacher/intern who would guide and aid his efforts in preparation.

What may these additional considerations be? The brief list following points out several.

- A need for greater facility in communication and language.
- A need for careful selection of a "tight" specific topic.
- A need for in-depth study and research of the subject.
- A need for skilled organization of the report material.
- A need for accurate timing in presenting the report.

These few guiding suggestions indicate that reporting is a learning activity which involves more mature speaking and planning skills. This may present a real challenge to the student and teacher; however, because of the value of this means of learning, as well as its usefulness in sharing knowledge, it affords an excellent opportunity to the child to use his speech abilities in a most realistic and meaningful setting.

Because of its individualized character, reporting can result in *either* a warm glow of success satisfaction *or* a demoralizing destructive sense of failure and chagrin. The help and guidance of an understanding teacher and the cooperative, diligent work of the student will spell the difference. Also because the activity is solo, it affords the reporter to examine and delve into a subject of his own choosing and interest. This allows a certain pacing to either the accelerated or slower student in his pursuing, at the level and depth of his ability, the subject of his choice.

Early experiences in reporting can enhance the learning of elementary research skills: the use of reference materials, the testing of ideas and concepts, and the developing of an adequate reporting of his work. Likewise, during the actual delivery of his oral presentation, the young speaker can learn to be aware of audience response to him as speaker. Their interest, attention, and positive reaction can serve as stimulator and reward. Likewise, their disinterest, inattention, and obvious boredom can be alert signals for him to change pace, spark his delivery, make use of voice and body—in short to employ the mechanics of good speaking.

Teaching Strategies

The following general suggestions may well serve as strategy guidelines for the middle-grade speech teacher. Perhaps it would be more correct to view them as instructional principles than as actual techniques.

1. It is most important that a clear reason or purpose be understood by the student. WHAT is the rationale behind his being asked to perform or present? What is he being asked to do? What is the specific assignment?
2. A clear understanding of the dimensions of his task is essential. Specific procedures and format are important in helping him see the WHY of the assignment: its usefulness, its particular function, its flexibility or adaptability that make it the best form of communication for the situation at hand.
3. It is imperative that the student have access to a wide variety of materials and that he know HOW to make use of them. These study skills are interrelated in the gathering of speech materials and information.
4. The gathering of facts, figures, and materials is not enough. An oral presentation needs interest content—illustrative materials. These props may cover a wide range of media that will give a change of pace and spice to the "message" communicated.

5. This consideration deals with the rehearsal of the presentation. Practice—alone, with the teacher, or before others—is essential if the finished product is to be effective.
6. Last of all is the matter of assessing the performance.

What did the student feel about himself and his presentation, and how did others see him in the role? Growth is dependent upon honest praise and criticism. Speaking is learned by speaking and evaluating, and improvement is based upon consistent effort to build on strengths and eliminate deficiencies and weaknesses.

In concluding this section on the intermediate teacher's work in speech learnings, a simple model plan is included as a guide for preparing other oral skills lessons (see figure 4.5).

Oral Language at the Upper-Grade Level

A quick review of the skills listed in the continuum for the junior high years will reveal that there are few *new* skills and abilities to be learned at this level. Rather, the learnings will become a refining and formalizing of many of the former acquisitions. In the area of listening and reading, this is described by the term "critical" which simply denotes a certain level of finer understanding. Perhaps it would be proper to refer to the more sophisticated speaking abilities as "critical speaking." The older student will continue to be involved in most of the earlier learned skills and activities, hence the upper-grade teacher will continue to be responsible for the strengthening of primary skills and for widening and elevating the degree of finesse involved. The social, utilitarian, and aesthetic functions of oral language will continually be emphasized in the school setting, and a higher level of expertise will be considered standard performance for the maturing young person. His expanded and enriched vocabulary, his wider range of voice quality, his advanced facility with standard speech, his ability to make use of the mechanics of oral communication, the degree of concept development and organization of ideas will be brought into focus in his spoken presentations.

Instructional Areas Emphasized

The teacher of oral language, be it the teacher in a self-contained classroom, team-teaching situation, or a departmentalized school, will probably be concerned with working in the following areas.

1. *Reporting* will still be an important oral activity in the advanced grades. Clarity and delivery will be assessed along with the development of the report—its material, organization, and style of presentation.
2. *Oral reading* in some sort of audience situation may be frequently used by the speech teacher as a means of enhancing the communications program. Voice,

Model Lesson Plan
Teaching Oral Demonstration

I. **Name:** Barbara Dach   **Date:** 10-9-74   **Grade:** 6   **No.** 1

   Subject: Language Arts (Oral Speech)   **Text:** Language We Use (6)

II. **Instructional Objective:** To teach oral skills in combination with a demonstration.

   Performance Objective: At the conclusion of the lesson period, the student should be able to plan and give a simple four-to-five step demonstration with oral description and directions so that members of the class can follow the process.

III. **Assignment:** Textbook reading: pp. 70-73, "Oral Presentation of a Demonstration—Suggested Procedures." Preparation of individual demonstration.

   Materials:
   textbook
   construction paper
   chart paper and felt pen

IV. **Procedure:**
   1. Introduce reading assignment.
   2. After reading, group work for preparing chart with "Guidelines for an Oral Demonstration."
   3. Present a sample Origami lesson illustrating an oral demonstration.
   4. Critique teacher's demo using chart points for checklist criteria.
   5. Discuss possible demonstration topics for student preparation for class presentation.

V. **Related Activities:**
   1. Use checklist for evaluation of science demonstration or art lesson explanation.
   2. Plan a P.E. activity in which someone demonstrates a particular game with three-to-four part directions.

VI. **Evaluation:** As a means of evaluating student performance, observe and record peer responses to the oral demonstration. Record comments in a brief anecdotal form.

VII. **Ongoing Activities:**
   1. Assignment: Students to listen to and critique an oral demonstration on TV or radio and bring to class for oral discussion.
   2. Students to volunteer to prepare a demonstration for lower-grade class (P.E., Science, or Art/Crafts).

   Comments: None.

Figure 4.5

expression, tone, pacing and phrasing, pronunciation and enunciation, combined with the reader's own projected enjoyment and appreciation of the written script will be important considerations.

3. *Dramatic productions* presented for adult audiences as part of the school's program for the year may give a limited number of students the opportunity to be involved in a live production to a live audience. Here, of course, the dramatics coach will emphasize the importance of diction, kinesics, stance, emotional tone—the whole gamut of expressional mechanics.

4. *Speeches,* the more formal presentation of an idea, a topic, a political or philosophical stance, a cultural or social problem, whatever is the stuff from which speeches are woven, may be written and delivered by students for various reasons. These give the aspiring candidate, the budding orator, or the proponent of a cause scope for using persuasion techniques to convince, to change, to influence his hearers.

5. *Class meetings* employing parliamentary procedures and form may give the speech teacher an avenue for instruction in rules of order, techniques of formal meetings, exact phrasing of words, and organizing resolutions and motions. These more adult activities appeal to certain adolescents and provide an outlet for oral communication in a structured setting.

6. *Debate,* with its dichotomies of *pro* and *con*—the necessity of taking a position and defending it while making use of rhetoric ability and oral powers to win a point—is a source of rich reward and enjoyment to the young speaker with a competitive, persuasive attitude. Here again, there are rules of the game to be followed in a formal structure.

7. *Storytelling* has been little emphasized at any previous level, and actually belongs no more here than at any earlier level. However, with increased speaking abilities, the young adolescent may make good use of his narrative powers. In his preparation and practice, the budding storyteller will remember:

   a. The importance of main ideas in the narrative.
   b. The secondary, supporting details of the story.
   c. The proper sequential order of the events of the tale.
   d. The power of vivid, picture-words and dialectic phrases.
   e. The power of using precise, specific language.
   f. The value of good organization: introduction, illustrative materials, body, and conclusion.
   g. The importance of feeling-tone, emotive quality, and appeal in the story itself.
   h. The causal aspect—relationships in time and space.

   The able storyteller will be one who seeks to develop a response in his hearers. This may be to awaken imagination, create clear perception and insights, to inspire enthusiasm and spontaniety, or to command concentration and attentiveness. In addition, he will have a keen desire to share with his listeners his life experiences, sensitivity to human moods and needs, and an element of sincerity and pleasure in his art. It is probably at this stage of his life that the older child may begin to be able to forget some of himself in his oral presentation and feel a sort of investiture of the character involved in his story. When this occurs, he begins to communicate his message indeed.

In planning for actual instruction in the art of storytelling, as well as the other areas of upper-grade speech development, the following lesson plan can serve the teacher/intern as a model (see figure 4.6, p. 106).

SUMMARY

The teaching of spoken language in its varied forms is a demanding and difficult task. The program to be planned, the identification and selection of skills to be taught, the development of instructional techniques and exercises, and the actual teaching with its need for interesting and activating students are problems requiring special study and preparation. Inasmuch as speech is a skills ability learned by the child even before the threshold of memory, he may often be unaware of his needs, or unwilling to change his speaking pattern, or unmotivated to make the consistent efforts necessary for improvement. Also because of the heavy curriculum load imposed in contemporary schools, as well as the teacher's possible uncertainty as to the real rewards resulting from the time requisite to speech development and refining, it is not surprising that often little is being done in the area of oral language instruction as a scheduled, planned activity throughout the elementary school years. There has also been a lack of good instructional material, guidelines, and basic teaching philosophy relative to oral communication at the lower levels. All these combine to cause a certain reluctance on the part of educators to attempt the necessary systematic program for this facet of language development and improvement.

At the least, it is hoped by the authors that this brief outlining of the skills involved, coupled with a certain amount of pragmatic materials and suggested strategies, will provide some stimulus toward teacher awareness of the need existing in today's schools, and with this awareness, a certain preparedness for handling the problems and preparing students with greater skills for communicating in today's world.

Selected Readings: The Speaking Vocabulary

BROMAN, BETTY L. "Too Much Shushing—Let Children Talk." *Childhood Education* 46 (December 1969):132–134.

BUYS, WILLIAM. "Speech Curricula for All American Youth." *The Speech Teacher* 15 (January 1966):25.

CAZDEN, COURTNEY B. "Suggestions for Studies of Early Language Acquisition." *Childhood Education* 46 (December 1969):127–131.

I. **Name:** Jo Ann King   **Date:** 11-20-74   **Grade:**   8 **No.** 1

    Subject: Language Arts (Oral Speech)   **Text:** <u>Language and Life</u> (8)

II. **Instructional Objective:** To provide an instructional period devoted to the mechanics of telling a story.

    Performance Objective: As a result of his learning, the student will be able to tell a story of his choice to a group, his presentation to be evaluated on a five-point rating scale.

III. **Assignment:** Read and be prepared to discuss in groups the section from the text on storytelling (pp. 18-27). Choose a story for telling and prepare it according to the seven-step plan.

    Materials:
        variety of storybooks, magazines, paperbacks
        recording: "Story Time"
        checklists

IV. **Procedure:**
1. Read assignment.
2. Outline seven steps of preparation.
3. Play recording and apply criteria in critique of performance.
4. Free activity time for reading and selecting stories for preparation and telling.

V. **Related Activities:**
1. Group practices of storytime sessions.
2. Preparation of flash cards for illustrating stories to be told (art).
3. Developing overlays to be used with the projector for storytime.
4. Preparing a flannel-board visual to accompany a story to be shared.

VI. **Evaluation:** Use the five-point rating scale to assess the effectiveness of student's storytelling.

VII. **Ongoing Activities:**
1. Sharing enough of a well-liked book to "sell" it to other readers.
2. Retelling a TV narrative or movie.
3. Identifying and classifying stories according to categories: fables, myths, epics, short stories.

    Comments: None.

Figure 4.6

CHING, DORIS C. "Methods for the Bilingual Child." *Elementary English* 42 (January 1965):22–27.

DICKENS, MILTON. *Speech: Dynamic Communication.* 2nd ed. New York: Harcourt Brace Jovanovich, Inc., 1963.

EISENSON, JON, and OGILVIE, MARDEL. *Speech Correction in the Schools.* 3rd ed. New York: The Macmillan Co., 1971.

IRWIN, JOHN, and ROSENBERGER, MARJORIE. *Modern Speech.* New York: Holt, Rinehart & Winston, Inc., 1961.

KEYSER, SAMUEL JAY. "The Role of Linguistics in the Elementary School Curriculum." *Elementary English* 47 (January 1970):39–45.

LINDBERG, LUCILE. "Oral Language or Else." *Elementary English* 42 (December 1965): 760.

LOBAN, WALTER. "Teaching Children Who Speak Social Class Dialects." *Elementary English* 45 (May 1968):592–599.

LOGAN, LILLIAN et al. *Creative Communication: Teaching the Language Arts.* Toronto: McGraw-Hill, Ryerson Limited, 1972.

ROBINSON, KARL F., and BECKER, ALBERT B. *Effective Speech for the Teacher.* New York: McGraw-Hill Book Co., Inc., 1970.

RUDDELL, ROBERT B. "Oral Language and the Development of Other Language Skills." *Elementary English* 43 (May 1966):489–498.

SMITH, DONALD K.; WEAVER, ANDREW T.; and ROBINSON, KARL R. "The Field of Speech: Its Purposes and Scope in Education." Official Document of Speech Association of America by action of the Administrative Council in Denver, Colo., August 18, 1963.

SMITH, E. BROOKS et al. *Language and Thinking in the Elementary School.* New York: Holt, Rinehart & Winston, Inc., 1970.

SIMONINI, R. C., JR. "Word Making in Present-Day English." *The English Journal* 55 (September 1966):752–757.

TIBBETTS, A. M. "The Grammatical Revolution That Failed." *Elementary English* 45 (January 1968):44–50.

WOLFRAM, WALTER A. "The Nature of Nonstandard Dialect Divergence." *Elementary English* 47 (May 1970):739–748.

THE DEVELOPMENT
OF LANGUAGE
THROUGH READING

A TEACHING/LEARNING MODULE APPROACH

In today's educational scene, the emphasis on teacher preparation is one of competency-based instruction. As a result of this focus, numerous institutions are entirely individualizing their course work basic to teacher certification. Most of this effort has culminated in the development of "learning modules" or individual packets for the student to complete in his professional training. The current authors have also been involved in this type of instructional programming at various levels. It is their feeling that such an approach to learning may have advantages for some students and for some types of learning experiences. However, they feel that a total or "all-or-nothing" changeover in educational program is a radical innovation which needs further study and evaluation.

In the present section, a modified modular program is presented. In the introduction to each chapter, (1) certain terminal performances are identified as the expected competency for each intern/teacher, (2) suggested learning experiences are listed for the student to undertake, (3) self-assessment, diagnostic materials are provided for preevaluation, and (4) posttesting instruments are included for the intern/teacher to determine if the satisfactory level of specified competencies has been reached. It is hoped that exposure to this type of learning-doing may provide both the instructor and the intern a current, pragmatic approach to teacher preparation in reading instruction.

THE DEVELOPMENT OF LANGUAGE THROUGH READING

5

THE READING PROCESS: A DEFINITIVE STATEMENT

The teacher of reading will discover that this third facet of language learning is perhaps the most complex and discrete of all instructional attempts. Certainly this is true at the beginning levels. Before examining teaching strategies, current programs, and the components of the instructional tasks themselves, the teacher/intern should have an introduction to the reading *process* itself. What is actually involved in the reading act? What are the basic linguistic, physical and psychological, progressive and interdependent steps necessary to successful reading? What happens *to* the child when he is reading? What takes place *within* him as he reads? These, and other like questions, need to be asked by the teacher of this important learning which is one of the most useful and valuable lifelong attainments of the student.

This chapter will give the reader an opportunity to explore some of the fundamental aspects of the reading process and of the teacher's role in teaching children to read. First of all, the teacher needs to understand and help her students who can already speak and listen, grasp the concept that reading is another form of communication; "That the words which are spoken can be recorded (encoded) in written form; and that what has been thus written can be read (decoded); and further, that what the child says, writes, and reads can be read by others."

This process of reading has not always been well understood. Indeed, current researchers have not yet discovered all that is involved in the developed skills of fluent readers, as will be discovered by even a cursory examination of the many, many studies being reported in the journals, abstracts, and publications available to teachers and students. Nor have these investigations yet fully explored all that is inherent in reading success—the motivational, perceptual, cognitive, and linguistic aspects embedded in basic living, being, and learning.

As the teacher/intern becomes involved in these topics, she will realize that there are many unanswered questions, conflicting ideas and ideologies, and not a little dogmatism concerning reading and learning to read. The instructor should, however, form some conclusions and opinions of her own as the facets of the reading process are examined. These, based on sound research and practice, will become the foundations for the teaching techniques, the instructional media, and the learning activities which will make up the framework of successful operation in the classroom. Therefore, it is important that time be given to identify the facets of the reading process, to analyzing its components and requirements, and to individually defining the concept and its terminology.

This, then, is the precise purpose of this chapter and the ones which immediately follow: to provide the reader with information and help for gaining clear insights into what is involved in the reading act and adequate instructional know-how for producing the desired reader. Thus a total look at the child will be taken so that the teacher will—hopefully—gain a feeling for him, his personal and academic needs, the importance of reading in fulfilling those needs—in short, his successful and happy progression in the school, home, and societal setting. This is a large task indeed; but such is the importance of learning to read well by the members of our society today.

A Multifaceted Process

What then are the components of this complex process? Various other writers have identified integral concomitants of the total. These include such terms as: "sequential, developmental, learned, learning, thinking, perceptual, sensory, response, conceptual, skills, interpretative," and on and on. These give the reader some idea of the varying emphases which have been given to the third vocabulary: reading. A brief look at each, or some of the terms describing the process, should suffice and give a clear understanding of each.

A sequential process. One of the first series of learnings with which the teacher of reading English deals is the concept of left to right progression of the writing of the language. Another sequence is that of the stringing together of our words in the order of our oral speech which is basic to the understanding of the thoughts and ideas expressed. Early in the beginning reading lessons the child will be introduced to the concept dealing with order from the top of the page downward in the sequence of line after line. These ideas will be reinforced often by the teacher's presenting ordering and seriating exercises for the young child to manipulate and categorize. This whole process of seriation and classification will be examined more fully under the section dealing with "Beginning Readiness for Reading."

A developmental process. The term as it refers to reading instruction, deals primarily with the order in which certain tasks and learning activities are presented in order to lead the student from the simplest skills to the increasingly more difficult ones required for independence and fluency. Some teachers and some authorities in the field have convinced themselves that certain primary learnings are to be presented in a precise order as prerequisites to success in new skills. However, careful research reports do not agree that reading is an absolute, *developmental tasks* syndrome. An examination of the differing programs currently being used in successful reading instruction will quickly focus on varying orders of presentation. However, beyond the mere program progression is the concept that there are basic skills and learnings involved which do develop within the student strengthening his skills and abilities in handling more difficult and discrete tasks. Hence, the idea of reading being a developmental process is a valid one. The length of words, the length of sentences and paragraphs as well as the story being read, the introduction of new words, the acquisition of decoding skills—these and other such instructional considerations are necessarily and basically matters of a progressing nature.

A learned process. The third facet of the process, that which deals with reading being a *learned process,* simply indicates that the ability to read is an acquired one. It must be taught or learned. It is not something inherent; it is the result of conditioning. Literacy, the ability to read and write, comes as the result of learning. It is because of this factor that the school has traditionally been given the primary responsibility for inducting the young into this societally learned process. The young child soon realizes that one of the family expectations is that he learn to read soon after attending school. More than one young first grader after a day or two of school has been heard to say with disappointment: "I didn't learn to read yet." The very word *learn* connotes that which is acquired by study, experience, or instruction. Certainly in learning to read, the student receives from all three types of input; and the aware teacher is concerned that through each channel—actual study, experience be it firsthand or vicarious, and instruction be it individual or group-oriented—the young learner will move easily and naturally into his full potential of this learned ability.

A learning process. The idea of reading being a *learning process* is closely related to its being learned. Who can deny the importance of "Reading to Learn" as well as "Learning to Read"? Neither is complete in isolation in contemporary education. Soon after the young student learns the mechanics and responses of reading, he begins to use this acquired skill to find new information, further knowledge, and expanded learnings. Along with his developing powers, come new tasks requiring reference skills and the use of more sophisticated tools—the dictionary, the encyclopedia, the card catalogue, the index, the glossary, and the subject matter text. He also faces increasingly difficult levels of recreational reading materials. There are those who would infer that reading "is on the way out," and that other media will soon take the place of the book, the periodical, the newspaper, or the letter. Certainly one would not minimize the effectiveness and value of these other media—the illustration, the animation of the film, the availability of listening and recording devices. Even these learning tools, however, require a level of learned "reading" to be effective in the classroom or carrel. Traditionally and currently, increasing demands have been made on the student's reading abilities as he progresses further up the ladder of academics year after year. Using his reading is a means of expanding his store of knowledge as well as strengthening his skills power as he continues to learn.

A thinking process. Clearly interrelated to and interdependent upon the child's being able to learn through reading is the concept of reading being a *thinking process.* If one examines the taxonomy of *comprehension* skills (see page 184 under "Skills of Reading" for a brief outline of the taxonomy), he will find a striking similarity to an outline of cognitive levels arranged in an ascending hierarchy. As the learner continues, he makes use of the various levels of cognition from the mechanical, knowledge kinds of responses to the insightful "ahas" of exciting application and critical evaluation. Reading is more than merely recognizing the words for which certain combinations of letters bring about a correct recall. It includes the whole gamut of thinking responses: feeling and defining some need, identifying a solution for meeting the need, selecting from alternative means, experimenting with the choices, rejecting or retaining the chosen route, and devising some means of evaluating the results. Certainly the reading act involves all of these suggested steps in the initial recognition of words, the forming of meaningful thought structures, the interpretation of the material, as well as the seeking for answers to specified tasks. Since reading is basically *communication,* all of the intellectual skills that are used in receiving and reacting to messages are necessary in the total process of understanding and assessing written materials.

A perceptual process. Basic to reading being thinking is reading as a *perceptual process.* One way of simplifying the term *percept* is to say that "a percept is the individual's response to a single stimulus, and that in the responding, some type of interpretation is taking place." Certainly this is not all that is involved, and some would question how a single stimulus could be so isolated. These may be valid, but for the sake of the discussion at hand, let us use the definition. In order for the child to make an interpretation of any input material, he will of necessity be affected by his past experiences. It will be these that give the tone to his response. It is safe to say that everything that has made the individual what he is will now influence his attitudes, feelings, thoughts, and reactions to what he is attempting to read. Without perception, there can be no actual reading. How can the reader attach meaning to orthography and symbol without the requisite background of experiences? It is this perceptual process that results in the child's organizing his input sensory data into meaningful segments and then into meaningful wholes.

What then determines the effective working of this process? Certainly there are numerous factors involved: physical and emotional well-being, psychological and intellectual development, societal and cultural conditioning, as well as the experiential total resulting from these factors. All will combine to affect the child's perception, and thus, the meanings which he *brings to* the printed material will be the result of each and all of these factors working together. Reading is not so much getting meaning *from* printed material as clothing the writing with the reader's feelings, ideas, meanings, and values.

A concept-forming process. If a percept is the organism's response to a single stimulus, the concept may be thought of as the fabric which results from the combining of many percepts. In other words, the greater the reader's store of percepts, the richer the resultant concept will be. Many experiences result in many percepts; many percepts result in a deeper level of concept formation. As the child's experiences widen, he is able to relate the same term or word to many more objects having like characteristics. Initially his concept of dog may relate to only his own pet, *dog* to him means just his dog. Later after seeing, petting, talking to, and being involved with various sized, haired, colored, breeds of dogs, he forms the generalized concept that includes all kinds of four-footed, barking, wagging, lapping, sniffing, and loving animals. *Dog* becomes a broadened concept, a generic term because of the richness of his experiences with many types of such animals.

Conceptualization, then, becomes the ability of the person to think on an abstract level. These vary from simple groups or categories to very complex patterns of classification. Labeling, or naming, is an important aspect of this process; hence, the value of adequate vocabulary development for word usage can be seen here. The wider the child's abilities to assign words to concepts, the greater depth of understanding; likewise, the more restricted his knowledge of words and terms, the more specific the communication between print and reader becomes.

A sensory process. Reading has further been called a *sensory process* in that the chief input stimuli make use of the visual, aural, and tactile senses. Literally a vast amount of respectable research has been conducted to discover the relationships between sightedness, hearing-listening abilities, and alternate learning modalities for those who may have visual and auditory deficiencies, or neurological impairments. Adequate visual maturity and acuity certainly are important considerations for fluency in reading. The ability to discriminate aurally is likewise an important factor in hearing tone, pitch, and intonation in spoken language. Closely allied to these physical skills is that of listening effectively. Through these learning modalities, the child channels the language input vital to success in reading.

A responding process. Since communicating is not a unilateral process, one can readily see the logic in saying that reading is a *responding process.* Not only does the writer have something to say, to tell, or to share; the reader must respond by being interested, by feeling the message being given, and by receiving and becoming involved with that which is being offered by the writer. It is this affective responding that makes reading such an important tool for communication. The whole subject of *motivation* is basic in this respect. It is the belief of the authors that individuals *are* motivated; the teacher then has the responsibility of discovering that motivation and using it as the framework of her curriculum. Far too often educators speak of "motivating learners" whereas it is probably more correct to say "interest students" or "activate children" or some such term. This is merely making use of the interests, likes or dislikes, hobbies, or attitudes of the student. He will respond more readily to the media and material which best focus on this affective domain in a positive manner, and he will reject that which reflects negatively.

In analyzing what takes place in the reading process, one is made aware that, because of the communication evident, the reader responds and interacts.

The reading process must bring about a response, an arousal, a resultant action, in which the reader feels the emotive quality of the material, so that he "smells, tastes, and touches" the descriptions related to these responses. He must experience the pathos, the hilarity, or the danger of the narrative by the appropriate reactions. His interest and reading taste must be so catered to and so captivated that he is carried along from page to page, topic to topic, or selection to selection without boredom or frustration. A vital facet of reading is interest.

A *skills process*. Another interrelated component of the total process of reading is that which deals with reading as a *skills process*. This facet has purposely been left until last to be discussed because so often it is given such prominence in reading instruction that one might think it is all that is involved. Indeed many reading programs stress the mechanics of the skills involved to such an extent that little time or effort is given to letting the child read. Frequently the reaction to this strong emphasis on skills acquisition is "We are doing so much to teach the child *how* to read, that we don't teach him *to* read!"

Certainly there are important basic skills to be well taught in reading classes. There are silent reading skills and oral reading skills which need to be given careful attention. These in some of the current skills continuums are almost innumerable, numbering not only into the dozens, but actually several hundred discrete skills. This has doubtless resulted from the contemporary emphasis on "behavioral objectives" or teaching goals being stated in measurable terms. Hence, each tiny decoding skill has been delineated and taught. Hopefully time will aid in some readjustment of this situation until a more realistic attempt at teaching reading skills will result.

A complete section will follow later in which important skills in reading will be identified and discussed at more length. Suffice it here to say that reading involves the use of specific skills.

Summary

In the preceding pages of this chapter the authors have sought to direct the teacher/intern to a serious, penetrating look at the entire reading process with its numerous related and interdependent components. This should aid in an attempt to adequately define the term "reading" as an understanding of what is involved in successful teaching. Each of the facets of the process focuses on an important concept by itself; however, each is interwoven in the total process so that none excludes or even overshadows the importance of the others. Reading is a complex process involving the person, his interests and tastes, his physical abilities, his emotional responses, his perceptual development, his depth of concept formation, and his skills in the mechanics of the reading act. All of these facets are influenced by the total store of experiences in the background of the learner.

THE READING PROCESS: THE PRAGMATIC APPROACH

As you begin this section of your reading instruction preparation, the material provided has been arranged to allow for your independent working with other intern/teachers and the faculty person directing your coursework. You will notice that the learning activities and informational content are included in the following order:

1. Performance Objectives or Learning Competencies.
2. Suggested Vocabulary List for your use.
3. Learning Experiences for your consideration.
4. Preassessment Instrument.
5. Postassessment Evaluation.

Learning Competencies

At the conclusion of your learnings related to the reading process you will demonstrate your competence by:

1. Stating in clear language a definition of reading as per the model provided in any of the reference readings.
2. Describing the nature and facets of the reading process as delineated by your authors or any other recognized authoritative source.
3. Discussing, either in written form or verbally, the value of reading as it relates to the academic, personal, social, and psychological development of elementary students.
4. Identifying and illustrating by examples, the phases of the reading process as discovered by your classroom involvement with elementary level children.
5. Defining and correctly using the professional terms used in this chapter.
6. Describing the basic paradigm of current reading instruction to a group of peers.

Vocabulary List for Chapter 5

The intern/teacher will likely meet the following reading terms in his work on finding out about the reading process. They will make a good basis for discussions, vocabulary drill, or writing tools.

AFFECTIVE	ABSTRACT	ABSTRACTION
COMPREHENSION	DEVELOPMENTAL TASKS	INTEGRATION
LINGUISTICS	PERCEPTION	PERCEPT
PERCEPTION	CONCEPT	CONCEPTUAL
READINESS	SENSORY	STIMULI
MODALITY	VISUAL	AURAL
HAPTIC	TACTILE	KINESTHETIC

Many of the terms suggested here will be found in the glossary entries of some current reading textbooks. Others will be included in a reputable dictionary of educational terms[1] and in a dictionary of learning or psychological terms.[2] It is well for professionals to use the language of their specialty with clarity and correctness. Many are included in the Glossary section of the text (see p. 363.)

Learning Experiences and/or Options and Alternatives

In your discovering the components of the reading process and your examination of their educational implications, you may wish to consider the following learning activities which have been designed to focus on the topic. Note that they are general enough and inclusive to the extent that they afford a variety of learners with viable options for arriving at the necessary level of competency for success in this area of study. Choose as many as you feel needful for your meeting standard performance.

1. Attendance and participation in an introductory seminar(s)—either one two-hour session, or two one-hour meetings—in which the faculty person will discuss the items included in this component as reflected in the statement of behavioral objectives.
2. Regular classroom involvement (minimum of one reading class per week) in which you are involved with reading students, either individually or in groups.
3. Arrange and schedule at least one interview-appointment with a reading teacher, reading specialist, or reading consultant in which you discuss the reading process and relevant programming to accomplish specified goals.
4. Either write a report of the interview (item 3), or arrange a session with several other interns and share with them verbally your findings from the appointment.
5. Read a minimum of two of the following sources:
   a. Bush, Clifford L., and Huebner, Mildred H. *Strategies for Reading in the Elementary School.* New York: The Macmillan Co., 1970. Foreword and Chapter 1, pp. 1–15.
   b. Durkin, Delores. *Teaching Them to Read.* Boston: Allyn & Bacon, Inc., 1970. Chapters 1 and 2, pp. 1–18.
   c. Dechant, Emerald. *Improving the Teaching of Reading.* Englewood Cliffs, N.J.: Prentice-Hall, Inc., 1964. Chapters 1 and 2, pp. 3–28.
   d. Zintz, Miles. *The Reading Process: The Teacher and the Learner.* Dubuque, Ia.: Wm. C. Brown Company Publishers, 1970. Chapter 1, pp. 1–19.
      NOTE: All of these authors examine the reading process, define it, pose questions, and offer opinions.

---

1. Carter V. Good, *Dictionary of Education* (New York: McGraw-Hill Book Company, Inc., 1959).
2. English and English, *Dictionary of Psychological and Psychoanalytical Terms* (New York: David McKay Co., Inc., 1958).

6. For your own retention and review, keep either reading cards (5 x 8), or outlined notes of your readings to be discussed with and examined by your master teacher and/or faculty advisor.
7. Other options you may wish to consider in completing these learning experiences:
   a. Preview a film of your choice which deals with the teaching of reading at the elementary level.
   b. Develop a set of word cards, a word game, or an alphabetized glossary of of the new words and terms you meet in undertaking this instructional module.

Preassessment Instrument

Before you undertake the actual learning experiences for this facet of your professional preparation for reading instruction, you may wish to diagnose your present strengths at the knowledge level of performance. Read the following evaluation for the purpose of assessing your areas of deficiency and your areas of satisfactory competence. This will guide you in the amount of effort you will need to make in order to complete this section of your course.

When you complete the evaluation, carefully analyze your responses, compute your total score. If you are able to get a "grade" of 45–50 points, this would indicate that with the reading assignments, you may be ready to proceed directly to the postevaluation and go on after its satisfactory completion to the next component.

Preassessment Evaluation   *NOTE: Carefully read each section of the following evaluation instrument before beginning. Note that the point-value of each task is stated.*

1. Define what the term *reading* means to you as completely and concisely as you are able. (10 points maximum)
2. Reading has been described as a multifaceted process. Some authors have listed as many as ten components of this total experience. Identify and briefly explain five of these partial processes. (15 points maximum)
3. Reading has been described as meeting numerous individual needs in the lives of people. Specify five important areas of needs which reading may help to meet, and briefly describe how the needs may be fulfilled through the reading experience. (15 points maximum)
4. There are many specific terms used in the literature dealing with the reading process. Below are ten such terms and their definitions. Match them correctly. (10 points maximum)

1. Affective

2. Abstraction

3. Comprehension

4. Developmental Tasks

5. Integration

6. Linguistics

7. Perception

8. Readiness

9. Sensory

10. Stimuli

A. The organism's response to stimuli in which some interpretation takes place.

B. Those things which impinge upon the senses of the organism.

C. Set: preparedness for action demonstrated by seeking behavior.

D. The scientific study of human language with its nature, structures, and modifications.

E. That which pertains to the input channels of communication, the sense modalities.

F. The concept of a sequential hierarchy of skills, each of which is basic to the learning of the next.

G. That component of the organism which is concerned with the emotive and normative being.

H. The ability to assimilate the reading idea or concept into the reader's experiential background.

I. The ability to gain meaningful ideas in response to reading.

J. The level of identification and understanding of relationships from symbolic objects.

Evaluate your total score by number of points correct on each item.

Note: This pretest serves two purposes: (1) it helps you to be aware of those areas about the reading process of which you already have sufficient knowledge, and (2) it points to other areas of knowledge which you will strengthen through the learning experience of this module.

After you have taken the preassessment test, you will probably have a much clearer idea of the expectations your instructor has for you. This previous awareness should prove most helpful in your knowing what you want to do, and how you want to meet, those instructional expectations. Select the learning experiences suggested, or discuss other contractual alternatives with your faculty advisor for approval to proceed. A schedule of progress can be developed for individuals, small groups, or entire classes according to the mutual agreement of student and professor.

The Postassessment for Final Evaluation

Now that the learning experiences have been completed for this component of your reading instruction course, you are ready to schedule your terminal evaluation for this section. Good luck!

Postassessment   *NOTE: This is the final step in your completing the module.*
Evaluation   *You will notice that each of the items is directly related to the*
stated objectives. If you have carefully done the learning experiences, you should
have no difficulty in successfully completing this step of the evaluation.

1. One author has stated: "The teaching of reading is a complex and vast field primarily because reading can be viewed from so many different vantage points." Discuss the statement as it relates to your readings and classroom experiences. (15 points maximum)
2. Room environment is important in the learning situation. Choose a grade level for consideration and choose one facet of the reading process which you wish to develop in your instructional program. Then describe how you would arrange your room for effective instruction. How would you meet the needs of your students? What use would you make of materials? bulletin boards? enrichment media? (10 points maximum)
3. Identify five facets of the reading process and specify a classroom activity which you have used or seen recently that was intended to strengthen each chosen phase of the reading process. (15 points: 1 p/process—2 p/activity)
4. During your work on this module, you have done reading from various sources and have met the names of people who are outstanding in the area of reading instruction. Name *five* such authorities. (5 points maximum)
5. Below are some true/false questions for you to consider. Determine the correct response. (Each correct answer is worth 2 points: 20 points maximum)
   a. Special emphasis should be placed upon the importance of reading as the major tool for acquiring education.
   b. Any printed expression stands for the spoken form of that expression.
   c. All of the breakdown in communication stems from the fact that language is symbolic.
   d. Beginning reading can only be intelligible to the student if it is based on familiar spoken language.
   e. That area of human personality which deals with one's feelings and values is called the cognitive domain.
   f. Stimuli are those things which impinge upon the senses of the organism.
   g. The organism's response to stimuli in which some interpretation takes place is called comprehension.
   h. Reading people use the term integration to signify the ability to assimilate the reading idea or concept into the reader's experiential background.
   i. Perception is the scientific study of human language with its nature, structure, and modifications.
   j. The level of identification and understanding of the relationships from interaction with symbolic objects is called abstraction.

Evaluate your total score by number of points correct on each item.

Intern Checklist

Name _____   Beginning Date _____

I. Preassessment: Date Taken _____   Score _____

II. Learning Experiences:

    1. Seminar(s)   Date _____ _____
                                                                (Faculty Signature)

                      Date _____ _____
                                                                (Faculty Signature)

    2. Readings: Author: _____   Date _____

                Author: _____   Date _____

    3. Classroom Work/Involvement: minimum one reading class per week.

        Week 1. _____   Dates _____
                     (Master Teacher's Signature)

        Week 2. _____   Dates _____
                     (Master Teacher's Signature)

        Week 3. _____   Dates _____
                     (Master Teacher's Signature)

    4. Interview _____   Dates _____
                     (Reading Person's Signature)

    5. Interview Report: Written? _____ or Oral? _____

                Date Completed _____

    6. Report of Required Readings: Date _____

        Reading Cards? _____ or Outlines? _____

    7. Options—List: a. _____   Date _____

                  b. _____   Date _____

III. Postassessment: Date Attempted _____   Score _____

Completion Date: _____   _____
                                                              (Intern's Signature)

                                            _____
                                                              (Faculty Signature)

NOTE: This checklist is a model for use. It provides for a sequential schedule for the module and a record of progress. Several learning experiences require a signature from your team leader, supervisor, or faculty advisor. When this is necessary, complete a similar checklist and hand it in to the appropriate faculty advisor.

Figure 5.1

Selected Readings: The Reading Process

The following authors discuss various aspects of the importance of reading in today's society and examine the total process of the reading act.

BARBE, WALTER B. *Teaching Reading.* New York: Oxford University Press, 1965. Chapter 2, "The History and Philosophy of Reading Instruction," pp. 37–70.

DEBOER, JOHN J., and DALLMAN, MARTHA. *The Teaching of Reading.* New York: Holt, Rinehart & Winston, Inc., 1970. Chapter 2, "The Nature of Reading," pp. 11–19.

JENNINGS, FRANK G. *This Is Reading.* New York: Teacher's College Press, 1965. Chapter 1, "What is Reading?" pp. 3–22.

MORRISON, IDA E. *Teaching Reading in the Elementary School.* New York: The Ronald Press Company, 1968. Chapter 2, "The Reading Process," pp. 22–50.

SMITH, HENRY P., and DECHANT, EMERALD V. *Psychology in Teaching Reading.* Englewood Cliffs, N.J.: Prentice-Hall, Inc., 1961. Chapter 1, "The Teacher's Interest in the Reading Process," pp. 1–20.

SPACHE, GEORGE D., and SPACHE, EVELYN B. *Reading in the Elementary School.* Boston: Allyn & Bacon, Inc., 1969. Chapter 1, "Ways of Defining the Reading Process," pp. 3–40.

STRANG, RUTH; McCULLOUGH, CONSTANCE; and TRAXLER, ARTHUR. *The Improvement of Reading.* New York: McGraw-Hill Book Company, Inc., 1967. Chapter 1, "Perspectives in Reading," pp. 3–39.

BEGINNING READING INSTRUCTION

THE READINESS LEVEL

RATIONALE

As a prospective teacher it is important that you be concerned with readiness of students for learning. As a future teacher of reading, you will want to know the most favorable moment for beginning to teach a child to read as well as for the teaching of each specific skill. The concept of reading readiness is not reserved for the beginning of reading instruction alone; it applies to each successive stage of reading development.

In our American educational system, starting to read has always been closely associated with starting to school. Somehow on this basis being six years old has seemed to signify starting times for both experiences. Since beginning reading ability was equated with a particular stage of development, it was "logical" to assume that if he had early difficulty in learning to read he was not ready to read. Following this concept, then, would lead one to also assume that the passage of time would automatically solve the difficulties in learning to read. However, other concepts have been accepted as relevant to readiness: (1) mental age, (2) perceptual development, (3) sensory discrimination, (4) language development, (5) emotional and social development, and even (6) instructional methods and procedures are important considerations.

Hence, readiness programs have been designed. Along with these, informal and formal assessment instruments have been developed. These have been based on psychological and sociological concerns. Today the whole idea of readiness has grown into an important facet of teacher education—Head Start programs, early childhood education, and preschool experiences have added new dimensions to the idea of preparation for beginning to read. So, it is important that you know about this area of education.

It was with this sense of the value of such learning, that the following module was constructed to offer you guidance in reading and learning experiences. As you complete the various components of this phase of your professional preparation, you will be introduced to new terminology, new concepts, new teaching strategies and correlated materials, and ways of evaluating and assessing a child's readiness to learn to read.

In order to measure your own present knowledge about the topic and apply it to the teaching situations, and in order to have a clear idea of the expected levels of proficiency you will need to successfully perform your teaching duties, carefully consider the performance objectives, the information provided, and the learning experiences. These will provide guidelines for you in your completion of this section.

Preassessment Instrument

Reading through the rationale for this facet of your coursework should have given you some clues as to the areas of study and experience you will be undertaking as you progress in this component of reading instruction. Before considering the performance competencies and the specific learning experiences suggested by the authors, it would be well for you to carefully read and react to the following questions which deal with reading readiness. If you are able to respond to most of these items, it is a good indication that you already have considerable background information and/or experience with young children and their readiness to begin formal instruction in reading. In today's society, with its numerous programs—day-care centers, early childhood learnings, Head Start activities— many interns/students have had work in the schools at beginning levels either as a volunteer helper, a teacher's aide, a tutor, playground director, or in some other paraprofessional capacity. Therefore, it may be that some will be able to spend very little time on this area of reading instruction, and can soon go on to another section of study. However, carefully consider each of the evaluative tasks here.

Preassessment Evaluation

1. What does the term *reading readiness* mean? Define it fully in the light of present-day concepts. (10 points maximum)
2. List and briefly describe at least five readiness factors which should be considered in assessing a child's developmental level. (15 points maximum)
3. Describe the differences between auditory and visual modalities. (5 points maximum)
4. What is the difference between auditory acuity and auditory discrimination? (5 points maximum)

5. Can you differentiate between visual discrimination, visual sequencing, and/ or visual memory? (5 points maximum)

6. Describe several procedures that a teacher might use to improve a student's auditory skills. (10 points maximum)

7. List and explain several activities you might use in seeking to strengthen visual skills of students. (10 points maximum)

8. Identify several reading readiness tests currently used in your area schools. (5 points maximum—1 p/item)

9. What are good times of the year for administering such readiness tests? Why? (5 points maximum)

10. What are several ways a teacher may use data for readiness tests in the instructional program? (5 p/item)

11. Identify and describe several published readiness programs. (5 p/item)

12. What are the basic purposes of reading readiness programs? (10 points maximum)

These assessment items should prove sufficient to alert the student to his entry-level knowledge relating to the subject of children's readiness to read, and to likewise show areas of deficiency or weakness which need additional work. The following section will briefly cover the topic of readiness, hopefully answering some questions and giving needed information. However, the student who is relatively unfamiliar with the concept of readiness should examine the reading list provided in this chapter and select available texts for further reading.

JUST WHAT IS READING READINESS?

Frequently one gets the idea from current literature and from the numerous published and packaged teaching materials that readiness can be attained by a single phase of development in the child. Hence some would assert that "knowing the letter names," or doing a program "of visual discrimination activities," or following a series "of auditory exercises" would ready the child for formal reading instruction. Such is not the case at all. The matter being that reading readiness is not a single, total entity, but rather a composite of a number of characteristic behaviors. Simply because a child is able to complete a commercial program, or recite the letters of the alphabet, or complete any one of a dozen other like tasks does not signify in one day that he is now ready to read. What then is meant by readiness?

First of all, it should be viewed as a sort of transitional *period* in the life of a boy or girl, not an overnight, sudden change from a nonreader to a beginning reading student. During this extended time (it might last from a minimum of several months to a total school term or longer), the child will continue to develop capacities and competencies, and yet may be deficient in some areas of total readiness. These handicaps will slow down some of his progress, but other strength areas will compensate to keep the learner moving ahead. Certain visual difficulties, or auditory discrepancies, or a lack of some coordinative competencies may affect specific skill performances important in the total reading process. However, these hindrances may not be sufficient to completely stop the mobility of the child; and as he continues to progress, his development in the deficient areas can be strengthened and nurtured by a carefully planned instructional program of readiness. Doubtless, his learning should be focused on his strength modality without detriment to the developing input channel until, little-by-little, he emerges into that stage of maturity necessary to becoming a reader. The progression may be painfully slow and labored, but gradually as each segment of learning is secured, the time comes when what he is "reading" communicates a thought, an idea, or a flash of imagination—anything so that he suddenly realizes that reading is actually "getting a message!" Not until that happens, and with some children it may take an extended period long after most others have become independent readers at their various levels, is reading truly occurring.

What then is readiness training? It is the teacher's sincere attempt to discover the individual's needs: physical, social, emotional, and psychological. On the basis of this diagnosing (for that is what it really is), the instructor provides a carefully planned series of experiences, activities, exposures—whatever is needed —to overcome the handicaps that retard the learner as he tackles the tasks of reading. This of necessity becomes a demanding responsibility for the caring teacher. The transition period from nonreading to reading (for this is what readiness is) takes into consideration each child and his particular abilities, deficiencies, and competencies. The child who already has learned to read, the quicker learner, the average child, and the slower learner, all come under her attention and awareness. For even the ones who seem more advanced may be actually using only one of the means of reading, and thus need to be introduced to the other valuable clues to be used in proficient reading. The visual child may be using only memory, or configuration, or pictorial clues without using the aural reinforcements of the sounds of words, the combinations of letters, or the structural clues for word recognition. All this is to simply say that nearly all students need continual and careful observation and assessment of their basic knowledge, their competencies, and their physical and psychological characteristics.

THE FACETS OF THE DEVELOPMENTAL PATTERN OF READINESS

Since the authors take the view that readiness is basically a *transition period* which covers the child's development in a number of areas, the reader may well ask: "What components, then, am I to be concerned with in getting the child ready for reading instruction?" A brief description of the following facets of readiness may suffice to get the alert student thinking and exploring each in fuller depth.

Mental age. Traditionally, learning to read has been equated with chronological age as if having been alive for a certain number of years automatically insured success in beginning reading. However, other than the fact that physical maturation often does have a relation with certain psychomotor skills and muscular accomplishments, chronological age probably is not so important as a consideration of readiness as mental age. This latter quotient considers mental maturity with chronological age, and some authorities have thought that an optimum MA for reading instruction could be approximately 6.5. It must be remembered, though, that this is only one consideration in assessing a child's readiness development.

If one bases readiness on maturation alone, later school entry would be the sole criteria for success. However, experience has shown this to be inadequate in and of itself. Permitting children to begin school at a later age has not eliminated the problems of early reading failure, for these "older" beginners have experienced the same difficulties in early academic failure as more immature students.

Perceptual development. Recent emphasis on children's perceptual development has focused on another facet of the readiness patterning. Perception, defined in simplest terms, is described as the organism's response to basic stimuli in which *some* interpretation takes place. This then examines the input channels for sensory stimuli, and in the case of reading, deals with the visual, aural, and haptic modalities. Hence when a child receives either visual, auditory, or kinesthetic-tactile impulses, he makes some type of interpretative response on the basis of his store of experiential background. If the input is unhindered and the student has had adequate primary or vicarious experiences, his percepts will be correct. We assume, so often, as teachers that children are perceiving learning as we do and as we intend them to. This may be incorrect, and they may be "reading" situations, activities, and experiences very differently from their viewpoint or perceptual base.

Much commercial material has been developed for enhancing and nurturing perceptual development: (1) visual sequencing, memory, discrimination; (2) auditory discrimination, memory, awareness, and expressing; (3) psychomotor activities—coordination, laterality, directionality, and body image. These programs may, indeed, enhance certain of these developmental phases in the sensory modalities and thus remove some of the hindering barriers to reading readiness; but singly or even in various combinations they may still be inadequate to effect the total transition to reading.

Language development. Recent linguistic awareness has emphasized again and again that language is spoken, and that our learning of all the language arts should be based on oral communication. Hence reading and writing vocabularies, to be meaningful and utilitarian, must be the spoken language of the learner. This has been the main thrust of the proponents of the organic or language-experience approach to total language learning. Their premise is that: "What I think, I can say. What I can say, I can write. What I write, I can read, and others can read." Certainly the degree to which a learner can understand language and express himself adequately in oral language will furnish a foundation for formalized

The "'experience story" approach has been a favorite with good teachers for many years. It provides an excellent beginning for using words in the reading context.

reading instruction based on standard language form. If, as one writer has expressed it, "When I think, I am talking to myself" is correct, then language is important to thinking. Albeit there are some recent linguists who are exploring the inherent quality of language vs. its being a learned capacity.

The whole basis of recent "catch up" programs for young children has been to provide an enriched environment for language growth as a requisite to school and learning success. Certainly facility with the language is an important ingredient in succeeding with most of the readiness tests currently being used.

Emotional maturity. Another area of concern to many educators is the child's emotional well-being and stability. Since the school milieu is often group-oriented, the learner is one of many and functions as a member rather than a sole individual. This naturally brings about a certain degree of affect possibility. Likes, dislikes, prejudices, biases, egocentrisms, feelings, attitudes, values—the whole gamut of emotive personality—all are tested in the classroom. If the child is too threatened or frightened or ignored, his whole emotional makeup can be shaken and the result will be traumatic indeed. To say that formalized learning requires a certain degree of emotional development and maturity is logical as one aspect of the child's readiness, and it needs to be objectively assessed through careful observation.

Reading is an individualized task; and the child's ability to work independently, quietly, with attention and concentration, is important not only to his own progress and success, but for the learning of others as well. Even in the group reading activities a certain modicum of behavior and emotional and physical control is needed for constructive learning and participation. The emotionally immature youngster frequently is damaged by too early emphasis on formalized learning tasks requiring behavioral control and responsibility. Hence observable emotional behavior furnishes the teacher with clues to developmental readiness in her students.

Social involvement and interchanges. The school is a social institution and the means of transmitting much of the cultural norms and expectancies to young learners. There are certain privileges, taboos, do's and don'ts, social amenities—in short, acceptable and nonacceptable behaviors—which find themselves, rightly or wrongly, in the school scene. The teacher, the peers, the curriculum itself, the activities are all affected by the mores and normative teachings of the society. The youngster's ability to learn and accept or reject such strictures affords the teacher with certain valuable insights into the child himself, his family background, and his early learnings whatever they may be.

This facet of the readiness pattern is closely allied to the emotional development of the student. Indeed, his social development will often be reflected in his emotive responses to situations and involvements—in short, his whole interaction with others. The give and take of daily being with the same group, the sharing, the resisting or submitting, the readiness with which such responses are made; each will indicate a degree of social maturity and conformity, if you like or dislike, in the young learner. Such behaviors, too, may affect his responses to the early activities and experiences introducing him to stories, role-playing, books, and later to actual reading on progressive levels. His tastes, interests, choices, and hobbies will determine his willingness and readiness to learn to read and then to read and become a reader.

Sex. One facet of readiness that the teacher must consider is that of sex differences between little boys and little girls. It is well substantiated that in the early school experiences boys do less well than girls in reading. Likewise, later on those who work with disabled readers in corrective and remedial programs will attest that there are some three times as many boys as girls in their special classes and/or clinics. What is the cause of this lack of reading success among boys in American schools? And, it must be noted that this is a phenomenon markedly present in the American educational scene. Studies of European schools tend to show that often the young male students there excel more than the girls. True there are some maturational differences, boys being somewhat slower than girls in the earlier years; but probably the big difference lies in the cultural expectations relating to the male role in American society. Some have suggested that the paucity of male teachers in the preschool, kindergarten, and primary levels is another factor of causation. Others have stressed that the kinds of tasks and activities which make up many of the readiness programs are more girl-oriented than boy-oriented. Whatever the etiology, certainly the point here is that teachers, being aware of the different degrees of success found between boys and girls in early school programs, should carefully assess beginning level skills and entry knowledge of their young students. A different measure of developmental readiness commensurate with each sex is not unreasonable to suggest for evaluating entry level competencies.

Many experienced professionals might suggest numerous other components of a child's being ready for reading, but this coverage will suffice to alert the intern to the multifaceted nature of the transition stages from nonreading to reading. Other readings and studies in depth, as the need may be felt by particular interns, can broaden and enhance this introduction to the topic.

EVALUATING AND PREDICTING READING SUCCESS

A thoughtful appraisal of the previous section should result in the student/intern's awareness that many of the characteristics suggested as components of readiness are actually difficult to measure by accurate, objective means. How does one assess such factors as emotional, social, environmental, and personality adequacies or deficiencies? Certainly this requires more than a paper-and-pencil test. Another inadequacy of many of the prepared tests is that they actually often measure just one facet of readiness while purporting to be total predictors of readiness in students. An examination and comparison of a number of the commercial tests will reveal that one may be a test of auditory discrimination, another chiefly a test of visual perceptual development, or yet another the drawing-copying variety for measuring the level of another aspect of hand-eye coordination. A list of some of these published tests is included for the intern's information. In the school setting copies should be available of several of these for examination and critiquing. Note the types of tasks involved and the stated purpose of the test for assessing and predicting a child's readiness. Many are far from adequate to give any total picture of the child.

Reading Readiness Tests

1. *Apell Test*, 1970. (An IBM marking test covering reading, language, and math readiness tasks.) EDCO-Dyne Corporation, Orange, California.
2. *Clymer-Barrett Pre-Reading Battery*, 1966–67. (Visual discrimination, auditory discrimination, visual-motor.) Personnel Press, Inc.

3. *Lee-Clark Reading Readiness Test*, 1962 revision. (Letter symbols, concepts, word symbols, total.) California Test Bureau.
4. *Lippincott Readiness Test* (including Readiness Checklist, test to accompany Basal Reading Series), 1965. J. B. Lippincott Company.
5. *Metropolitan Readiness Tests*, 1966. (Word meaning, listening, matching, alphabet, numbers, copying, total.) Harcourt, Brace, & World, Inc.
6. *Murphy-Durrell Reading Readiness Analysis*, 1965. (Sound recognition, letter naming, learning words, total.) Harcourt, Brace, & World, Inc.
7. *Valett Developmental Survey of Basic Learning Abilities*, 1966. Ages 2–7. (Motor integration and physical development, tactile discrimination, language development, verbal fluency, conceptual development.) Consulting Psychologists Press.

NOTE: These are but a few of the many published reading readiness tests being used currently. The intern should be able to secure copies of several of these for critiquing.

Recently a number of teacher-observation checklist-types of evaluative instruments have been developed. These are to be used subjectively by the teacher for recording certain behaviors in a number of areas of development. These cover a wide gamut of observable (and some not so observable) responses expected from young children. Even though some of the teacher-prepared checklist forms may be incomplete, they do add a dimension necessary to total assessment of the child. As indicated earlier, the commercially prepared tests are limited to the extent which they are capable of measuring some aspects of readiness. Observation checklists, likewise, are not adequate solely in and of themselves. Probably a combination of several would be most effective; however, it should be noted that time and situation will dictate what the teacher will be able to do within the available resources. Certainly a heightened awareness and a sincere desire to properly and accurately assess a child's progress and level of readiness transition should result.

Nothing has been said and is often not said when reading readiness is being considered, about the child's attitude toward books themselves. Perhaps one very good indicator is the interest he shows toward and about books and their contents. His curiosity and evident desire are important criteria, based to be sure on his past experience with and exposure to pictorial and printed material—a valuable clue as to his feeling about reading and his desire to be able to participate in it.

TEACHING MEDIA FOR READINESS TO READ

Due to the importance of readiness factors, and because of the wide range of components to be dealt with during the transition period, the publishing houses have provided a broad selection of programs and materials for school and home use. These range from manipulative devices, to kits of activities, to workbooks.

Some deal with a single aspect of readiness, while others seek to cover a much wider range of components. Needless to say some are more effective than others in reaching the objective sought. Here, as with the testing materials, no single medium will prove successful in moving all or even most children from nonreading to reading. The learning environment that provides a variety of kinds of materials for the child's involvement and discovery plus an atmosphere conducive to inquiry and participation should be a most effective laboratory for readiness learning. The following list of materials and programs is by no means all-inclusive, but will show the variety of materials provided in one city district and its schools and early-childhood centers.

Readiness Materials

1. *Building Pre-Reading Skills* (Ginn & Company)
   a. Kit A, Language
   b. Kit B, Consonants
2. *Try: Experiences for Young Children* (Noble and Noble)
   a. Task 1, 2, 3
3. *Let's Look at Children; Let's Look at First Graders* (Educational Testing Service)
4. *Peabody Language Development Kits* (American Guidance Service, Inc.)
   a. Level 1, Level 2
5. *Developing Vocabulary of Self and Others* (American Guidance Service, Inc.)
   a. DUSO Kit D-1
6. *Sounds I Can Hear* (Scott, Foresman)
   a. House
   b. School
   c. Neighborhood
   d. Farm and the Zoo
7. *Listening Skills Program* (Science Research Associates)
   a. Primary Level, 1a, 1b, 1c
8. *Sullivan Reading Readiness Materials* (Behavioral Research Laboratories)
9. *Perceptual Motor Materials* (Teaching Resources)
10. *Continental Press Reading Readiness Program* (Continental Press)
11. *Audio Flashcard* (EFI)
    a. Reading Readiness Series
12. *Bank Street Readers* (The Macmillan Company)
    a. Teacher's Guide to Readiness Experiences and the Preprimers
13. *On Our Way to Read* (Harper & Row)
14. *Fun With Tom and Betty* (Ginn & Company)
15. *Outset Sound Filmstrip Program* (Guidance Associates)
    a. Listen There Are Sounds Around You

    b. Look About You
    c. People We Know
    d. Places to Go

A brief look at these and/or others currently used in public schools will reveal that they cover a broad scope of readiness activities related to specific transition components: sensory, perceptual, kinetic, visual and aural, discriminatory, and developmental.

Learning Experiences

In order for you to meet the expected competencies of this component of your course, a number of learning experiences have been suggested. Some of them are readings, some are participations in classroom activities, some deal with assessing readiness levels, and some relate to actual preparation for teaching readiness skills. This variety of learnings provides the student with good coverage for learning the theoretical basis for the readiness transition and also the practical aspects of working with children and the curriculum prepared for young students.

1. Attend and participate in an introductory seminar to be conducted by the faculty person designated.
2. Participate in a workshop session which will be a preparation session for developing teaching materials, instructional aids, or usable ideas for readiness activities.
3. Arrange an observation in your assigned school in which you will have opportunity to observe and complete an evaluative checklist assessing a student's level of readiness. (Several model checklist forms are included in this chapter and can be reproduced for your use.)
4. Administer a readiness test to either a single student or a small group. After giving the test(s), correct it and analyze the results. (Copies of a readiness test can be obtained from your school or the testing office, or your curriculum center.)
5. On the basis of the results of the data from the test administered, develop a prescriptive instructional plan, either for one lesson or a week of work focused on a specific area of weakness.
6. Work at a regular assignment at the preschool or kindergarten level for a period of at least one (1) week. During this time, you can implement your testing, planning, and actual teaching.
7. Select additional readings from professional textbooks that deal with the aspect of reading readiness.
8. Develop a personal glossary of new terms you have discovered during your work on readiness.

9. Design a bulletin board which will be usable in a K-primary classroom for introducing or strengthening a readiness concept of learning.

USABLE FORMS FOR IMPLEMENTING LEARNING EXPERIENCES

On the following pages, a number of model forms have been included for your use as you work through the activities and learnings of this phase of your course on reading instruction. These may be used as is, or the students or class may wish to modify or change them for a particular situation or purpose. They are meant only to aid the intern in recording observation materials, organizing data, or for planning and assessing actual instructional practices or materials.

A quick glance through these will alert the student that the first several of these are forms for analyzing and recording the behaviors of young children which are in the transition stage. These range from very simple to a more complete type of assessment.

Specific school districts have usually adopted a particular inventory form for use by their teachers and psychometrists. Many of these are very detailed and not only identify numerous specific tasks for the child to respond to and for the teacher to observe and record; but also provide a scaled and weighted marking system for getting a numerical quantitative score for prediction and assessment placement. The student may be able to obtain a copy of such an inventory as:

- The *A B C Inventory to Determine Kindergarten and School Readiness*, 1965, Norman Adair and George Blesch. Muskegon, Michigan.
- The Betty Caldwell Inventory (Standardization Edition).
- The *Developmental Task Analysis*, 1969, Robert E. Valett. Fearon Publishers, Belmont, California.

An examination will easily show that each of these developers has identified many behaviors and arranged them in some sequential order in an ascending hierarchy to determine skills and maturational levels purported to be related to readiness. These would appear to be based on some continuum of the dimensions of growth and development factors including performance or behavioral objectives for perceptual/conceptual skills. These normally include an outline of such competencies as follow.

- Visual-Motor Skills
  1. Gross Skills: Crawling, walking, running, jumping, balancing, skipping, dancing.
  2. Fine Skills: Holding crayon, chalk, pencil and brush. Traces, draws, copies, paints, colors. Cuts, pastes, tears, folds, joins, ties. Buckles, buttons, hooks, laces.

A Very Simple Form for Recording Certain Readiness Factors

Child's Name: _____   Teacher: _____

(Check each blank and date it when the child accomplishes the observed competency.)

Yes	Date	
_____	_____	I know my full name
_____	_____	I know my address
_____	_____	I know my telephone number
_____	_____	I can skip with correct rhythm
_____	_____	I can lace and tie my shoes
_____	_____	I know the names of the basic colors
_____	_____	I can count to thirty (30)
_____	_____	I can write (manuscript) my name
_____	_____	I can copy a simple picture
_____	_____	I know some words which rhyme
_____	_____	I can follow simple directions
_____	_____	I speak clearly (all the sounds)
_____	_____	I often share with others
_____	_____	I like to help and work with others
_____	_____	I like to be a "helper" in the room
_____	_____	I appear to be happy at school
_____	_____	I can recognize and name the letters of the alphabet
_____	_____	I like to look at and talk about books
_____	_____	I like the read aloud and story times

Comments:

Figure 6.1

- Visual Perceptual Developmental Tasks
  1. Body Image from Parts to Whole: Names parts of head and face on self or model or in drawing or puzzle. Names parts of body as pointed to on self, model, drawing, or puzzle.
  2. Figure-Ground Perception: Tracing, coloring, selecting boundaries of a particular picture, object, or categories of objects that overlay or are hidden by others.
  3. Spatial Relationships: Sees directionality—over, under, up, down, behind, in front, before, after, left, right, next to, between, among, across, inside, outside, in, on, below. Moves according to direction to form pattern, traces path in maze, connects by marking, positions in group.
  4. Position in Space: Notes likeness, difference, changes of same objects, drawings, positioning, completeness.
  5. Visual Memory: Names from memory objects or pictures seen. Observes picture and recalls components. Recalls additions to objects, pictures. Visually records figures, forms, symbols, and sequences.
  6. Discrimination: Likenesses, differences, sizes, shapes. Colors, hues, contrasts, additions, omissions.
- Auditory Perception Developmental Tasks
  1. Aural Identification: Hears familiar sounds and identifies sources. Repeats words, sounds, from aural model.
  2. Auditory Discrimination: Compares and contrasts sounds as to volumes, pitch, intensity, rhythm, sameness or contrast.
  3. Auditory Memory and/or Sequencing: Repeats series of sounds, digits, names, from hearing. Repeats rhythm patterns by tapping, clapping, saying, or singing.
  4. Haptic (Tactile-Kinesic) Skills: Without looking, find objects, tiles, figures or different shapes; or like shapes. Select from a set of like objects, shapes, or tiles another of same or like size. From textured objects, select one that is the same, or different: smooth, soft, rough, hard, slippery.

This outline continuum of perceptual skills will afford the intern a set of skills for which to observe, for which to develop performance objectives, and/or from which to plan specific lessons or units of work for readiness development. Beside the perceptual skills the student should also be aware of *cognitive* levels and the skills related to them. Hence, an outline of these levels and consistent competencies have been included here.

CONTINUUM OF COGNITIVE SKILLS FOR READINESS DEVELOPMENT: THINKING TASKS

- Finding Relationships: Finding likes and unlikes.
  1. Connecting pairs of pictures which are related: hand/arm, car/garage, foot/shoe (verbally or drawing line).

Children in the primary grade setting need aural input as well as visual clues in learning to unlock words.

2. Identifying opposite of concept pairs when given a word: large/small, hot/cold, loud/quiet.
3. Supply causal factors from depicted actions. Picture—girls crying. Why? Broken doll.
4. Predicting outcomes from picture clues: what will happen?
5. Cause-effect relationships from oral stimulus. Story told or read: Why did it happen? What might have happened if. . . . ? Predicting next event in sequence.
- Classifying and Seriation Tasks: Organizing, arranging, grouping, sorting; according to color, use, sex, size, age, texture, condition, attributes, names. Likewise the negative of the above conditions can be considered: this is *not* _____.
- Meaning and Understanding: Comprehending clues—recalling, listing, identifying, naming, describing—from a hearing of a story and then remembering single events, items, or main topics or meanings.
1. Divergent thinking: from clues of categories, can name examples—food (cereal, bread, milk, fruit, etc.). Recognizing and identifying categories to which it does *not* belong, or naming another category or set to which it might also belong: Orange is good, but also a fruit, or something which is round.

Reading Lesson Observation: Analysis

Name _____ Observation Date _____

Teacher Observed _____

School _____ Grade _____

Instructional Objective: _____
_____

Behavioral Objective(s): _____
_____
_____

Basic Skill Involved: _____

Material(s) Used: _____
_____
_____

Activity(ties) Used in Lesson: _____
_____
_____

Size of Group Observed: _____

Subskills Involved in Lesson: _____
_____
_____
_____

Comments:

_____   _____
(Teacher's Signature)   (Intern's Signature)

NOTE: This form is a model for reading observation, to be used as tool for evaluation.

Figure 6.2

140

Intern Checklist

Name _____ Beginning Date _____

I. Preassessment: Date Taken _____ Score _____

II. Learning Experiences:

   1. Seminar(s)   Date _____ _____
                                                                      (Faculty Signature)

                      Date _____ _____
                                                                      (Faculty Signature)

   2. Readings: Author: _____ Date _____

                Author: _____ Date _____

   3. Workshop Attendance: Date _____

   4. Classroom Work/Involvement: minimum one week.

                                            _____
                                            (Master Teacher's Signature)

   5. Readiness Test: _____
                               (Name of Test)

       Dates: Administered _____ Analyzed _____

   6. Program Outline Submitted: _____

                                            (Signature of Supervisor)

   7. Observation Date: _____

       Checklist Completed: _____ _____
                                                  (Initial)

   8. Option: _____

       Date _____ _____
                                            (Signature of Supervisor)

III. Postassessment: Date Attempted _____ Score _____

Completion Date: _____ _____
                                                    (Intern's Signature)

                                                          _____
                                            (Faculty Signature)

NOTE: This checklist is a model for your use. It provides a sequential schedule for the module and a record of your progress. Several of the learning experiences require a signature from your team leader, supervisor, or faculty advisor. When necessary, complete a similar form and hand it in to your faculty advisor.

Figure 6.3

2. Convergent thinking: from a categorizing clue, child can identify other objects which also belong, or find or name other objects that do not belong. Sorting assortment of objects and classifying according to: size, shape, and color; or plants, birds, animals, people, and fish; or stone, plastic, cloth, wood, and metal. Selecting and identifying all things that have one common attribute; all that have two attributes that are common; or three.

From these examples of skills and competencies, the intern/teacher will think of many more activities and areas of development that may be necessary or related to various readiness transition factors. Many of the commercial as well as teacher-prepared materials have been focused on teaching and strengthening these abilities in young children. The teacher's guide will usually furnish the clues as to the purpose for using media in specific ways to reach particular objectives as observation and diagnosis reveal them. Likewise, the intern will be aware that not only in the areas of perceptual and cognitive development, but also in the development of language abilities, the young child is to be observed and evaluated. Therefore, a skills continuum of language skills is included here.

THE DEVELOPMENT OF LANGUAGE SKILLS

- Following Oral Directions: Carrying out instructions requiring one or two steps.
- Giving Oral Directions: Can give simple directions to another, both one- and two-step processes.
- Identifying Named Objects: Using complete sentences to identify objects, or pictures of objects, or to select each as directed orally. From picture clues, work sheet, can identify objects, actions, and respond with a statement which is a complete, correct sentence. Can respond to oral questions: "Is this a _____," by using a complete sentence to state, "No, this is not_____."
- Using Language to Describe: Responsive and Creative Skills
  1. Selecting an object or a picture from an assortment or group in response to a verbal description of same.
  2. Describe an object or picture as it is examined, using some describing words in complete sentences.
  3. Selecting an object at random, the description will be given clearly enough for another child to identify it. (A sort of "I Spy" type activity.)
  4. From a short, descriptive, oral narrative, the child can pantomime the character's action, stance, manner.
- Correct Sentence Structure, Tense, Case: Grammar/Syntax
  1. Using visual clues with oral description of same, child can select the picture depicting correct tense, action, number.
  2. Using pictorial clues, the child will describe the action using proper tense, number.

3. Given oral sentences in which either the verb or noun are omitted, the child supplies missing word and repeats complete sentence correctly.
4. Uses pronouns with correct number and person to describe incident, picture.
5. Correctly constructs simple, complex, and compound sentences in retelling story, describing picture or objects.
- Original Creative Language Expression: Creates story from being given a picture, the beginning of a story or incident, or a subject/topic to tell a story about.
- Using Sequence Correctly: Arranges pictures, incidents, or happenings in proper order to relate a story.

Postassessment for Final Evaluation

As a means of assessing your learning during this section on Reading Readiness, the following evaluation instrument is designed to evaluate your knowledge level of the topic.

Postassessment Evaluation   *NOTE: Carefully read each part of the evaluation before attempting response.*

1. Define the term *reading readiness*, citing an authoritative source from which you drew the material for your definition. (10 points)
2. List five readiness vocabulary terms important to understanding the concept, and briefly discuss each as it relates to the topic. (10 points)
3. Give the names of four reading readiness tests, and briefly list the facets of the transition each is purported to assess. (10 points)
4. Identify ten observable behaviors that you would expect to find in young children as indicators of their readiness to read. (20 points)

Evaluate your total score by number of points correct on each item.

NOTE: The following Preschool Inventory was developed by the Stockton Unified School District, Stockton, California, and is reprinted here by permission of the District Office as an example of the type of inventory that is being developed by professionals at the District Level and used by teachers in assessing the developmental patterns of young children.

INSTRUCTIONS TO TEACHERS

A *Preschool Profile* including behavioral objectives and *Able Scale* should be kept for every child who attends preschool. At the end of the school year the complete booklet should be placed in the child's cumulative folder for the kindergarten teacher. The booklet should be sent to the preschool office if the child leaves the class before the school year ends. The summary sheet and comments on the back should be done in duplicate. This duplicate record (the yellow sheet) for each child should be sent to the preschool office as soon as the preassessment is completed. It will be returned in the Spring for the postassessment. After completion it should be filed in the preschool office.

The child who seems *unable to cope* with school situations and varies in his development from other children of his age, should be referred to the child development specialist for diagnostic testing and evaluation. As early in the year as possible the principal and parents should be consulted. Home and family background should be obtained as well as a complete health history in an effort to better understand the child's problems. The school nurse should be consulted and further health examinations arranged if it seems advisable. If there is a family social worker or school counselor available, they should be consulted. A conference should be held with those concerned to determine future plans. A report containing all available information about the child should be prepared and sent to the preschool office.

The Able Assessment Scale

The ABLE SCALE has grown from a need for a simple informal system for assessing the development of young children in the Stockton Unified School District. The information it provides should be useful for informal screening, helpful in keeping school personnel aware of a child's strengths, needs, and progress, desirable for use in parent-teacher conferencing and valuable for use in planning a child centered environment.

The ABLE SCALE is designed to assess performance of young children in four areas of child development:

> A—ART
> B—BEHAVIOR (social)
> L—LANGUAGE
> E—EMOTIONS

It provides a focus for observing a young child and a basis for considering:

> Is he working and playing with others?
> Is he communicating through language, art, and behavior?
> Is he in tune with his environment?
> Is he fulfilling the possibilities which lie within him?
> Is he able to cope with his world?

It should be recognized that any ABLE SCALE rating is merely an indication of how the observer sees the child but after several observations have been made in a variety of situations, certain patterns of performance may become apparent. A discerning observer, using the ABLE SCALE should also become aware of the child's:

Actions	Attention	Confidence	Perception	Self-expression
Aptitudes	Attitudes	Interests	Persistence	Uniqueness

Use of the ABLE SCALE requires that school environment and activities be planned to provide the child with opportunities for interaction with others and self-expression through language and art. This does not suggest that he be pressured to participate, but the choice should be there for him, if the observer is to note his actions. The child should not necessarily be expected to communicate through an art media, but the opportunity to enjoy satisfying art experiences should be provided. Speech problems may prevent language communication. This should be noted on the Preschool Record under speech development.

A nine point scale suggests stages for indicating the child's level of development in each area of the ABLE SCALE. A child achieving on the sixth level will be a cooperative, contributing member of a group. He will be able to use words meaningfully to express himself in phrases, simple and compound sentences. He will be able to draw or paint pictures, that include two or more forms that relate to each other or to a ground line or both to compose a picture such as, for example, a house by a tree on a hill. A child may perform on a high level in one area and a low level in another depending on interests and past experience. Opportunities should be provided to help him strengthen the weaker areas. A child who is performing on the sixth level or above in each of the four areas of the ABLE SCALE should be ABLE TO COPE successfully with kindergarten. It would be unusual for a preschool age child to function consistently on the ninth level in all areas. He would most certainly be considered in the gifted range. Children may move through some stages rapidly and linger longer in others. Sudden or unusual changes in a child's performance should serve to alert those working with him to search for clues to causes for the change.

THE ABLE SCALE
A—ART
B—BEHAVIOR
L—LANGUAGE
E—EMOTION

CHILD'S NAME _____

SCHOOL _____

LINE GRAPH

Low	1	2	3	4	5	6	7	8	9	High
A										
B										
L										
E										

Assessment dates: Pre_____ Post_____

To indicate a child's stage of development in each of the four ABLE SCALE areas, the evaluator should consider a range of nine points with step one (1) at the lowest extreme and step nine (9) at the most advanced level. Descriptive phrases have been included with each step to guide the evaluator. After close observation, a line drawn under an appropriate phrase in each area may be used to indicate assessment of child's

ABLE SCALE Revised form 8–18–71 developed by Helene H. Nixon, Preschool Education Consultant, Stockton Unified School District, 701 North Madison Street, Stockton, California 95202.

accomplishment. It is assumed a child will have mastered stage underlined and those preceding it reasonably well. He or she may operate at other levels temporarily. A line graph may be used to compare performance, strength, and needs at beginning and end of period. Pre- and postdates should be recorded.

UNDERLINE CHILD'S LEVEL OF DEVELOPMENT IN EACH AREA

RED—Preassessment   BLUE—Postassessment

ART	BEHAVIOR (SOCIAL)
1. Scribbles	1. Avoids participation
2. Controls marks	2. Functions alone
3. Draws shapes	3. Plays parallel
4. Formulates designs	4. Interacts with individuals
5. Invents own symbols	5. Shifts group to group
6. Relates forms—groundline	6. Contributes to group
7. Creates variety images	7. Participates in extended projects
8. Portrays much detail	8. Leads successfully
9. Applies advanced principles to variety of media with gifted artistic expression	9. Assumes responsibility for welfare of others in constructive complex group activity
LANGUAGE	EMOTION
1. Vocalizes	1. Withdraws—anxious
2. Imitates vocally	2. Is overly aggressive
3. Uses words meaningfully	3. Displays tenseness
4. Says words in phrases	4. Becomes over stimulated easily
5. Talks in simple sentences	5. Maintains composure—usually
6. Includes compound sentences	6. Cooperates willingly
7. Speaks in complex sentences	7. Sees self positively
8. Narrates using wide vocabulary	8. Directs self well
9. Comprehends and communicates complicated ideas clearly with gifted verbal expression	9. Copes successfully with own feelings and most situations arising, exhibiting poise and stability

INDIVIDUAL STUDENT PROFILE

School _____   Name _____

Program _____   Birthdate _____

Parents _____   Date Entered _____ Age_____

Lives with _____   Date Left _____

Address _____   Attendance Regular ____ Irregular____

Phone _____   Teachers _____

STOCKTON UNIFIED
SCHOOL DISTRICT
PRESCHOOL PROFILE
SCHOOL YEAR _____

ABLE SCALE GRAPH

	1	2	3	4	5	6	7	8	9
Art									
Behavior									
Language									
Emotions									

SPEECH DEVELOPMENT

Pre	Post	Check (✔) items that apply
		No verbal communication
		Completely unintelligible
		Hearing problem
		Stuttering (nonfluency)
		Vocal problem
		Articulation problem (baby talk)
		Single words intelligible
		Intelligible if listener knows topic
		Readily intelligible

BEHAVIORAL OBJECTIVES

°		Affective	Cognitive	Psycho-motor
1	a			
	b			
	c			
	d			
2	a			
	b			
	c			
	d			
3	a			
	b			
	c			
	d			
4	a			
	b			
	c			
	d			
5	a			
	b			
	c			
	d			
6	a			
	b			
	c			
	d			
7	a			
	b			
	c			
	d			
8	a			
	b			
	c			
	d			
9	a			
	b			
	c			
	d			

° RED—represents accomplishment at school entrance in affective, cognitive and psycho-motor domains. The ABLE SCALE preassessment should also be done in red.

BLUE—indicates gains during period child attended the preschool program.

NUMERALS (1 2 3 4 5 6 7 8 9) refer to objectives. Letters (a b c d) refer to criteria for objectives.

DATE:_____

COMMENTS:
> (Include information regarding child's health, dental care, general well-being, special interests, needs, parent participation and test results if any tests were given).

ETHNIC GROUP _____

LANGUAGE—spoken by family _____

LANGUAGE—spoken by child _____

STOCKTON UNIFIED SCHOOL DISTRICT
STOCKTON, CALIFORNIA

(Preschool Instructional Objectives Stated Behaviorally)

It is expected that 90 percent of all children four years or older who attend preschool classes regularly for at least eight months will successfully achieve one or more of the four criteria listed for each objective with 90 percent accuracy. A box preceding a criterion marked with one diagonal line ▱ indicates progress toward completion. A cross ⊠ indicates successful accomplishment.

> RED—represents accomplishment at school entrance
> BLUE—represents gains during period child attended class

AFFECTIVE DOMAIN

1. Given teachers, parent helpers, and volunteers who relate well to children, the child will be able *to accept the adults on the teaching team* and show this acceptance.
   - ☐ a. By willingly staying with them
   - ☐ b. By interacting with them
   - ☐ c. By participating in activities with them
   - ☐ d. By encouraging others to participate

2. Given a teaching team that is responsive to the needs of children, the child will be able *to reflect interest in school.*
   - ☐ a. By indicating a desire to attend regularly
   - ☐ b. By showing a desire to be on time
   - ☐ c. By communicating ideas, needs and feelings spontaneously
   - ☐ d. By responding positively to routine procedures

3. Given preschool teachers who value and nurture a positive self-image in children, the child will be able *to reveal feelings of self-worth.*
   - ☐ a. By expressing a desire to save own creative paintings, drawings, woodwork, etc.

Behavioral Objectives developed by Helene H. Nixon, Preschool Consultant and State Preschool Staff, Stockton Unified School District, 701 North Madison Street, Stockton, California 95202 (Revised Edition 8-18-71)

☐ b. By performing confidently in dramatic play

☐ c. By exhibiting an "I can do" attitude

☐ d. By volunteering to help other children in the class

4. Given a systematically arranged preschool classroom the child will be able *to indicate awareness of organization of environment.*

☐ a. By going to a designated special interest area

☐ b. By selecting materials independently

☐ c. By using materials appropriately

☐ d. By putting things where they belong when finished

5. Given challenging learning opportunities, the child will be able *to exhibit a desire to discover information.*

☐ a. By observing people, places, or things

☐ b. By asking questions

☐ c. By exploring or experimenting

☐ d. By studying pictures, books, models, maps, or diagrams

6. Given opportunities for group activity, the child will be able *to demonstrate that he values peer relationships.*

☐ a. By interacting with one or more children

☐ b. By showing consideration for other children

☐ c. By initiating group activity

☐ d. By working cooperatively as well as constructively with a group to the successful completion of a project that continues over a period of two or more days

7. Given the opportunity to participate in the planning of preschool experiences, the child will be able *to choose.*

☐ a. Things to do   ☐ c. Persons to be with

☐ b. Places of interest to go   ☐ d. Procedures to follow

8. Given conservation minded adult models, the child will be able *to communicate concern for care of surroundings* by avoiding waste and destruction.

☐ a. Of own belongings

☐ b. Of things belonging to others

☐ c. Of materials and equipment provided by community

☐ d. Of natural resources

9. Given teachers and parents who are interested in parent involvement in school affairs, the child will be able *to contribute to the home-school relationship.*

☐ a. By delivering messages to the home

☐ b. By delivering messages to the school

☐ c. By encouraging parents to visit school

☐ d. By encouraging teachers to visit homes

COGNITIVE DOMAIN

1. Given objects, models, pictures or felt cut outs, the child will be able *to label* (using complete sentences—This is a _____.).

☐ a. 8 toys

☐ b. 8 foods

☐ c. 8 pets

☐ d. 8 colors

2. Given objects, models, pictures or felt cut out symbols, the child will be able *to classify*.
   ☐ a. *Set I*   ☐ b. *Set II*
      8 colors   8 shapes
      8 foods   8 family
      8 pets   8 wild animals
      8 toys   8 transportation
   ☐ c. *Set III*   ☐ d. *Set IV*
      8 homes   8 community helps
      8 clothing   8 plants
      8 utensils (food)   8 school supplies
      8 furniture   8 facial discrimination

3. Given spatial positions, the child will be able *to identify these positions* correctly when demonstrated, using equipment, objects, pictures or symbols.
   ☐ a. *Set I*   ☐ b. *Set II*
      on—off   above—below
      in—out   over—under
      up—down   coming—going
      top—bottom   push—pull
   ☐ c. *Set III*   ☐ d. *Set IV*
      beginning—ending   around
      in front of—behind   beside
      before—after   between
      near—far   through

4. Given five tags, cards, placemats or containers labeled with first names of children in class, the child will be able *to recognize own name*.
   ☐ a. On name tag   ☐ c. On placemat
   ☐ b. On name card   ☐ d. On container

5. Given objects, models, pictures or felt cut out symbols, the child will be able to *arrange items in natural sequence*.
   ☐ a. Big, middle size, little
   ☐ b. Large, medium, small
   ☐ c. First, middle, last
   ☐ d. First, last, second, next to last

6. Given objects, models, pictures or felt cut out symbols, the child will be able *to match items in pattern arrangement*.
   ☐ a. → → → →   ☐ c. → ← → ←
   ☐ b. ← ← ← ←   ☐ d. ← → ← →

7. Given measuring tools and things to manipulate, the child will be able *to compare more and less*.
   ☐ a. In quality (hard, soft, rough, smooth)
   ☐ b. In quantity (number, weight, length, volume)
   ☐ c. In intensity (color, sound, temperature, speed)
   ☐ d. In suitability (clothing, utensils, tools, machines)

8. Given tables, chairs, placemats, cups, napkins, plastic spoons, forks, and other manipulative objects, symbols, and numerals, the child will be able *to perform number operations* through five.
   - ☐ a. One to one matching
   - ☐ b. Counting
   - ☐ c. Recognition of numerals (1–2–3–4–5)
   - ☐ d. Matching each numeral correctly to a set of that quantity

9. Given logical causality (if-then) relationships and an understanding, helpful adult, the child will be able *to solve simple problems.*
   - ☐ a. In construction
   - ☐ b. In science
   - ☐ c. In mathematics
   - ☐ d. In human relations

PSYCHOMOTOR DOMAIN

1. Given space and a designated line the child will be able *to display gross motor coordination by jumping.*
   - ☐ a. Forward, backward, sideways right, sideways left over line on ground
   - ☐ b. Forward, sideways right, left over rope (or yarn) raised 1 inch
   - ☐ c. Two inches forward, sideways right, left
   - ☐ d. Three inches forward, sideways right, left

2. Given a large light weight rubber ball (8 to 15 inches in diameter) and three bean bags, the child will be able *to manipulate objects* adequately.
   - ☐ a. To roll ball 8 feet
   - ☐ b. To kick ball and chase it 8 feet
   - ☐ c. To bounce ball three times
   - ☐ d. To throw three bean bags hitting large target 5 feet away three times

3. Given an inclined board, steps, ladder and jungle gym, the child will be able *to climb.*
   - ☐ a. Five feet of a 30 degree inclined board
   - ☐ b. Five steps (large hollow blocks can be used if steps are not available)
   - ☐ c. Five steps of a ladder
   - ☐ d. To top and bottom of jungle gym

4. Given a balance board 6 feet long and a chalk line or a string stretched along floor for a distance of 6 feet, the child will be able *to maintain physical balance.*
   - ☐ a. As he walks the length of the board
   - ☐ b. As he turns around and walks back to starting point on balance board
   - ☐ c. Walks length of chalk line or string, forward and backward
   - ☐ d. As he hops on one foot length of chalk or string line

5. Given the opportunity to use five senses, the child will be able *to perceive things that are the same or not the same.*
   - ☐ a. By looking only to match eight objects one to one into four groups
   - ☐ b. By listening only to match eight sounds one to one into four groups
   - ☐ c. By touching only to match eight textures one to one into four groups
   - ☐ d. By smelling and tasting only to match eight foods one to one into four groups

6. Given a mirror, another child, a mannequin (large paper doll) or paper and paint, crayons, chalk or pencil, the child will be able *to provide evidence of development of body image* by identifying (pointing, drawing or naming correctly).

☐ a. *Set I*	☐ b. *Set II*	☐ c. *Set III*	☐ d. *Set IV*
hands	eyes	hair	forehead
head	ears	tongue	eyebrows
face	nose	teeth	eyelids
stomach	mouth	neck	eyelashes
back	elbows	shoulders	cheeks
sides	knees	chest	lips
arms	fingers	hips	chin
legs	toes	wrists	fingernails
feet	heels	ankles	toenails

7. Given choice to use right or left parts of body, the child will be able *to show development toward lateral dominance* (laterality).
   - ☐ a. Using hands (playing games requiring throwing or using tools)
   - ☐ b. Using feet (kicking ball or stomping with one foot)
   - ☐ c. Using eyes (looking through kaleidoscope or tube)
   - ☐ d. Using ears (listening to watch or sea shells)

8. Given a singing model, musical accompaniment, rhythm instruments, scarfs, streamers and other props, the child will be able *to express self through patterns of axial and/or locomotor movement.*

☐ a. push	☐ b. bend	☐ c. sway	☐ d. slide
pull	stretch	walk	march
rise	twist	run	gallop
fall	turn	leap	skip

9. Given a variety of visual, tactile, art, and manipulative materials, the child will be able *to coordinate eyes and hands in small motor activity.*
   - ☐ a. To produce three types of clay modeling
   - ☐ b. To create a collage using at least three different materials
   - ☐ c. To construct something with wood and nails using, at least, three different tools correctly
   - ☐ d. To feel, match, trace on paper and cut out with scissors a circle, a square and a triangle.

THE CONTEMPORARY SCENE

INSTRUCTIONAL METHODOLOGY
AND READING APPROACHES

7

Current reading instruction is probably as complex in theory and structure as any single area of elementary curriculum. Yet, little has been done to help the classroom teacher or the college student visualize the overall scope of the entire contemporary program of teaching children to read. As a result, a blurred picture and a confused hesitancy frequently cloud a total clear focus needed by today's teacher of reading.

It should also be noted that there has been a recent proliferation of materials, methods, devices, techniques, gadgets, systems, and strategies in the area of beginning reading. Actually a recent author (Aukerman, 1971) has identified about 100 approaches to beginning reading instruction. These can be classified under many different categories which further compounds the difficulties in formulating a clear, concise picture of the situation in today's schools and their attempts to teach beginning reading.

It is incredible, but often true, that children who have been taught by almost all of these methods, approaches, and combinations of such, have learned to read. Many of these deserve to be considered, and the future teacher certainly should have a nodding acquaintance with a number of these being currently used in the public and/or private schools. You will not be called on to teach via *all* of these strategies during your entire teaching career, but you will hear about them, read about many of them, and see a number of them in actual use even in one school district alone.

After having taken an overview of the process of reading itself, it seems logical that the teacher/intern take a second global look. This time the scene will cover reading instruction as it is currently being undertaken in American schools. In order to get this molar view, some sort of model or paradigm is needed so that

153

the whole picture with its component levels can be studied as a unit. Such a curriculum model has been developed by the authors and included here.

THE READING PARADIGM

The development of curriculum models has become a popular contemporary aid for analyzing the structure of a specific segment of the curriculum. Such schematic devices have been developed for many areas of the teaching field. They afford the student to see at a total look the structure of a teaching area—mathematics, science, history, or reading instruction. This total look will help him to discover the various component facets of the teaching rationale, the necessary implementations for a designated program, and the various strategies and techniques which are consistent with a particular program and its philosophy of education.

The authors have attempted to plot the basic levels of a schema to show as clearly as possible the (1) modalities of learning through which reading takes place, (2) the strands of methodology of reading instruction, (3) the current approaches to the teaching of reading, and (4) the administrative schedules by which the instructional programs are implemented. The paradigm (see figure 7.1) reflects chiefly the early years of reading instruction, beginning reading through the primary grades. Some implications and practices however may be traceable through the whole continuum of instruction.

Learning Modalities

Authorities, as has been discussed, have described reading as being a perceptual as well as a sensory process. Both ideas involve the impinging of sensory stimuli and the response of the organism to its awareness of these stimuli. These responses are naturally affected by the experience, knowledge, and conditioning of the individual in his present "life space" as he views his total being.

The concept most relevant for reading teachers in this first level of the model is that "instruction can be successfully channelled through any *one*, or combination of more than one, of the several modalities as shown in the paradigm: the visual, aural, or haptic inputs." The teacher/intern should note, however, that there is good research evidence that learners have varying strengths of modalities through which the process takes place more easily and permanently. This implies that it is important for the instructor to know which modality is a more open channel for effective teaching approach and practice. Some authorities would recommend teaching to the child's strength while others would advise making use of the weaker input channel in order to strengthen the total of the child. The present authors suggest that in the beginning, it is far better to use the modality which is strongest. Later, certainly, attention should be focused on his weaker learning channels in order to help him develop at an adequate rate

A PARADIGM: CONTEMPORARY READING INSTRUCTION

I. LEARNING MODALITIES
(Input Channels)

VISUAL	HAPTIC	AURAL
Perceptual/Conceptual	Kinesthetic/Tactile	Phonogram/Ideogram

II. TEACHING METHODOLOGIES
(Two Strands)

HOLISTIC	ATOMISTIC
Global/Analytic	Synthetic/Decoding

III. CURRENT READING APPROACHES
(Instructional Strategies)

Whole Word	Alphabet Bases
Sight Vocabulary	New Alphabets
Linguistic	Phonic-Linguistics
Language Experience	Color Coding

ECLECTIC APPROACHES

Basal Reader
Programmed Reading
Reading Labs
Multimedia

IV. ADMINISTRATIVE/SCHEDULING PROGRAMS
(Implementation Plans)

Intraclass Grouping	Interclass Grouping
Staggered Day	Block Programs
Learning Centers	Team Teaching
Nongraded	Learning PAKs
Open Classrooms	Platooning
Individualized Reading	

Figure 7.1

and to his fullest capacity. If the child is evidently visual in aptitude, by all means make use of this strength and employ an approach to his beginning reading that is basically oriented to a sight vocabulary program. On the other hand, if the student's visual memory is weak, but his auditory memory is stronger, it is logical to make use of his heightened ability and present an initial reading program that is based on phoneme-grapheme associations. If neither of these modalities is sufficiently strong to form the basis of instruction, some program which makes use of haptic input should be tried. Sensory activities making use of touch, muscle usage, or kinesics may start the learning toward reading. Some teachers have effectively combined exercises and activities in their instructional programs which make use of any and all modalities.

Teaching Methodology

The reader will note the second level of the paradigm which deals with the two basic strands of methodology in reading instruction: a holistic type of instruction or an atomistic one. In other words, we are concerned with either a global approach to teaching which has traditionally been termed "analytic" in contrast with that more decoding type of approach that has frequently been referred to as "synthetic." Following one of the two methodologies, the teacher will choose her materials and teaching strategies which are consistent with the method employed.

Global. In the beginning reading instruction, the materials will be concerned with the very least, whole words; better yet with meaning segments; and better yet with complete sentences, simple paragraphs, or short stories.

Atomistic. Initial teaching making use of this strand of methodology will make use of a program based on the building blocks of language, the graphic symbols or phonics combinations which record the sounds of the language.

The basic difference is one of philosophy as to how children best learn, and knowledge of their learning modalities. The visual learner will probably do better with the global method, whereas, the aural learner will profit more from an atomistic, sound-based methodology. Philosophically the question is: "Should learning be presented in gestalt fashion, from the total form, and then allow the learner to analyze the constituent parts?" or "Should instruction be given in basic small parts from which the entire word, phrase, or sentence will be constructed?"

Naturally, as in most theory, there are seldom absolute, "black-and-white" programs or positions. Today there are many instructional programs which make use of both strands of methodology, though they are primarily one or the other.

Because English is not a particularly phonemic language, and because of a sincere desire to make reading instruction as meaningful an experience as possible, American teachers in general for some decades have used a global, whole-word, or see-and-say approach with beginning students of reading. The emphasis is now changing.

On the other hand, reading has also been traditionally taught for centuries in many countries of the world via a synthetic, alphabet-based approach. Words were not learned by memorizing them after seeing them a sufficient number of times to recognize them, but by learning the phoneme-grapheme relationships and thus being able to unlock unfamiliar words. The child thus learned the graphic symbols of his orthography and learned to assemble them and organize them in proper sound sequence to form known words in his vocabulary. Thus reading became a means of building from small parts toward complete whole words, then phrases of language, and finally entire sentences. With the present emphasis on this latter methodology, many American teachers are once again employing phonics instruction as a means of teaching decoding skills to young learners.

Current Approaches to Teaching Reading

The reader will note that at Level 3 of the paradigm there is a list of various types of contemporary reading programs. It is by no means complete, but gives examples of the kinds of instructional approaches being used in many schools today. Frequently it is difficult to identify a particular reading program or approach as belonging to a specific pure methodology, either holistic or atomistic. The experts who have developed instructional programs have often made use of a combined, or eclectic methodology, for teaching reading. However, several approaches which are basically "either/or" in beginning instruction have been listed as belonging to one of the two main strands of teaching. Within this phase of teaching, the various skills and mechanics of reading instruction are developed either through the use of whole words, phrases, sentences, or stories; or basic skills are taught via material which emphasizes single letters (vowels or consonants) or combinations which record speech sounds (digraphs, diphthongs, clusters, etc.) from which words and written language are built.

Global Approaches. Any reading methodology which makes use of a teaching strategy that deals primarily with whole words, ideas, or sentences—in short, with teaching reading by using visual memory, sight vocabulary, pictures and words, or basic word lists—can be included in this holistic strand of method. The Language Experience approach, the *total language* or Linguistic approach, and many Basal Reader approaches are global in their beginning learning experiences. They start with the child's visual ability to recognize a set of words from which his materials are composed. The basic rationale behind this emphasis is that learning should be as meaningful as possible; hence nothing less than an entire word should be used; that is, since these morphemes express in language a small component of meaning they should be the least of instructional segments from which teaching proceeds.

Atomistic approaches. Any reading approach which begins by teaching the child letter-sound relationships (phoneme-grapheme), and then proceeds to use those sounds as building blocks for larger reading tasks can be included in the atomistic family. Such an approach, from parts to wholes, has more recently been called a decoding methodology. Some of these alphabet-based reading programs include the new phonemic alphabets such as i/t/a, the phonics programs, and the coded approaches which make use of colors and/or diacritical markings as pronunciation, or "'sounding out" clues. The recent so-called First Grade Reading Studies and the emphasis on decoding by such researchers as Chall in her *Learning to Read: The Great Debate* have done much to popularize atomistic programs in the early stages of reading instruction.

Eclectic approaches. The model provided lists four types of reading instruction which make an early use of both global and atomistic methodologies. These four are basal reading labs, and multimedia programs making use of a variety of visual, aural, and haptic (manipulatory) educational materials and devices. These four types of instructional programs generally make use of a combination of learning modalities as well as blending the strands of methodology.

Many of the more recent reading programs have been called "multisensory" approaches, thus signifying that the authors are emphasizing the importance of making use of every input channel possible in reading instruction. In fact most researchers agree that there is no "best" or "one" way to teach reading, but that a combination of several programs is probably most effective in successful learning. The present authors suggest that this best combination should be (1) some reputable basal reading program to provide the sequence and structure for teaching skills, and (2) two or more enrichment types of approaches, preferably self-selected individualized reading, making use of good trade books and contemporary reading materials, and (3) a language-experience, organic program which makes use of the children's own language and original stories. One of these should give an *early emphasis* on decoding skills. If such a program is followed as outlined above, this could be done by the teacher in the language-experience instruction, or if the basal readers chosen have a phonics base, the decoding skills can be taught via that material.

Administration and Scheduling of the Instructional Program

Once the basic teaching program and the materials to accompany it have been selected, the next step becomes one of deciding how the classes are to be scheduled, what modes or groups are to be used, and what will work advantageously to provide for the growth and success of each student involved. Hence, the fourth level of the paradigm deals with implementing the first three phases of the instructional pattern. Various plans, schedules, and programs have been developed through the years. Each of these is an attempt to improve or enhance reading instruction. The authors have identified seven such administrative strategies which are aimed chiefly at better teaching and learning. These have often been referred to as "methods or approaches to teaching reading," but the terms are misnomers, for they are actually just scheduling devices to assist in a more convenient or satis-factory means of carrying out the learning programs.

The mechanics of these seven types of scheduling devices can be classified under four headings. The categories include (1) the grouping of students—either homogeneously or heterogeneously—according to their abilities, achievements, in-terests, or educational needs; (2) the provision for the numbers of students that are to be taught during various periods of time; (3) the allowing of students to progress at varying rates through levels of learning, difficulty, or time periods; and (4) the provision of additional personalized and self-selective reading pro-grams to accommodate a level of individuation not otherwise possible. In some schools and school districts, these and like plans have been modified and com-bined to meet specific needs of the community and areas involved. In each in-stance, though, this level of education can be recognized as implementive, organi-zational plans developed to specifically improve and facilitate the reading instruction program.

At least the model presented here is an attempt to clarify for the intern/teacher current trends and innovative practices as they fit into the trimodalities, the methodologies, the specific reading approaches, and last of all the administra-tion of the reading instruction itself. Within the suggested structure, there is ample scope for additional combinations, curriculum modifications, and plans for imple-mentation. The intern or teacher who has a well-defined philosophy of education, or a particular learning theory or favorite teaching strategy, will readily see possi-bilities of interjecting his own practice and theory which will be consistent with the framework, or skeletal outline, presented here, and he should be able to identify and relate current practices with specific or eclectic educational theory.

THE CONTEMPORARY SCENE: HOLISTIC APPROACHES

Again, as you consider this facet of your professional preparation, you will note that the following material has been programmed for you in a modified modular form and is presented in the following sequential order.

1. Performance Objectives and/or Learning Competencies.
2. Suggested Learning Experiences with Contractual Options.
3. Preassessment Instrument.
4. Postassessment Evaluation.

Performance Objectives

When you have completed the work on this module, you should be able to:

• Interpret the reading paradigm by describing the four levels involved in the contemporary instruction of reading as per the model provided on page 155.

- Identify and briefly describe a minimum of four reading instruction approaches which can be classified as global (holistic) in methodology.
- Analyze and assess a current reading program being used in your assigned school. The evaluation to be recorded on a provided form (see figure 7.2, page 161) to be submitted as part of your postassessment of this module.

Suggested Learning Experiences with Contractual Options

Here is a list of learning experiences for you to consider and undertake. Unless they are otherwise designated, consider that they are requisite to your completing the module.

1. For further reading choose *one* of the following selected texts with chapter(s) as indicated.
    - Aukerman, Robert C. *Approaches to Beginning Reading.* New York: John Wiley & Sons, 1971. Chapter 6 or 7 or 9 only.
    - Durkin, Dolores. *Teaching Them to Read.* Boston: Allyn & Bacon, 1970. Chapter 6, "Materials for Teaching Reading," pp. 105–144.
2. For those who desire or need a group session with the university instructor, a discussion seminar of the topic will be scheduled and announced. Attendance optional.
3. Prepare a one-week lesson plan for use with a basal reading program, and teach a reading group using materials, strategies, and/or programs which are global in methodology. The demonstration to be observed and rated by the master teacher, team leader, or university instructor. The written plan is to be submitted as part of your postassessment. (The Demonstration Checklist is to be marked and returned also. See figure 7.4, p. 164.)
4. Examine the reading program materials being used in a local school to check the introductory materials in the teacher's manual for a statement of the basic philosophy of methodology and approach, and use figure 7.2 as a model for recording.

Optional Learning Experiences

1. Secure a set of basic Dolch Word Cards and give a "card flip" test to a minimum of two students in your reading group. Note the words they cannot recognize and analyze them for similarities or differences. (Optional)

and/or

2. Plan an activity with your group which will provide suitable background for developing a language experience chart story. Discuss the incident, elicit suggested materials, work with them to "write" their story, and make a model of the story for them to use in rewriting their activity.

Reading Program Analysis

Intern: _____ School: _____

Program Analyzed: _____ Date _____

Grade Level: _____Publisher: _____

Type of Grouping: 1:1 _____ 4-6 _____ 7-10 _____ Class _____

List Materials Used in the Program: _____

_____

_____

Do You Assess This Program as Being Basically _____ Global? _____ Atomistic?

Explain Why: _____

_____

_____

_____

With What Type of Learner Would You Feel Best About Using This Program?

Slow? _____ Average? _____ Accelerated? _____

Why Would You Make This Decision? _____

_____

_____

_____

Rate The Material on The Continuum Provided:

Excellent_____ Superior_____ Adequate_____ Fair_____ Poor_____

Explain Your Basis of Rating The Program: _____

_____

_____

_____

Signed _____

Figure 7.2

Preassessment Instrument

After you have examined and thoughtfully considered the competency-based performances for this component, you may feel that you would like to take the pretest to evaluate your own knowledge and ability. If so, schedule the examination time and undertake the tasks. If your score is twenty points out of the possible twenty-five, you will probably opt to immediately schedule the postevaluation and complete this phase of your coursework.

Preassessment Evaluation   *NOTE: This assessment of your previous knowledge about current approaches to beginning reading instruction will (1) identify areas where you will need little new learning, and (2) help to show you areas where you will need to concentrate your time and effort.*

1. Aukerman, in his recent book, has stated that he had identified and categorized, with explanations, more than 100 contemporary approaches to beginning reading instruction. List as many approaches and specific programs as you can. (5 points maximum)
2. Reading people have frequently referred to instructional methodology as being (1) analytic or synthetic, (2) holistic or atomistic, or (3) global or decoding. The three sets of terms mean the same thing. Choose any set and define what is meant. (10 points maximum)
3. From your list in Item 1, select three beginning reading approaches which you would call basically holistic, analytic, or global. (5 points maximum)
4. From your list in Item 1, select three beginning reading approaches which you could classify as being basically atomistic, synthetic, or decoding in nature. (5 points maximum)

Evaluate your total test score by number of points correct on each item.

Postassessment Evaluation   *In order to assess your performance on this component:*

1. Submit your *completed* Intern Checklist with copies of all required materials attached.
2. Attend and participate in a summarizing seminar to be scheduled with the instructor.

THE CONTEMPORARY SCENE: ATOMISTIC APPROACHES

You have already examined a number of approaches to beginning reading instruction. These were chiefly those programs which made use of a holistic or

Intern Checklist

Name _____ Beginning Date _____

I. Preassessment: Date Taken _____ Score _____

II. Learning Experiences:

   1. Readings: Journal Article: _____ Date _____,

           Text: Author _____ Date _____

   2. Lesson Plan: Date _____ _____
                                       (Staff Initial)

   3. Group Attendance: Yes _____ No _____

   4. Option:

     (a) Dolch Word Flip Test   Date _____ _____
                                                       (Initial)

     (b) Language Experience Chart   Date _____ _____
                                                       (Initial)

   Note: Have your supervisor initial the activity chosen/completed.

III. Postassessment:

   1. Work sheets, Reports, Forms: Submitted? _____

     Dates: Lesson Plans   Date _____

            Program Analysis   Date _____

            Option   Date _____

   2. Summarizing Seminar: Date _____ Rating   E   S   U

Completion Date: _____ _____
                                          (Intern's Signature)

                                    _____
                                          (Faculty Signature)

NOTE: The following form is included as a model to be used for keeping a record of progress on this portion of the course. It has been designed to provide a sequential pattern for the learning experiences and/or activities. When a similar checklist is completed, it is to be submitted to the instructor as one part of the postassessment.

Figure 7.3

Demonstration Checklist

Date: _____

Intern Demonstrating: _____

School: _____ Grade Level: _____

Number in Group: _____ Boys: _____ Girls: _____

Note to Observer: Please rate the intern on four criteria by making an X in the appropriate column. Then assign an overall assignment for the lesson observed.

Criteria	Excellent	Good	Fair	Adequate	Poor
Lesson Planning					
Use of Materials					
Teaching Performance					
Children's Interest					
Overall Assessment					

Comments:

_____
(Evaluator's Signature)

NOTE: A model performance form for use in evaluating the reading lesson as planned and taught.

Figure 7.4

global introduction to learning words, sentences, and/or paragraphs and short stories. In other words these were total language approaches and were found mainly in instructional programs which are commonly called basal reading approaches, linguistic approaches, language experience approaches—in short, any teaching approach that uses sight vocabulary for its base of instruction.

In the current component, you will be identifying and examining those teaching programs which can be classified as "from parts to whole" or atomistic. These instructional approaches made use of the *parts* of words; that is, the letters of the alphabet, phonic segments (blends, clusters, digraphs, and diphthongs), principles of learning such as syllabication, compound words, inflectional endings, and affixes. These are all commonly called "decoding skills." It is from these linguistic segments that the child in learning to read is led into the whole components: words, phrases, sentences.

In this phase of your coursework, you will be looking at those instructional practices and teaching strategies which introduce reading from the atomistic base; and you will also be learning those principles which may be modified for your own teaching use as you seek to present reading to children via a decoding emphasis.

Recent research findings have influenced many educators to reappraise reading methodology, and to again recognize the value of using many approaches

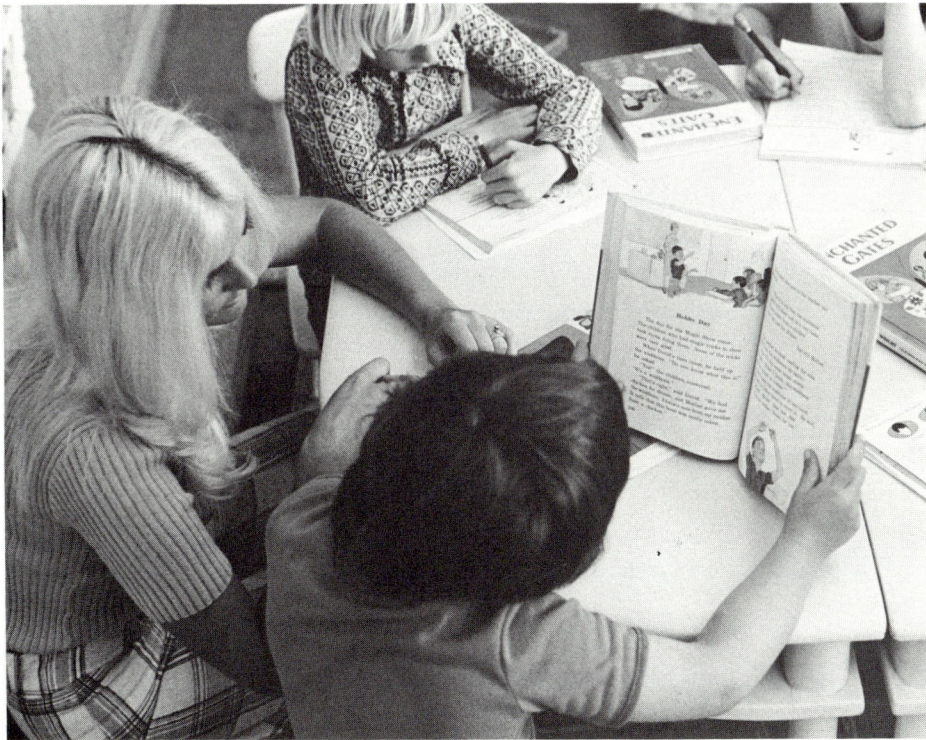

Teachers often find that some aspects of reading instruction can be handled easily in the group setting; however, the need for individual help and diagnosis is equally valuable.

to strengthen and broaden their instructional program. In an effort to make use of fine materials and to assist many kinds of learners toward reading success, both strands of methodology are blended to provide for the visual and the aural learner. Hence, an early focus on decoding skills should be included in any *good* teaching program for today's reader. Chall, in reviewing some fifty years of reading research, concludes that most important of all is the *teacher;* this is the prime ingredient to a child's reading success. Her second conclusion is that there is actually no one "best" way to teach reading, but that probably some good basal reading program should form the framework of instruction. Then this basal reader would be enriched and enhanced by one or more approaches, and *one* of them should give an early emphasis to *decoding.*

This would encourage the intern/teacher to examine reputable companies' basal reading series with their accompanying manuals, workbooks, and activity materials. Let this be the skeleton of the learning program, but not the total approach or material for the formal instruction in reading. Combine with this (1) some form of self-selective, individualized approach, and (2) frequent use of the organic or language-experience approach. This combination of sound, sequential skills learning, plus the double thrust of letting children choose their own level and interest area of trade books for actual reading, and the use of their own original, creative stories should provide for the needs of all students and lead to their not only learning *how* to read, but also their learning *to* read and enjoy it.

Preassessment Instrument

Before you continue work on this particular facet of your professional preparation, it might be helpful for you to preassess your competencies in the area of decoding skills. Here are several questions, general ones, which should help in discovering how much you already know, and which areas you may wish to spend more time and effort in.

Preassessment
Evaluation

1. What skills are included in the area of phonics instruction? List and describe five or six.
2. How many phonics generalizations do you know? Which of these relate to teaching about vowels? Consonants?
3. What is a blend? Cluster? Digraph? Diphthong? Contraction? A compound word? Macron? Breve?
4. Can you give examples of phonic elements in initial, medial, or terminal positions?

5. Differentiate between the meanings of the terms phonic, phonetic, and phonemic.
6. What is the *schwa*? Where would you find one?
7. Are you able to briefly describe the following decoding-oriented reading programs?
   a. The Sullivan Program   d. Phonetic Keys to Reading
   b. Distar   e. i/t/a
   c. Words in Color   f. Speech to Print Phonics
8. What professional helps on using a decoding approach do you know well enough to recommend to another teacher?

These few questions should provide you with a quick assessment of your own learnings at the knowledge level. Perhaps after perusing them, you feel it necessary to do some reading for further information on this phase of reading instruction. The following suggested sources, briefly annotated with specific chapters or sections, will give you a number of choices for some basic study.

Reading List for Phonics/Decoding

AUKERMAN, ROBERT C. *Approaches to Beginning Reading*, Wiley, 1971. This is a comprehensive text examining and categorizing more than a hundred reading programs. An excellent source book.

CHALL, JEANNE S. *Learning to Read: The Great Debate*, McGraw-Hill, 1967. Note particularly chapter 4 which deals with the debate regarding systematic vs. incidental phonics instruction.

CORDTS, ANNA D. *Phonics for the Reading Teacher*, Holt, Rinehart, & Winston, 1965. The first 3 chapters of this useful tool provide the teacher with a rationale for using the phonics approach.

DEBOER, JOHN J., and DALHMANN, MARTHA. *The Teaching of Reading*, Holt, Rinehart, & Winston, 1970. Chapter 5B provides the reader with a variety of useful exercises, activities, and teaching aids for teaching phonics skills.

DURKIN, DELORES. *Teaching Them to Read*, Allyn & Bacon, 1970. An excellent text for examining most phases of the entire reading process and instruction.

HEILMAN, ARTHUR W. *Phonics in Proper Perspective*, Charles E. Merrill, 1968. A handy little book which provides the intern/teacher with numerous helpful suggestions for using phonics.

SCHELL, ROBERT E. *Letters and Sounds: A Manual for Reading Instruction*, Prentice-Hall, 1972. This recent paperback furnishes the intern/teacher with a step-by-step guide to teaching children at any age the sounds of the English language as a basis for reading via a decoding process.

Performance Competencies

In order to assess your progress in this important area of reading instruction at the elementary level, you should have some signposts to indicate your completion of certain tasks and your mastery of sequential skills and competencies for teaching children to read. The following performance objectives can serve as such indicators of your progress.

- Identify a minimum of four reading instruction approaches which can be classified as atomistic (synthetic) in methodology as per the Reading Paradigm.
- Define each of the vocabulary words pertinent to this module as per any recognized glossary.
- Pass a proficiency test in phonics principles to demonstrate your ability to apply generalizations in learning situations.
- Prepare a daily lesson plan on a specified phonics skill according to the model provided.
- Teach a demonstration lesson in reading which involves introducing a decoding skill as per the teacher's manual of a recognized atomistic reading approach.

Learning Experiences

Following is a list of planned learning experiences which you are to undertake. If they are not specifically listed as optional activities, they are intended to be included for your completion of this module.

- Select from any of the recognized textbooks on reading instruction, the chapter(s) dealing with atomistic approaches to reading. While reading, keep reading cards for your future use and/or review.
- Review the reading programs being used in your own school setting, and list those which are basically atomistic in approach: alphabet based, phonics-decoding, i/t/a, on your intern checklist form.
- While you are completing this module, keep a record of the different decoding skills used in your reading work; this list should be stapled to your checklist and submitted as part of your postassessment.
- Using the following Vocabulary List, write a brief definition for each word. Then check your answer with the reading glossary or any other recognized source to determine your score.

Suggested Vocabulary to Learn

As a professional educator, you will need to know the "language" of your specific areas of specialization. As a teacher of reading, you will discover that there is a whole body of terms which has particular relevance and meaning in this facet of the curriculum. An extensive glossary of such words and terms is included as Part Six of this textbook. Refer to it and use it freely as you have need.

Here is a list of words which refer to those reading skills and approaches included in this module.

ATOMISTIC	DECODING	SYNTHETIC
PHONICS	PHONEMIC	PHONETIC
SYLLABICATION	SYLLABIZING	SYLLABIFICATION
STRUCTURAL ANALYSIS	SCHWA	PHONEME/GRAPHEME
LETTER/SOUND RELATION	GENERALIZATION	AFFIX
PREFIX	SUFFIX	BLEND
BREVE	MACRON	DIACRITICAL MARK
DIGRAPH	DIPHTHONG	ROOT
INFLECTIONAL ENDING	COMPOUND WORD	CONTRACTION

PHONICS PRINCIPLES WHICH ARE VALUABLE IN TEACHING READING

The careful teacher should follow a set of basic principles of learning and instruction at all times. These will strengthen skills and enhance the student's learning in both the cognitive and affective areas. A set of principles does not specifically set forth teaching strategies or precise practices for the teacher to follow step-by-step. Instead, it offers a set of evaluative criteria or guides for measuring not only the teacher's effectiveness and the soundness of her instruction, but it also provides a measure of student exposure to systematic, sequential coverage of materials and skill learnings. The following guidelines should be examined and considered as the intern/teacher approaches reading instruction from a phonics-decoding base.

1. Visual training should be given simultaneously with work on auditory skills. This should not be an "either/or" approach.
2. If a child is to profit from phonics instruction, he must be able to discriminate between language sounds which are similar as well as those which differ greatly.
3. The teacher who would teach phonic facts and aid the student in recognizing and then applying generalizations must include only those which will result in the child's becoming an independent reader.
4. If teaching via a phonics approach inhibits the child in becoming a meaningful reader, it should be discontinued.
5. Teaching strategies which result in the child's relying on a single method of word attack is poor.
6. Many phonics generalizations are so severely limited in application that they are practically useless in reading instruction.
7. A continual program of diagnosis and prescription to assess student progress and need is basic to teaching phonics skills.
8. Even a child being introduced to phonics generalizations is no guarantee of his being able to transfer that knowledge to application level in actual reading experiences.
9. Instruction in phonics should follow a prescribed continuum of sequential learnings; it is not a hit-or-miss process.
10. The intern/teacher who would succeed in reading instruction through a phonics-decoding approach must first know the total program of learning.

Some may ask what are the best steps to follow in introducing phonics teachings. Certainly an examination of a number of reliable and well-used programs will show that there is not general agreement on all points. However, the authors feel that the following suggested order of introducing the basic steps of such a program is a sound one. In the next chapter, a skills continuum is included for teaching the basic steps of success in reading, but since the topic of teaching via an atomistic methodology, and specifically using a phonics-decoding approach, is being considered here, the following step-by-step introduction of various phonics learnings is suggested.

PHONICS INSTRUCTION: SEQUENTIAL STEPS

A sound program of teaching reading using a decoding base is listed in the suggested order of introducing new learnings.

1. A sound assessment of the student's abilities in auditory discrimination, auditory sequencing, and auditory memory, followed by a prescriptive program to meet needs in any of the three aural areas.
2. Introduction of the consonant letters and their related sounds in the following order:
   a. The regular consonants in their initial position.
   b. The consonant blends and clusters in the beginnings of words. (*bl, br, cl, cr,* and *spl, spr, str,* etc.)
   c. The consonant digraphs in initial positioning. (*ch, sh, th*)
   d. The substitution of beginning consonant sounds/letters.
   e. The consonant sounds in their terminal position.
   f. The terminal consonant blends and digraphs.
   g. The recognition of silent consonants. (*mb, ps, pn,* etc.)
   h. The irregular consonant sounds. (soft *c* and *g,* etc.)
   i. The nonphonemic patterns of words.
   j. The consonants in basic sight words.
   k. The consonant sounds in contractions.
3. The introduction of the vowels and their related sounds as follows:
   a. The sounds of the short vowels with generalizations giving clues for pronunciation.
   b. The long sounds of the vowels and the generalizations which affect them.
   c. The combining of vowels to form digraphs. (*ea, ie, oa,* etc.)
   d. Combinations of both long and short vowel sounds in words.
   e. The diphthongs. (*oi, ou, ow,* etc.)
   f. The basic generalizations and exceptions.
   g. The variant sounds of double o. ($\overline{oo}$ and *oo*)
4. Some authorities separate *structural analysis* and *phonics analysis* in their programs of instruction; however, it seems reasonable in considering decoding

skills and their introduction to students to combine them as clues to unlocking new words in reading. The following order of approaching the various steps is suggested:

 a. Examining compound words.
 b. Finding root words and separating affixes from them.
 c. Adding inflectional endings. (plural forms, tense, etc.)
 d. Doubling final consonants before endings.
5. Syllabizing or syllabication of words.
 a. Accented syllables in words.
 b. Teaching generalizations for syllabizing.

The preceding steps in phonics instruction represent a sequential presenting of learning tasks for reading. Examine them and note that they merit inclusion in the teaching program of today's schools. The authors believe that this is a logical order for introducing and teaching these clues for student use in reading.

Self-Assessment in Phonics Knowledge and Application

In order for the intern/teacher to evaluate his own competency in understanding and applying phonics principles in reading, the several following assessment activities have been included for your use. Note that some nonsense "words" have been used in an attempt to help the student "feel" what young children face when they are facing unknown written forms of words. These have also been used by the authors to provide an example of the types of experiences to be used by teachers in seeking to elicit from students their concepts of phonics learnings. Hence generalizations are formed and used in attacking new vocabulary.

Before attempting the evaluative tasks, briefly review the following generalizations and then apply them for verification of your pronunciation choices.

CONSONANT GUIDES

NOTE: Perhaps the simplest way for children to define and identify the consonants is to state that they are all the letters of the alphabet that are not vowels. This excepts: a, e, i, o, u, *and occasionally* w *and* y.

Consonant Generalizations

1. The consonant sounds are much more regular in the letters they represent than vowels: Note the beginning words of the following as examples.

b in bit	*d* in dab	*f* in far
h in his	*j* in jar	*k* in kick
l in lamb	*m* in man	*n* in nice
p in pat	*r* in rat	*t* in tag
v in vine	*w* in wag	*y* in yet
	z in zoo	

NOTE: Even with these usually regular consonants, there are exceptions in pro-nunciation when they may be silent, or when combined with other letters they may represent other sounds.

2. B is silent in a word or syllable when it follows M, or when it comes before T. (bomb, numb, and debt, doubt)
3. C usually has the sound of K, but often when followed by *e, i,* or *y* it has the soft sound of S. (cat or cry and city or cyst)
4. D sometimes represents the sound of T. (packed, snapped, etc.)
5. G, like C, has two sounds: the hard, regular sound and the soft, J-sound when followed by *e, i,* or *y.* It is silent when followed by N. (gag or go, gem or gentle, and gnat or sign)
6. H is silent at the beginning of some words, or when it follows G, K, and R in some words. (hour or heir, and ghost, khaki, and rhyme)
7. K is silent when followed by N at the beginning of words, and often helps to distinguish certain homonyms. (knit or knock and need/kneed, knot/not)
8. L is often silent when followed in a syllable by M or K (calm or almond and talk or folk)
9. N is usually silent when preceded by M in the same syllable. (hymn, solemn, etc.)
10. P when followed by N or S at the beginning of words is silent. (pneumonia, pneuma and pseudo or psalm)
11. S also represents the Z and ZH sounds in certain words. (pins or tags and pleasure or leisure)
12. T is a silent letter in the syllable when it comes before CH and sometimes when it follows S. (witch, catch, or notch and castle, whistle, or listen)
13. W sometimes serves as a silent vowel when combined with O in a syllable, (bow, low, know, etc.)
14. X has no sound of its own, but represents (1) KS in mix and axe, (2) GZ when followed by a vowel or a silent H as in examine and exhaust, and (3) Z when it begins a word such as xylem and xylophone.
15. Y occasionally combines with vowels or consonants and then serves as a vowel also. (hey, say, or may and spy, fly, or shy)
16. W and Y also combine with some vowels and modify their normal sound or form diphthongs. (saw, few, or sew and how, boy, or howl)

NOTE: The phonetician, a technical analyst of speech sounds, frequently refers to some consonant sounds as being voiced *and some as being* unvoiced. *These are consonant pairs, linguistically formed in the same manner, and difference in sound occurs because the consonant is voiced or unvoiced. Examples of these sounds include:*

Voiced	*Unvoiced*
B in big, nibble, or dab	P in pill, ample, or sip
D in bed, drag, or dog	T in tag, battle, or but
G in gone, giggle, or big	K in kiss, cork, or kinky
V in voice, river, or dove	F in fat, doff, or fig
Z in zoo, dazzle, or buzz	S in sing, fist, or miss

Although the vowel sounds are much less regular than the consonant sounds, there are some few generalizations which can be helpful as a first attempt at pronouncing or unlocking new words. The following list should provide a good review for the intern/teacher, as well as providing guides for introducing generalizations to children in the actual learning situation.

HINTS FOR LEARNING VOWELS

In a One Syllable Word, or the Accented Syllable, Usually . . .

1. A single vowel which is not followed by a consonant is long. (no, by, or be and *si·*lent, *me·*ter, or *vi·o·*lin)
   This is often referred to as an "open syllable" in phonics.
2. A single vowel which is followed by a consonant is short. (pet, man, or big and *sil·*ly, *bon·*net, or *sam·*ple)
   This is frequently called a "closed syllable" by some teachers.
3. If two vowels are together, the first is long and the second is silent. (boat, neat, roams, or receive)
4. If there are two vowels, one being terminal *e*, the first is long and the final *e* is silent. (fade, site, rode, mete, and flute)
5. Vowels in the unaccented syllables often take the schwa (short *uh*) sound. (*a·*lone, sys·*tem*, eas·*i·*ly, gal·*lop*, and cir·*cus*)
6. When vowels are combined with R and L, their normal short and long sounds are modified—the R and L control. (bar, fur, or bare, fore and all, pull, smell)
7. Vowels combined with V are an alert signal—they may be either long or short. (*riv·*er, *ro·*ver, *sev·*en, *cov·*er, *di·*ver)

Certain Important Vowel Combinations Represent the Same or Almost Identical Sounds. These Include:

1. The *al* and *aw* sounds: all, call, fall and caw, awl, awning.
2. The *oi* and *oy* sounds: noise and voice and boy, loyal, and royal.
3. The *oo* combination is pronounced as in hood, look, and took or as in room, tool, doom.
4. The *ow* combination can take the long *o* sound as in tow, low, and crow or it may sound like *ou* as in how, now, brown, cow.

One other area of practical phonic knowledge should be included here for review before applying these principles in an evaluative activity for measuring ability to use phonics in unlocking and pronouncing new words. This is that facet of learning which deals with breaking words into their component parts and/or syllables. The following generalizations will serve as guides for instruction as well as a brief review of specific principles for application.

PRINCIPLES FOR SYLLABIZING

1. Compound words are normally divided between the two word parts as well as between syllables within either of the base words. (bread·bas·ket, col·or·blind, on·ward, and e·ven·tem·pered)
2. When words contain double consonants between vowels, the division is usually between the like consonants. (pup·pet, dag·ger, com·mon, drib·ble)
3. When two unlike consonants come between two vowels, the words is usually divided between the consonants. (mem·ber, fur·ther, or·gy, and cur·tain)
4. When two vowels are divided by a single consonant it is usual to begin the second syllable with the consonant. (di·rect, si·lent, fa·vor, ru·mor, se·lect)
5. If a word ending is consonant -le, the last syllable usually begins with the consonant. (dou·ble, sim·ple, wrig·gle, whi·stle)
6. Affixes (prefixes and suffixes) are normally considered to be separate syllables. (dis·abil·i·ty, de·valu·a·tion, un·hap·pi·ness, self·ish)
7. Vowel diphthongs and digraphs are considered to be single sounds and are not usually divided. (dis·*ease*, trai·ler, broad·en and moun·tain, show·ers)
8. Consonant blends, clusters, and diphthongs are considered as one recorded sound, hence are not divided usually. (mon·*ster*, whe·*ther*, cen·*tral*, in·*scribe*, ex·*pl*ain)

After this quick review of the phonics principles governing the consonant and vowel sounds and the division of words into component sounds, you should be able to work through the following exercise with little difficulty.

**Word Analysis
Skills**

1. In the following groups of nonsense words, state the type of vowel found in the underlined, accented syllable and the generalization leading you to try this type of vowel first.
   a. *ib*net, *lad*fin, *pod*cum, *lub*dub
   b. *ho*mic, de*ba*, *li*sid, *fu*doc
   c. *dai*f, an*suic*, *boe*dong, *fee*rin
   d. *de*de, *bi*fe, re*ni*ke, *sa*de

e. *ser, lerdnt, hirnik, burdiss*

f. *garleb, gare, kar, kare, var, vare*

2. Give the sound in the unaccented syllable (accented syllable underlined) and state the generalization.

   *stub*ble, *ap*ron, be*come*, *mad*ame

3. In the following groups of words, divide the words into syllables. Give the generalization which led you to try this division first.

   a. hodlent, sadfin, libter

   b. ligent, hosec, lagor

   c. lieble, inble, hoacle, listle

   d. lebbet, hottan, fillen

   e. desant, reband, linting

4. Some consonants have more than one sound. In the case of "g" or "c" these sounds are called either hard or soft. If you met a strange word (represented by the nonsense words which follow) which would you try first, hard or soft sound of the "g" or "c"?

   cest, caft, cish, comp, cimp, cuve, geds, gakt, gife, gomp, gist, gume

Now that you have completed your work this far in this section of the course-work, it might be well for you to again refer back to the "Reading List for Phonics/ Decoding" at the beginning portion of this section. Several of the listings are particularly useful as a handbook for teaching with a phonics approach. Again, it should be emphasized to all teachers, that there is no ONE way to teach children to read. An early emphasis on decoding is important in that it provides the child with some unlocking skills, but as soon as possible the child should be encouraged to read with the fluency and freedom that marks the independent reader. Many fine teachers follow the practice of augmenting or strengthening their basal program of instruction with a phonics-based strand of reading. The authors recommend this practice.

Postassessment for Final Evaluation

As a final checkup for the student to determine his ability to apply knowledge, the following postassessment is included. If you are able to handle this exercise with comparative ease and accuracy, it is one indicator that you have learned the material in this section satisfactorily.

Postassessment
Evaluation   *NOTE: Here are a number of principles and generalizations and below them are also a number of examples which illustrate the statement. Each example in a group must be consistent in order for it to be the correct response. Match the number and letter.*

1. When two consonant letters represent a single speech sound a consonant digraph is formed.
2. When two or more consonant sounds are fused in such a way that neither identifiable letter sound is lost, it is called a blend.
3. Two vowel sounds which are combined to glide smoothly from the first into the next forming a single new sound is a diphthong.
4. The vowel sound in an unaccented syllable, or one with diminished stress, is called the *schwa*.
5. If there are two vowels in a word or accented syllable, one of them being a final *e*, the first is usually long and the terminal *e* is silent.
6. When there is a single vowel in a word or accented syllable not followed by a consonant, it usually has a long sound.
7. If two vowels come together in a word or accented syllable, the first is usually long and the second is silent.
8. When a single vowel is followed by a consonant in a word or accented syllable, it usually has the short sound.
9. If a vowel is followed by an *r* or *w* in a word or accented syllable, its sound is said to be controlled or modified.
10. Often when the letter *c* is followed by *e, i,* or *y*, it has the soft sound.
11. The digraph, *th*, sometimes has a voiced sound.
12. When the letter *g* is followed by certain vowels it has a soft sound in some words.
13. When the letter *o* is doubled in certain words it has an extended or long sound.
14. The *th* digraph represents an unvoiced sound in some words.
15. The short sound of the double *o* (oo) is heard in pronouncing certain words or syllables.
16. Some consonants, when followed by, or in combination with other letters, are silent.
17. When the letters *le* are preceded by another consonant, the syllable is formed by the consonant *-le*.
18. Words with double consonants are usually divided between the like letters.
19. Affixes are normally divided from base words to form separate syllables.
20. The letter *v* is sometimes referred to as a "signal" because it affects the vowel pronunciation adjacent to it.

a. try, fling, bright, splash
b. ate, line, mole, mute
c. beautiful, gallop, alone, circus
d. room, coo, hoot, bloom
e. visit, motion, rotation, nation
f. but, man, let, vim, tamper
g. rabbit, meet, closed, this
h. book, look, wood, hood
i. mit·ten, cor·rupt, of·fer
j. jaw, cork, mark, third
k. cell, cycle, race, cinder
l. groin, town, round, toys
m. bomb, knee, gnaw, psychology
n. await, meat, frown, row

o. ro·ver, liv·er, di·ver, o·ver
p. white, which, rang, witch
q. rage, judge, genie, gist
r. am·ple, rum·ble, sub·tle, rat·tle
s. south, thistle, mirth, thank
t. meet, road, steam, brain

u. mother, these, those, rather
v. coat, book, leap, reed
w. re·do, mak·ing, un·lock, us·able
x. vital, paper, rodent, decent
y. bloom, took, plow, doing
z. kitten, single, rope, bale

Intern Checklist

Name: _____ **Date** _____

I. **Preassessment:**   **Date Taken** _____ **Score** _____

II. **Learning Experiences:**

    1. **Reading: Author:** _____ **Chap.** _____

            Title: _____

    2. **Review of programs which are ATOMISTIC in approach:**

            Title _____

            Title _____

            Title _____

            Title _____

    3. **Daily record of decoding skills kept?** _____ **Attached?** _____

    4. **Lesson plan (attached to form) and lesson taught?** _____

            Date used: _____

    5. **Vocabulary list sentences written?** _____ **Date** _____

            Attached to form? _____

III. **Options contracted:** _____

    Forms included with this checklist for your folder? _____

IV. **Postassessment:**

    1. **Work sheets, checklist, etc., submitted—Date** _____

    2. **Test scheduled?** _____ **Date** _____ **Time** _____

    3. **Test taken?** _____ **Score** _____

    Completion date: _____

                                    _____
                                      (Intern's Signature)

                                    _____
                                      (Faculty Signature)

NOTE: The following model form is to record your progress on this module. It follows the pattern of learning experiences. As each activity is completed, check and date the proper space, secure signatures if necessary, and affix lesson plans, analyses, etc., before handing it in as part of the postassessment.

Figure 7.5

8

BASIC READING SKILLS
INSTRUCTIONAL IMPLICATIONS

RATIONALE

Reading has been called a skills process. This infers that it is similar to any other skill that is learned, and it is actually a complex skill developed from many component abilities. Before one can begin to teach someone to read, he should first recognize what these skills are, and how they are learned.

It is the purpose of this chapter to help you discover what the basic skills of reading are, the best sequence of teaching them, and how they can be taught most effectively. You will be examining the various developmental skills necessary for children to become independent readers. These abilities may be classified under four basic headings: (1) word recognition skills, (2) comprehension skills, (3) vocabulary skills, and (4) the study skills. You will discover that these are called by various terms, but they basically all refer to the child's ability to unlock words or decode, to get meaning from his reading, and to use his ability to read for gaining information on his own.

In order for these foundation skills to be developed, the teacher needs, again, to recognize the facets of the reading process, their interrelatedness and their developmental interdependence. Reading is not merely saying words, it is getting the message of those words; and it is getting the message for specific purposes—not only getting meaning *from*, but bringing meaning *to*, printed symbols.

Within each of the broad classifications of skills, there are numerous specific abilities to be learned by the student, numerous levels of understanding, and various kinds of reading "tools" to be used in independent studying. These considerations, then, will be the framework of this phase of your learning experience or module of work.

WORD RECOGNITION SKILLS

In the previous chapter, which dealt with various approaches to reading instruction, you were introduced at some length to the whole phonics-decoding methodology. As was pointed out, this is only *one* approach to beginning reading, and stress should be placed on the word *beginning*. Actually, once the child has begun to read, he should rely less and less on decoding processes. Reading should increasingly become a visual process, and his sight vocabulary should continue to increase so that his eyes instantly recognize the words from memory. If he meets unfamiliar words, he will continue to use phonics clues as a *first* attempt at unlocking the new word; however, an overreliance on just this one word-recognition skill will inhibit not only his speed, but his getting meaning from written communication. As soon as possible, other means of developing reading skills should be introduced and taught. This process of word analysis, or decoding, can be graphically depicted with its components and subskills. Note figure 8.1 for details. Since this

WORD RECOGNITION SKILLS			
PHONICS ANALYSIS (Symbols-Sounds Relationships)		**STRUCTURE ANALYSIS** (Words and Variant Forms)	
CONSONANTS	**VOWELS**	**SYLLABIZING**	**WORD PATTERNS**
BLENDS	LONG	ACCENTS	PHONEME FAMILIES
CLUSTERS	SHORT	AFFIXES	COMPOUND WORDS
CONSONANT DIGRAPHS	DIPHTHONGS	ENDINGS	CONTRACTIONS
	VOWEL DIGRAPHS	DIACRITICAL MARKINGS	

Note: The student will discover when examining various programs of reading instruction that the order in which the skills and subskills is introduced varies somewhat. Therefore, the above schema does not fix a particular sequence to a particular learning and its introduction.

Figure 8.1

subject was examined earlier, this brief mention of the first of the reading skills, "Word Recognition, Word Attack, or Word Unlocking," as it is interchangeably termed, will be sufficient in the present chapter. In studying the basic skills, the student/intern may wish to refer back to the facets of phonics decoding as not only an approach to reading instruction, but as a basic skill to be taught early in the reading process.

Basic Sight Words

Many basal programs of reading instruction are built on a controlled vocabulary list in which words are introduced in order and in small numbers from story to story. These lists of frequently used words have been compiled as a result of word count studies and purport to be the requisite vocabulary for building reading skills. Naturally there is considerable debate as to their value and relevance to contemporary beginning readers. Probably the most well-known of these lists is the Dolch Basic Word list of the 220 most common words. These are still widely used as a test of children's knowledge of sight vocabulary, either singly or in sentences.

Students of phonics principles have also developed a list of words which do *not* follow the common generalizations and must be learned from memory. A partial coverage of these is included here for the intern's analysis. As you pronounce them, note how they would be pronounced if you followed the basic principles.

A PARTIAL LIST OF NONPHONETIC WORDS

across	again	aisle	already
another	any	anxious	bear
beauty	been	bind	both
bough	bread	brought	build
busy	buy	captain	calf
chief	clothes	coming	cough
couple	cousin	cruel	dead
debt	do	done	doubt
dove	dozen	earn	eight
eye	father	field	find
freight	friend	four	garage
get	ghost	give	glove
gone	great	guest	guide
have	heaven	heart	high
idea	isle	instead	kind
knew	knife	know	language
laugh	leather	light	live
lion	love	machine	measure
mild	mind	mischief	move
Mr.	Mrs.	neigh	neither

none	ocean	office	often
once	onion	other	ought
patient	piece	pull	push
quiet	ranger	ready	right
said	science	school	shoe
sign	soften	some	son
soul	special	steak	square
sure	sword	their	they
thought	to	ton	touch
two	use	vein	view
was	wash	weight	were
what	who	wild	wind
woman	would	you	young

NOTE: This partial list or the complete list is frequently used by teachers as an assessment of a child's knowledge of sight vocabulary.

In the beginning stages of reading, the child who is taught by way of visual clues, a sight-memory approach, often learns to find valuable associative help from the illustrations accompanying new words as they are introduced. This progressing from the pictorial clue to the written word is often accomplished solely through the mental transfer from one to the other. A simple form of using the cloze procedure for reading instruction is the substitution of an occasional picture instead of a word. This practice, called *rebus reading*, is frequently used in the early stages of reading and allows some children to read the known words and the simple pictures with a greater degree of fluency and meaning than stopping to puzzle over a word and trying to unlock it by one of the several means he may have learned.

In short, then, one can safely affirm that whether the need is for decoding abilities or for strengthening sight word usage, the result should be the same, *instant recognition of words.* Another area of skills for attacking or unlocking words is that of *concept association.* Visual and aural clues have been discussed, but little has been said about those clues for identifying new words via a contextual and/or conceptual sense. Children often substitute most any word in an attempt to "get through" their reading assignments. This injecting wild guesses, or even any word which may have the same beginning sound as the correct one, reflects the child's lack of getting the message from his reading. Once he recognizes that words should be sensible and reasonable, he is furnished with another means of meeting new ones: "Does the word supplied fit? Does it make sense? What is it saying?" This method of attack relies on his previous experiential background for helping him get the gist of the text. It supplies the "blank spots," the unknown words, with responses that are associated with consistency to what he is reading. Thus, the context furnishes valuable associative clues to be tried, retained, or rejected.

THE SKILLS OF COMPREHENDING

Reading without meaning is mere word calling and defeats the purpose of the act which is to communicate with the material being read. Some would even say that getting meaning while reading is more important than correctly pronouncing the words as written. Hence, teaching children to get meaning from their reading is a major responsibility in education. Adults seem prone to assume that because children are saying a number of words correctly they are also comprehending what is written. An examination of this broad term, *comprehension,* shows that there are a variety of skills included in this getting-meaning, thinking process just as there were a number of types of skills in word-identification. Only when we realize that comprehension is such a complex ability, made up of these numerous component skills, will we be able to adequately teach children to understand written material. Just as a careful teacher works with students on many word-attack recognition skills, so must she work on the variety of comprehension skills.

An impressive number of experts in the area of reading instruction as well as in the area of children's development and intellectual growth have used numerous terms in describing comprehension. A brief look at some of these descriptive words clearly shows a strong relationship to the facets of the thinking process itself. Note some of the definitive expressions: "techniques of understanding, cultivation of thinking, imagining, reflecting, reasoning, analyzing, evaluating data, searching for relevance, identification of sources, synthesizing findings, judging, clarifying meanings, critical organizing . . ." and numerous others. Indeed some have likened the taxonomy of comprehension skills to the levels of the cognitive structure. Figure 8.2, p. 184, arranges the components and their subskills in a graphic schema with four basic facets of reading for meaning: Literal, Interpretative, Critical, and Specific.

Reading and Interpretative Comprehension

When reading at this level of understanding, the child is involved with tasks which require his getting meaning from directly stated facts. He also deals with happenings, information, and ideas included in reading materials. Sometimes teachers may seem to overstress this level of getting meaning, but it must be remembered that these skills are basic to what might be termed "higher level" comprehension tasks. Even if one might view literal comprehension as being a first-level category, it should be recognized that there are a number of reading experiences which require getting meaning that range from very easy to much more difficult competencies. These include (1) reading for stated details, (2) reading for comparisons or contrasts, (3) reading for sequence or order, (4) reading to get

THE SKILLS
OF
COMPREHENSION

LITERAL READING	INTERPRETATIVE READING	CRITICAL READING	SPECIFIC READING
STATED:	INFERRED:	ASSESSED:	PURPOSED:
FACTS-DETAILS	COMPARISONS AND CONTRASTS	REAL OR MAKE-BELIEVE	FOLLOW DIRECTIONS
COMPARISONS AND CONTRASTS	SUPPORTIVE DETAILS	FACT OR OPINIONS	LOCATE AND USE INFORMATION
SEQUENCE AND ORDER	ORDER AND SEQUENCE	ACCURACY AND ADEQUACY	SUMMARIZE
MAIN IDEAS	TOPIC IDEAS	VALIDITY AND WORTH	RELATE TO LIFE
CAUSE AND EFFECT	LITERAL OR FIGURATIVE LANGUAGE	RELEVANCE AND APPROPRIATENESS	ANALYZE AUTHOR'S STYLE AND SIGNALS
TRAITS AND CHARACTERISTICS	CAUSE AND RESULT	VALUE AND DESIRABILITY	SYNTHESIZE DATA AND TRUTHS
	OUTCOMES AND PROBABILITIES		

APPRECIATIVE READING

AFFECTIVE RESPONSES

FEELING TONE: INTEREST, LIKE OR DISLIKE, BIAS, FEAR, ANGER, AMUSEMENT

IMAGERY: WORD PICTURES, VISUALIZE SENSORY STIMULI—HEAR, FEEL, SENSE

CHARACTER IDENTIFICATION: EMPATHY, SYMPATHY, SENSITIVITY, PROJECTIONS

LANGUAGE RESPONSE: LINGUISTIC SKILLS—SEMANTIC DIMENSIONS

Figure 8.2

main ideas, (5) reading for descriptive characteristics, and (6) reading to discover cause and effect.

In considering the steps just listed, it should be pointed out that the reader will not only need, in most instances, to identify and recognize the purposes for which he is reading; but he will later need to be able to recall and verbalize these component levels of understanding.

Reading and Inferential Comprehension

When the reader makes inferences, he is conjecturing or hypothesizing as a response which synthesizes the literal meaning of what has been read, plus his personal experiences, his store of knowledge, his creative imagination, and his intuitive transfer. Some reading material, particularly narrative fiction, may lead the reader into more widely divergent conjectures; whereas the analytical, factual type of materials normally results in more convergent inferences or hypotheses. Sometimes in order to determine the depth of a student's inferential understanding, the teacher may require a rationale for the inferences made from the reading tasks. Whatever the immediate objective of the assignment or response, thinking at a creative level is involved. Comprehension at this level has been noted to include reading for the purpose of making an inference relative to (1) comparisons or contrasts not directly stated, (2) details not included which might have supported the passage, (3) the sequential order of events not fully included, (4) the stating of the main idea, (5) deciding on literal and figurative language used, (6) what is the cause and result, and (7) outcomes and probabilities. This phase of comprehension, drawing conclusions from inferred information, is an important test of what the child has read *into* the material covered. Some have expressed literal comprehension as "reading the lines," and inferential comprehending as "reading between the lines." This kind of creative interpretation of reading in which the child goes beyond the stated information reveals a depth or originality and imagination, but his should be reasonable deductions, not mere fantasizing without foundation.

Reading and Critical Comprehension

In critical reading, the student reaches a higher level of skill than in either of the previous two categories discussed, for here he reads literally what the author is saying while also interpreting what has not been written, only inferred. However, a third facet of meaning-getting is involved in critical reading; a combination of inquiry, evaluation, and searching. Here the reader is challenging and assessing in order to discover truthfulness and authenticity, bias or honesty, propaganda or objectivity. He uses the content and weighs it against his own experiences, comparing it with authoritative criteria: (1) the teacher's information, (2) other writers on the same topic, and (3) creditable experts with whom there is contact or access. These external and internal criteria, then, become the basis for judgment by the reader at his level of competence. Certainly these skills, inherent at this level of comprehension, are reaching far deeper than the mere calling of words, or even skimming for surface information. As the schema in figure 8.2 indicates, there are several component skills inherent in critical comprehension. They include the reader's evaluation of (1) what is real or fantasy, (2) what is fact or opinion, (3) the accuracy and adequacy of what is written, (4) the validity and worth of the content, (5) the relevancy and appropriateness of the material, and (6) the value and desirability of the message of the writer. Critical reading has sometimes been confused with, or used interchangeably with, creative reading, but the present writers feel that the latter criteria belong more in the realm of interpretative comprehension and appreciative comprehension than in the area of critical reading and comprehension.

It seems that teaching children to read and comprehend critically is of utmost importance in contemporary times. The media are being used constantly to influence thinking at all levels, hence it is urgent that young readers learn to differentiate and evaluate critically and clearly. Too often, it seems, educators have been content to teach the mechanics of reading without stressing or teaching for *readers* who function at this higher level of comprehension. Even very young children can exhibit clear thinking and make sound judgments regarding the materials they are reading at their commensurate levels.

Reading and Specific Comprehension

A fourth level of meaning-getting in reading deals with specificity in language use and reading for a particular purpose. First of all, a word about words and the facility of language. Many students seem to be almost impoverished in their knowledge of, and use of, the facile, beautiful expressiveness of our language. Reading can enhance the child's awareness of the clarity and force inherent in well-chosen words. The whole crux of meaning rests on the writer's ability to use language well, and then on the reader's being able to forcefully grasp the meaning conveyed by the author's succinct, clear expression, information, or description. Sometimes one single word makes all the difference, and the misreading (literally or figuratively) of that single word destroys or loses the whole pith of meaning.

What then are the facets of this level of specific comprehension? The following brief descriptions based on the material from the schema will suffice to alert the student/intern to the need for careful work in this interesting and utilitarian phase of reading instruction. Besides the clarity of correct word meaning and usage, the student reads for specific reasons. This is reading with intent and purpose and can become an incentive factor. This is reading for meaning in order to (1) follow specifications or directions, (2) find needed information and then apply it correctly and usefully, (3) capsulize or summarize large amounts of material into the condensed form of an outline or summary, (4) relate written material to life situations, problems, or needs in order to discover solutions, (5) carefully examine the author's style, pattern of writing, mode of expression, and (6) synthesize informational data, truths, segments. This level of understanding is primarily one of application and synthesis via meaningful reading activities and experiences.

The Main Objective: Appreciative Reading

Important as each of these areas of comprehension is as a separate entity, the main significance of each singly, and of all four in combination, is that the reader shall develop an appreciation for meaningful reading. Comprehension must result in affective responses from and within the reader as a person. This is the aesthetic impact of reading upon the reader; the sensitization of the individual to the artistic elements of the message as well as to his personal response to the literary quality of the form, style, and structure of the material. All of this results in the development of interests and tastes in selecting reading material and finding satisfaction and value from it. This is the appreciative enjoyment that results from the discovery of the right message at the right time for the right individual. And here the teacher plays an important role. Studies have shown that not only is the teacher the most important single factor in the child's successful learning to read, but reports indicate that the teacher is likewise the most important influence on the child's learning to read what is commonly called "literature." Certainly the teacher who introduces and shares worthwhile reading material with children will discover early her power of influence in nurturing a desire for and a delight in reading in young learners.

Four areas of affective qualities result then from appreciative comprehension: (1) Feeling Tone, the emotive reactions of the person to the material he is assimilating; (2) Developing Imagery, the visualizing and internalizing of the graphic picture-language employed; (3) Character Identification, the being at one with the people and their situations; and (4) Response to Language, recognition of the skill and artistry of the writer and his use of the semantic dimensions. Helping young readers to be increasingly aware of these components of the appreciative skills and strengthening them is an important and rewarding responsibility of the teacher of reading for depth of meaning.

BUILDING READING VOCABULARY

It has been estimated that young children entering school bring with them a vocabulary of from some two thousand words ranging upward in some cases to as many as ten to fifteen thousand words. It is upon the foundation of the child's spoken vocabulary that the teacher begins to build the transition skills leading from the oral use of language into the reading of the printed word. Therefore, it becomes an early responsibility of the teacher to assess the child's previous exposure to language and his present facility in using his vocabulary. Some children normally use the words regularly met in the classroom and its situations. Others will have learned words and expression that are neither usable in the class, nor for that matter, even in the books they will meet. In either instance the good teacher will seek to nurture and enhance the vocabularies of all the children, adequate or inadequate at the start.

The building of a reading vocabulary will make use of any and all of the word recognition skills and the comprehension skills. The basal program which the teacher uses as the framework of her reading program will introduce new words in a sequential pattern as one means of enlarging the child's reading word list. The writing of experience chart stories will make use of the spoken language of individuals and groups. The read-aloud times will provide opportunities for introducing new listening vocabulary which then can be used in students' speaking and writing and reading. Upper primary and intermediate students soon begin to make use of their reading skills to seek information from their other textbooks: science, history, mathematics, health. Likewise, the specific vocabulary of these content areas proves a valuable source of new words and terms for the growing, developing reader. From the independent, recreational reading done, new words are met and learned so that from all these means of input, the child's usable reading vocabulary may increase many hundreds of words in a single year.

Just as in the other basic reading skills examined with their subskills, so vocabulary building skills include a number of component competencies. Figure 8.3 shows the various facets and their interrelatedness with one another. Note that the building of reading and writing vocabularies is seen as developing from and through the child's listening and speaking abilities. Then with his newly acquired and strengthening word attack and comprehension skills, plus the introduction of the vocabulary building subskills, the young reader is encouraged to use his growing reading competencies and is reinforced by his successfully handling the component skills. ·

The recent emphasis from linguistics which deals with morphology, lexicography, and etymology in many of the elementary language arts textbooks, may have a positive effect on children's vocabulary growth, not only in its scope of breadth, but also in the depth dimension. Certainly any means of interesting and fascinating young learners with the power and beauty of words and language is to be valued and used well. Just as work on comprehension skills should culminate in the reader's appreciation of reading, so work on building vocabulary should result in the learner's awareness of and love for precise, descriptive, beautiful diction. Here again the teacher's attitude toward language will be reflected in the types of assignments and activities that youngsters are expected to complete, and their response will be commensurate to the teacher's enthusiasm and interest in the language to be learned and shared. If the teacher views such learnings as exciting discoveries, the children will participate with eagerness and willingness. On the other hand if the teacher is really disinterested or poorly prepared, the tasks re-

READING VOCABULARY-BUILDING SKILLS

LISTENING VOCABULARY
SPEAKING VOCABULARY

READING VOCABULARY

RECOGNITION CLUES	DEFINITIONAL CLUES	LINGUISTICS CLUES
COMPOUND WORDS	SYNONYMS	ROOTS AND AFFIXES
CONTRACTIONS	HOMONYMS	INFLECTIONAL ENDINGS
HYPHENATED WORDS	ANTONYMS	DERIVATIONS
INFLECTIONAL CHANGES	CONTENT AREA WORDS	ETYMOLOGY
CONFIGURATION	DICTIONARY USAGE	MORPHOLOGY
CLOZURES	THESAURUS	LEXICOGRAPHY

Note: As the learner progresses further into vocabulary-building skills, he can be introduced to new component abilities as a means of new experimentation with learning and
using expanded reading words and terms.

Figure 8.3

lated to vocabulary expansion and enrichment will become tasteless, boring exercises to be endured with low tolerance and little success.

The dictionary and thesaurus, instead of literally fulfilling the meaning of the
word (a storehouse or plain where treasure is stored), become impoverished,
dearthy tomes to be used for contrived, stilted assignments of "looking up words
and writing sentences about them!" The intricate, invigorating search for hidden
meanings and gems of understanding inherent in the roots of many words will be
overlooked and ignored. As a reminder of the precision and richness of the building blocks of our language, the authors have included a brief listing of some of the
more usable roots and affixes commonly found in many of the English words.

A LIST OF COMMON PREFIXES

GROUP 1: Negative prefixes that mean *no, not,* or *opposite,* and
reverse the meaning of the root word.

	Prefix Element	Illustrative Example
	un	unfinished, unlike, untrue
Level 1	dis	disagree, disable, dislike
	in	incorrect, indecent, inevitable

A LIST OF COMMON PREFIXES (cont.)

	Prefix Element	Illustrative Example
Level 2	anti	antisocial, anticlimax, antiaircraft
	non	nonsense, nonfat, nonessential
Level 3	de	deactivate, deflect, denude
	il	illicit, illegal, illogical
	im	imbalance, immoral, impossible
	ir	irreconcilable, irreverent, irreversible
Level 4	a	amoral, atheistic, asocial
	an	anarchy, antonym, anacronism

The student/intern will notice that the negative prefixes have been arbitrarily categorized into four levels. This offers only a suggested order of introduction, and the teacher can readily see that there is a slight progression of difficulty from Level 1 and continuing on through Level 4.

A LIST OF COMMON PREFIXES

Group II. Prefixes that indicate *amount* and/or *number*.

	Prefix element	Meaning	Illustrative Example
Level 1	uni	one	unity, uniform, unicycle
	bi	two	bicycle, biweekly, biped
	tri	three	triplets, tricycle, triune
	quad	four	quadraped, quartile
	semi	half	semicircle, semester
	multi	many	multimedia, multiply
Level 2	mono	single	monopoly, monologue, monogamy
	du	double	duet, duel, dual, dubious
	dec	ten	decimal, decade, decimate
	prim	first	primate, primer, primary
	hemi	half	hemispheric, hemitrope
	cent	hundred	century, centipede, centile
Level 3	di	separate	diverse, direction
	kilo	thousand	kilometer, kilogram
	milli	thousand	milligram, millenium
	proto	first	prototype, protoplasm

Note that here again, the numerical/quantitative prefixes have been levelled to show a suggested order of introducing them to students. Certainly this is no fixed order, for the best time to introduce any learning is when the need for it arises, but for review and study, these prefixes may be taught in groups as listed above.

A LIST OF COMMON PREFIXES

Group III: Prefixes that are introduced incidentally or specifically as per the meaning indicated in Column 2.

	Prefix element	Meaning	Illustrative Example
	a	state, condition	aflame, aloud, afire
	ex	1. out, outside of	exit, exclude, expose
		2. former	ex-athlete, ex-wife
Level 1	re	1. again	repeat, redo, revive
		2. back, backward	refrain, retract, renounce
	in	in, into, within	invite, include, indepth
	com, con, cor	together, with	communicate, connect correspondence
	pre	1. in front of	preservice, prefix
		2. before	premature, preface
		3. early	preschool, prevent
Level 2	inter	between	interim, interspace
	super	above, beyond	superstar, superior
	sub	under, below	submarine, subway
	post	after	postwar, postscript
	pro	1. in favor of	pro-American
		2. forward, outward	provide, proceed, protrude
	ab	away from, off	absence, abstain, abduct
	ad	to, toward, near	advent, admit, advance
Level 3	ante	before	antebellum, antecedent
	circum	around	circus, circumvent
	intro	inward, within	introduce, introspect
	dia	across, through	diameter, diagonal
	extra	beyond	extraordinary, extrapolate
	out	out, beyond	outmode, outwork, outworn
Level 4	pan	all, whole	panorama, panacea
	per	fully, throughout	perfectly, percent
	peri	around, enclosed	periphery, perimeter

Numerous activities can be built around words using many of these common prefixes. They have been arranged in four levels for the teacher's convenience.

Level 1 elements are normally considered to be less difficult to introduce and use than the succeeding levels.

Not only are the prefixes a fertile source for building vocabulary, but the common suffixes, as well, afford the teacher valuable opportunities for working with words. These segments supply meanings, give clues for understanding, and can afford the intern many structural clues for word recognition, comprehension, and for enriching his vocabulary. A brief review list has been included here.

A LIST OF COMMON SUFFIXES

GROUP I: Suffixes whose meaning is indicated as shown.

	Suffix Element	Meaning	Illustrative Example
Level 1	ful	full of	careful, hopeful, awful
	less	1. without	doubtless, helpless
		2. unable to be acted upon	dauntless
	ness	condition, state	closeness, goodness
	ly	1. in a manner	quickly, early, neatly
		2. every	nightly, daily, monthly
	th	ordinal number	tenth, fifth, ninth
	ty	1. amount, degree	plenty, thirty, paucity
		2. condition, quality	priority, eventuality
Level 2	able, ible	able to be	edible, readable, capable
	en	small, little	mitten, kitten
	et, ette, let	diminutive	dinette, playlet, leaflet
	en	to make	weaken, liven, enliven
	ling	young, small	duckling, nursling
	ish	as, like	owlish, freakish, childish
	ous	full of	noxious, dangerous
	y, ly	like, full of	likely, dewy, mighty, only
Level 3	acious	full of, with	gracious, vivacious
	ary, ory	place, area	armory, granary
	ate	to make, to be	ameliorate, irritate
	ative, ive	tending toward	lucrative, defensive
	fy, ify	to make, to have	fortify, magnify, deify
	ward	in direction of	awkward, forward, inward
	ure	being, function	leisure, manufacture
	wise	toward, direction of	clockwise, otherwise

A LIST OF COMMON SUFFIXES (cont.)

	Suffix Element	Meaning	Illustrative Example
	arium, orium	place, area	solarium, terrarium
	fy	to have, make	purify, clarify
	ice	being, quality	suffice, incise
	ic	form, character of	gastric, heroic
Level 4	id	condition of	turgid, vivid, fervid
	ism	belief	aetheism, deism, marxism
	ize, ise	to make	pauperize, scandalize, advertise
	some	full of	winsome, lonesome
	ule	small, little	miniscule, granule

Another group of suffixes which is very usable and important when introducing students to this technique of vocabulary expansion, is noun suffixes with various meanings. A list of these follows.

A LIST OF NOUN SUFFIXES

GROUP I: Noun suffixes whose basic meaning is a *being who is*.

	Suffix Element	Illustrative Example
	ant	defendant, servant
	ent	superintendent, dependent, existent
Level 1	er	user, buyer, builder
	ian	Marxian, custodian, humanitarian
	or	inventor, actor, debtor
	ee	trustee, guarantee, employee
	eer	volunteer, engineer, auctioneer
Level 2	ier	cavalier, cashier, bombardier
	ist	botanist, artist, liberationist
	ster	youngster, oldster, prankster
	art, ard	laggard, braggart
Level 3	ess, tress	mistress, seamstress, actress
	ice	novice, poultice

Yet another grouping of suffixes should be included for consideration by the intern/teacher of reading vocabulary. This listing is used in forming a wide variety of words common to the language.

A LIST OF NOUN SUFFIXES

GROUP II: Noun suffixes denoting *condition* or *state of being*.

	Suffix Element	Illustrative Example
Level 1	ance, ancy	vacancy, acquaintance, relevance
	ation	relation, limitation, rejuvenation
	ence	existence, independence, excellence
	ion	ambition, confusion, fusion
	ition	condition, repetition
	ment	establishment, amazement, development
Level 2	dom	freedom, wisdom, martyrdom
	hood	statehood, parenthood, boyhood
	ship	leadership, hardship, friendship

Of course, valuable as the affixes are, they would be of little value without the basic root words to which they are added. For though they supply a meaning element, it is the root word that gives the basic meaning to the term being studied. Many of our root, or base, words have been taken from the Greek and Latin languages. Many, many thousands of our English words are based on a rather limited number of basic roots, plus the affixes, with the varied derivative forms.

LIST OF LATIN ROOTS

	Root Word	Common Meaning	Illustrative Example
	annus	year	annual, annuity, anniversary
	bellum	war	bellicose, belligerent
	campus	field	champion, camp, encamp
	capit	head	capital, recap, caption
	corpus	body	corpse, corporal, corpuscle
	dies	day	dial, diary, dietician
	greg	flock, herd	gregarious, segregate
Level 1	home	man	homage, homogeneous
	ignis	fire	igneous, ignite
	lumen	light	illuminate, luminary
	lun	moon	lunar, lunatic
	naso	nose	nostril, nasal
	nomen	name	nominally, nomination
	persona	person	impersonate, personalize
	sol	sun	solarium, solar, parasol

A LIST OF LATIN ROOTS (cont.)

Root Word	Common Meaning	Illustrative Example
animus	alive	animate, animosity
denti	tooth	dental, dentist, indent
fid	trust	fidelity, confidence
genus	kind, origin	genes, genesis, original
jus	law, right	justice, jurisdiction
lingua	language	linguistic, bilingual
lit	letter	illiterate, literature
loc	place	local, locate, relocate
manu	hand	manufacture manicure
mort	death	mortify, mortician
ped	foot	pedestrian, pedals
ora	pray, speak	oracle, oratory, oral
temp	time	temporal, contempt
verb	word	verbose, proverb, verb
vita	life	vitality, vitamin, invitation
alt	high	altar, altimeter, altitude
belle	pretty	embellish, belladonna
bene	good	beneficent, benefit, benediction
clar	clear	declare, clarify, clarion
grat	pleasant	ingrate, gracious, gratuity
grav	heavy	grave, gravity, gravel
honor	repute	honorable, honest
magnus	large	magnitude, magnify
mal	bad	malign, malice, malignancy
novus	new	novitiate, novel, novice
sacer	holy	sacrosanct, sacred, sacrament
arch	chief	archenemy, monarch
biblio	book	Bible, bibliographic
cracy	government	autocracy, democracy
demo	people	demographic, democrat
gam	marriage	polygamy, monogamous
hemo	blood	hemotologist, hemorrhage
idio	personal	idiot, idion
logue	speech, word	logical, logistical
mechan	machine	mechanical, mechanic
neuro	nerve	neurotic, neurologist
osteo	bone	osteopathic, osteology
petro	stone	petrified, petrol
phobia	fear	claustrophobia, phobic

Level 2 (rows: animus through vita)

Level 3 (rows: alt through sacer)

Level 4 (rows: arch through phobia)

A LIST OF LATIN ROOTS (cont.)

	Root Word	Common Meaning	Illustrative Example
Level 4	pod	foot	podiatrist, tripod
(cont.)	polic	city	politics, police, metropolitan
	pseudo	false	pseudonym, pseudomorph
	techno	art, skill	technology, technique
	tome	to cut	tonsilectomy, anatomy
	toxic	poison	toxemia, toxic, antitoxin
	zoo	animal	zodiac, zoology

The Latin roots shown here are but a portion of the total, but even this list should alert the student/intern to the possibilities of many vocabulary building activities which can make use of these basic word segments. Likewise, the Greek roots provide many clues to the original meanings of many of our contemporary English words. See the following list for these.

A LIST OF COMMON GREEK ROOTS

	Root Word	Common Meaning	Illustrative Example
	angle	corner	triangle, angular
	anthropo	mankind	misanthropic, anthropology
	astro	star	disastrous, asteroid
	bio	life	biology, biopsy
	cardio	heart	cardiac, cardiology
	centric	center	centrifugal, egocentric
	chrom	color	kodachrome, chromatic
	chrono	time	chronology, synchronize
	dyna	power	dynamic, dynamo
	eu	earth	geography, geometric
Level 1	graph	draw, write	graphics, graphite
	helio	sun	heliotrope, heliostat
	hydro	water	hydroplane, hydraulic
	logy	study of	technology, psychology
	micro	small	microbe, microscope
	peri	around	perimeter, periphery
	phos, photo	light	phosphorus, photo
	scope	see	telescope, microscope
	tele	far	telegraph, telephone
	theo	God	theocracy, theology
	therm	heat	thermometer, thermal

A LIST OF COMMON GREEK ROOTS (cont.)

Root Word	Common Meaning	Illustrative Example
auto	self	autonomy, automobile
cycle	wheel	cyclometer, tricycle
derm	skin	dermatologist, dermal
hetero	different	heterogeneous, heteronym
macro	large	macron, macrocosm
meter	measure	odometer, chronometer
metry	measurement	symmetry, optometry
mega	great	megalopolis, megaphone
odont	tooth	orthodontistry
ortho	straight	orthodox, orthography
pedi	child	pedagogy, pediatrics
patho	feeling	sympathy, empathize
physio	nature	physical, physics
psycho	mind	psychometry, psychotic
phono	sound	phoneme, phonogram
iatric	medical	psychiatric, geriatric
sphere	round, circle	spherical, atmosphere
sym, syn	together, same	synthetic, sympathetic

Level 2

Again, this is only a partial list of the many Greek roots which are frequently used in the structuring of English words. However, a careful analysis of many common words will show that they have been built from some of these root words and added onto and expanded with either suffixes or affixes. Some may think that children are not interested in or by such learnings, but if a teacher has interest and value in this phase of morphology and etymology, he can easily spark vocabulary learnings by talking about and helping children discover words and their fascinating evolution. It was only a few years ago that a little elementary school girl won a national spelling test by correctly spelling "antidisestablishmentarianism." Students all over the country hearing about this wanted to know what the word means. Such incidents can become the reason for taking a look at basic meanings as they are revealed through the study of word parts. Note the number of prefixes and suffixes added to the base word *establish*. What *does* it mean?

THE REFERENCE OR STUDY SKILLS

Almost before children have really become independent readers in our American schools they are pushed into using reading skills for learning purposes. New areas of the curriculum require reading for locating information. This utilitarian aspect of reading instruction is commonly referred to as teaching study skills, or the use of reference tools. This skills area is one that continues throughout the lifetime of most individuals. With our current emphasis on "lifelong learning," more and more adults are continuing to go to school, or are going back to school for further education and/or training in their field of work or profession. It is amazing how many of the basic study skills which were learned in early school years are suddenly called into use again. This is just by way of saying that beginning in the primary grades and continuing on through adult education, the learner at any age makes use of his abilities in purposeful reading. More and more as the child progresses from grade to successive grade, his reading material is changing from mere narrative material to the content material related to many subject areas of school curriculum. Less and less is reading instruction based on literary material, and more on content subject matter, as he reaches and continues through the intermediate grades, junior high school, and on through secondary years. Even in basal reading programs, more and more materials are being drawn from the subject matter fields. This growing trend has shown that many young learners need specific training in handling this type of material at each level. Hence today's reading teacher is concerned with teaching this area of skills perhaps more than at any other time in the history of the public school.

This emphasis on functional reading means that the reading teacher will not be teaching reading just during a specified period set aside for reading instruction.

Children need to be familiar with new words before meeting them in the context of reading materials. The alert teachers will make use of many opportunities for introducing vocabulary to students.

It may certainly well be that she will have set times for such teaching, but more and more, she will also be reinforcing specific learnings in which reading is used in almost every other subject area. It is a truism that each type of subject matter material has its own particular vocabulary and concepts, its own system of logical sequence, its unique relatedness to other areas of the curriculum, and a special technique for presenting the material with its basic principles and assumptions. It is likewise true that the elementary teacher who recognizes these differences in subject areas will need, therefore, to often disrupt an ongoing learning to reteach, or emphasize, a taught skill from reading's word recognition skills, its comprehension skills, its vocabulary learning techniques, and now from its methods of getting and using information—its reference or study skills.

Just what then is meant by the term "study skills"? The writers like to think of them as those abilities which are basically an integrated part of the reading process, but which are primarily used when the reader is mastering content materials. Certainly this skills area is not separate from the other reading skills, but is perhaps best thought of as an application of those other skills in specialized tasks for deeper learning in other curricular areas. Figure 8.4, which follows, presents a schematic arrangement showing that study skills stem from the other basic reading competencies and branch into important components of interrelated learnings.

Purposeful Reading

Reading for a purpose entails a number of skills which have to do with finding and organizing information for further use in the academic setting. These will be considered briefly in the order presented in the schema.

Following directions. Probably no single reading skill is more often used by youngsters and adults alike than that of following written directions. From simple art or science directions, to model-building, to completing school assignments, to following a pattern, to using recipes and do-it-yourself kits, to highly professional formulas—the whole gamut of experiences in modern life makes use of the reader's ability to interpret and follow directions on boxes, cans, kits, covers, lids, books.

In the school scene where the learning of this important ability begins, the students follow teacher-written directions from the chalkboard, from work sheets, or independent tasks in his contracts, learning centers, task cards. In each area of the curriculum they encounter intricate directions for carrying out work, for checking results, and for examining and using new processes. This is particularly true in arithmetic and science. In the social science areas of geography and history, they follow instructions to trace time lines, routes, to find areas and analyze material. In taking exams, following directions is of prime importance. Many times students have failed in crucial evaluative situations because they incorrectly or incompletely read and followed stated directions. It is a good practice for teacher and group to read directions orally and to discuss them for clarification in order that there is no misunderstanding or confusion about specifics.

WORD RECOGNITION SKILLS		
COMPREHENSION SKILLS		
VOCABULARY SKILLS		
STUDY SKILLS		
PURPOSEFUL READING	**REFERENCE TOOLS**	**SPECIALIZED READING**
FOLLOWING DIRECTIONS	DICTIONARY	CONTENT VOCABULARY
LOCATING INFORMATION	ENCYCLOPEDIA	CONTENT READING
ORGANIZING MATERIALS	INDEXES	GRAPHS
EVALUATION AND SELECTION	CARD CATALOG	TABLES
NOTE-TAKING	READER'S GUIDE	MAPS
OUTLINING	HANDBOOKS	CHARTS

Note: The Study Skills have been divided into three strands of reading skills: (1) reading for a purpose, (2) using reference tools, and (3) undertaking specialized reading tasks involving subject materials and graphic representations of data.

Figure 8.4

Locating information. Beginning in the lower primary grades the student should be introduced to this utilitarian reading skill. In the present day, students at all levels quickly become aware of the many sources of information available. Likewise, the student/teacher is certainly aware that all levels of reading in books of the content fields require pupils to search for and synthesize materials and information from a wide variety of sources. How, then, does one teach these component study skills of locating information?

Beginning in the primary grades, the teacher guides young students in a number of tasks which require the use of this competency and reinforce and refine the technique. The following list of graduated skills should suffice to alert the intern/teacher to the numerous ways to help the pupil develop location techniques of (1) finding specific words, phrases, or sentences which answer specific "Who, What, Where" questions; (2) finding page numbers, pictures, or titles; (3) using tables of contents, indexes, and glossaries; (4) learning to alphabetize and using alphabetized lists; (5) using captions, italicized words, bold-faced print, paragraph headings; (6) learning to skim and scan rapidly, to use summaries, outlines, and study questions; (7) using study guides, notes, reports, and abstracts; (8) learning to use footnotes, bibliographical entries, and documentation evidence.

Organizing materials. A third facet of purposeful reading skills deals with the student's learning to arrange and organize the results of his reading in some usable order. This *developed* skill begins in the early experiences of school with such tasks as were mentioned in the section on readiness activities: putting objects in series, classifying, categorizing, sorting, arranging. At the beginning reading level it takes the form of (1) arranging pictures in the proper sequence to tell a story; (2) placing word cards in the chart holder to form simple sentences; (3) deciding which sentences in an experience story should come first and which should follow in a particular order; (4) listing stories which belong in a group because of a common theme or topic; (5) classifying ideas, items, or topics according to headings; (6) select topic sentences and arrange them in order for simple summaries; (7) arrange data or materials into tables, graphs, charts, and graphic figure forms; (8) develop note-taking abilities and outlining skills from their reading in content areas.

Evaluating and selecting. Assessing the appropriateness of information and/or material for meeting specific needs requires the decision-making process of selecting the best or most fit. This important skill is basic to many of the other abilities being considered in this section. The intern/teacher will discover many usable strategies as well as many opportunities for developing students' competencies in this reading area. When need for making judgments and selections arises, the students can make the choices of words, pictures, techniques, sentences, paragraphs, or even selections. They can be given opportunities to make selections which answer questions, complete statements, give important information, need to be remembered because of their utility, or expand a concept or complete an assignment in another curriculum area. Evaluating and synthesizing, as well as application, are high-level skills in the cognitive domain and can be strengthened in this area of reading instruction. They are basic to later critical reading and critical thinking.

Note-taking and outlining. In order to use material and information communicated through reading, the student needs to capsulize and condense. Taking notes for recall or future use is an important study skill. These may be in the form of narrative summaries of the content, or a sequence listing of facts, figures, processes, or procedures. From these notes, students often outline important steps in graduated order. Probably this technique is used more often than any other throughout the middle grades, junior high school, secondary school, college levels and even in graduate school work. Reading and then condensing the information for easy retrieval is a most valuable ability to be taught and learned and used from early years on through life.

Using the Reference Tools

A second category of skills for study can be referred to as knowledge of and use of reference tools. These special compilations of helpful materials in their individualized formats are a valuable source of information on many topics. The reading teacher is usually responsible for introducing these aids and teaching young students how to use them effectively. A quick glance back at Figure 8.4 will remind the student/intern of the various guides, handbooks, anthologies, and almanac type materials available to the young researcher.

Dictionary usage. An important reading skill to be learned is that of the dictionary usage. Dictionary skills are sequential in nature and develop from very simple tasks to much more discrete and extended ones. Several companies have published graded sets for student use. These begin with picture dictionaries, continue through beginner's level, junior, intermediate, high school, and adult publications.

The teacher should be aware that there are certain requisite abilities basic to instruction in the dictionary. These include (1) the student's knowing the alphabet in its proper order, (2) his understanding that words often have multiple meanings, (3) his realization that letter sounds vary in particular situations, (4) his knowledge of diacritical markings for pronunciation guides, and (5) some knowledge of root words and their expansion by inflectional endings and derivations. Following these primary understandings, the student will be introduced to a variety of other learnings relative to the developmental skills of dictionary usage. Some of these step-by-step competencies are (1) knowing the names of the letters of the alphabet; (2) knowing which letters in general belong in each quarter of the alphabet; (3) recognizing guide words and their purpose; (4) understanding the pronunciation key provided; (5) alphabetizing using initial letter, then to the second and third letters as needs arise; (6) selecting the proper meaning for the situation; (7) properly pronouncing the word as indicated by the markings; (8) choosing the preferred and/or secondary pronunciation; (9) identifying idioms, colloquials, dialect; (10) learning new word meanings; (11) recognizing abbreviations, special forms; (12) discovering special sections of the dictionary: foreign words, geographical data, biographical information, dates; (13) correctly spelling words and using the dictionary as the model for such. Certainly this is not an all-inclusive listing of dictionary skills to be taught and learned, but it can serve as some measurement of the coverage being given in actual school situations. It should be mentioned, too, that most publishers provide a teacher's guide for instructional purposes. These accompany the graded dictionaries and suggest appropriate approaches, correlated tasks, and activities for teacher usage. Likewise, many of the spelling and language textbooks include dictionary skills as part of their program. The important thing to be emphasized is, that as with any other skills area, there are definite learnings to be introduced and stressed in each level of schoolwork. This is not something incidental to be left to chance, but should be included regularly in the planning of units of work in reading, spelling, and language arts. The skills, then, can be used and reinforced in a meaningful setting when the student is involved in content areas of work: science, mathematics, history, geography, health.

Most school districts provide multiple copies of dictionaries for each classroom. Some even have a sufficient number for each student to have his own desk copy as a means of cultivating continued usage and nurturing the "dictionary habit." If each room has several levels of dictionaries in sufficient number to allow free use as need arises, it should be adequate. Since the students in any group will have varying needs and abilities at any given time, a coverage of *levels* seems more desirable than to have copies of all the same edition for all students in a given situation. Ideally, there must be easy access to an unabridged copy for the advanced or interested students' use.

Using encyclopedias. As soon as the child is beginning to use his reading abilities for functional uses, he can be introduced to the encyclopedia as an important reference source. In introducing a set, the teacher will explain its individual format, whether it is arranged alphabetically, by eras of time, or by large subject area with component topics. Some encyclopedias have an indexed volume for finding information in several cross-referenced volumes. Whatever the format, it should be carefully introduced for easy student use. Several parallels to the dictionary may be noted: alphabetized topics, guide words, cross references, both are books of facts, both serve as authoritative sources, and both need to be used as intended for optimum help.

At a time when technical knowledge is flourishing, and research is widely being carried out, these early learnings in the elementary grades are valuable in laying a foundation for discovering information, expanding learnings of important topics, carrying on independent library research activities—in short, for developing the kinds of inquiring minds that search and probe for satisfying answers.

Using the index and table of contents. Most textbooks have specific sections which are planned to facilitate the reader's use of them in obtaining information as easily and quickly as possible. Yet, many adults plunge into books without even scanning these important aids in order to find out how and where specific data or documentation is to be found. Likewise, many secondary and college students suddenly come to the realization that they need additional help in using reference tools. If they were introduced in early years to such helps as the table of contents, index, and glossary sections of textbooks, the coverage was either so light that they easily forgot it, or else not at all. Hence they spend valuable time and effort hunting aimlessly for information when these guides could furnish clues for immediate location. The teacher at any level can and should, when introducing a book, direct the student's attention to those listings of key words, topics, or subject areas especially prepared for guiding the reader in his search for specific material. This thorough knowledge of each author's organization and format can prove to be an invaluable help in the student's getting the message and information available in a given text. The teacher will often find suggestions for introducing the index and table of contents in the manuals of the textbooks and workbooks accompanying the series. Filmstrips or films, too, have been prepared as teaching aids to reference skills, as have transparencies and overlays for projection use in teaching groups. These provide explanations, illustrations, and activities for presenting these learnings with the additional interest element of audiovisual media.

The teacher in today's school is faced with more than just teaching a body of facts or knowledge. The contemporary task is in preparing and teaching students how to find knowledge when it is needed with as much ease as possible. This facility is far more valuable than merely storing up knowledge as some additive process to be drawn from at some future time. With the modern explosion of all fields of knowledge, it is impossible to think that students can accumulate enough learning to suffice them for life. Education must be viewed as a process rather than a product.

The card catalogue. Frequently graduate students in the college or university scene admit reluctantly that they have never actually learned to adequately use many of the tools of the library. These learnings begin first of all with the shelving arrangements, and the way books are categorized for easy selection. The first experience for very young children is to discover where the "Z" or easy to read books are kept. Later they will learn to differentiate between the fiction and nonfiction sections. Fiction is shelved in alphabetical order of the author's last name, while nonfiction is arranged according to the Dewey Decimal System or Library of Congress Classification. The following general numbers give broad clues for finding materials within a broad category:

000 — General Works
100 — Philosophy
200 — Religion
300 — Social Sciences
400 — Language
500 — Pure Science
600 — Applied Science
700 — Arts and Recreation
800 — Literature
900 — Biography, Geography, and History

Even young children can be introduced to the card catalogue and its various keys for finding specific works. They should be introduced to the author card, the title card, the subject card, and the "See also" cross-reference listings for related subjects. Various other types of listings can be used as they are available: (1) The Reader's Guide, (2) Yearbooks, (3) Biographical Dictionaries, (4) Geographical Sources, (5) Handbooks, (6) Manuals, (7) Bibliographies, and (8) Audiovisual Catalogues. Certainly all children will not use these frequently in the elementary grades, but if such holdings are in the school or public library where they will be working, it is well for them to be made aware of such helpful tools.

Specialized Reading

A third area of the study skills is concerned with certain specialized skills in reading. These include:

- The learning of specialized vocabulary which belongs specifically to each of the content areas of the curriculum in both elementary and secondary schools. In each subject there are words and terms which need learning: the science terms, the math vocabulary, the special language of the social sciences. Even in such areas as physical education, there is a certain amount of necessary reading which involves words and terms with discrete meanings as they are used in that phase of learning. The instructors in these areas, if the students are in a departmentalized program, will share some of the responsibility for teaching these terms, but the reading teacher will also help in this regard. The teacher who works in a self-contained classroom, will of course, be the sole instructional source to the particular class with which she works.

- Reading graphs, maps, tables, charts, and figures as part of the content area learning experiences is another important area of instruction which belongs in the area of elementary reading. True, many of these specialized tasks will be introduced and taught as part of several of the subject material assignments; but these competencies are actually reading skills and need teaching just as any other facet of the program does. These distinctive skills which are frequently needed by the young student as he works in different kinds of learning materials become an important segment of the reading program. No elementary teacher should feel that the job is completed just because a reading period has been scheduled daily in a selected reading book. It remains for the teacher, also, to give additional care and guidance in direct learning experiences which develop these specialized reading skills. Here there is no pleasurable narrative to carry the young student along in recreational reading, but a purposive objective—to get information, retain it, perhaps follow some directions, answer specific questions, organize and present facts, figures, or explanations. There may be a whole spectrum of tasks requiring specialized reading tasks basic to success. Hence this plea that reading teachers recognize this important phase of instruction and carefully plan for a variety of meaningful activities which will provide a setting for introducing these specialized study skills. Further, to assess progress in the use of such abilities, and reteach and review them frequently is of equal importance.

A word should also be said here relative to the concepts which young readers meet in these specialized areas of content materials. The learning of the specific vocabulary is important, indeed, but the teacher must also be aware of the concept load of the texts. The levels of reasoning required in handling some of these materials are often advanced and the student will need help and direction to be able to grasp and assimilate the content. It should be noted that each of the subject areas has its own particular patterns of reading. For example note the following:

1. *Arithmetic.* The student will need to:
   Read numerical symbols, singly and in combination.
   Read various kinds of graphs—bar, line, and circle.
   Read for following directions in problem solving.
   Read for information to explain new processes.
   Read illustrative materials—bills, accounts, tables.
   Read story problems involving a number of purposes—to get the setting of the problem; to get the data of the problem; to discover what he is to do or solve for; to sort out extraneous material; to decide what process he is to use.
2. *Youth Literature.* As soon as the child can begin to read, he must be given opportunities and encouragement to select from the great body of children's literature, the trade books; but here again he will find varying patterns of materials which include beautifully illustrated picture books, with little text; short storybooks at all levels; poetry in various forms—haiku, limericks, couplets, cinquains, free verse, lyric and epic poems; biographies of famous and contemporary figures; plays, dialogues, monologues, dramatic scripts; short fiction works, novels, mysteries, story collections; interesting nonfiction stories and books dealing with numerous topics and areas.
   The young reader will soon discover the wide range of materials and styles used in each of these types of materials commonly called juvenile literature.
3. *Science.* In reading the science materials the student will be introduced to reading by giving directions for experiments to be done which describe formulas to be followed, loaded with facts, details, and explanations; diagrams, classifications; descriptions of scientific problem-solving tasks; technical details for understanding scientific processes.
4. *History and Geography.* In using the materials for the social sciences, the student will cover a wide range of readings which can include simple narratives giving historical data; the lives of people and their accomplishments; analytical materials relating to cause-effect relations; content requiring comparison/contrast understandings; reports containing chronological and sequential orders of events and dates; varied readings requiring critical reading skills—fact and opinions, differing and sometimes conflicting viewpoints of the same happenings, propaganda, principles, theories, debatable practices; technical reading and interpretation of informative data from almanacs, atlases, charts, graphs, maps, globes.

This brief résumé of the varieties of materials and skills requisite to content area reading should suffice to alert the upper primary, intermediate, junior high, and secondary teacher of reading to the requisite competencies basic to success by students at these levels.

SUMMARY

This chapter has covered a wide spectrum of reading skills:

1. Word Recognition Skills with its numerous subcategories of (1) the Phonics Analysis Skills involving the consonants and vowels, and (2) the Structural Analysis Skills with the major components of words and their variant forms, principles of syllabizing, and patterns of words in our language.
2. Development of Sight Vocabulary and the importance of visual process in reading.
3. The Comprehension Skills which include (1) Literal Reading, (2) Interpretative Reading, (3) Critical Reading, and (4) Specific Reading with a number of subskills for each component, each of which focuses ultimately on the affective responses from appreciative reading.
4. The Vocabulary Building Competencies which are based on the student's listening and speaking vocabularies, and include the facets of (1) Recognition Clues, (2) Definitional Clues, and (3) Linguistic Clues.
5. The Reference or Study Skills, building on the other skills areas and utilizing (1) Purposeful Reading, (2) Reference Tools, and (3) Specialized Reading relating primarily to the content areas and the need for knowing how to approach them.

THE MODIFIED MODULAR APPROACH FOR STUDENTS

The following suggested learning approach is prepared for your use in working through this section of your course. It is an alternative approach for increased on-site involvement with actual school children in the classroom.

Behavioral Objectives

At the completion of the suggested learning experiences included in this module, you should be able to:

1. Identify the basic skills categories for reading as outlined in the skills continuum of the Program of Reading (used in the school you are assigned, or as per the author's list).
2. Select a particular skills area of reading, and list the component abilities with 90 percent accuracy as outlined in the chapter.
3. Develop a Weekly Reading Lesson Plan based on a behavioral objective(s) as per the Model suggested.
4. Write behavioral objectives containing specified variables (5) based on stated reading skills, the model provided by the instructor being the means of evaluation.

5. Develop an instructional plan, using the instructor's model with six parts, for teaching a lesson to introduce or strengthen a specified reading skill.
6. Administer a placement or level test from a reading program currently being used in the assigned school to determine a student's reading placement as specified by the Instructor's Manual.
7. Teach a planned lesson for skills development, the model lesson plan being the instrument for assessment.
8. Use professional terminology relating to basic reading skills as demonstrated on a written vocabulary task; the definitions as stated in *A Glossary of Reading Terms* (see Part Six).

Learning Experiences

In completing this module, it will be necessary for you to be involved in a variety of learning experiences which will familiarize you with the basic reading skills. Certain of these experiences are designated as prerequisites, others offer you alternative options.

1. Attend an introductory seminar conducted by the university instructor, time and place to be announced.
2. Obtain the Teacher's Manual for the basic reading program being used in your assigned school and for the level of teaching you are involved in. Read the manual noting: (1) the stated teaching objectives of the program; (2) an analysis of the program's skills sequence; (3) the means of evaluation provided in the program materials; (4) the teaching strategies and activities employed. (The reading notes may be handed in to the instructor or shared with your intern group at a specified time.)
3. Use the Weekly Lesson Plan model and outline a projected week's instruction. (See figure 8.7.)
4. Use the Model Lesson Plan form to develop a specific skills based reading lesson. (See figure 8.8.)
5. Teach a reading group using your Weekly Plan and including a lesson developed in Task 4.
6. Observe a reading lesson directed by your master teacher and fill out the Reading Skills Analysis Form for the lesson.
7. Choose *one* of the following authorities for further basic reading:

   - Bush, Clifford L., and Huebner, Mildred. *Strategies for Reading in the Elementary School*, Macmillan, 1970. Chapters 4, 5, and 6, pp. 48–126. (Skim for content.)
   - Durkin, Delores. *Teaching Them to Read*, Allyn & Bacon, 1970. Chapters 13 and 14, pp. 322–402. (Skim for content.)

Intern Checklist

Name _____ Beginning Date _____

I. **Learning Experiences:**

1. **Seminar Attended:** Date _____ _____
(Faculty Initial)

2. **Readings: Author:** _____

Chapters: _____ Date _____

3. **Obtained copy Reading Program:** _____ Date _____

4. **Obtained Teacher's Manual:** _____ Date _____

Name of Reading Program: _____

5. **Developed Weekly Plan:** _____ Date _____

6. **Designed Lesson Plan:** _____ Date _____

7. **Taught Reading Lesson:** _____ Date _____

_____
(Supervisor's Signature)

8. **Observation Date:** _____ **Analysis Done** _____

Type of Lesson? _____ Date _____

II. **Other Activity:** _____

III. **Postassessment: Date Attempted:** _____ Score _____

Completion Date: _____ _____
(Intern's Signature)

_____
(Faculty Signature)

NOTE: This is a model to be completed as a checklist for part of your postassessment for this module. Keep accurate records, get signatures when necessary, and then clip a similar form to the final evaluation.

Figure 8.5

Reading Lesson Observation: Analysis

Name _____ Observation Date _____

Teacher Observed _____

School _____ Grade _____

Instructional Objective: _____

_____

Behavioral Objective(s): _____

_____

Basic Skill Involved: _____

Material(s) Used: _____

_____

_____

Activity(ties) Used in Lesson: _____

_____

_____

Size of Group Observed: _____

Subskills Involved in Lesson: _____

_____

_____

_____

Comments:

_____   _____
     (Teacher's Signature)   (Intern's Signature)

Figure 8.6

Weekly Reading Lesson Plan

Teacher's Name: _____   Group or Class: _____

Instructional Goal Code No.: _____   Date: _____

Entry Skills: _____

Behavioral Objectives Code No.: _____

_____

_____

      Materials   **Teaching Steps**

Teaching Materials

Reinforcement Materials

Review Materials

Evaluation and Comments

Figure 8.7

Suggested Model for Preparing Lesson Plans

I.   Name: _____ Date: _____ Grade: _____ No.: _____

     Subject: _____ Text: _____

II. Instructional Objective: _____

    _____

    Performance Objective: _____

    _____

III. Assignment: _____

    _____

    Materials:

    _____

    _____

    _____

IV. Procedures:

    1. _____

    2. _____

    3. _____

    4. _____

V.   Related Activities:

    1. _____

    2. _____

VI. Evaluation: _____

    _____

    _____

VII. Ongoing Activities: _____

    _____

    _____

    Comments:

Figure 8.8

Postassessment   *NOTE: The purpose of this task is twofold: (1) to assess your*
No. 1   *present strengths in this area of reading instruction, and (2) to*
identify areas of weakness in which you will need more effort. Read each section
carefully.

1. Most authorities agree that there are several broad skills areas to be developed
   in reading instruction. Identify five of these. (10 points maximum—2 pt/skill)
2. One of the more recent terms being used by reading people is "Skills Continuum." Describe what the term means, and then choose one broad area with
   subcategories to illustrate the concept. (15 points maximum)
3. In emphasizing "teacher accountability" educators are recognizing the importance of properly stated *behavioral objectives.* Choose a specific reading
   skill taught in the elementary school and write a behavioral objective following
   standard format. (10 points maximum)
4. In planning for a specific reading lesson, the teacher should think through various steps of her instructional time. List the necessary steps (7) to be included
   in a well-planned lesson. (10 points maximum)

Postassessment   *NOTE: This is to evaluate your progress and knowledge on*
No. 2   *this Module. You have been working with Basic Reading*
Skills, and now it is time to assess your exit behaviors and determine your level of
performance.

1. Competency-Based Education, many agree, must be built on clearly and correctly stated performances which can be observed and measured. Reading
   skills can well be scrutinized in this manner. Select a basic skill, state an instructional objective, and then list the components (variables) you would want
   to include in writing a behavioral (performance) objective. (15 points maximum)
2. Based on your readings as well as your actual classroom work, list the major,
   or broad, skills areas (5) to be taught in reading instruction. (10 points maximum—2 pt/area)
3. From your experiences in working with the Reading Program, select a Basic
   Skill and then list under that heading as many sub- or component skills as you
   are able. (10 points maximum)
4. Here are some terms which are often met by reading people when considering
   reading skills. Define each briefly. (25 points maximum—5 pt/term)
   a. structural analysis   d. schwa
   b. decoding   e. etymology
   c. comprehension

9 SUGGESTIONS, ACTIVITIES, MATERIALS, AND MEDIA FOR PLANNING CREATIVE READING INSTRUCTION

Creative teaching is the key to a successful learning situation for both the instructors and the students. When fresh new ideas are gendered in the planning, the result is interested, excited learners involved and participating in imaginative activities. This often proves to be an incentive which sparks a desire to know and to do. Such interaction with stimulating media and teaching approaches "turns on" children under the guidance of an enthusiastic, vibrant learning specialist.

The authors desire, in this chapter of the text, to provide unique, suggestive ideas which may be used to reinforce the reading skills. However, more than that, because of the shortness of space here and the impossibility of including a sufficient number of such suggestions, it is hoped that these may serve as germinators of many more such teachable ongoing activators. By no means are these to be thought of as being originals from the authors, for how does one discover something that some other person has not thought of or done? These have been gathered through years of working with children in the classroom as well as working with teachers at all levels.

Their inclusion is for the purpose of providing suggestive activities for developing high-interest, purposive experiences for reading instruction. These stimulators may be used in the classroom with an entire class, a reading or activity group, or some with individual children. Hopefully they will provide enrichment for more able students, pleasure and success for remedial learners, and meaning and variety for the children who are moving forward at the expected level.

THE IMPORTANCE AND VALUE OF USING READING ACTIVITIES

It should be remembered, that any recreational activity that is to be used for furthering education must have a clear purpose for use with children at their

214

appropriate level of work. Such teaching-learning materials should likewise be matched to the optimum time and environment for the desired learning. Such activities will prove of maximum value only as they are planned and adapted by the instructor to balance and enhance the curriculum for the diagnosed, specific needs of children. Further, probably the greatest accrual from the use of educational games is that they provide an opportunity for using and transferring previously learned concepts into pragmatic experiences. This utilization of previously learned skills in a relaxed, recreational, pleasure situation allows children to enjoy learning without stress or fear of failure save the competitive dislike of losing the game. Such activities should be planned so that there is a maximum opportunity for each participant to respond frequently in a controlled time situation, and also to allow each child opportunity to see and hear and assess each response of any player. The teacher, aide, or helper who directs the activity should be alert to guide in correcting wrong responses lest the habituated skills be negatized.

Not only do the children involved profit from these types of enrichment activities, but teachers as well have an opportunity to observe and evaluate student performance easily and incidentally. Once the students know the mechanics and rules of the game, the teacher can give full attention to each as he performs and thus assess his competencies in a natural, relaxed setting. This type of continuing diagnosis via direct observation is valuable in not only evaluating progress, but also in discovering areas of additional need as a guide for instructional planning.

Not only can an enriched program of reading instruction help to form reading skills habits and become the basis of continuing observational assessment, but such an activity-expanded program becomes an interesting, varied classroom technique. This change-of-pace approach provides freshness and variety in the regular class sessions of instruction and can be utilized in a number of situations which lead into teaching times as well as bridging from one skills learning to another, or from one type of reading lesson to another, or even from a totally different curriculum experience as an introduction to a more formalized lesson period. The flexibility of reading games or activities also provides for varying group sizes in ongoing learnings which free the teacher for individualized or small group situations.

Inasmuch as a number of very fine authors have compiled and published recent books which deal entirely with games and activities, the present writers feel that it is sufficient to alert the intern to these sources rather than seek to include in the present chapter sufficient examples to be worthwhile. The following list of such works should provide the intern with information for finding and using some of these valuable little books.

Several Recent Reading Activities Books

1. California Reading Association, *Fresh Teaching Ideas for Teaching Reading*, 1970. This little book is exactly what is stated in the title, a compilation of instructional ideas contributed by more than 200 professors, consultants, special-

The creative classroom provides for the recreational and pleasurable aspects of reading. This reading corner illustrates a thoughtful teacher's invitation to students to read.

ists, and classroom teachers who are involved with reading. The suggested activities and games cover a wide spectrum of skills including Auditory Analysis, Phonetic Analysis, Structural Analysis, Alphabetizing, Sight Words, Vocabulary Comprehension, Sentence Comprehension, Paragraph Comprehension, Story Comprehension, and Remediation.

2. Selma E. Herr, *Learning Activities for Reading*, 2nd edition, Wm. C. Brown Company Publishers, 1970. An activity book covering nearly fifty different phases of reading instruction. Teachers will find interesting materials and techniques for activating students of reading at all levels of the elementary school. Numerous illustrations offer excellent clues for following the suggestions for developing materials and media. A very practical and useful tool for student/intern or in-service teacher.

3. Sandra Nina Kaplan, Jo Ann Butom Kaplan, Sheila Kunishima Madsen, and Bette K. Taylor, *Change for Children, Ideas and Activities for Individualizing Learning*, Goodyear Publishing Company, 1973. Although this recent publica-

tion deals with many areas of teaching in the elementary school setting, there are numerous usable ideas for reading instruction. The chief focus of the authors is on room environment and organization. The development and use of learning centers in meeting individual student's learning needs is thoroughly covered with many descriptions of media and teaching strategies for each type of center suggested. This is a fine "How to Do It" activity book for implementing classroom change and activities.

4. David H. Russell and Etta E. Karp, *Reading Aids Through the Grades* (Three Hundred Developmental Reading Activities), Bureau of Publications, Teachers College, Columbia University, 1959. Although this little instructional guide has been around for a number of years, it has, and still continues, to offer teachers innovative ideas for varying the reading program. Basic skills and learning areas are grouped in four categories: The Readiness Program, the Primary Grades, the Intermediate Grades, and the Higher Grades. Nearly every facet of learning at these levels is included, and numerous ideas for strengthening skills and maintaining growth as well as introduction to sequential skills is covered.

5. Evelyn Spache, *Reading Activities for Child Involvement*, Allyn & Bacon, Inc., 1972. This is a unique collection of some 500 suggested activities for reinforcing reading skills. The author has provided a rationale for each skill, stating its importance, its need for reinforcement, an understandable definitive description, and the performance objectives for each. Clear directions for making materials and using them is an important part of this usable little book. The coverage of all skills areas is excellent: readiness, word perception, language and vocabulary development, location skills, content reading skills, and comprehension/interpretation skills.

6. Stockton Unified School District, Stockton, California, *Gamble, Games And Manipulatives Bring Learning Enjoyment*, 1972, compiled by Cheryl Crothers, Chris Edwards, Marie Dhority, and Barbara Waters. This is a fine example of the development of curriculum materials by local school districts and provided for use by the teaching staff. These teachers feel that children learn to cope with printed words through a variety of ways: via audio, visual, and tactile media. In order to understand and retain abstract concepts requisite to reading success, they have provided many suggestions for the developing of and constructing of many manipulative devices. The handbook offers a wide variety of suggestions for teachers desiring to create materials for varying the paper-and-pencil approach to the skills areas of reading. These games and enrichment activities are for the enhancement of instruction of any reaching approach: basal, language experience, linguistic, phonic.

This list of recent books of suggestions for teaching activities in reading instruction can alert the teacher/intern to the number of such publications currently available. Most of the materials to be used are easily obtainable, and the preparation is simple enough to be feasible for even the busy teacher or student to create. The cost of making and using such media is relatively small.

On the other hand, publishers and commercial firms have become increasingly aware of the salability of such products in the modern public school. Hence many activity kits, games, recordings, manipulatives, and such teaching devices have become commonly available at most any outlet source. The following short list of some of the better-known materials will provide examples of the variety of teaching aids that can be purchased for classroom use.

Commercial Aids, Devices, and Games

1. *Adhere-O-Learning Aids*, Adhere-O-Learning Aids, Wilmette, Ill. Flannel-board cutouts for phonics learnings.
2. *Basic Phrase Cards*, Garrard Publishing Company, Champaign, Ill. Flash cards using the basic word phrases.
3. *Consonant Lotto and Vowel Lotto*, Garrard Publishing Company, Champaign, Ill. Simple card game for learning basic consonant/vowel sounds.
4. *Controlled Reader Materials*, Educational Development Laboratories, Huntington, N.Y. A pacing machine with interesting filmstrip stories, quizzes.
5. *Dolch Basic Sight Cards*, Garrard Publishing Company, Champaign, Ill. Flash cards of the basic vocabulary words.
6. *Dolch Basic Phrase Cards*, Garrard Publishing Company, Champaign, Ill. Flash cards using the basic vocabulary in phrases.
7. *Everyday Language Skills*, F. Owen Publishing Company, Dansville, N.Y. Graded charts for reading skills.
8. *Flash-X*, Educational Development Laboratories, Huntington, N.Y. Individual tachistoscopic device: words, symbols, etc.
9. *Go Fish*, Remedial Education Center, Washington, D.C. A reading game.
10. *Group Sounding Game*, Garrard Publishing Company, Champaign, Ill. A fun approach for small group activity learning basic sounds.
11. *Language Master*, Bell and Howell, Inc. Magnetic tape word cards for recording and playing back.
12. *Linguistic Blocks Series*, Scott, Foresman & Company, Chicago. Lettered blocks for making words, phrases, etc.
13. *Listen and Do*, Houghton Mifflin Company, Boston, Mass. Recordings with accompanying work sheets.
14. *Phonics We Use, Learning Games Kit*, Lyons and Carnahan Co., Chicago, Ill. A fine kit of games involving vowels, consonants, digraphs, diphthongs, blends, etc.
15. *Phono-Visual Materials*, Phono-Visual Products, Washington, D.C. Visual aids combined with an aural base for reading.
16. *See and Say Consonant Game*, Milton Bradley Company, Springfield, Mass. An oral-aural approach for learning the regular consonant sounds.

17. *Sight Vocabulary Solitaire*, Gerrard Publishing Company, Champaign, Ill. A solo activity.
18. *Short Vowel Drill*, Remedial Education Center, Washington, D.C. Interesting activity for strengthening knowledge for short vowel sounds.
19. *Syllabascope*, Woodcrafters Guild, Washington, D.C. A word analysis activity with cards provided.
20. *Tach-X*, Educational Development Laboratories, Huntington, N.Y. Letter, numeral, word filmstrips for use with tachistoscope.
21. *Word Analysis Practice Cards*, Harcourt, Brace & World, Inc. New York. An inductive approach using structural clues for decoding.
22. *Word Wheels*, Webster, McGraw-Hill, St. Louis, Mo. Comprehensive drill activities covering all phases of word structure.

This is by no means a complete listing of the many, many commercially prepared materials available to classroom and teacher, but is a selection which covers the types of enrichment materials which can be purchased currently. During the recent funding which was made available under the Elementary and Secondary Education Acts, many schools acquired a considerable amount of this type of merchandise, and numerous classroom closets have sizeable quantities stacked and stored awaiting use. Most media centers, as well, have been able to purchase such teaching hardware and software, and it is being used by teachers in expanding their instructional programs with individuals, small groups, and/or total class modes.

COMMON MATERIALS FOR TEACHING AN ALTERNATIVE PROGRAM

Sometimes interns/teachers need just an alert to spark their imaginations and thinking to realize the vast amounts of usable, everyday materials which can provide an alternative approach for reading instruction. The following list of common articles and environmental materials is an example of such. Certainly these are note books, workbooks, flash cards, or similar materials, but the creative teacher will be able to find opportunities to use them productively in incidental teaching situations for stimulating students to read. These are suggested for use *with* a developmental program for enlivening and interesting students in reading many kinds of materials and are merely representative of the resource material available.

1. *Advertisements:* From newspapers, magazines, and catalogues. Note descriptions, dimensions, prices, comparisons, and contrasts.
2. *Advertising:* On billboards, signs, shop windows, truck sides, and atop buildings.
3. *Airline schedules:* Note places, times, descriptions, connecting points, and alternate routes.
4. *Bulletin boards:* Read the captions, questions, descriptions, bookjackets.

5. *Calendars:* Note the illustrations, important dates, anniversaries, happenings.
6. *Catalogues:* From merchandising houses and mail-order stores.
7. *Classified sections:* Of magazines, weeklies, and newspapers. Read personals, lost and found, employment ads.
8. *Comic strips:* Single cartoons, strips, and books.
9. *Directions:* From models, science experiments, repairs.
10. *Directories:* Telephone, personnel, and special groups. Note names, addresses, variant spellings, etc.
11. *Do-it-yourself kits and materials:* The descriptions, directions, materials.
12. *Driver's manuals:* Rules, laws, signals, requirements.
13. *Envelopes:* The addresses, postmarks, stamps.
14. *Excerpts:* From articles, stories, descriptions, essays.
15. *Familiar objects:* Note names, manufacturers, dates, patents, contents.
16. *Field trip reports:* The summaries, sequences, events.
17. *Filmstrips:* Read the captions, labels, directions, explanations as film is turned.
18. *Games:* The boxes, directions, alternative rules, plays and combinations possible.
19. *Greeting cards:* All kinds—birthday, Christmas, New Year's, get-well—with their verses and sentiments.
20. *Grocery materials:* Cans, boxes, cartons, bottles, packages, and labels of all kinds. Use to make a shopping list.
21. *Handbooks:* Simple guides for making things or doing things.
22. *House advertisements:* Note locations, streets, areas, and descriptions.
23. *Holiday materials:* Posters, descriptions, prices, places, events, participants.
24. *Headlines:* Use just the bold-faced print of newspapers, magazines, posters.
25. *Illustrations:* Pictures, graphs, tables, drawings, photographs with captions or descriptions.
26. *Indexes:* For any common subject or area: from books, complete volumes, sections.
27. *Indicators:* All kinds of signalling devices, guages, thermometers, barometers.
28. *Insignias:* Make a collection of Clubs, Lodges, Groups, trademarks, military, sports.
29. *Invitations:* To parties, events, socials.
30. *Jackets from books:* Use instead of the book for interest, author, title, illustrator, and short résumé.
31. *Jingles:* Familiar rhymes, limericks, and short poetry.
32. *Jokebooks:* Any bit of humorous anecdote in newspapers, youth publications, magazines, or books.
33. *Labels:* From clothing, food, appliances, or furniture which give information and directions.
34. *License plates:* Note numeral combinations, letters, states, and dates.
35. *Letters:* Personal, business, informal correspondence.

36. *Library material:* The Dewey Decimal System Breakdown, card catalogue, reading guides, indexes, shelving codes.
37. *Logs:* Of a trip, voyage, camp-out, expedition, field trip.
38. *Lunchroom signs:* The foods, prices, daily menu.
39. *Lyrics of familiar songs:* Folksongs, westerns, populars, ballads.
40. *Magazines:* Stories, jokes, poetry, advertisements, articles, news items, pictures, and captions.
41. *Mail:* Post that comes—brochures, advertisements, announcements, notices, schedules, periodicals.
42. *Manuals:* The guides, instructions, and handbooks for any subject or activity plus for ordinary usages.
43. *Manuscripts:* For plays, presentations, books, articles, assemblies.
44. *Maps:* Not only in textbooks, but road maps, maps and guides for travel, trips, foreign places, tours.
45. *Menus:* School cafeteria or restaurant.
46. *Mimeographed materials:* Covering any subject and any length to provide a different media for reading.
47. *Movie information:* Titles, actors, plot lines, settings, schedules, theatres, ratings, directors.
48. *Motorcycles:* Advertisements, descriptions, stories.
49. *Museum brochures:* Display information, subjects, people, guides and locations, eras.
50. *Newspapers:* All sections—society, vital statistics, ads, sports, entertainment, education, news—for names, places, events, people.
51. *Neighborhood bulletins, newsheets:* For announcements, happenings of interest, schedules, honors.
52. *Notebooks:* Containing notes, outlines, summaries, quotations, data.
53. *Notices:* This could be school notices from teachers, administration, office. Printed bulletins from public sources: sales, events of interest, scheduled happenings.
54. *Obituaries:* Of famous people from newspapers, newsmagazines.
55. *Observation reports:* All kinds—classroom, playground, community, scientific, medical, behavioral.
56. *Occupational information bulletins:* Descriptions of jobs, requirements, openings, advantages and limitations, regions and locations.
57. *Office materials:* Announcements, regulations, warnings, take-home bulletins.
58. *Opinionaires:* Survey results from any level of education, community, society.
59. *Original or creative writings:* Individual, group, or class compositions on any theme, topic, or subject and making use of any literary style: poetry, prose, fiction, nonfiction.
60. *Overhead projections:* Of student work, examples or illustrative pictures, data, graphs, tables, or of teacher-given points of interest or information.

61. *Packages:* From grocery or department store. Note brand names, contents, merchants, guarantees, warnings, and directions.
62. *Paintings:* Works of art—all media—with captions, artists, titles.
63. *Pamphlets:* Descriptions, information, instructions, on most any subject and/ or area of interest.
64. *Parliamentary rules and procedures:* For use in class meetings, assemblies, introductions, presentations.
65. *Passports:* Read data, information, visas, endorsements, places, official names.
66. *Passenger lists:* From tours, flights, passages, expeditions, trips.
67. *Patriotic materials:* Pledge of Allegiance, Declaration of Independence, Gettysburg Address, Preamble to Constitution, Laws and Legislation, Bills, Rules and Regulations, Creeds, Statements, Speeches.
68. *Periodicals:* For all ages and levels—news, literature, humor, continued stories, dramatic scripts.
69. *Pets materials:* Their food, their care, description.
70. *Photographs, albums, reports, illustrations:* Using the captions, descriptions, or explanations for reading.
71. *Picture postcards:* Noting the places, details, and descriptive notes as well as personal messages from the sender.
72. *Plaques:* Inscriptions, memorabilia, dedications, presentations, honor selections, memberships.
73. *Plays:* Scripts for dramatic participation, role playing, pantomime, radio and TV casting, assemblies, programs, special occasions.
74. *Play situations:* Activities, games, competitions, recreational events, playground fun, physical education—reading rules, requirements, sequences.
75. *Plots:* Of books, stories, situations, plays, musicals.
76. *Pockets:* On books, AV media, check-out equipment and materials which give data.
77. *Postage stamp albums:* Descriptions, dates, places, people, commemorative data, amounts.
78. *Postmarks:* On letters, cards, magazines, papers, advertising.
79. *Posters:* In the classroom, library, hallways, offices, playground—announcing, describing, inviting, campaigning.
80. *Predictions:* Horoscopes, future happening information, astrological information.
81. *Price tags:* For comparing, making up shopping lists, work on numerical values.
82. *Principal's rulebook:* The Do's and Don'ts of conduct and deportment while at school.
83. *Programs:* The handouts at assemblies, plays, shows, exhibitions, competitions. Read for names and roles.
84. *Proofreading:* Any written material—editing, correcting, evaluating correctness.

85. *Puppetry scripts and directions:* Booklets or scripts on making and using puppets, and dialogues or monologues for presentations.
86. *Puzzles:* Requiring reading of directions for working, or crosswords, codes, jumbled scripts.
87. *Questionnaires:* Inquiries, surveys, forms to be filled out, opinions to be stated.
88. *Radio logs:* For stations, programs, times, dates.
89. *Railway schedules:* Of tours, regular runs, connections, times, dates.
90. *Rebus materials:* For getting context clues in reading.
91. *Recipes and cookbooks:* For measurements, sequence of process, new vocabulary words.
92. *Reports:* Of class meetings, field trips, experiments, projects, activities.
93. *Record album covers:* Titles, performers, lyrics.
94. *Recreation materials:* Posters, announcements, competitions, camps, programs, results, awards.
95. *Real estate signs:* Advertisements, descriptions, agents, addresses.
96. *Riddles-quizzes, puns, and other word games:* Fun with words.
97. *Sales slips, receipts, contracts:* Technical and factual materials related to merchandising.
98. *Scenarios:* For TV and radio productions, plays.
99. *Schedules:* Of school events, community happenings, room activities.
100. *Scout (girl and boy) handbooks:* For awards, creeds, procedures.
101. *Scrapbooks:* Of pictures, events, topics, history, geography, family happenings, community events.
102. *Seasonal happenings:* Pictures, announcements, representations, festivals, symbolism.
103. *Secretarial reports:* Minutes, notes, recommendations, motions, pollings.
104. *Sentiments:* For special occasions, anniversaries, presentations, receptions.
105. *Serials:* Either in periodical or book form.
106. *Signs:* Road, street, buildings, traffic, room and office, classroom.
107. *Skits:* For reading or presentation.
108. *Slogans:* For elections, projects, campaigns, groups, clubs, advertising candidates.
109. *Snack bar posters:* Signs, menu offerings, prices, orders.
110. *Social events:* Invitations, announcements, reports, descriptions, calendars.
111. *Solutions:* To puzzles, games, problems, riddles.
112. *Songs:* The words of familiar melodies often make good reading.
113. *Souvenirs:* Realia, keepsakes, remembrances, curios in displays with descriptive information.
114. *Speeches:* Addresses, reports, introductions, presentations, for special occasions in school and community.
115. *Sports materials:* In newspapers, sports magazines, Sunday supplements, school newspapers, announcements of events, rallies, games.
116. *Stamps:* Postage, rubber, seals, signatures.

117. *Statistics:* Tabular and quantitative information relating to a specific topic or situation.
118. *Syllabuses:* Class schedules, curriculum areas, statement outlines.
119. *Synopses:* Of stories, articles, plays, literature.
120. *Task cards:* Contracts, individual learning units, job cards, for modular scheduling or departmentalized classes.
121. *Tax forms:* Revenue reports.
122. *TV guides:* For program scheduling, descriptions, casts.
123. *Telegrams:* Succinct, terse language—summaries.
124. *Term papers:* Original reports, documents.
125. *Tests:* For all purposes of qualifying: driver's license, performance speed, especially noting directions and regulations.
126. *Theater programs and advertisements:* Posters, casts, synopses, settings.
127. *Theater tickets:* Informational data.
128. *Thesaurus:* Word knowledge, vocabulary expansion, synonyms, and related terms.
129. *Tickets:* Traffic citations, admissions to performances, sales slips, sports events, dramas.
130. *Timetables:* For buses, trains, ferries, flights, passages, tours, trips, outings.
131. *Toys:* Wrappings, descriptions, directions for assembling and using.
132. *Travel brochures:* Trip descriptions, city and area tour points of interest, places of interest, brief summaries of important events and special sites.
133. *Touring itineraries:* Schedules, places, accommodations, restaurants, inns, hotels, transportation facilities, and guide assistance.
134. *Treasure hunt lists:* Directions for finding articles, and further instructions in sequence.
135. *Tricks and magic:* Booklets of "How to Do" with descriptive information.
136. *Trip-tics:* Commercially prepared itineraries for auto travel—AAA schedules.
137. *Tubes:* Shaving cream, toothpaste, cosmetic, and medicinal; descriptions of usage, dosage, treatment, and guaranteed results.
138. *Tutoring material:* Directions for assisting and teaching another.
139. *Unique or unusual captions, titles, or subjects.*
140. *Valentines:* Humorous, rhymed, sentimental.
141. *Vehicle code book:* Regulations, signs, signals, laws, responsibilities, obligations, and prerequisites.
142. *Vending machines:* Products, costs, operating instructions, and limitations.
143. *Verses:* Couplets, limericks, jingles, quatrains, cinquains, haiku, ballads, epics, sonnets—all types of poetry.
144. *Vignettes:* Miniature character sketches, incidents, happenings in narrative form.
145. *Vocational folders:* Brochures with job descriptions, qualifications, remuneration, advantages and opportunities.

146. *Want-ads:* In newspapers and periodicals.
147. *Warranties:* Guarantees, claims, and character.
148. *Weather reports:* Predictions and changes.
149. *Wedding announcements, invitations, reports.*
150. *Whimsey:* Humorous, fanciful narrative.
151. *Who's Who listings:* For various professions and areas.
152. *Wills and testaments:* Real or fanciful such as class will.
153. *Wrappers:* Candy bar, popsicles, sandwiches, gum, nuts, or chips—for contents, amounts, descriptions.
154. *"Y" programs and schedules:* Sports, classes, camps.
155. *Zoo signs:* Descriptions of animals and their habitats.

Common as many of the above-listed materials may seem to be, the imaginative teacher will discover ways of providing many of them for use in the classroom, home, or school assignments. Many of them can be displayed or arranged in an interest center, learning station, or for incidental use as the need arises. They should often spark conversation, writing topics, or be used as a means of getting reluctant readers to examine and decipher their meaning and intent. Some students have developed such inhibiting barriers against books and the usual media, that it is nearly impossible to instruct them with traditional materials.

Certainly there is a wide divergence of applicability of some of these suggested alternative materials which would be inappropriate for some age levels. No attempt has been made by the authors to "grade" or classify them as to suitability for specific ability levels, but the creative teacher should be aware of many situations in which some of these different reading materials could be used for variety and activation. The next section will describe some activities in which some of these materials may be utilized in unique settings for developing language skills, especially reading.

ACTIVATING INDEPENDENT READING EXPERIENCES

The following suggested activities are certainly not intended to be used as *the* reading program, but are meant to help catch the attention of students. Once their interest is captured, their skills can be extended and developed. Such learning experiences hopefully may be more appealing and meaningful to young learners as an alternative to a more traditional program by itself.

Eye-Catchers and Interest-Arousers: A New Kind of Book Report

1. After reading your story, recast the characters from members of the class. Either rewrite the story placing classmates in the various character roles, or describe particular characters and specify why you think certain student friends fit the

role assigned. Exchange your rewritten stories or characterizations for others to read and discuss.

2. After reading a book or short story, decide how you will convince the class that this particular selection should go on the "Best Sellers List" of your classroom. Analyze what there is about it that makes it a candidate for becoming one of "The All-Time Greats."

3. As you read, think about the characters of your book or story. Let your imagination roam and feel that you are going to personally meet these "people." Decide which ones you would like to meet, which ones you would *not* like to meet, and those whom you would feel neutral about. What would you say to them? What would you like to do with them? Why did you feel this way?

4. Plan a "shopping trip" for Christmas gifts from the bookstore. Think about the book you are reading or have just read. Would you like to give this to a friend as a gift? To what type of person would you give it? Why did you choose this one? To whom would you not give it? Why? Write a letter to the person to whom you are going to "give" the book and tell him/her why you chose the book for him/her and what you liked about it that would appeal to them.

5. When you have finished your book, make "tongue depressor puppets" of the characters (stick puppets). Using a cardboard carton as a stage, give a show using the characters of your story and tell what is happening from the book or story you have read.

6. Use the titles or dust jackets of the books you have read and make a collage of them for a room display, bulletin board, or reading center decoration.

7. If you like art work, design a newspaper or magazine advertisement of your book. Your purpose will be to *sell* it to new readers and appeal to their sense of need for reading this same title.

8. While reading your book or story, or after completing it, write a letter to one of the characters involved. You may want to tell him/her how you feel about them and what they did, or how you reacted to a particular situation in which they were involved. Ask them questions about their behaviors, or why they played a certain role, or who or what influenced them to make certain decisions. You may wish to commend them or criticize them for certain actions.

9. Arrange a panel discussion from several people who have read the same book or story. Take "pro and con" positions about the plot, the style, the characters, the setting, and the outcomes. Discuss its merits, purposes, or message for today's young readers. Decide if the book should be selected for an "Award Winning List."

10. Pretend you are the author of the story or book you have just read. Find out as much as you can about the person and then prepare for a TV interview or "talk show." Be able to talk about yourself and your book. Why did you write it? What prompted the characters? the setting? the plot line?

11. When you have finished your story or book, think about the ending. Did it conclude the way you thought it should? What other endings might have oc-

curred? What influenced the outcome? Could it have ended otherwise? Re-write the ending as you may have wanted it to be, and share it with a group or the entire class.

12. Using a shoe box, construct a diorama of the main setting or a particular scene of your story or book. Visualize the buildings, the landscape, the positioning of characters and other objects as realistically, or as fancifully, as you can.

13. How did you "feel" about the story or book while you were reading it? When did you have these strong feelings? What were the emotions that you recall most clearly? Were you happy and did you laugh? Did you feel depressed or sad? How about being disappointed or disgusted? Did the story cause you to feel angry or impatient with the characters and situations? Why did you feel this way?

14. Decide that you will be the illustrator of a picture book. What characters did you most like to depict? Why did you have them look like you did? Which scene did you enjoy most while you were drawing or painting? Did you enjoy the author's story from which you drew your illustrations? Find out about "yourself," the book's illustrator, and be able to give some personal facts from your autobiographical data.

15. As you read your story, was there anybody in the characters who made you think of yourself and how you might have acted? Did you think of anybody you know as you read? What character made you think there was a similarity to them? This is called *identification* and *projection*. Why did you identify with a certain character? What feelings did you project with others? When, in the story, did you identify? What was the situation, or why did you feel very like the character?

16. Find pictures, or words, or scenes that remind you of the story you have just read. Make a poster or collage of these to depict the individuality and unique-ness of your book as you interpreted and "saw" it.

17. If you liked the book you read, think about the reasons why. Choose a charac-ter and make a "campaign" poster for him/her and ask voters to select or vote for your candidate. List specific reasons for their voting for this person and why he should be selected.

18. Pretend that you are on a selection committee for choosing the "best" book for sealing it in a vault or capsule to be opened a century later. What book would you pick? Why did you choose it? What about its message would you want future readers to share?

19. Write a letter to someone, imaginary or real, that you think would enjoy or ap-preciate your choice of "best" book. Write them a letter telling them why you selected the book and them, and what you think they will like about your favor-ite book.

20. Imagine that you are a movie scenario writer, and have been employed to write the scenes for your book. Decide which sets should be used. Will you need all the characters introduced by the author? What changes will be neces-

sary for filming? Which roles will you modify or delete? What can you cut, and yet tell an interesting story without marring the action?

21. Using a long strip of wrapping or butcher paper, make a "graffiti fence" for students to use in describing their book, its characters, or their reactions to it. Let it stay up for an extended time (several weeks) as they write on it after recreational or assigned reading.

22. Select the part of the book you found most exciting. Practice reading it, and then tape record the selection which was so interesting that you could hardly wait to hear the conclusion. Play it to the class as a "selling gimmick" so they will want to read it also.

23. Arrange for an author-emphasis week. After reading your book, write a letter to the author telling him/her what you liked most about the story. If there were things you thought about the book which should have been different, explain to the writer why. As different class members read their letters together, new writers will be introduced with their books.

24. Role play one of the characters of your book, and tell your friends all about yourself: your home, life, experiences, friends. Don't expose what happens to you at the conclusion of the book, but ask your peers to read all about you and discover your fate for themselves.

25. Assume you have been hired as a photographer by the author of the book to illustrate it with actual pictures. Decide on five or six of the best scenes you want to "take" and write them down. Then describe each scene in detail as you would capture it for best illustrating the important parts of the book.

26. When you have finished your book, think about the kinds of people who might *not* like it. Why would it not appeal to them? Are there specific incidents or characters to which they would react negatively? Is it the general philosophy or tone of the author?

27. Draw enlargements of the characters of your book, freehand or projector copied, and using either the projector or your drawings, introduce the characters one by one to your audience. Tell enough to interest the others to become acquainted with these "people" themselves.

28. Assume the role of movie director of the book you have just read. Select the "actors" from your classmates for each of the parts in the movie. Your job is then to convince the classmates that they should take the parts. Tell them why you chose them, why you think they are best fitted to fill the role. In other words, *sell* them the part and the book as well.

29. Prepare a short commercial for a TV appearance in which you will attempt to attract buyers for the book you have just read. Persuade as powerfully as possible in a brief appearance.

30. Imagine you are the local librarian who presents a brief review of a new book at intervals. Decide what you will say in your "spot announcement" on the radio: about the author, the book, the plot, the characters, the setting, and/or the conclusion.

31. Use the "cliff-hanging" device with your book. Lead up to a very crucial point in the narrative, then simply stop—tell no more. Your classmates will have to read it for themselves in order to discover the solution.

32. Write an actual script of a story or scenes from your book, assign parts and put on a dramatic production for the remainder of the class or another group, or as a program feature.

These are far removed from the traditional book report that has often done more to turn off readers than to encourage them. The ideas suggested here are not limited to any particular age or level of student. They can be adapted and modified by imaginative teachers to fit appropriate ages and types of reading materials. The plea, of course, is to interest young readers, and give them creative, meaningful outlets for sharing books with one another without the drag of an assigned résumé of the books read.

ORAL READING: PURPOSES AND ACTIVITIES

Despite recent opposition to its inclusion and use in the instructional program, oral reading has once again become a respectable facet of contemporary teaching. This is probably largely due to the emphasis from the linguists that language is an oral activity, and that all the skills of listening, reading, and writing are to be based on spoken communication. Even so, most readers spend much more time in silent rather than in oral reading; but there are situations and occasions when it is necessary to read aloud. Good oral reading, like good speaking, is a learned ability based on practice and habituation, hence to be an accomplished reader requires direction, correction, and instruction. So there is a definite place for teaching oral reading skills in the school setting, *but* it must be for a significant purpose.

Purposes for Oral Reading

As indicated, when we read orally, there must be a reason for our doing so. For example, we prepare some materials to be read to a group of our peers, a social group, a class group of professionals, or in an organization. Often these are short, prepared announcements, bulletins, minutes, resolutions. Or we may read a telephone message, a definition from the dictionary, an interesting item to share from a newspaper or periodical, a snatch of poetry or humor from a book, a critique of some production—whatever, our purpose is to share with others something that we feel is valuable, interesting, amazing, or humorous. Some have seen oral reading as having a variety of purposes including (1) to entertain—audience reading, (2) to set a feeling tone, create a mood, (3) to share for a social or personal response, and (4) to relay information, a conveying of fact or data. This, then indicates that many speaking qualities and skills are combined with basic reading skills to result in a good oral reader. This is a combining of linguistic patterns of voice: tone, volume, intonation, stress, pacing, and variations. Beside voice patterns, the oral reader is using good breathing to correlate with eye span and voice span, and he is being audience-aware in order to adjust his tempo and presentation to their needs. His gestures, body movements, facial expressions, in short his use of *kinesics,* are all combined with voice and reading abilities to interest, hold, and inform his audience. Oral reading, then, is audience reading to fit a particular situation and fill a purpose.

Oral reading and young children. It has been estimated that beginning readers, first grade and second grade students, probably do more aural/oral reading activities than children at any other level of work. This is a clue to teachers of one important purpose for planning oral reading experiences: that of habituation in responding to printed symbols by thinking of and saying the word represented. This association of printed word, meaning, and encoding language is an important one in foundational reading tasks. Whether the material be a printed book from a basal reading series, a lesson from a programmed kit, or a language-experience chart story of the children's own creating, the activity of oral reading will help them in word recognition, phrasing and clustering words in thought units, and the interpretation of mood and meaning. This combining of objectives insures that both the visual and locomotor skills develop; that students will gradually need less oral reading and will make use of more silent reading activities. One of the objections to oral reading has traditionally been concerned with too much vocalizing in reading, which of course can slow down rate if continued indefinitely. However, to exclude oral reading experiences entirely can be cheating the child of an important activity for demonstrating his ability and success in having learned to read. Through this exercise, he can gain personal gratification and satisfying reinforcement.

Oral reading and sharing experiences. Sometimes the classroom has reading material which must be shared due to the fact that there is a limited supply of copy. In this event, oral reading takes on a new meaning in which the reader has something important to be shared with his classmates and friends. Perhaps it is a library book, or a supplementary reader, or it may be an article from a magazine or newspaper. Whatever the source, this provides a valuable reason for the child's preparing a reading selection for presentation to others. If the teacher has asked for specific information, or for clarification of an opinion or viewpoint, or for some authoritative source for settling a difference or dispute about some point, the child will be afforded an opportunity to read for a definite purpose and share his findings with his peers. And, of course, throughout the school day there will be opportunities to read bulletins, announcements, academic or committee reports, invitations, minutes of class meetings, or even directives from administration concerning procedures on the playground or in the building. The alert teacher will use such incidents for providing students ample opportunities for sharing through oral reading experiences.

Hearing literature through oral reading. Whenever good literature is shared orally, both listeners and reader can enjoy a shared experience. This group feeling of appreciation often proves to be a contagious activity as students are allowed the opportunity to express their own enthusiasm about stories and books. As others hear the descriptions of characters and their conversations, there is a certain "coming to life" of reading materials. Likewise the reader profits from the experience as he finds himself communicating humor, pathos, or lively narrative. This feeling of "getting through" is important. Good oral reading can begin with the teacher's serial reading. This day-by-day sharing develops a heightened interest in, and a pleasurable association with, the stories and characters of the books read. It serves as an introduction to literature, a study of the mechanics of writing—plot, narrative, style, characterization—and it can deepen the personal relationships between teacher and students.

Diagnosis and prescription through oral reading. When the teacher desires to use oral reading as a basis for evaluating the child's progress in word recognition, or his developing comprehension, it should usually be in a private, one-to-one situation. This takes place continuously and provides many samplings in order to determine needs, strengths, interests, and instructional direction for the child. In making use of such learning/teaching situations, the teacher will normally use some observation, checklist type of informal reading inventory for guiding her/him in looking for certain types of needs and for systematically recording them. Such reading errors as substitutions, reversals, wild guesses, regressions, omissions, and repetitions are commonly discovered through such use of the oral reading situation. This can offer the teacher valuable clues as to *why* children are not successfully progressing in reading activities: "*why* mispronunciations, lack of meaning, inability to handle inferences or analogies, improper phrasing, or inattention to punctuation signals are occurring." As a result, the teaching program can be adjusted to deal with specific skills areas or deficiencies. Procedures for meeting these individual needs can likewise be planned by arranging for group and/or solo activities. This listening to oral reading by the teacher often reveals the important element of *why* in a way that silent reading cannot.

SITUATIONS FOR ORAL READING ACTIVITIES

In planning for instruction in oral reading, and specific instruction is needed just as in any other skills area, the teacher will certainly want to be aware of the interest areas of the readers. If a basal program is used, the instructor's manual will offer suggestions for oral reading activities from time to time. However, this is insufficient material to be used, and with the wealth of fine children's books available today as well as the periodical literature of good quality, the instructional program should be planned to include using such media for oral as well as silent reading. The oral reading for an audience situation should be planned carefully so that maximum satisfaction will accrue both to the reader and his listeners. Some simple guides can insure smooth performances.

 1. Allow the child to prepare for his own presentation.
 2. Offer guidance in selecting the material to be used.
 3. Let the story or selection choice be made by the student.
 4. Discuss "cutting" the selection or story for the oral reading presentation.
 5. If the reading is for a special program, guide in the material chosen to be used.
 6. If the reading is to be a group effort, democratically decide where each presentation is to end and begin.
 7. After silent reading, listen for mispronunciations or weak areas where help is needed.
 8. Allow for ample time to practice and prepare the reading.
 9. Discuss performance standards for the reader as well as the listeners.
10. Allow for original writing selections to be shared as oral readings if so desired.

Following these and like procedures will enhance the oral reading program. Some attention should also be given to what is in good taste for audience reading, and what may be embarrassing or unsuitable for certain occasions. Some materials may be of a personal nature that may be offensive, and some humor may be better not included in the oral readings.

What then are the audience situations or learning experiences which will be most suitable for oral reading? In what context may it be most valuable to use this facet of reading instruction? The following brief descriptions may guide the teacher/intern in preparing opportunities for children to read aloud to one another or in special events programs.

 1. Any situation which can be correlated with other language or creative arts learnings; in dramatic situations, combined with art or music, or as an integral part of any form of expressive arts.
 2. Reading verse or poetry which should always be shared as an oral activity either by individuals or groups.
 3. Choral readings provide a beautiful channel for oral expression. These can be planned in several ways: in a simple solo reading followed by the refrain type of response provided in some poems; by assigning a line to be read by each child, or by small groups in turn; an antiphonal situation in which the chorus is divided in two sections and one responds alternately with the other; and entire group or unison reading.
 4. Selecting characters for each person in the story to be read. These read the actual conversation set apart by the quotation marks, and a narrator fills in the description and situation.
 5. A narration situation as a backdrop for a pantomiming individual or group of performers.
 6. The characters and narrator for presenting a puppet show in which the "actors" are silent and readers furnish the dialogue.
 7. Reading dramatic script, either published or written by the children from

familiar stories or books, in a quiet, relaxed setting for the sheer enjoyment of the conversation and humor.

8. Couple-group, or aural-oral, reading as it is sometimes called. The entire group is divided into couples who simultaneously read to each other "knee to knee" or facing each other. Each reads a paragraph or section at a time while the other acts as audience and corrects, assists, or monitors. This negates the routine "round robin" type of taking turns reading, and provides ample opportunity for each to have a number of frequent turns at reading.

9. Role-playing, creative drama times which are based on situations from the reading material. A narrator or narrators can provide the background and situation for the free action of the exercise in interpretation.

10. Recording activities in which the cassette or tape recorder is used for oral reading practice by either an individual student or the group participating. In either event this offers the reader(s) excellent opportunity to hear and critique the performance. Discussion usually follows in which the good is highlighted and the need for improvement is noted with suggestions to follow and an opportunity for demonstrating and practicing is available.

11. Use of recordings and script in which the student reads along with the support of the voice provided.

12. Total class oral reading in which each "does his own thing." Children soon forget the others reading aloud too, and probably find it not too unlike many situations in real life at home or elsewhere where numerous sounds blend together in a "harmonious chorus"! The teacher quietly moving around the room is afforded opportunities to listen and observe while students participate.

13. Using the reading corner for a couple or small group to read to one another as a recreation or reward situation while other work is going on in the room.

14. A learning center(s) arrangement in which there can be an oral reading table, circle, pillows, or carpeted area to which children can go for reading aloud.

15. Actual lesson times and instruction situations which call for oral reading to: find answers to questions posed by the teacher or students; discover facts for verifying statements; discover and articulate the sequences of events being discussed; clarify from an authoritative source; practice good reading aloud which may include proper phrasing, expression, cadence and intonation, or pronunciation; share a bit of vivid description, humorous fun, or characterization; or provide information relating to any area of the subject matter being studied.

Probably, the intern will recognize by now that silent and oral reading are not an either/or situation, but actually a combining of many activities and situations which necessitate the use of and blending of both. Certainly a good instructional program will include generous amounts of each as the situation and material seem best fitted for their being used.

The students will need to use and learn both processes in the instructional program. Remember oral reading is actually an extension process in skill involvement. Silent reading can be thought of as a seeing and thinking process, and oral reading is a seeing, thinking, and saying process which involves both decoding and encoding of language.

THE DEVELOPMENT
OF LANGUAGE
THROUGH WRITING

10

THE DEVELOPMENT
OF WRITTEN LANGUAGE

WRITING, THE FOURTH VOCABULARY: THE THEORETICAL APPROACH

Writing: Freezing the Oral Tradition

Writing is the act of recording, through graphic symbols, the thoughts of man. This act is considered by many to be the most abstract of all the language skills. When one considers the level of symbolism that is involved in the act of writing, one can understand that consideration. Oral language, or the codifying of sound to represent thoughts, desires, ideas is, in the act of writing, made graphic. Writing then is, in fact, making graphic symbols from oral symbols. It is one of the supreme achievements of man. It is also one of the most difficult skills that we as educators must teach our students.

For thousands of years man relied on the oral tradition, word of mouth, to preserve his collective knowledge, mores, laws, and the necessary accoutrements of culture. This form of record keeping was, at best, unreliable. The retelling of those ideas years, or even months later, often was most apt to be changed significantly from the original as it was stated. This oral tradition, by word of mouth, was by its very nature the essence of fluidity. An accurate, systematic approach of preserving the experiences and the thoughts of man, for the benefit of those that followed, simply did not exist.

In its evolution, the creative mind of man saw the need to more accurately preserve the thoughts and ideas that occurred. Thus, in this process, man devised a way of marking on stone, clay, skins, bark and other surfaces that which he deemed necessary to preserve. Very possibly the first of these markings were pictures or drawings that were meant to convey a message. Later these pictures

237

were probably made symbolic and represented acts and ideas in an abstract way. Eventually the concept of a codified system of markings was developed to record ideas. From that, the ultimate achievement occurred—the alphabet.

With this supreme tool the "oral tradition" became frozen in print. Now the thoughts, the ideas, the laws, the collective knowledge, the mores, and all the musings of man could be written and preserved. Man could communicate over great distances, in both time and space. The fluid of the oral tradition became solid through the pragmatic creativity of man's mind when it devised an alphabet and provided man the tool he needed for writing.

HISTORICAL DEVELOPMENT OF WRITING

Our English Alphabet: Beginnings and Development

Quite frankly, the beginnings of writing have been lost in the mists of time. The alphabet, however, as we know it in the English language, seems to have emerged to its present state over the centuries in a traceable manner. The name *alphabet,* is in fact a combination of the first two letters of the Greek system, *alpha* and *beta.* While the ancient Greeks are credited with the invention of having symbols stand for speech sounds and thus creating the alphabet, those inventive people are said to have borrowed the concept that is basic to it. Phoenician merchants visiting the shores of Greece in the early centuries displayed this remarkable concept to their hosts. The Phoenicians in turn are believed to have found the idea in early North Semitic cultures. Beyond these Semites, the veil of time has been drawn. The idea of written symbols for speech sounds was, nevertheless, refined by the Greeks into their alphabet. It then moved to Rome and the Latin. From Rome the idea transferred itself to Northern Europe and, eventually, to the English language.

The Age of Calligraphy: Writing as an Art

The use of the alphabet in early times was, by and large, reserved for a relative few. Universal education and the right to read and write by the masses were unknown. Aside from certain of the ruling classes and segments of the religious community very few were afforded the skills of reading and writing. As a result, the use of the written word was sparse. The scribe, or the professional "writer of words," was an important member of the community that was large and affluent enough to afford him. His livelihood was earned by using his skills of writing and selling them to those who had need of his skills. His position in the evolution of Europe and elsewhere is undenied.

The written word was so valued and considered such a magnificent achievement that for a period of time (and in some quarters even today) handwriting was thought of as an art form. The art of calligraphy, or beautiful writing, had been practiced in the Middle and Far Eastern cultures for centuries. It found itself in the western cultures as well. The calligrapher was an important member of the early Church in Europe, for example. The ornate and illuminated manuscripts of those days are highly prized by collectors today and demand impressive prices in the art market. The church calligrapher spent uncounted hours copying the Bible, prayers, and other religious documents so that the word of Christ could be taken as far as man could carry the written word. These ornate and beautiful examples of the use of symbols for speech sounds were and are highly prized as an art form. As a pragmatic tool of written communication, however, it had obvious and severe limitations.

Some attempts at block printing were done. This involved carving words on a flat surface, most often wood, to represent a page of print. Then that piece of carved wood was inked and pressed against paper. The results, although satisfactory at the time, hardly proved to be revolutionary.

Moveable Type and the Printing Press: A New Door Is Opened

The real revolution in the use of the alphabet, and thus creating a climate for its universal use, happened in Germany in 1450. The inventive mind of Johann Gutenberg devised moveable type. That was that each letter of the alphabet was separately forged and kept in multiple copies. They could then be slotted in place to form a page, then be reused to form other words and pages. The need to carve the master block for printing became obsolete immediately. The handwritten manuscripts so carefully done by calligraphers became examples of an art form, no longer considered a pragmatic way of reproducing written materials. An age had ended, and a new era had begun. The reproduction of writing by a moveable alphabet in the printing process was the first ray in the dawning of a new era.

With the invention of moveable type and the subsequent refinements of that invention, the phenomena of written, printed language came within the grasp of all who would seek the skills and controls to understand. In our modern era, those skills and controls are considered a necessary life tool.

Preservation of Learning, Transmission of Culture and Belief

With that remarkable facility, writing, man has kept a record of his follies and achievements over the centuries. His great discoveries have been kept for posterity. His mistakes, likewise, are on record so that, hopefully, they may not be made again. With this incredible ability, the ability to freeze speech sounds in graphic form, the cultures of man have advanced, modified, and grown. Messages can be shared over the centuries, across oceans and vast continents. Fleeting ideas can be recorded, embellished, and shared. All beliefs and religions can be recorded.

Probably no cultural tool has been more important to man in his ascendency to his prime role on this planet than his ability to write and have that written message understood by its receiver. Therefore, as teachers of children, our emphasis on written language is well placed. The ability to write (and to read) may well be the cornerstone of our society.

READINESS FOR WRITING

To assume that all children are ready to write at a given "magic moment" in time, is as naïve as expecting all children to be ready to read at a certain time. The human child is a vastly complex organism. He grows and matures at varying rates, and is ready for certain educational experiences at various times. We, as teachers, need to be acutely aware of this. Presenting a child with a task that he is not able to successfully complete can be a very damaging experience.[1]

What kinds of clues can we look for in order to determine whether or not a child is ready to write? The following cluster of readiness factors may be considered before we can expect writing to occur.

1. Is he able to function at a listening and speaking level in the English language that contains a vocabulary that will allow him to listen and to respond at a fluid level?
2. Is his visual discrimination at a level that allows him to see differences in sizes and shapes?
3. Is he successfully engaged in reading activities?
4. Are his small muscles developed enough to handle the writing equipment he will use?
5. Has he had sufficient experiences with handwriting skills so that he can, in fact, write?
6. Is his overall maturation at a level that will permit an attention span long enough to complete a writing experience?
7. Has he displayed "handedness," a preference for using one hand over the other?
8. Does he possess the necessary intelligence to abstract at the level needed to write?

If, to the teacher's satisfaction, the youngster has met the above requirements, the probability is very good that he is ready to begin the task of learning to write. If he has not, it would be wise to delay his initial writing until an assessment later on assures the teacher that he is ready.

It is not uncommon for teachers to operate with readiness activities for months

---

1. Education Center, Cincinnati Public Schools, "Handwriting," *The Primary Manual*, 1967, pp. 66–73.

and in some cases years with specific youngsters before they are able to begin writing. This readiness activity is a wise investment. To attempt to induce writing in a youngster before he is ready to write, can cause problems that may take years to solve.

THE NECESSITY OF TEACHING WRITING SKILLS: MECHANICS

Without question one must know the skills of handwriting before one attempts to write. The important issue of handwriting and the skills involved in that act are therefore discussed in another section of this book, as befits its importance.

It stands to reason, however, that the first task the teacher must face in helping children cope with this last, and most abstract vocabulary, that of writing, would be to help the child learn and utilize the alphabet. This important learning is the key to all that follows. He needs to know that letters stand for speech sounds; he needs to know that the English language is somewhat phonetic; and he needs

Models of writing for students to examine and to reproduce are very important in written language in the early years of learning. The relationship between reading and writing appear very evident.

to know that there is a system of markings that do relate thoughts and ideas to others. There are various approaches to helping children learn to utilize the alphabet (see figure 11.1, p. 270) and most school districts offer aid in the form of courses of study and/or study aids to enhance the teaching and learning of this all important tool.

The preschool and primary teacher will utilize the manuscript style of writing to introduce the child to writing. She does this for two essential reasons: (1) the reproduction of these printed letters requires two muscular movements, a straight line and the circle movement, rather than the complicated system required in cursive writing, and (2) the manuscript print resembles very closely that which the child finds in his printed reading material, and therefore configurational confusion is much less a problem. The cursive approach to writing is usually not attempted by most teachers until the child has reached the end of the third grade and in many cases not until he has reached fourth grade. If small muscle development is slow, and the youngster has difficulty with the intricate problem of manipulating his pen or pencil even at that age, it is best to let him continue manuscript writing until he is ready and comfortable with the cursive approach.[2]

Many authorities decry the change from manuscript to cursive at all. They maintain that configurationally cursive and manuscript are two separate languages, and that children are often confused when they make the transfer from one to the other. Research does tell us that speed in writing is not an issue. People are able to write as rapidly with manuscript print as with cursive writing. Probably the major issue in requiring children to change from manuscript print to cursive writing is family and peer pressure. It may be kind of a "rite" of growing up and becoming mature. Mothers and fathers are often anxious to see their child "write" rather than "print," and the child often thinks cursive is for "grown-ups" and will want to have the skills that will allow him to recreate cursive writing.

Probably the first attempt at writing will be for the child to recreate his name. This comes after considerable readiness (both muscular and visual), of course, and it comes at various times for various children in a given class setting. After he is able to print his own name, he goes on to print his address and telephone number. Possibly the names of his friends, various areas and articles in the classroom are labeled and he is given opportunities to recreate these labels and names. He is at all times under the direction of his teacher and a regular portion of each day is given over to the development of these skills. Careful planning and execution on the part of the teacher is essential at this stage. While it is important that his first attempts at writing be integrated with other language skills, particularly reading, time needs to be specifically set aside for initial learning experiences with writing.

2. Mildred Donoghue, *The Child and the English Language Arts* (Dubuque, Ia.: Wm. C. Brown Company Publishers, 1971), pp. 260.

It is always important that the child see that the skills of writing are useful to him. He needs to understand that what he is learning is of immediate use to him. We, therefore, give him opportunities to write words that are involved with his ego. His name, his address, his phone number, his friends—these are all related to his ego and are important to him. Asking the child to write, especially in the early years, about that which does not affect him directly, is often an exercise in frustration.

The experience story (see figure 11.5, p. 277) is likely to be the first real writing of an expository nature that the youngster does. It gives him a chance to write complete thoughts in sentence form, and to share his thoughts, in writing, with others.

This technique requires that a common experience (a class project, a field trip, a party) be discussed by the class. The teacher, then, asks the children to dictate a "story" about the experience to her. She, in turn, writes it on the chalkboard for all to see and to read. When she is finished the children copy it. The teacher is able then to evaluate the progress (both in handwriting and content) that the children are making. This technique is a favorite of primary teachers but can be successfully practiced in the middle and upper grades as well.

FORM AND USAGE: FORMAL AND INFORMAL WRITING

As children develop the skills of writing and are apt to use the skills more and more, it is important that we, as teachers, point out that there is more than one level of writing. The adult uses one level of writing when he makes out the shopping list or takes notes in class. He uses quite another level when he writes a letter to a prospective employer or composes a term paper at the university. One is for consumption by others, whereas the other is not. One is more formal, more structured, and needs to be correct in all elements. The other is informal, less structured, and can serve its purpose by speaking in fragments. If we are to help children understand that written language is of value to them and can be used as an everyday life's tool, this difference needs to be made clear.

Some teachers clearly state that a written assignment in class will be read and evaluated. They allow children time to write a first, second, and even a third draft before they turn in a paper of a more formal structure. Teachers will often make themselves available to children to help with structure, spelling, grammar, and other technical aspects, so that when the final draft is ready for evaluation, the child has prepared the document to the best of his ability. The teacher can then correct, comment, offer suggestions, and return the paper to the youngster for a final (if necessary) rewrite. This more formal approach to writing is exemplified by children writing letters, reports, reviews, critiques, and the like. It is a time for planning by the teacher, a time of utilizing various aids such as the dictionary and models of form. This kind of experience is a formal kind of experience—the teacher prepares a lesson, requests an assignment, and evaluates the outcome.

Guidance and structure are required; children will not learn to write correctly without help. The "incidental" approach will not suffice in situations of this nature. An examination of the illustrative lesson plans in the following chapter will give examples of the structure needed for teaching of this nature.

Children, likewise, need to know that a less structured, less formal kind of writing has value, too. Jotting down notes, making lists, sending notes to friends, or any writing of a personal nature exemplifies this kind of writing experience. The teacher usually does not see this kind of writing for the purpose of evaluation. She does not prepare lessons, specifically, to induce this kind of writing. This kind of writing experience can truly be called "incidental." Our major job, as teachers, is to make sure opportunities and reasons for this kind of writing occur. Informal writing is a large part of the adult's writing experience. To not provide opportunities for its growth is in many ways, cheating children of a written language experience.

ORGANIZATION AND PATTERNS IN WRITTEN LANGUAGE

When the child begins to write in a formal manner, he needs to know that structure is important. He needs to know that there is a "correct way" of doing it, and he needs help in knowing the "correct way." English is a systematized language. To operate with the English language using writing as the medium, requires knowledge of the system and opportunities of working within it.[3]

While most authorities in the field of language development for children decry the use of formal grammar being taught at the elementary school level, certain elements of "quasi grammar" do need to be taught. Children do need to understand the elements of a simple sentence, and the idea that a sentence is a full thought. Some children in the middle and upper grades may be ready for experiences with complex and even compound sentence structure. While formal grammar lessons probably are not necessary, it would be dangerous to assume that children will learn these concepts without teacher assistance.

Without question, children need experiences with the various kinds of sentences—the declarative, the imperative, the interrogative, the exclamatory—and how they are punctuated. Whether or not the names of these sentence forms are used when children learn about them is an issue open to argument. The important point being that children learn that sentences can do several things for the writer when he uses them to communicate.

Examples of these kinds of sentences, and the punctuation that accompanies them, can be presented in the very early years of the child's school experience. Most children very quickly learn the value of the period, the question mark, and the exclamation point as well as the comma. They just as quickly learn to utilize them in their early writing attempts.

---

3. Robert Evans, "A Glove Thrown Down," *Elementary English,* May 1967, pp. 523–527.

The paragraph is another concept that children need to encounter as they learn to write. As with the sentence, they have had experience with the paragraph through reading. The concept needs reinforcement through teaching while they learn to write.

Most children are not yet ready for paragraph construction before the middle grades. They may have recreated paragraphs while copying experience stories and the like, but they are not likely to be able to compose one until the end of third grade or until fourth.

The major issues for the youngster to understand when he begins to compose a paragraph are that one indents from the margin so that the reader will know that the writer has "changed the subject," and that the sentences all talk about the same thing in the paragraph.

The authors remember visiting a student teacher in a third grade. The task for the afternoon was to introduce the concept of a paragraph. The student teacher gathered her group in a semicircle in front of her chair and began by discussing several articles that had been brought in by the children that week for sharing. The theme of share-and-tell that week was "My Favorite Toy." The counter had a collection of trucks, toy automobiles, dolls, several games, and a whole assortment of favorite toys.

The student teacher had chosen, at random, three toys: a doll, a truck, and a small racing car. She held the toys up and led a discussion about each. When she had drawn a lengthy discussion (about twenty minutes) about the toys, she announced that the group was going to write about the toys. They were, she said, going to write descriptions about the toys—tell something about each one. The children seemed quite excited about this, as each one had joined in the discussion and had much to offer. Then the student teacher made her major point. "Each toy needs to be described separately. We're going to write several sentences about each toy. Then when we start to describe the next toy, we'll let everyone know by starting a new paragraph."

At this point the student teacher went to the chalkboard and wrote the word "paragraph." She went on to explain how a paragraph is a group of sentences that talks about one thing. She explained that when the subject changed, a new paragraph was started.

The student teacher produced a large chart that she had prepared the day before. The chart contained several short paragraphs describing common pets: a dog, a cat, and a canary. She and the children read it together. At each change of subject, the student teacher pointed out, the first sentence of the new paragraph was indented. "This," she said, "tells our eyes that a new set of ideas is coming. It tells us we are going to read about something new." She reviewed the lesson, placed the toys on display, passed out paper, and the children began to write.

The student teacher moved among her pupils, encouraging, answering questions, pointing out mistakes. The results were more than satisfactory. Each of the children, at their own level of writing, produced three paragraphs. Some were quite involved, some of only two or three sentences, but the seed of a concept had been planted. Now all it needed was care and feeding. This kind of teaching could only enhance this most abstract of the vocabularies, that of writing.

THE STRUCTURE OF THE COMPOSITION

As the youngster progresses through the grades and the skills of writing (for example, handwriting, sentence structure, punctuation, paragraph construction, spelling) become more and more set, we offer him additional opportunities to use his increased ability to write. He writes in all areas of the curriculum. He makes reports in the social studies and in science. He responds, in writing, to his experiences with literature. He outlines, he abstracts, he composes creative and original pieces. His language milieu increasingly utilizes the printed page and the written word.

As his facility with written language grows, and additional requests to write continue, it is most important for us, as teachers, to remember the continuing need to help him see and understand the various structures that are needed to compose and otherwise use the skills of writing.

When, for example, he is asked to do a report for the social studies, what help can we offer him as to the structure of a report? How does one write a report? What comes first, second, and so on? These strategies need to be carefully thought out by the teacher and prepared in a workable lesson plan designed to give the youngster the additional skills he will need to write the required report.

Outlining, likewise, has a structure and an approach. It is a skill that needs specific directions to develop. How does a teacher work with a group of youngsters in such a way that the skills of outlining become part of the child's language world? As with other forms of composition, the child needs direct instruction. The skills of composition will not develop unaided. Good, planned, specific lessons need to be prepared so that the youngster will see and understand the structure and the skills required. He needs opportunities to apply those skills so that he can, at a practical level, see their application.

The chapter following this one offers specific plans for helping children develop the skills of writing. Some of them offer guides to teaching the structure of composition. It would be good now to examine the following plans and see how structure of composition is developed through specific lessons.

For Preschool and Kindergarten

Primary Level

Intermediate Grades

Upper Grades

For the beginning teacher it is comforting to know that these skills develop slowly. We need to accept what the child gives us in terms of written language, but always look toward his greater facility with the written word.[4]

Creative Writing

Any time a youngster puts pencil to paper and composes an original statement, he is creating. Creative writing then, in the broad sense, would mean any composition a youngster writes; be it a letter, a report, a review. In common educational jargon, however, the term "Creative Writing" implies another meaning. The implication involves the artistic use of words, the writing of fictional stories, of writing poetry, of "painting pictures with words."

This kind of writing, the initial attempts of children to utilize the art of language in a written form, is probably one of the most delightful experiences with writing the child will have. It is certainly a favorite of teachers. Flights of the imagination are always a welcome break in our very practical world. But, like any creative art, creative writing needs a kind of structure, a kind of form that will contain the creative ideas of those who write.

Most creative writing falls into the category of expository writing. That is, the most usual media for expression will be sentences and paragraphs. The need to understand these mechanics and knowledge of how to use them is explicit. Good language teaching is required (see figure 11.3, Original Writing, page 273; figure 11.6, Creative Writing Experiences, page 279). Despite common myth, creativity is not exclusively a spontaneous act.

Poetry and verse writing also need form. The meter, the number of lines, and the rhyme of a poem or verse need to be pointed out to children. All of these elements need to be recognized by the teacher and strategies planned for the teaching of them.

Getting ready for a creative writing experience is most important. There

---

4. "For Punchier Prose," *Grade Teacher*, April 1966. Reprinted from *Readings in the Language Arts*, ed. V. D. Anderson et al. (New York: The Macmillan Co., 1964), pp. 137–141.

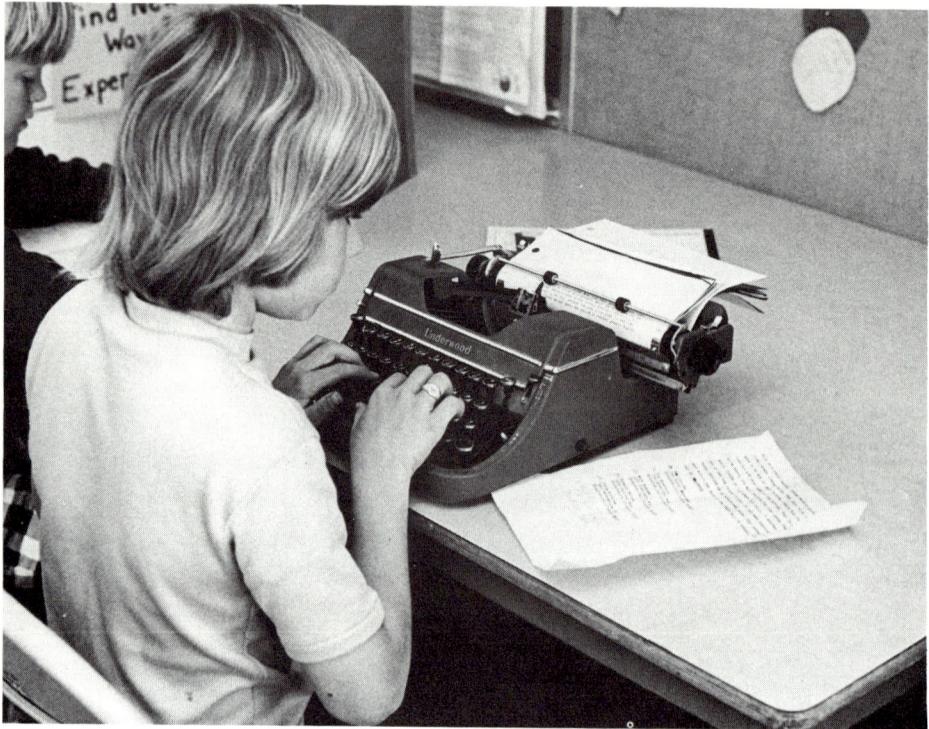

Experiences with written language, for the creative teacher, come in many forms. The excitement of using a typewriter can enhance the child's original writing efforts.

should always be a relaxed, happy atmosphere when we ask children to write in a creative, artful way. The act of creating, for children, should be a joy.

Any experience with creative writing should begin with a time for motivation to write, a reason to write, and an assurance that children have the background that will allow them to write. The motivation can be as simple as holding up an evocative picture to be discussed and then written about. Or, it can be as involved as a walk in the woods or park nearby and coming back to the classroom to record the thoughts about it. It is imperative to know that a period of "input" take place before we ask children for creative "output" in written form. Creativity obviously cannot take place in a vacuum. We, as teachers, must provide the student materials with which to create.

It should be a matter of concern that we offer the young writer the necessary form into which he can channel his efforts. Will we suggest sentence and paragraph form? Poetry or prose? Whatever we suggest, we need to provide him the requisite tools with which he can give vent to his creative endeavor. Perhaps this will be in reinforcing and refining his ability to use proper sentences and develop good paragraphs. Perhaps we will offer him models of fine poetry, excellent prose, or fascinating drama of which he will make use. The issue is, of course, that he be helped to acquire the necessary skills and controls to create well. Our job as teachers is to help him develop those skills and controls.

Unfortunately, or perhaps fortunately, the creative urges do not conform to the clock. Creative work many times demands time. We need to allow that necessary time! Let the assignment come in when he is ready to submit it, only then will he truly succeed. It is conceivable that for some, several days of working on a project in spare time will suffice. For others extended, planned time is necessary for the fruition of the creative process in written language. We should expect and make provision for the extra time dimension for good writing.

Sometimes, the young writer may finish his original assignments, and then want our assessments and comments. We, as attending adults, will give him the help he seeks. Often it will be mechanical assistance: sentence structure, the proper wording, paragraph clarification, or spelling and punctuation assistance. When we have worked over and discussed his work with him, he may need to correct or redo the task. Often the writing of several drafts of his creative work is necessary before he is ready to submit the final, polished efforts of his writing.

With creative writing, more than with most other forms of writing, we need to stand ready to accept. Creativity operates at various levels with various children. Not all are equally creative as not all are equally intelligent. That being the case, evaluation is an extremely difficult problem to overcome. Shall we reward the creative child for a natural endowment, and punish the child with less creative potential? Certainly not! We need to accept his efforts as a personal statement and respond to them as such. To "grade" a creative effort of an elementary student is unthinkable.[5] Creating with the written language is a delightful and important achievement. Regular opportunities for creative writing should be assured as we plan for the language curriculum.

THE IMPORTANCE OF WRITTEN MODELS

When a child composes with the written word, he is engaging in one of the most abstract activities that language can provide. Because of this, he needs all the assistance possible. He needs encouragement and he needs success. He needs help with the skills of writing and he needs instruction to help him cope with the structure and form required when he writes.

Certainly one way to help the child cope with the intricacies of the written word is to provide him with written language models. As the youngster begins to

---

5. Alvina Burrows et al., *New Horizons in the Language Arts* (New York: Harper & Row, Publishers, 1972), pp. 205–208.

write, he has already had experience with the printed page in his initial attempts at reading. He has seen language represented in print. He has had experiences with sentences and with paragraphs in his reader and in various other contexts. We can assume then, that he is not totally unfamiliar with the concept that words strung together in a prescribed manner will communicate.

To recreate the phenomena of words communicating ideas when they are written in a prescribed manner is another matter; thus, the necessity of written language models to accompany good teaching practices. The child's language milieu in his classroom needs to contain written language in all forms. Aside from the labels and names that are attached to the various bulletin boards and displays about the room, what written language models do we need to provide? The following suggestions should be considered.

The alphabet. From the time the youngster first begins to write, all the way to the more sophisticated composition of the upper-grade student, an example of the alphabet in correct order needs to be in view. For the primary grades the alphabet needs to be in manuscript form. For the middle and upper grades, both manuscript and cursive need to be displayed. The alphabet, in clear view, is a primary resource for any child learning to write. He should be encouraged to consult it often, as he writes. This tool, along with regular lessons in the skills of handwriting, is of primary importance when we ask a child to write. Commercial alphabets are readily available and most school districts provide them for every classroom.

Models of sentence form and punctuation. When we ask a child to write a sentence, we need to provide him with a model of how a sentence is constructed. He needs to see sentences that make a statement, ask a question, show excitement. He needs to see the punctuation that is required of each of these kinds of sentences. Many good teachers construct these sentences on tagboard and display them in a prominent place so that children can utilize this model when they write.

Proper paper heading. Most teachers like to have children organize a paper heading in a specific way. The heading usually requires the student's name, the date, a margin, and a title, among other data. If this is a requirement, a model of how a paper needs to be organized should be on display.

Paragraph construction. When the youngster begins to compose to the extent that paragraphs become a tool of communication for him, he needs a visual model of how one is constructed. He needs to see that a paragraph is a collection of sentences telling about one idea. He needs to see that the first sentence of a paragraph is indented. He needs a visual model as a point of reference when he writes using paragraphs as part of his structure.

Model letter forms. One of the favorite writing exercises, for teachers and students alike, is the writing of letters. Letters of thanks, letters to ill classmates, letters of inquiry—they pour forth from classrooms at all grade levels. Letters are a meaningful, personal way of communicating with the written word. That is probably why they are so popular with students and teachers. It is always good to have a model of a letter available for the youngster. He needs to see the proper form of a letter: the return address and the date, the greeting, the body, the salutation, and finally the signature, and where each belongs on the paper. This model can be on tagboard and displayed in front of the class as a teaching aid, or in the case of the middle- and upper-grade student, it can be a mimeographed paper to be distributed to each child.

Model outlines. Outlining is not usually introduced before the upper grades. When it is introduced, however, the concept that an outline is the skeleton of a composition is often a difficult concept for some children. Certainly the need for a model outline is evident. The involvement of numerals, upper- and lowercase letters, and other elements of the outline can be a source of confusion.

Many good teachers will provide a model of an outline on the chalkboard or on tagboard as they present the concept of outlining. They will often, too, provide a mimeographed outline model to students along with the parent composition so that students may study the outline form and the composition from which it came.

Poetry and other special forms. The meter of a line or a stanza of poetry, the rhyming pattern of it, and the special form and structure of poetic writing need modeling before a student attempts to write a poem. Modeling for poetry certainly demands that the student hear poetry as well as see it before he begins to write. The teacher, then, needs to provide ample opportunity for her students to hear poetry so that the cadence, the lilt, and the music of a poem can be appreciated for what it is, and to understand it as a special kind of writing. Favorite poems then can be placed on the chalkboard, or can be written on tagboard to be used as a visual model for the child who will write.

Any special form of writing needs to be modeled for children so that they can have visual reinforcement of the teaching that precedes it or goes with it. Address forms, note taking, and lyric writing, among others, demand their written forms as models so that children can learn from them.

A good teacher knows that real learning comes from children having many experiences geared toward a concept or an idea. That is what teaching is all about, providing experiences for children and helping them learn from them. Certainly in any attempt to develop writers, one experience children need is the opportunity to examine models of writing. These models can, and do, provide a real service in helping children learn to use writing as a regular language tool.

SETTING CONDITIONS FOR WRITING IN THE ELEMENTARY SCHOOL

When we ask children to write in our classrooms, we need to remember that the act of writing, like speaking, is an output activity. We are asking children to put forth ideas in a structured manner, for evaluation and comment.

The experienced teacher knows that when we ask children to operate in an output activity, particularly an activity such as writing, certain conditions need to be present. To insure a successful experience with writing for elementary students, what conditions need to be present? The following certainly need consideration.

A reason for writing. Since writing is an output activity, input must occur before a child can effectively attempt writing. A pencil, a paper, and a child are simply not enough to spark the urge to write. What will the child write about? Does he have enough information to share with the written word? Is he motivated to write? These questions must be considered before we ask children to compose.

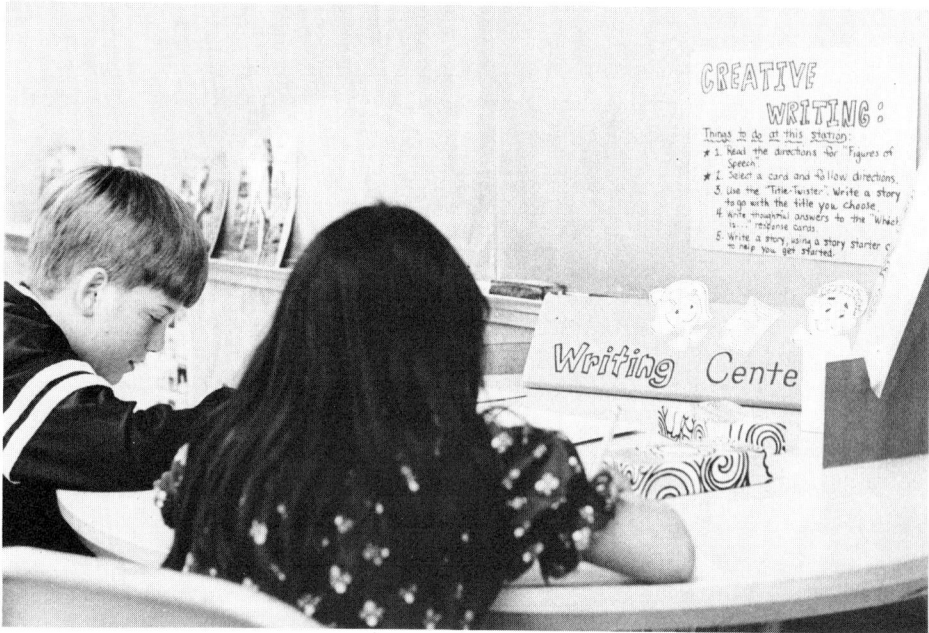

Setting conditions for written expression is necessary: a clean surface, proper tools, adequate lighting, and—most of all—something to write about are imperative.

Many good teachers arrange experiences simply to provide ammunition for the child to use when he writes. Field trips, science experiments, visitors from the community, a creative activity, children's literature, films—all are common experiences that teachers utilize so that the youngster will have something to share on paper. The child needs to be motivated to write, and he needs something to write about before we ask him to put pencil to paper to compose.

The necessary equipment. When the youngster has had experiences that will provide for the output activity of writing and is motivated to write, the equipment he needs should be readily available. He needs properly lined paper, sharpened pencils, a smooth, clean surface upon which to write, and a properly lighted and heated environment.

A quiet, relaxed atmosphere. When a child composes by writing, the classroom environment needs to be conducive to this activity. The usual hustle and bustle of the classroom needs, for the time being at least, to be quieted. The young writer needs this lack of noise to think, to consider words, to organize ideas, and to get them on paper. He needs as little distraction as possible. The wise teacher will make sure that the time for writing is a quiet time.

Ample time. When one creates, and composing with words is a creative activity, one needs time. Often a young writer will need more time than the space allowed in the daily plan the teacher has prepared. If this is the case, give him that time! Let him work with his composition until he is satisfied with it. Let him complete it at his own rate. When he has completed it, accept it and give it the consideration it requires.

A skillful, understanding, professional teacher. When a child begins to compose at any level, he needs encouragement, he needs acceptance, he needs understanding. He needs a teacher who is readily available to him to assist with spelling, punctuation, structure, handwriting, and all the mechanics of writing that he is struggling with. He needs a teacher that knows all children are not equally gifted with language ability. He needs a teacher who knows and understands that often girls are more fluent with words than are boys in the elementary school. He needs a teacher who knows that readiness to write and the background experiences necessary to write differ within the class, thus affecting the child's ability to compose with words.

Acceptance of a "first draft." It is a rare youngster in the elementary school who completes a composition of any nature in a satisfactory manner the first time. No matter how hard he may try or the amount of time he is allowed to use, the hurdle of mechanics in writing is often too high to surmount the first time.

The wise teacher then will expect a considerably less than perfect "first draft" of any composition that she may request from children. She will accept it, work with the youngster on the refinements that are needed (spelling, sentence structure, paragraphing, handwriting, punctuation), and allow him a chance to make the corrections and submit a "second draft" and sometimes a "third draft."

Some teachers advise children to simply get ideas on paper for the "first draft," disregarding many of the elements of structure that will be apparent in a later draft. The "second draft," then, is a child's refinement of the "first draft," and the "second draft" is presented to the teacher so that comments and corrections can be made.

The important issue, however, is that most children are not able to successfully complete a "perfect" composition the first time around. They need time and help in arriving at a finished product, and that often calls for more than one attempt.

SUMMARY

When we expect children to write, we expect them also to perform at the highest level of language abstraction. We ask them, in fact, to take sound abstractions (speech) and put them into graphic symbols (writing). It is one of the extreme achievements of man.

Before we ask a child to write, we need to be sure that he has an adequate background of language experiences that will allow him to be successful with this new task. We need to be certain that he has an adequate listening, speaking, and reading background before he attempts to compose with written language.

Certainly we need to help the youngster develop the immediate tools he needs in order to write. He needs to be familiar with the English alphabet and the linguistic syndrome that surrounds the tasks of writing. The tasks of handwriting and spelling are certainly tools he needs before he attends to this new ability.

The child needs to know the many forms that written language can take. He needs examples of these forms, and he needs encouragement to recreate these forms.

Good, planned, sequential teaching procedures need to be a part of the youngster's induction into the skills of communicating with written language. Without careful induction into this realm of language, frustration and failure are likely to occur.

Selected Readings: The Writing Vocabulary

APPLEGATE, MAUREE. *Easy in English.* New York: Harper & Row, Publishers, 1960.

CARLSON, RUTH KEARNEY. "An Originality Story Scale." *The Elementary School Journal* 65 (April 1965):366–371.

DUNN, MOIRA. "Writing Poetry in the Elementary School." *Elementary English* 45 (March 1968):337–341.

EVERTTS, ELDONNA L., "Composition Through Literature." *The Instructor* 75 (March 1966):105–108.

FARRELL, JOHN. *The Creative Teacher of Language.* Toronto: McGraw-Hill, Ryerson Limited, 1965.

FOWLER, MARY ELIZABETH. *Teaching Language, Composition, and Literature.* New York: McGraw-Hill Book Company, Inc., 1965.

FUNK, HAL D., and TRIPLETT, DEWAYNE. *Language Arts in the Elementary School: Readings.* New York: J. B. Lippincott Company, 1972.

GOLUB, LESTER S. "Stimulating and Receiving Children's Writing: Implications for an Elementary Writing Curriculum." *Elementary English* 48 (January 1971):33–49.

HUNTER, ELIZABETH. "Fostering Creative Expression." *Childhood Education* 44 (February 1968):369–373.

LOBAN, WALTER D. *The Language of Elementary School Children.* Research Report No. 1, National Council of Teachers of English, Champaign, Ill., 1963.

LOGAN, LILLIAN et al. *Creative Communication: Teaching the Language Arts.* Toronto: McGraw-Hill, Ryerson Limited, 1972.

McKEE, PAUL. *Reading: A Program of Instruction for the Elementary School.* Boston: Houghton Mifflin Co., 1966.

ROBINSON, HELEN. *Reading and the Language Arts.* Chicago: University of Chicago Press, 1963.

RUSSELL, DAVID. *Children's Thinking.* Boston: Ginn and Company, 1956.

SMITH, E. BROOKS et al. *Language and Thinking in the Elementary School.* New York: Holt, Rinehart & Winston, Inc., 1970.

TINGLE, MARY J. "Teaching Composition in the Elementary School." *Elementary English* 47 (January 1970):70–73.

11

THE CHILD AND
WRITTEN LANGUAGE
THEORY INTO PRACTICE

Since the child's use of written language becomes such a milestone event in his learning life, it is vital that the instructional program be planned and carried out most effectively. In communicating through writing, the crux of the activity lies in the degree to which it allows the child to pour out his ideas, experiences, or fantasies. The writing experience can become an exhilarating, creative pleasure, or it can be an assigned task with the elements of boredom and drudgery ever present. Certainly any teacher hopes it will be the former, for once the child tastes the heady delight of creating with words, the desire to continue to experience his spontaneous expressiveness becomes almost cyclic. Rarely is he content to let the response wither; but rather repeats the experience frequently, spurred on by the excitement of a "stretched" imagination seeking release through the medium of original written expression. It may take the form of some memory to be recorded, a sensory stimulation to be relived, an experience to be recalled, or just a sheer fantasy from the flight of the imagination which he wishes to capture. Whatever the purpose, the writer will find sufficient motivation to carry him along where fact or fancy may lead.

In order to achieve the full satisfaction possible from writing, the child needs the guidance and understanding of a supportive teacher. Fluency with words is insufficient in and of itself. The student needs to be aware that he has something to say that is important, and then he needs the skills and tools to say it well as he perfects and polishes the expression which is emerging through his words as they flow and run over themselves in the sparkle of the creative process. But before there can be productive, rewarding output from the young writer, there must of necessity be commensurate input, the replenishing of ideas, sensations, experiences, and imaginative content. This, then, becomes part of the teaching situations provided by the teacher to encourage good written expression. What then before children write happily, freely, and creatively?

PRELIMINARY TO CHILDREN'S ORIGINAL WRITING

Even before the child has acquired the manipulative skills necessary to allow for the mechanics of writing, he has felt the urge to express through words. Happy the one who has been encouraged and freed to do so, and then has had the assistance of another who could capture and record for him in writing the uniqueness of his own creative impulse. However, children are not all sufficiently able to express themselves readily with spontaneous words because they are not sufficiently free from inhibiting fears and shyness. Nor are they adequate in skills necessary for fluently communicating with words, nor do they all have sufficient inner strengths and awareness for rich expression in writing. Therefore, it becomes necessary for the teacher to develop a certain degree of sensitivity to the needs of children as they struggle to adequately express themselves. This sensitivity should result in a recognition that children have a need to express themselves, and that in order to do so they must have many rich experiences as a base for their interpretative perceptions, many opportunities to use and stretch their imaginations, numerous meaningful activities for using words, good models for and sound instruction in communication skills. In other words, basic to good writing is a stimulating environment, an interesting instructional program, and a climate of acceptance.

Not only does the teacher need an awareness of the students and their personalities, she also needs to have a clear sense of the purposes for teaching written expression. In thinking through the instructional program and planning for balanced activities and skills learnings, what may emerge in the teacher's thinking as the basic instructional objectives of the program?

INSTRUCTIONAL OBJECTIVES FOR WRITTEN EXPRESSION

The following broad goals or purposes of teaching written language can assist the teacher in planning for learning experiences and enriching activities for stimulating and fostering good writing by children. The instructional program should:

1. Provide a sound base for teaching the mechanics of written language: legible handwriting, standard spelling, adequate punctuation, proper sentence structure, and unified paragraphs.
2. Stimulate students to develop a "writing conscience" which utilizes good written procedure in all work.
3. Give the student many opportunities to express himself adequately: his personal thoughts, intimate feelings, and affective responses, ideals, values, attitudes, interests, aspirations, and aesthetic concepts.

4. Activate and maintain interest in and appreciation for all forms of writing: prose, poetry, humor, description, reporting, and informational.
5. Provide appropriate instruction for children who display creative literary talent to develop to their full capacity.
6. Give ample, supportive encouragement to all children to recognize and use good written expression as a viable form of communicating ideas, information, feelings, and personal experiences.
7. Provide many good models of excellent writing: literature, reports, essays, and classics as well as samples from the children's own writings.
8. Set standards of correctness as well as form and style for evaluating performance and a level of acceptability.
9. Allow for continuing evaluation of work in order to recognize progress and diagnose for further instruction.
10. Develop a high level of performance in all aspects of written language: functional writing, social writing, instructional-utilitarian writing, and creative and original writing.

In planning for children's writing experiences, the teacher should consider the following five-step developmental process for nurturing involvement with recorded language.

Step One: Cultivate awareness of the situations or problems which can most effectively be resolved or handled through written language.
Step Two: Allow time and opportunity for germination and conceptualization before expecting action from the young writer.
Step Three: Expect ignition to take place as the spark is touched off; momentum results from the ideas as they generate force and action.
Step Four: Effect *completion* and *closure* as the writing takes form and is corrected, polished, and perfected.
Step Five: Provide opportunity and time for communicating and sharing of the writing; a time of excitement, pleasure, and reward for the writer and listener alike.

IMPORTANCE OF TEACHER ATTITUDE

The reader will certainly have already recognized the authors' feeling that the teacher of written skills is of prime importance in the total instructional program. It is the teacher who will set the stage for many activities and experiences for writing input previous to expression. It is the teacher, likewise, who will recognize that writing, like reading, is a developmental process related to and dependent on the child's intellectual, emotional, social, physical, aesthetic, and linguistic growth levels. Further, it is the teacher who provides the climate conducive to children's writing—the understanding, accepting, guiding instruction, as well as sincere pleasure in the expressed ideas of the students. This teacher will recognize that there is a time for direct instruction and guidance to be provided, and that there is also a time when all that is necessary is to allow for freedom of expression to take place. In conducting the teaching/learning times, the teacher might well consider the following tasks helpful.

1. Allow for exchanging ideas. Some children need help from others in getting started. Let them talk together and make suggestions to one another as a means of initiating action.
2. Provide stimulating activators as a beginning place; many types of "starters" can be used to excite, stir the imagination, or spark the writing sessions. An extensive list of such materials is included on pp. 262–263.
3. Encourage fresh, original ideas by recognizing unique or creative ways of expression and using them as models or examples.
4. Assist children in written expression when it is needed, for they often have ideas or concepts, but lack the ability or vocabulary to express them clearly or forcefully.
5. Guide the writing experience by being available to suggest and to help students as they are writing.
6. Encourage and activate those students who have more difficulty in expressing themselves through writing by doing a group composition or by decreasing the amount expected.
7. Assess the written work as to its originality, force, correctness, and completeness. Students' use of a self-correcting checklist or teacher-student conference is preferred to teacher marking.
8. Schedule times for writers to share their compositions with small groups, another individual, or the entire class by reading them aloud or "publishing" them in a class bulletin or newspaper.
9. After diagnosing areas of need, form groups for special skills instruction in mechanics of writing.
10. Introduce new learning materials or skills instruction to the entire class, small groups, or individuals if time permits.

In considering the role of the teacher in fostering written language, it should be evident that children often need guidance and direct instruction as well as an opportunity to practice their skills. These the teacher provides along with an atmosphere of acceptance and appreciation for creative efforts.

PERSONAL CORRECTION OF ORIGINAL WRITING

An oft disputed question is: "What is the best way to correct a child's written composition?" And of course, there are many shades of answers which cover the whole spectrum from "Don't correct it at all" on one hand to "Correct every bit of written work and mark each error so that the child can make the necessary rewrites." The present authors feel that if the composition is of the original, creative type of writing, the first priority is free expression of ideas, and the teacher should not make numerous red pencil marks on it. However, this does not eliminate the need for legibility and correctness if the material is to be shared with others. How then does one correct written work? Note the following suggestions for evaluating children's compositions.

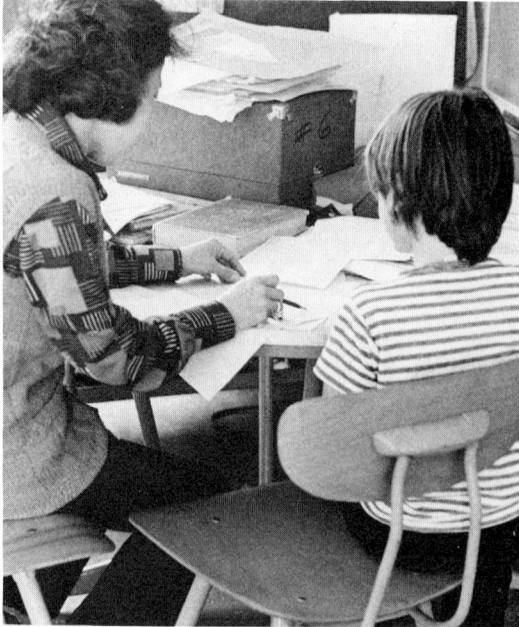

A climate of acceptance and facilitation are important components of a successful writing program. A co-operative individualization between teacher and writer is often helpful.

1. A one-to-one or small group interview-discussion time for evaluating original writing could be focused on such assessment questions as:

   Is what you wrote original?
   Did you use an old idea and give it a new form?
   Were you able to say what you wanted to say?
   Did you use enough descriptive words?
   Are your sentences complete and clear?
   Does your writing have style: pulse, imagery, and color?
   Is your content true or make-believe?
   How did you feel about writing this?
   Did you use any sensory appeals in your writing?
   How could you improve your composition if you rewrite it?
   Did you use punctuation signals where needed?

Does your title say what the composition really is?
Do you see any misspelled words?
Have you used capital letters where needed?
Would somebody else enjoy reading your composition?

2. Sometimes have peer correction in which couples work together to correct their respective papers. Allow quiet discussion and interchange as they question and suggest to one another.

3. Develop a simple checklist form commensurate with the age of your students for them to use as a "'proofreading guide device" for evaluating and correcting their own papers. The questions from no. 1 above can furnish clues for the areas of examination: punctuation, capitalization, spelling, sentence structure, title, and content could be the main categories with subcomponents for each.

4. Group correction in which the teacher leads in a review proofreading activity calling attention to their titles and asking what we remember about each word (capital letters), asking each to look at the beginning paragraph (is it indented?). Then examine each sentence (does each begin with the necessary uppercase letter?). Is there closing punctuation for each sentence (period, question, or exclamation mark)? Does direct conversation have enclosing quotation marks? Do you see any misspelled words? If this type of correction-review activity is followed rather systematically, it should develop a proofreading conscience in students before they submit work.

5. Socialized correction in which a volunteer offers his composition to be projected on the screen. He then reads it aloud and "discovers" any errors in grammar, spelling, or form. When he is finished "correcting" to the group, other members may see additional items for correction. If a projector is not available, the teacher may copy the paper on the board exactly as it is written and then allow the student to follow the same procedure. As the student examines his paper, the others in the group or class examine theirs for like errors and make the necessary corrections.

These attempts at teaching a sense of responsibility for evaluating and correcting should prove much more meaningful than for the teacher to follow the traditional route and mark each error, pass the paper back, and require recopying. Obviously, the more students can be helped to discover their own level of performance, the more they should develop some *locus of control* awareness. Also, the finding of their own errors can be treated as a positive behavior and takes the sting of criticism from the usual correcting procedure.

EXPERIENCES FOR ACTIVATING WRITTEN EXPRESSION

If the readers will note the reading list at the conclusion of this chapter, they will note a number of very fine reference texts which provide almost unlimited suggestions for interesting and activating students to do original writing in many forms. Hence, here there are only suggested categories of "sparking" the writing programs rather than specific, detailed activities. One is usually tempted to expand on the more creative aspects of original writing and identify ways of using children's interests and motivation to spur written communication. However, the teacher must not exclude the utilitarian purposes of writing, and seeking to discover means to "glamorize" the instructional program. Certainly writing stories, poems, descriptions, and even riddles and jokes may be more fun than attempting to report, outline, summarize, or write letters and complete forms. However, teaching written expression involves these functional aspects as well as the aesthetic and creative phases of the program.

SENSORY ACTIVITIES FOR ENRICHING AND EXPANDING WRITING

All kinds of sensory experiences which help young writers to feel language are important starters for instructional purposes. Making use of aural, visual, tactile, olfactory, and gustatory input provide additional dimensions for written expression. The teacher who can explore sensory elements with children will discover that their responses involve a heightened level of expressiveness.

Aural sensitivity. There is something exciting and sometimes mysterious about sensing through auditory channels without the additional input of sight, touch, smell, or taste. Common sounds made from familiar objects take on a new depth of meaning when the listener uses only hearing clues. New, descriptive words are suddenly needed to define or identify what has been heard.

Visual stimulation. All kinds of pictures, both abstract and realistic, from line drawings to gay, splashy posters, can be used to help children "see" words and phrases for describing experiences, feelings, incidents—both real and imaginary—and/or actions as they respond to pictorial media. The picture file for such instructional uses can include all categories of graphic art: people, animals, sports, places, scenery on land, sea, sky, or underground. Pictures depicting seasons, holidays, festivities, foreign lands, mountains, forests, and clouds are usable media for turning children's thinking and imaginations loose to see and sense.

Tactile dimensions. From earliest childhood, the developing youngster explores and senses with his hands, face, lips, and skin. The textures of materials, their weight or lightness, their firmness or softness, their size and shape—all such felt qualities can provide the child with descriptive material for a written activity. Any object that can be handled, touched, or sensed through feeling will serve for adding the tactile dimension for sensory description in writing.

Olfactory sensations. Any odor that is unusual or distinctive or any aroma that is pleasant or tantalizing, and the object or material from which the scent comes, is important in adding another descriptive quality to be included in written composition. These can delight and awaken memories of exquisitely vivid associations, or they can remind one of unpleasant, repugnant sources as well.

Gustatory experiences. The sense of taste can evoke such a number of descriptive words and expressions—the ones that are good, delicious, yummy, sweet, creamy, delectable, or the flavors that are sour, bitter, acid, puckery, nasty, medicinal, too salty, peppery, or spicy. Describing each and comparing or contrasting it with other tastes can be the basis for a number of interesting, sensory-focused written exercises.

As a result of exposure to and heightened awareness of the additional dimensions derived from sensory stimulation, the young writer will make use of picturesque descriptions by using carefully chosen words and phrases to convey exact and varied meanings. He will need to learn synonyms and related words for describing and defining his sensitivity expansions, hence his written expression will have the additional impetus of personal, feeling involvement. And, of course, this will increase the child's interest and investment in good written language.

USING LITERARY EXPERIENCES FOR ENHANCING WRITING

Inasmuch as the authors have included a separate section of this textbook to the use of good youth literature in enrichment and expansion of the language arts instructional program, it is sufficient here to merely give a brief listing of some of the ways literature can be effectively used for sparking original writing by young learners. As the teacher shares books of many varieties with the children, ideas will be born to both instructor and students. These need to be expressed and "frozen" so that others can share them. What better way than in original, creative writing forms? These may take the shape of poetry, original stories from groups and individuals, fantasies and make-believe tales, brief descriptive vignettes of characters or incidents, varieties of reports, articles or whatever. The important thing is to stimulate children for expressive writing, and then provide the mechanics and opportunities for them to write.

Setting the Mood for Writing Poetry

As the teacher shares poetry with children it may take on many forms, styles, or moods. Consider the following forms of poetic expression that children of various ages may utilize in seeking to share an experience, a feeling, a response, or mood.

Forms of Poetry

1. A *single line* of expressive writing may be the first attempt of the child to write a poem. Sometimes these sparkle and shine with a simplicity and beauty that astonishes the adult. Encourage any such effort; it is the basis of poetry.
2. A rhymed *couplet* seems to fit the writing needs of some children who think

poems need to rhyme and follow a certain cadence pattern. If this suits them best, let them use it and later expand it into other forms and modes.

3. *Free verse* with its free style, may not seem to some to be actual poetry. But, what is poetry? It is a freeing of children's thinking and feelings so that they let go with words and "paint a picture" of the thing they see or feel. It doesn't have to follow a form or rhyming pattern, it just has to express with beauty, clarity, or force the felt, free-flowing of the idea. Perhaps the true criteria is if it does something to the reader or listener. Does he feel the emotion, see his own pictures, or let his own songs sing inside him? Then, and only then, can it be called poetry despite its form or lack of it.

4. The simple, four-line *quatrain,* usually with alternate lines which rhyme, suits some children. It is brief enough and structured enough to provide them a certain definable pattern that they may need as a vehicle to express their poetic impulses. It may aid the teacher in first attempts to guide young writers in expressing their words like a recurrent tune. This form especially aids in the rippling, dancing quality that words have as they keep in tune with and in harmony with the music of poetry.

5. The *limerick* is often thought of as a humorous, light form of expression. It, too, with its set pattern of rhythm and rhyme, can provide the necessary boundaries to guide a more reluctant writer to make first attempts at feeling and expressing himself in poetry. Some first-line starters can be suggested by the class or group: "There was a young man of . . ." or "There once was a woman of . . . ." The fun and humor of situations and people lend themselves nicely to this simple form of poetry.

6. Japanese *haiku,* with its single nature theme, its three-line, seventeen syllable form—five syllables, seven syllables, and five syllables—has started some children along the route to expressing themselves in poetry. It is unrhymed and paints a delicate, sensitive picture of a season, a growing, living phenomenon —a flower, creature, a tree—and the writer's description, response, or feeling about the subject.

7. The *tanka* is an extended form of poetry also borrowed from the Japanese who have delighted in one person providing the original haiku, and the respondent providing an additional two lines of seven syllables each, thus forming a five-line version. This can provide an interesting and stimulating writing session with two groups participating with each other; one doing the original three-line stanza and the other developing and expanding it with the additional fourteen syllables.

8. The Korean *sijo* form of poetry is not so well known as haiku, but provides an equally viable form of expression for young poets. It is a three-sentence poem which is divided into six lines of seven or eight syllables each. Thus each sentence has from fourteen to sixteen syllables. Since the structure is even more flexible than haiku, it can provide an excellent form for early introduction of poetry to children.

With each of the three oriental forms of poetry just discussed, the most difficult task is for children to keep language simple and yet be able to effectively
express their feeling and imagery. Each form provides an opportunity to examine symbolic and abstract language which are certainly basic to oriental expression and poetry. Even elementary children can be aware of this level of
symbolic language and communication, and it enhances their pleasure in using
these literary forms.

9. Another form of simple poetry is the *cinquain*. This verse of five lines is unrhymed syllabic pattern of 2-4-6-8-2 syllables respectively. A simple pattern
or composition is as follows: Line 1: a single noun; Line 2: descriptive adjectives; Line 3: related participles to the word; Line 4: a statement about the word;
and Line 5: one summary word to express the experience, emotion, or mood.

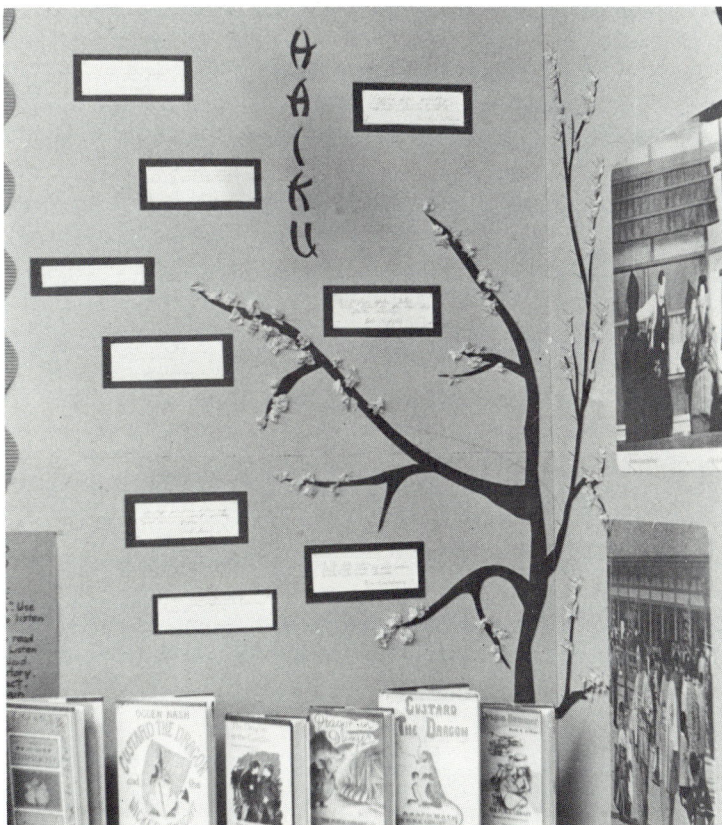

A creative climate in the classroom sets the mood for a
variety of successful experiences in poetic expression.
Children's poetry should be *seen* and *heard*.

Other poetic forms which may be used in the school setting are the six-line stanza, or *sextet,* and the fourteen-line *sonnet,* or any variation of the patterns discussed. The important consideration is that the child's poem is a word picture of his world and his feelings within that world. It must loosen his spirit, let him touch the sky. Or it may be a flowing along of his strange or vague feelings about himself and his situation or solutions to it. It can bring the inside-self out into the light and warmth of the sun for clarification and examination, and send it inward again, freshened and cleansed after asking questions without expecting answers or even being answered. It can be a sharing of delight, or a calm look at oneself. But whatever, it is an unforgettable experience in communication through writing.

WRITTEN EXPRESSION AND NARRATIVE WRITING

As the teacher shares stories with children, opportunities are provided for excitement, adventure, pathos, mystery—all the affective responses which can be vicariously shared in the circumstances and lives of the characters who live in storyland. From these identifications and projections, they are often provided the materials for their own original writings. Think of the wide spectrum of subjects dealt with in children's books and stories, and then realize that these are the very things that children themselves like to write about.

1. Young children often write about themselves—their thoughts and feelings, hopes, desires, problems, and their hurts.
2. Children enjoy and often write about the animals who are their pets: descriptions, personifications, conversations, and adventures.
3. Since children enjoy all kinds of action, any kind in fact, this is often the subject matter of their original, creative written expression.
4. Children appreciate and enjoy humor, and often want to share funny things in their stories. The ridiculous and laughable situations and involvements of life often form a thread of humor in their narratives.
5. Most children are alive with sensory stimulation; hence, they like to write about the things that their senses detect. These sensory messages often deal with strong, earthy likes or dislikes.
6. Children frequently write about nature and its phenomena: the seasons, weather, storms, clouds and sky, growing things, flowers, trees and leaves, wildlife. The variety is unlimited in its scope and interest appeal to the young writer.
7. Not only do children enjoy reading and hearing and writing about action; but they also frequently write about beautiful, quiet, lovely things. They express their deep, inner thoughts on a very philosophical level at times. The abstract quality of their expressions is interesting and thoughtful. Such themes as life and death, responsibility and maturity, peace and happiness often are handled in a very natural and beautiful simplicity.
8. Modern technology, with its space-age breadth, is also a favorite topic for

young writers. Their science fiction with its supernatural, extrasensory touch is often particularly well done.

9. The future and eternity, the mystique of the unknown frequently appears in children's writing, both poetry and prose, and they seem to enjoy delving into a realm beyond the prosaic limits of the actual.

10. Pure fantasy, utter make-believe, is sometimes handled so plausibly and convincingly that it delights the reader and listener as well as the writer himself. Made-up names, nonsense words, neologisms, and onomatopoeic words flow from the minds and pens of youthful writers in such a way that the adult reader is amazed and delighted with the skill and art reflected.

11. One last area of subject interest to children when they write is characterization. Whether it be the product of sheer imagination, or the description of a particular individual, or even a combination of several "known" people, children seem insightfully adept at such descriptions. Further their stories and incidents and poems are often built around a particular character or characters.

WRITING TECHNIQUES AND DEVICES

Not only will the intern/teacher need to be aware of the fertile areas of writing which seem to especially interest and intrigue children in their writing efforts, likewise there are certain literary devices which can be introduced for use by the young writer. This brief listing will refresh the memory of the intern or teacher and can provide the learner as well with several technical dimensions for improving or expanding written language expression and literary skills. At the beginning the young child will manipulate and play with words in a sort of joyous abandon; but as he matures, he becomes aware of writers' use of techniques in their writings. He begins to seek knowledge about these devices, and having learned about them, wants to employ them in his own written compositions. This developing of style, using of words for specific purposes and mixing the colors of language in order to more effectively express, is a learned skill. Therefore the teacher needs a modicum of expertise in order to answer questions, point out examples, and work with the young writer to guide and suggest.

Alliteration. From the early "jingle" stage of poetry or the "tongue twister" the child has become aware of the repetitive use of words with the same beginning sound to express thoughts or ideas. This euphonious device calls attention to particularly melodic combinations of sounds: "the sheen of soft, summer sunlight," or "wonderful, welcoming words."

Antithesis. Sometimes words or phrases describing a person or incident are placed in such a position that a comparison is actually a contrast: "The length to which he went was dwarfed by the insignificance of the task."

Assonance. Whereas alliteration makes use of the same initial sound, usually a consonant sound, assonance makes use of vowel sounds placed in different parts of words: "nice, spicy rice" or "the hostess with the mostess."

Imagery. Images are often classified as related to the five senses: visual, aural, tactile, olfactory, or gustatory. Hence any use of word pictures evoking these sensory images are called literary imagery.

Historical present. Elementary schoolchildren often use this technique of placing the reader in the past of history by using the present tense verb. This transporting process is effective in writing dramatic scripts for TV or radio presentations.

Metaphor. Children, without instruction and guidance, seldom make use of the metaphor device in their writing. This speaking of one object as if it were another is a somewhat sophisticated technique for making writing vivid.

Onomatopoeia. The use of words which express their own sound is a writing strategy which often adds a strength and depth to descriptive expression: "boom, crack, bow-wow."

Personification. This figure of speech gives to things or ideas the personality or qualities of humanity; the attributing of human life to inanimate objects.

Rhyme. The likeness of sounds in a variety of words, particularly at the end of lines of poetry or sentences, requires a certain auditory skill as well as handling of words.

Rhythm. The flow and melody of language, or its cadence and intonations, is important as a writing tool. Children often seem to feel the pulse and surge and vibrations of language and seek to express it in writing their own compositions.

Word order. The ability to change word orders, or to invert them in such a way as to express with clarity and force, is an important and valuable device. The alert teacher will introduce times for experimenting with word order in constructing sentences by the youthful writer.

The teacher can, by introducing such literary techniques and encouraging the students to use them, add a certain flavor and zest to children's writing. This can keep their composition from becoming monotonous, stereotyped, or stale.

One device which was not included in the previous list was the use of the *simile*. This often overused device is an easy one for the child to use. Hence, if young writers are not cautioned, it can result in worn-out, cliché language rather than an improvement and enrichment of their written expression. The simile is marked by the word "as" and expresses a comparison or likeness. Too many "light as a feather," "warm as toast," "tall as a beanpole," types of expressions are marks of poorly written work.

The seasoned teacher is aware that good writing does not develop quickly, but is a process requiring time and consistent effort. When the creative concept occurs, it should quickly be put down on paper in its raw freshness. However, the maturing child soon discovers that rewriting, polishing, and refinement are needed before he is ready for sharing his composition with others.

LEVELED SKILLS FOR TEACHING WRITTEN LANGUAGE

In order to picture the whole spectrum of skills taught in this fourth vocabulary, written language, it is helpful to examine groups of skills thought to be consistent with the development and abilities of children at the Primary Level, the Intermediate Level, and the Upper-Grade Level. These basic skill categories with their component competencies not only show the progression of learnings, but also furnish the intern/teacher with a guide for articulating his own teaching objectives as well as the competency-based goals for students. The skill groups are considered under two headings: The Mechanics of Written Language and Composition, and The Skills of Written Composition. Each section has illustrative lesson plans.

The Mechanics of Written Language and Composition

Primary Level Learnings

During the first years of the school scene, the student will be introduced to a number of written tasks which he will be expected to master.

Alphabet. All letters are to be learned in both upper- and lowercase forms.

Words. Single letters will be written in proper sequence to form words. Printed or written models as well as oral dictation may be used for learning to put letters together to form known words.

Capitalization. The uppercase letter forms will be learned for the following uses:

1. Proper names—people's names and titles; places—cities, towns, states, areas or countries; and geographical sites—rivers, mountains, lakes, seas, oceans, bays.
2. Days—of the week, holidays, and names of the months.
3. Titles of stories, books, newspapers, or magazines, as well as poems, verses, songs, or plays.
4. In written forms—greetings and closures in letters, invitations, thank-you's, acceptances.
5. In writing initials and at the beginning of sentences.
6. In direct address of persons such as father, mother, aunt, or uncle.
7. In writing the pronoun, I.

Punctuation. The meaning signals will be learned in this level of work in the following situations:
1. Period—as sentence closure, at completion of request or command, after initials, and after titles such as Mr., Mrs., or Ms.
2. Comma—used in dates, addresses, in series, to show direct conversation, and in greetings and closings of personal letters.
3. Question mark—to end sentences asking questions, or following single interrogative words (Where?).
4. Quotation marks—to enclose direct quotations or conversations, or for titles of stories, poems, plays, magazines, or reports.

Model Lesson Plan
Teaching an Introduction to the Letter P

I. **Name:** Paula Prentice   **Date:** 11-15-75   **Grade:** 1   **No.** 16

   Subject: Written Language   **Text:** Alphabet Animals

II. **Instructional Objective:** To introduce the letter P in its written form and with its associated sound.

   Performance Objective: As a result of the lesson and activities, the student will write the letter P correctly and name and write three words (pop, pup, and pet) using the letters.

III. **Assignment:** Alphabet Animals, pp. 33-34.

   Materials:
   teacher's manual and exercise books—Alphabet Animals
   pencils and crayons
   record player and record: "Paula Porcupine"

IV. **Procedure:**
   1. Review letters: b, d, and h for form.
   2. Play recorded story about "Paula."
   3. Use chalkboard and exercise books for writing P and p.
   4. Use page 34 exercise for writing and practice.

V. **Related Activities:**
   1. Art lesson for drawing Paula's habitat.
   2. Sharing circle for feeling and talking about quills.

VI. **Evaluation:** Use the children's exercise books to evaluate their writing of letter P as well as the names and words suggested. Note interest and participation in "suggested activities."

VII. **Ongoing Activities:** Play the "I Remember" game, using the jingles for each learned letter.

   Comments: Note any students needing additional work on writing (alignment, size, formation) and reschedule for reteaching.

Figure 11.1

I. **Name:** Maria Garcia   **Date:** 9-22-74   **Grade:** 1   **No.** 22

     Subject: Written Language   **Text:** <u>Alphabet Animals</u>

II. **Instructional Objective:** To assist students in completing their information form: name, address, and telephone number.

     Performance Objective: Each student will correctly write and spell his name and address with phone number as per the model furnished by the teacher.

III. **Assignment:** Find the page in <u>Alphabet Animals</u> which records the beginning letter and name of each student and then complete the writing assignment.

     Materials:
         paper, pencils, crayons
         <u>Alphabet Animal</u> exercise books
         telephone directory

IV. **Procedure:**
         1. Each child finds the page for his letter-name.
         2. Distribute "information cards" to each.
         3. Assist when needed as circulating room.
         4. Individually "interview" each child with card.

V. **Related Activities:**
         1. Introduce telephone directory and use.
         2. Play the "looking up names" game.

VI. **Evaluation:** Check each card for filing in information folders. How well did students follow directions? Write the assignment? Was writing legible, neat, correct?

VII. **Ongoing Activities:** Write letters "to each other" using a neighbor's information card for address, etc. Exchange and use social correction for assessing work.

     Comments: None.

Figure 11.2

5. Exclamation mark—to indicate statements or commands containing strong feeling or emotion.
6. Apostrophe—to indicate the possessive forms and for forming contractions.

Indenting. Words in addresses or titles, and at the beginning of paragraphs, or in chart stories.

While the child is in the several grades of the primary level, he will be introduced to these learnings as needs arise, and continue to use them as foundations for further language experiences at upper levels of work. His skills mastery will widen and include more and more situations for using these learned tasks.

Intermediate Level Learnings

During the middle grades, the student will be expected to do an increasing amount of written work in the functional setting of his classroom and daily work. Reports, assignments, taking notes, beginning outlining, filling in forms, providing information—a host of tasks will require the daily use of written language. As a result, not only the earlier basic skills will be needed, but additional uses of vocabulary forms, capitalization, and punctuation will be introduced. The following are examples/situations:

Alphabet. The skill of alphabetizing and using alphabetical order for locating information, using the dictionary, and arranging sequences will be learned at several levels of difficulty: initial letter only; first two letters; and arranging according to the first three letters.

Capitalization. The use of capital letters will include all of the primary level skills and several new situations will probably be required: names of languages and ethnic groups of people, religions, names of schools, buildings, stores or firms, and companies or corporations; names of churches, clubs, or organizations; names of continents, regions, or areas; names of roads, railways, routes; names of ships, planes, or trains; religious names, sacred writings or persons, and of deities; and capital letters in organizing series or simple outline forms.

Punctuation. The student will continue to use all of the previously learned signals and be introduced to new ones as follows:

1. Periods—after abbreviations, in outline forms, after numerals, in series of bibliographies.
2. Commas—in taking notes, in outlining, in written conversation, when last name is written first, to separate parts of bibliographical entries, to set off parenthetical materials, to separate transitional words in sentences, and to set off phrases in apposition.
3. Colon—in the greeting section of a business letter, in writing time, in introducing a list, and in writing a play.

I. **Name:** Melanie Greenburg   **Date:** 4-3-75   **Grade:** 4 **No.** 4

    Subject: Written Composition   **Text:** <u>Form and Usage</u>

II. **Instructional Objective:** To review and clarify sentence types: declarative, interrogative, and exclamatory.

    Performance Objective: Students will recognize and compose written sentences illustrating each of the three categories with appropriate closing punctuation.

III. **Assignment:** Complete work sheet identifying sentence types. Review textbook (pp. 12, 15, and 21) discussion and assignment.

    Materials:
        work sheets: sentence identification
        textbooks
        paper and pencils, sentence posters

IV. **Procedure:**
    1. Pretest skills level with work sheet.
    2. Correct and discuss in class.
    3. Reading assignment and group discussion (3).
    4. Chalkboard exercise—original sentence sharing.

V. **Related Activities:**
    1. From reading selection (current assignment), identify and write illustrative sentences.
    2. Role-playing use of sentence types for expression.
    3. Film viewing and tally of sentence types used.

VI. **Evaluation:** Teacher observation checklist of group activity as well as diagnosis from pretest worksheets for pupil needs.

VII. **Ongoing Activities:** Writing of "radio scripts" for sharing for use of varied sentence forms.

    Comments: Assess participation and interest evidence for affective tone in learning.

Figure 11.3

4. Hyphen—in separating syllables of words, when dividing words at ends of lines, in writing some compound words.
5. Indenting—in writing outlines, subtitles, or topic headings in a report.

Upper-Grade Learnings in Written Language

The teacher will be aware that language curriculum follows a spiral model. It begins on a narrow base, and year-by-year expands as it progresses upward from level to level. Thus it continues to utilize previously learned skills and competencies as it introduces new ones and widens the scope of learned abilities. Hence, at the upper-grade levels, some new learnings that are presented as learned skills are reinforced and strengthened. Note the following:

Capitalization. Additional geographical names and locations, names of monuments or buildings, political parties, government titles and positions, government departments, documents of importance, and names of family relationships.

Punctuation. Some additional uses may be introduced.

1. Commas—for clarity in sentences, as interrupters for emphasis or effect, as showing introductory elements in sentences, for dividing compound sentences, to set off phrases and clauses in certain sentences.
2. Semicolon—for use in sentences with other punctuation, and separating independent clauses in compound sentences.
3. Italics—for denoting titles of books and for emphasis of particular words, also for transliterated terms commonly used (*vis-à-vis, vice versa*).

Admittedly, many skills continuums may contain many more specific skills listings; but this should alert the student/teacher to a briefly stated, sequential ordering of the basic skills important in the mechanics of written language.

The Skills of Written Composition

In outlining the skills to be taught for written language, it should be noted that there is a difference between *objective* writing and *subjective* writing. Likewise, it should be noted that skills for objective writing are more easily defined and listed than for subjective writing. The very nature of the latter lends itself much more easily to the originational, creative aspects of written expression—poetry, description, stories, drama, and various types of prose writing—hence, some of the more rigid restraints governing objective writing may easily be waived to provide for variety and flexibility to the writer. However, the reader will note that many of the following skills relate equally to both aspects of written language.

Primary Level Learnings

As soon as the child begins to compose, either with the guidance and help of his instructor, as a group activity, or as a solo effort, he will become aware of a number of learnings and skills essential to clear expression. These foundational learnings will continue to be used and refined throughout, not only his academic era, but all of his life whenever he uses the medium of written communication. These skills areas are considered under the headings: Vocabulary, Sentence Structure, Composition Form, and Evaluation.

Vocabulary. The student will learn to transfer the words from his listening, speaking, and reading vocabularies to written form with a growing respect for accuracy and clarity. He will also discover words and terms which express affective quality and sensory impressions, and begin to use them in composition writing. His ability to use variant forms of words will be correctly reflected in his writings, synonyms, and vivid, color words.

Sentence Structure. In forming his written sentences in "experience chart" stories or original writing, the primary student will:

1. Relate the cadence and intonational patterns of spoken language to the need for punctuation and capitalization in his written expression.
2. Begin to incorporate simple sentences and more complex forms into his writing.
3. Begin to avoid the run-on sentence type of writing by overusing connectives.
4. Use complete sentences in his writing.
5. Discover a "feeling" for vivid, descriptive words and language and begin to use it in his written communications.
6. Become aware of proper sequence in writing of happenings and use simple paragraphs as a means of closure.
7. From orally relating an event, begin to "outline" events in chronological order and then transfer this to written expression.
8. Begin to develop simple plans for written composition: main ideas, topic sentences, and organizational patterns.
9. Develop a single subject in his story, description, or narrative (single paragraph).

Composition Form. As the student becomes involved in learning experiences related to written language, he will:

1. Observe the beginnings of form on teacher-prepared chart stories, chalkboard work, or from printed materials—title, spacing, margins, size of letters, alignments.
2. Begin to follow suggested manuscript forms—headings, margins, titles.
3. Learn and use a simple form for a friendly letter.
4. Be aware of simple poetic forms and use them in composing original verse— limericks, couplets, quatrains.

Model Lesson Plan
Letter Forms

I.   **Name:**   Mr. Ted Bloomington   **Date:**   10-17-74   **Grade:**   3   **No.** 7

    Subject: Written Expression   **Text:**   <u>Language We Use</u> (3)

II.   **Instructional Objective:** To introduce students to the basic form of a personal letter.

    Performance Objective: The student will recognize and name the basic parts of a personal letter: inside address, greeting, message, and closing as per the model provided.

III.   **Assignment:** Pp. 17-18, language text, and composing a group letter to be written thanking recent visitor to the classroom.

    Materials:
        textbooks
        paper and pencils
        envelope forms

IV.   **Procedure:**
        1.   Read and discuss letter form.
        2.   Compose a group letter to express thanks.
        3.   Copy letters and address the "envelopes."
        4.   Select good work for display and sending.

V.   **Related Activities:**
        1.   Sharing experience of recent letter from a friend.
        2.   Use filmstrip: "Letter Writing is Fun."

VI.   **Evaluation:** Examine work for freshness of thought and expression. Using text model for format and spacing, judge the level of work: Excellent, Superior, Good, Fair, or Poor.

VII.   **Ongoing Activities:** Arrange a "twin" room with another teacher for letter-writing exchange of personal letters to be acknowledged and answered.

    Comments: An excellent opportunity to use a learning experience for expressing personal feelings.

Figure 11.4

Model Lesson Plan
Reporting

I. Name: Selina Hodges   **Date:** 1-15-75   **Grade:** 1   **No.** 4

    Subject: Written Expression   **Text:** <u>Learning About Letters</u>

II. Instructional Objective: To strengthen writing skills: narrating and recording an incident using correct form.

    Performance Objective: Following the teacher model, students will copy and correct their "story" about Mickie Monkey—noting capital letters, closing punctuation, and simple sentences.

III. Assignment: Use lesson 10 from <u>Learning About Letters</u>—<u>M</u> animals. Discuss and write a group story about Mickie Monkey.

    Materials:
        lined paper, pencils, crayons
        exercise books: <u>Learning About Letters</u>
        notes from zoo field trip

IV. Procedure:
    1. Refer to "log" from recent zoo trip.
    2. Discuss and describe the monkey moat and island.
    3. Build an experience story about the monkeys.
    4. Copy and read the story and correct it.

V. Related Activities:
    1. Read the incident from <u>Mr. Stubbs</u> about the escape.
    2. Use the monkey puppets <u>to role play</u> activities.

VI. Evaluation: Collect stories. Note form, legibility, and correctness (capital letters, closing punctuation, sentence structure).

VII. Ongoing Activities: Show a film: "Day at the Zoo" and discuss "local color" and the monkey habitat. Talk about colors, sounds, smells (sensory input).

    Comments: Note those students who habitually respond—more important, those who are quiet and unobtrusive. Seek to draw them into more active participation in the next language experience story activity.

Figure 11.5

Evaluation. In order to begin at earliest levels to help students develop responsibility for correcting and assessing their written language, the teacher will guide the student in:

1. Looking over his own work after completing it, then using planned language lessons for assisting in *self-improvement* correction.
2. Noting misspelled words by comparing them with a word list, beginning dictionary, or teacher's assistance list from the chalkboard.
3. Building his own "Writing Vocabulary List" from words he uses and needs.

Intermediate Levels of Language Learning

During the continuing process of learning written composition, the student will strengthen his previously acquired skills and knowledge, and he will be introduced to more discrete competencies as well. This expanding and refining experience should be embedded in many relevant and interesting activities throughout the entire school day. Learning all aspects of language is a full-time task and cannot be limited to a separate period for each of the strands of instruction. There will be specific time slots alloted to introducing new skills, but the reinforcement of these abilities will best be continued in all written activities to which the child is exposed. The competencies which are often expected of middle-grade students include the following items.

Vocabulary. As the learner uses written language in his many daily experiences, he will:

1. Develop a feeling for, and an ability to use appropriately chosen words, both at the connotative as well as the denotative levels of meaning.
2. Increase his written vocabulary to be more nearly commensurate with his speaking and reading vocabularies.
3. Vary his use of words to eliminate undue repetitiveness.
4. Learn to choose words which avoid vague or indefinite meaning, and use exact, clear words in expressing his message.
5. Avoid using overworked, tired clichés and redundant overwordiness.

Composition Structure. The intermediate student will build his sentences, paragraphs, and short compositions by:

1. Varying his sentence structure by using simple, complex, and compound sentences.
2. Controlling the overuse of connectives and avoiding run-on sentences by wise use of "and" or "but."
3. Building sentences that clearly and vividly describe incidents, people, or places.

Model Lesson Plan
Creative Writing

I. **Name:** George Kaspian   **Date:** 10-5-75   **Grade:** 4   **No.** 2

    Subject: Creative Writing   **Text:** <u>Slithery Snakes</u>, etc.

II. **Instructional Objective:** To provide a stimulating learning situation for sparking original composition.

     Performance Objective: Given an activator, students will respond by identifying five descriptive words about the object and then write an original story involving the object and using the words.

III. **Assignment:** To write an original composition (poem, short story, descriptive narrative) centered in an activator.

     Materials:
     box of sensory-provoking objects
     paper and pencil
     recording of soft background music

IV. **Procedure:**
     1. Use the "grab box" for selecting an article.
     2. Group oral discussion and description for starters.
     3. Individual "grabbing" of an article activator.
     4. Composition and writing time.

V.   **Related Activities:**
     1. Play "Game Chains" for identifying words.
     2. Use recorded story for model of form and content.

VI. **Evaluation:** Particularly note colorful words, unity of narration, clear description, and original "twists" in expression.

VII. **Ongoing Activities:** Self-correction and refinement for polished production of class newspaper inclusion.

     Comments: None.

Figure 11.6

4. Organizing his topic by arranging subtopics logically or sequentially.
5. Planning paragraphs before beginning to write.
6. Using a new paragraph for changing speakers when writing dialogue or conversation.
7. Demonstrating a growing knowledge and skill in controlling written language for particular purposes.
8. Constructing each paragraph in an expository composition or written report on the basis of each phase, aspect, or division of the particular topic being included.

Manuscript Form. The instructional program will include various forms of writing. The student will learn to:

1. Use Roman numerals, alphabet letters, and Arabic numerals in sequencing outlines.
2. Follow a model for writing various types of letters, for inviting, inquiring, replying.
3. Develop a simple chart form for memos, bulletins, announcements, lists, outlines, or recording.
4. Recognize and use a variety of poetic forms, story forms, dramatic forms, and reporting forms.
5. Follow simple standard conventions in all assigned or required written work.
6. Take notes from written or oral presentations without copying verbatim.

Assessing Competencies. In developing his "language conscience," the student should be encouraged to follow the procedures suggested below:

1. After proofreading a first draft of a composition, the student will be responsible to correct, revise, and rewrite a final copy.
2. Use oral reading of his composition to test for complete sentences, clarity of expression, and logical meaning. Then to apply proper punctuation to assist a reader in interpreting what he has written.
3. Use the dictionary or form model for comparing usage, spelling, format, and written mechanics in order to make corrections.
4. When editing written language, the student should consistently use a simple code of symbols to indicate each type of error ("sp" for a spelling error, / to show need for space or division, ¶ to show need for paragraph).

Upper-Grade Written Language Skills in Composition

Normally the student will have been introduced to most of the basic skills of written composition by the time he reaches the upper elementary grades. Hence much of the instructional program may be diagnostic to alert the student and teacher to specific areas of competency which do not need continued emphasis or

Model Lesson Plan
Writing

I. **Name:** Norman Browning   **Date:** 11-23-74   **Grade:** 5   **No.** 12

Subject: Written Expression   **Text:** Language Here and Now

II. **Instructional Objective:** To provide a learning setting for instruction in formal letter writing.

Performance Objective: Students will follow a model for writing a formal letter of inquiry, application, or replying and correct their letter using the class checklist form.

III. **Assignment:** Read the section on formal letters from the textbook, pp. 77-78. Select a purpose type and compose a short letter.

Materials:
textbooks
paper and pencils, and business envelope forms
wallcharts of letter-type forms

IV. **Procedure:**
1. Discuss wall charts noting specifics.
2. Read and discuss text suggestions.
3. Select letter type and compose letters.
4. Volunteer for projected letter—socialized correction.

V. **Related Activities:**
1. Construct bulletin board of display work.
2. Prepare pages for class "model" book for writing.

VI. **Evaluation:** Brief dictated quiz on letter parts. Examine letters for correctness and form. Note content, expression, clarity, force.

VII. **Ongoing Activities:** Compose and send actual letters of inquiry and request for materials for current social studies unit on transportation.

Comments: Seek to relate written work to all phases and areas of the curriculum.

Figure 11.7

Model Lesson Plan
Sharing

I. Name: Mary Lynn Morrison   **Date:** 11-2-75   **Grade:** 8   **No.** 8

Subject: Journalism   **Text:** <u>Writing and Reporting</u>

II. Instructional Objective: To provide learning experiences focused on an interview report situation.

Performance Objective: The student will interview a professional person for a minimum of ten minutes, make notes, and compose a brief interview-report for the class newspaper.

III. Assignment: To schedule an interview, hold it, make notes, and write an interview description as a result.

Materials:
handbook of interviewing/reporting techniques
reporters' pads, pencils
format model for the "paper"

IV. Procedure:
1. Make appointments for interviews of choice.
2. Conduct interview session and take notes.
3. Organize and do rough-draft copy for critiquing.
4. Correct and polish report for publication.

V. Related Activities:
1. Compare literary styles of several well-known reporters from clippings.
2. Do some background "research" on the profession of interview candidate.

VI. Evaluation: Group critiquing and sharing of rough-draft reports. Set group standards of quality necessary for submitting for publication and acceptance.

VII. Ongoing Activities: Role play different interview reporting situations: police, politician, celebrity.

Comments: Things to note: lead questions, note-taking techniques, topic sentences, conclusion.

Figure 11.8

I. **Name:** Mr. Tim Worthington   **Date:** 11-7-75   **Grade:** 6   **No.** 11

    Subject: Written Expression   **Text:** Today's English (6)

II. **Instructional Objective:** To provide a relevant setting for organizing and writing a written report on selected topic.

    Performance Objective: Following standard form, the student will organize a written report and compose it for class information sharing and critiquing.

III. **Assignment:** Review information on report writing from chapter 5, pp. 173-175 of English text. Prepare rough draft of report.

    Materials:
      English textbook
      reference sources for report information
      report form model for brief draft
      paper and pencils

IV. **Procedure:**
     1. Oral presentation of model report: assess.
     2. Reread textbook discussion: purposes/procedures.
     3. Use "brief draft" form for organization.
     4. Complete rough draft for preliminary evaluation.

V. **Related Activities:**
     1. Listen to recorded brief reports from last year's class.
     2. Compare and evaluate dittoed reports to model.

VI. **Evaluation:** Assess for clarity, logical sequence, strength of support material included, sources of information, interest, and sentence structure.

VII. **Ongoing Activities:** Begin class "textbook" of written report models for reference table usage.

    Comments: Emphasize self-responsibility for proofreading and improvement before submitting reports.

Figure 11.9

reteaching, or to particular deficiencies which need attention and improvement. Providing the student with a variety of meaningful activities for using language in its written forms, of course, will be a vital facet of the teacher's planning and preparation. In each area of written composition instruction, there will be ample need and scope for expanding and refining skills. Note the continuum that follows for suggestions.

Above all else, written language experiences should provide an element of delight. Here children have illustrated a favorite poem.

Written Vocabulary and Word Usage. The older student can be helped in his use of words by:

1. Expressing ideas found in his own opinions, experiences, and imaginations.
2. Exploring the creative aspects of figurative language usage of simile, metaphor, antithesis, personification.
3. Expanding ideas and concepts by examining attitudes, interests, feelings of oneself and others.
4. Clarifying ideas and vocabulary through the study of people, places, and events.

Structure Development. As the student continues to build on the previously learned skills of composition, his work will be chiefly one of refining abilities to write. The following suggested competencies should be considered by the intern/ teacher.

1. Expository writing should be focused around the following skills: ability to clearly explain a process or topic, clarity in organizing data or information, fully developing a subject or topic, and supporting a position or opinion.
2. Paragraph development should include: unity of subject matter; clear topic sentence; variety of coverage—with facts, incidents, examples, or reasons; and cohesiveness and coherence—order of importance, chronological order, logical order, and order of location.
3. A variety of composition forms should be used and experimented with—narration, exposition, description, characterization, communication.

SUMMARY

Teachers have often asked themselves: "What is the difference? What makes some written composition by children drab and dull? Why do some write with force and clarity so that what they say is sparkling and spontaneous?" These and like questions can be answered. Creative expression in writing is the result of a number of factors: depth of the child's insight, his native ability, his creative capacity, his awareness of relationships, his facility with words, his grasp of the skills and mechanics of writing, his mental imagery and skill in recording and recreating it for others. Further, the child's written composition will reflect the skill and sensitivity of his teacher. If that instructor is perceptive and accepting, the classroom will be a reflection of the attitude of the teacher. There will be a climate of safety for children to express their ideas and feelings. There will be many stimulating activators for the slow starters. There will be ample time for children to explore, examine, think—time to create. There will also be good teaching that provides the impetus for writing and then supports it with good teaching of skills and mechanics necessary for excellence in written expression. There will be scheduled time for refinement and rewriting; and there will be time for sharing and enjoyment of the original, creative writing done by fellow students within the class.

The teacher of written language is the most important single factor toward success. The patience and encouragement supplied by the teacher are invaluable

Model Lesson Plan
Outlining

I. **Name:** Bellamy Roundtree   **Date:** 10-27-75   **Grade:** 7   **No.** 13

Subject: Functional Writing   **Text:** How to Use Language (7)

II. **Instructional Objective:** To review and refine skills required in writing an outline from written materials.

Performance Objective: The student will prepare a five-point outline in written form following the class model for indentation, labeling, and sequencing.

III. **Assignment:** Discuss uses and values of outlines for guiding in writing, pp. 25-31. Outline article of choice.

Materials:
textbooks for model and information
assorted short articles for outline materials
outline blanks for student use and pens

IV. **Procedure:**
1. Groups (four) discussion and demonstration.
2. Selection of articles for couple-writing tasks.
3. Correction and refinement of doubled groups.
4. Assessment and selection for volunteer displays.

V. **Related Activities:**
1. View film (Britannica): "Outlining Simplified."
2. Compare various means of markings used in outlining.

VI. **Evaluation:** From one-page, ditto handout, individuals will prepare an outline, step-by-step.

VII. **Ongoing Activities:** From prepared outline, the groups will write an original story, report, or essay following the outlined sequence, plot-line, or data as designated.

Comments: Stress the logical order, brevity, and clarity.

Figure 11.10

Model Lesson Plan
Poetry

I. Name: Heather Symington   **Date:** 10-7-74   **Grade:** 5   **No.** 7

    Subject: Written Language   **Text:**   <u>Haiku Is Fun</u>

II. Instructional Objective: To introduce haiku form and provide instruction in original writing of a poetic nature.

    Performance Objective: After the discussion and introduction of haiku form (5-7-5), students will write an original haiku poem following the prescribed model.

III. Assignment: To select a nature theme (season, animal, flower, or plant) and compose and write an original Japanese poem.

    Materials:
       books of haiku poetry for sharing
       scansion model—large chart
       paper, pencils, pictures

IV. Procedure:
    1. Read-aloud time of haiku poetry.
    2. Discussion and instruction time—form.
    3. Chalkboard listing of suggested themes.
    4. Group composition time—individual writing.

V. Related Activities:
    1. Art lesson for illustrating poems.
    2. "Televised" art show with audience reading of haiku.

VI. Evaluation: Work toward fresh, clean expression of each "miniature." Count syllables for the rhythm patterns. Note symbolism and picturesque word selection.

VII. Ongoing Activities: Compare other poetic forms (Korean sijo, couplets, quatrains, cinquains). Try writing examples as a group composition with the teacher.

    Comments: A good opportunity to emphasize feeling of beauty and aesthetics.

Figure 11.11

aids to guiding the child through the developing steps from cognition to communication, through the very personal, imaginative, individualistic levels of creating. First of all, the child must be stimulated and alerted to the sheer joy of recording free ideas, then led into the experiment of creating with words. Later he will be guided into the intricacies of form and style which require a certain self-evaluation; and it must be emphasized that early assessment must come from the writer himself. Later, when he has experimented, explored, attempted, and communicated, he will be strong enough to have some external evaluation from teacher and friends as he begins the more difficult task of developing correct form and style as well as organization and writing conventions. If this is enforced too soon, it may be destructive and harmful to the embryonic writer.

It is well to remember that children differ as widely in their writing abilities and linguistic developments as in any other phase of their complex progression: physically, emotionally, socially, and academically. Hence, every freedom must be allowed each child to create within the climate of his abilities, desires, and interests. The product of their endeavors will likewise differ greatly—in the amount produced, the flow and style of their expression, their use of words and description, their level of refinement, and their need of stimulation and encouragement. For the teacher who will dare to open the door to good written expression, the reward and the satisfaction will be commensurate with the effort expended.

Selected Readings: Written Composition

Please note the following fine selections which deal with many aspects of children and writing. They offer a rich variety of subjects and suggestions for sparking young students in using written language.

APPLEGATE, MAUREE. *Easy in English, An Imaginative Approach to the Teaching of the Language Arts.* New York: Harper & Row, Publishers, 1960.

BEHN, HARRY. *Cricket Songs, Japanese Haiku.* New York: Harcourt, Brace & World, Publishers, 1964.

BURGER, ISABEL N. *Creative Play Acting.* New York: A. S. Barnes and Company, 1950.

BURROWS, ALVINA T. *Teaching Composition—What Research Says to the Teacher.* National Education Association, No. 18, 1969.

CARLSON, RUTH KEARNEY. "The Sunset Is a Pretty Pink Dove—Children's Voices in Poetry." *Elementary English,* October 1969, pp. 748–57.

CARLSON, RUTH KEARNEY. "Seventeen Qualities of Original Writing." *Elementary English* 38 (December 1961):576–579.

CURRY, LOUISE. *Teaching with Puppets.* Philadelphia: Fortress Press, 1966.

DURLAND, FRANCES C. *Creative Dramatics for Children.* Yellow Springs, Ohio: Antioch Press, 1952.

EARLY, MARGARET. *Language Face to Face, Developing a Language Centered Curriculum at the Heman Street School, Arts Center.* Syracuse, N. Y.: Syracuse University Press, 1971.

English Curriculum Study Center. *Project English: Written Composition—A Guide for*

Teachers in Elementary Schools. Bulletin No. 101965. Athens, Ga.: University of Georgia Press, 1964.

GEORGE, MARY YANAGA. *Language Art, An Ideabook.* Scranton, Penn.: Chandler Publishing Company, 1970.

HOFSTELLER, ARTHUR N.; ANDERSON, LORENA A.; and FRAME, RUTH. *Cooperative Evaluation of Proficiency in English and Creative Writing.* Kanawha County Schools, Charleston, West Virginia, 1962.

JORY, JOAN. *Nonsensical Nuances of ABC's.* Alameda County Schools Department, 224 West Winton Avenue, Haywood, California 94544, 1968.

KOCH, KENNETH. *Wishes, Lies and Dreams.* New York: Chelsea House Publishers, 1971 (paperback: Random House, 1971).

Kids (a magazine written for and by children). Write to Box 30, Cambridge, Mass. 02139, for sample copy.

LEWIS, RICHARD. *The Moment of Wonder, A Colection of Chinese and Japanese Poetry.* New York: The Dial Press Inc., Publishers, 1964.

LOGAN, LILLIAN M.; LOGAN, VIRGIL G.; and PATERSON, LEONA. *Creative Communication, Teaching the Language Arts.* Toronto, Canada: McGraw-Hill Ryerson Limited, Publishers, 1972.

MARKSBERRY, MARY LEE. *Foundation for Creativity.* New York: Harper & Row, Publishers, 1963.

McCORD, DAVID. "Excerpts from 'Write Me Another Verse.' " *Horn Book,* August 1970, pp. 364–69.

MIZUMURA, KAZUE. *I See the Winds.* New York: Thomas Y. Crowell, Publishers, 1966.

Northwestern University Curriculum Center in English. *Project English: A Teacher's Experience with Composition.* Evanston, Ill.: Northwestern University, 1965.

PEASE, DON. *Creative Writing in the Elementary School.* New York: Exposition Press, 1964.

PETTY, WALTER T., and BOWEN, MARY. *Slithery Snakes and Other Aids to Children's Writing.* New York: Appleton-Century-Crofts, 1967.

REDKEY, NANCY. "Free Writing for Fluency." *Elementary School Journal,* May 1964, pp. 430–33.

SCOTT, LOUISE BINDER. *Learning Time with Language Experiences for Young Children.* New York: McGraw-Hill Book Company, Inc., 1968.

SMITH, JAMES A. *Setting Conditions for Creative Teaching in the Elementary School.* Boston: Allyn & Bacon, Inc., 1966.

STICKLAND, RUTH G. *The Language Arts in the Elementary School.* Boston: D. C. Health and Co., 1969, Chapter 14.

TORRANCE, E. PAUL. *What Research Says to the Teacher: Creativity.* Washington, D.C.: National Education Association, 1963.

———. "Creative Thinking of Children." *Journal of Teacher Education,* December 1962, pp. 448–60.

WALTER, NINA WILLIS. *Let Them Write Poetry.* New York: Holt, Rinehart & Winston, 1966.

WILT, MARIAM E. *Creativity in the Elementary School.* New York: Appleton-Century-Crofts, Inc., 1959.

WOLFSON, BERNICE J. "Creativity in the Classroom." *Elementary English* 38 (November 1961):523.

12

THE MECHANICS OF
WRITTEN LANGUAGE
HANDWRITING AND SPELLING

SECTION I ■ HANDWRITING, THE UTILITARIAN TOOL: THE THEORETICAL APPROACH

Learning to form letters is a skill. This skill is important, as it is one of the tools children need in order to communicate with written language. We need to think of handwriting as a means to an end, not an end unto itself.

The old, and in some places still hallowed, belief that all handwriting be absolutely uniform and beautiful by a specific standard, has been pretty much discarded by most authorities. The major issues with handwriting are, or should be, (1) can it be read easily, (2) is it legible, since it is a form of communication, and (3) can it effectively communicate what the writer wishes to communicate?

Like all skills, learning handwriting needs specific teaching. It cannot develop properly with children unless its development is carefully guided. The teacher, therefore, needs to plan and execute in a professional way so that children will develop facility with this skill.

READINESS FOR HANDWRITING

The teacher who works with preschool, kindergarten, and primary grade youngsters knows the importance of readiness for handwriting. She knows that quite often the small muscles that operate for handwriting are not sufficiently developed to handle a pen or pencil with the necessary dexterity for handwriting. Therefore, one of her major jobs, particularly in preschool and kindergarten, and quite often in the first grade, is to provide activities that will develop these small muscles needed for handwriting. Cutting and pasting, scribbling, drawing and painting—all manner of manipulative exercises are provided for the youngster so

290

Handwriting requires careful teaching and modeling by the instructor. Many times this instruction, as in many other areas, needs to be individualized.

that his small muscles can become "educated" enough so that he can approach the task of handwriting successfully at a later time.

Along with manipulative exercises, the teacher of young children will provide many opportunities to distinguish between sizes and shapes. Visual discrimination is necessary for reading, as discussed earlier, but it is likewise equally necessary for the skills of handwriting.

Many preschool and kindergarten teachers know that readiness to write comes at different times for different children. Some children are quite able to recognize and recreate their names, names of familiar classroom objects, and the like at the end of kindergarten or the beginning of first grade. Others need continuing readiness before they are able to attempt this task.

The youngster in the preschool and the kindergarten-first levels needs to see handwriting utilized. He needs to see ideas written, to dictate experiences to the teacher so that she can transcribe them on the chalkboard for him to examine and perhaps to read back to the teacher. Much of the readiness provided for beginning reading will provide a readiness for handwriting as well.

The chalkboard in the classroom is a fine place to extend readiness activities. Small groups of children can be placed at the chalkboard and comfortably utilize the large muscles while training the small muscles by drawing circles and straight lines necessary for later manuscript writing. Drawing at the chalkboard or making stick figures are other activities that can enhance readiness for writing.[1]

Dr. Jerry E. King, specialist and authority in early childhood education at the University of the Pacific, suggests several points for observation to determine whether or not a child is ready to begin the task of learning the skills of handwriting. He recommends we observe for the following:

1. Does the child use symbols in his drawings? For example, roof on a house, windows in the house, proper sizes and shapes in his drawings.
2. Does he color with reason? Are the colors he uses sympathetic with the real world?
3. Is his hand-eye coordination able to allow him to pick up objects easily, throw a ball with some facility? Is he able to throw a ball?
4. Does his hand-eye coordination allow him to successfully put simple puzzles back together?
5. Can the youngster walk a "walking beam" successfully?
6. Is he able to turn the pages of a book with facility?
7. Does the child play at writing? Does he scribble and pretend that it is writing?
8. Can he reproduce circles and squares after viewing them?
9. Can he correctly manipulate the crayon and other writing tools?
10. Can he follow line patterns with scissors? Can he cut out shapes and patterns?

If the majority of these tasks can be successfully completed, the youngster is ready to begin initial instruction in handwriting.

MANUSCRIPT WRITING

Manuscript writing describes that kind of writing commonly called "print script." It most closely resembles that print found on the printed page that the youngster encounters in initial attempts at reading. In another chapter of this book the rationale for the use of manuscript writing for young children was offered. In today's elementary schools, approximately 85 percent of our teachers use manuscript writing as the method of inducing writing in young children. This instructional trend began in the United States in the early 1920s and has continued to the present.

The student of teaching may well ask the reasons for this wide acceptance of the manuscript approach for beginning handwriting. The reasons are clear. The simple line, circles, and spacing requirements meet the muscular needs of the young child as he recreates the various letters via this medium. This approach, likewise,

---

1. Paul C. Burns et al., *The Language Arts in Childhood Education* (Chicago, Ill.: Rand-McNally & Co., 1971), pp. 336–341.

aids him in an early expressing of his felt need to communicate with the written word.

Handwriting, as pointed out earlier, is a skill which develops gradually. It needs that gradual development as a refining process. It will not develop by itself, unaided. Some learn the skills of handwriting easily. Some find it a long and arduous task. As we know, children develop at various rates. The growth and development pattern of writing reflects that variance of growth. Natural aptitude is another variable, which the teacher will note as she assesses individual student differences.

In response to these observations the teacher will plan an instructional program which will seek to meet the needs of these differences by providing opportunities for the youngster to learn forms and, by practicing basic movements, recreate those forms; and by providing many experiences for the child to use his newly acquired writing skills in meaningful and interesting activities.

The Skills of Teaching Manuscript Writing

Always and constantly in learning to write, the child needs examples of manuscript letter forms before him. These models are a basic reinforcing element as he learns to write. These models of and by themselves, however, are not adequate to induce complete learning. Direct instruction becomes mandatory. The following modeling agents need to be considered by the teacher for beginning writing instruction.

1. All manuscript letters are made with straight lines and circles, or parts thereof.
2. All letters start at the top; not with a beginning upstroke.
3. All strokes are made separately. The writing instrument is lifted slightly before the next stroke begins.
4. All but five letters end at the base line. The exceptions are g, j, p, q, and y, which extend below.
5. All capital letters and tall letters are to be written two spaces high. Small letters use one space.
6. Space between letters varies according to formation. Those letters using the circle are closer together, and the vertical letters are spaced farther apart.

These brief guidelines will assist the teacher in the basic consideration needed in beginning handwriting instruction.

Introducing the Letters

Many teachers like to group letters according to their stroke patterns in introducing them to children. The following clusters may aid the teacher in such grouping.

Uppercase Letters

1. Straight lines and circles are used in forming: C, G, O, and Q.
2. Straight lines only are used in forming: E, F, H, I, L, and T.
3. Half circles and straight lines are used to form: B, D, J, P, R, and U.
4. Straight lines and slanting strokes are used in forming the following: A, K, M, N, W, V, X, Y, and Z.

Lowercase Letters

1. Half circles and straight lines are used with f, i, l, t, and u.
2. Straight lines and counterclockwise circles are used in forming: a, c, d, e, g, o, q.
3. Straight lines and clockwise circles are used to form p and b.
4. Straight lines combine with part circles to form h, j, m, n, r, and y.
5. Straight lines with slanting strokes are used to form k, v, w, x, and z.
6. In writing the letters S and s, the writer uses two half circles connected.

In introducing these early writing experiences and learnings, the thoughtful teacher will make use not only of individual instruction, but will also use the group setting for teaching many of the letters and their formation. As soon as the students have learned to write the letters, they may begin to use them to copy words, sentences, or even short stories from their class-developed experience chart stories. They may also want to copy short poems or stories from printed sources. Each of these, or like activities, will afford them opportunities to use their newly acquired abilities.

Additional Techniques for Manuscript Writing

Not only good teaching practices, but reliable research findings as well, have indicated that certain instructional procedures need to be considered in the program. These can add immeasurably to the success of learning as children are induced to write. Briefly stated, they include such matters as: positioning of the paper; method of holding the pencil; lighting and vision of the writer; and posture and seating while writing. Each of these considerations is briefly examined here.

Position of the paper. In manuscript writing, the paper is placed squarely on the desk so that downward strokes are pulled directly toward the child. This aids the child in keeping his writing of manuscript vertical on the page without a slant to the letters. As the child writes down on his practice paper, he continues to push it away from his chest so that he is comfortable. With the paper correctly placed straight on the desk, it makes little difference if the child is right- or left-handed as long as he holds his pencil correctly.

Method of holding the pencil. The manner in which the student holds his pen or pencil is important for writing comfort. A few simple suggestions, if followed at the beginning of the child's learning to write, can make the physical act of writing a relaxed experience resulting in a feeling of pleasure. On the other hand, if the child is tense and uncomfortable, the feelings he associates with handwriting can frustrate and hinder his progress. Note these simple guides.

1. Youngsters need practice writing at the chalkboard before writing in smaller script on paper at the desk. This can aid in developing free arm movement and will facilitate the child in keeping his hand below the writing line.
2. The learner needs to grasp the pencil or pen with his thumb, the index and middle fingers in an extended position.
3. The pencil or pen should be held loosely; never gripped tightly.
4. In order for the writer to clearly see the lines on which he is writing, he should hold the writing hand well below the line.
5. Normally the child will grasp his pencil about an inch from the tip; however, the left-handed child should hold the pencil farther from the tip—about an inch and a half.

Lighting and vision of the writer. To be effective in writing, the child needs normal vision, whether with or without correction for abnormalities. Not only is his normal vision important, but the light which falls on his paper is a requisite for success. If the lighting can be arranged for the right-handed child so that it falls over his left shoulder and vice versa for the left-handed youngster, it allows maximum illumination for his task.

Posture and seating while writing. By rule of thumb, it can probably be assumed that the child "fits" the desk; he is comfortable while seated; his feet reach the floor without strain; the desk surface is smooth and easily within his reach; and his spine is comfortably straight while he is writing.

The Left-Handed Child and Writing Instruction

Mention has been made of the sinistral, or left-handed, child. However, a few words should be included here for the teacher's consideration. Individuals may be classified as "handed" if they show a strong preference for using one hand more than the other. The range goes from dominant right-handedness through mild degrees of right-handedness and left-handedness, and the mild phenomenon of ambidexterity (using both left and right hands with equal facility) to dominant left-handedness. The average classroom may have several children who can be classified as left-handed; however, the majority of elementary children in our society are definitely right-handed. It is most important, though, that if a child is dominantly left-handed, he should be taught as a left-handed writer. Psychological studies have shown again and again that to change a dominant "lefty" by *forcing* him to use his right hand in writing can cause serious emotional problems. However, if the preference for the left hand is mild, he can be encouraged to utilize his right hand with apparently no damage.

Preschool, primary, and kindergarten teachers need to consider the possibility of giving children a *preference test* to determine the extent of handedness of each child. No person is completely "either/or" in his preference as to handedness. Therefore simple tests can be effective in discovering the child's handedness preference. As in all activities, the child should be allowed to use either hand easily. Some test areas might include the following simple activities.

- *Throwing a ball.* Instruct a child to throw a soft ball to the teacher. Note which hand he uses in throwing.
- *Catching test.* Standing very near the child, toss or hand a small object. Note the hand with which he receives it.
- *Cutting test.* Instruct the child to cut out circles drawn on a piece of paper. First with one hand, using scissors; then the other. Note the more expert hand.

Careful observation of the child while performing simple tasks such as using fork and spoon, stringing beads, reaching for articles, playing with blocks, winding yarn into a ball will give the teacher additional information about the child and his hand preferences.

Hints for Teaching the Left-Handed Writer

The following simple instructive hints should afford the teacher information for constructively helping the "lefty" in his early writing experiences.

1. The student should be encouraged to hold his pencil about an inch and a half from the point while he is writing.
2. He should be encouraged to keep his writing hand well below the line of writing.
3. The pencil or pen needs to be held loosely.
4. He should place his writing paper farther to the right-hand side of the desk for comfortable positioning. This facilitates greater arm movement.
5. The left-handed writer needs much practice at the chalkboard before writing on paper.
6. Ball-point pens and pencils should be used so that the writer does not smudge his writing.

It is important that the authors reiterate that the young writer's beginning experiences with actual handwriting be in the manuscript tradition. These early writing tasks should also be conducted in a relaxed atmosphere; but not allowed to fall into the "incidental" approach. Attitudes about and toward writing experiences are often formed in these beginning exercises and can continue to affect and influence later feelings about other learning activities which make use of handwriting as a functional tool.[2]

---

2. E. A. Enstrom, "The Relative Efficiency of the Various Approaches to Writing with the Left Hand," *The Journal of Educational Research*, August 1962, pp. 573–577.

Evaluating Manuscript Writing

Probably no area of elementary curriculum is more difficult or subjective to evaluate than children's handwriting efforts. In this respect, it is often felt to be good to foster some sort of writing "conscience" in which the child is encouraged to assess his own progress and success. Hence, after completing an assignment or writing activity, the student can be directed to examine his own efforts. A sample model such as the large letters on the chalkboard or bulletin board, or the actual handwriting book itself can be used for this comparison. This comparing of their own work with the provided model will show which letters or words need improvement and practice. The child should be encouraged not to erase or write over the writing that is below standard. Rather, he should be encouraged to rewrite those letters and words that are causing difficulty.

In evaluating their work, children should not compete with others; but should strive to improve their own work. It is easier, therefore, for the teacher to make commendation for progressive effort rather than on the basis of group improvement. Individual help is thus given to those students needing particular attention in specific areas.

Evaluative Criteria

Most teachers have found that students who "self-check" their own writing progress improve most rapidly. This checking by individual students of their own handwriting has proven to be one of the best incentives for better form. One of the most successful practices followed by good teachers in helping children to assess their own work is to provide them with specific criteria with which they can judge their skills. Such criteria can be clearly written on some sort of chart form (chalkboard or tagboard for permanence) where they can be easily seen.

Most criteria lists should include at least the following checks for manuscript writing.

Spacing consideration. In making use of his newly acquired and growing skills, the young writer will want to combine individual letters into words, and his words into meaningful sentences. It is important then that he knows how to space the letters in words, and what space to leave between words. The "round" letters are usually written more closely together, whereas straight letters need a bit more space between them. A good rule to follow is to leave the space of two fingers between words when using the wide-lined primary paper that allows for tall letters of about one inch in height.

Slant considerations. Most handwriting programs currently in use stipulate that there should be no slant in forming the letters in manuscript print. Hence, all straight lines are to be made perpendicular to the lines of the paper. If the teacher desires, a ruler can be used to check the vertical lines of the various letters used.

Formation considerations. Inasmuch as manuscript or print script is composed chiefly of round circle forms and straight lines, one criteria for comparison is to see if the circles are in fact round and the straight lines or segments are actually straight. Another consideration is to see that all letters are formed correctly according to the model provided. They should also show a uniformity of size in relation to each other. The uppercase letters (capitals) and the lowercase *b, d, f, h, t* should extend up to the top guideline from the base line of the writing. (Note the exam-

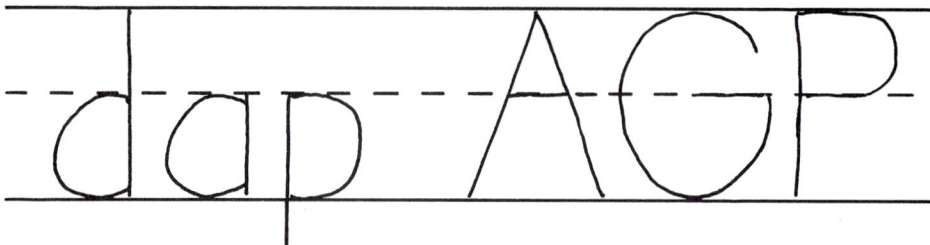

ples.) The other lowercase letters extend upward to the dotted lines of the writing paper approximately midway. Thus the proper height is attained by the young writers. In using this primary-lined paper, it is important to skip one line between each line of writing so that one does not interfere with the next line of writing.

Alignment considerations. A fourth criteria for judging correct writing is that of uniformity of letters as to their positioning on the base line. "Good" writing has this criteria of uniformity for legibility's sake.

These four considerations, then become basic to both the evaluation of children's handwriting by the teacher or by each student as he assesses his own work. Proofreading of paperwork can be effectively encouraged by taking a few moments for such examination by the students before handing in papers or before filing them in their individual work folders for progress comparison.

A Skills Continuum of Manuscript Writing Skills

Contemporary educators in many areas of the country have recently become interested in formulating some sort of skills continuum to be followed in the instruction programs of the various subjects of the elementary and secondary curriculum. These sequential listings of abilities identify competencies beginning with simple and progressing toward more difficult tasks. An example of one such suggested hierarchy of skills could include items from the following example.

Skills Continuum: Manuscript Writing (K through Grade 2)

During his early experiences in formal handwriting instruction, the child should progress through the following skills:

1. Demonstrate that he can hold a piece of chalk, crayon, or a pencil in a comfortable manner while writing.
2. Demonstrate that he is developing the left-to-right progression skills: by placing a series of pictures in left-to-right position and sequence; by following a simple maze pattern with crayon and then with pencil; and by tracing numerals and letters first with crayon and then with pencil.
3. Show that he can trace a series of geometric figures such as a circle, a square, a straight line, and a triangle.
4. Show that he can draw such figures as a circle, a square, a straight line, and a triangle.
5. Demonstrate that he can visualize his name and write the manuscript letters in proper sequence. (Correct formation and size should be stressed.)
6. Demonstrate the correct way of holding a pencil, a crayon, or chalk in order to write legible symbols, letters, or actual words.
7. Form both upper- and lowercase letters to copy teacher-written words and sentences on lined paper.
8. Write from dictation words or sentences using proper letter form and spacing.
9. Demonstrate his ability to utilize handwriting skills by composing original

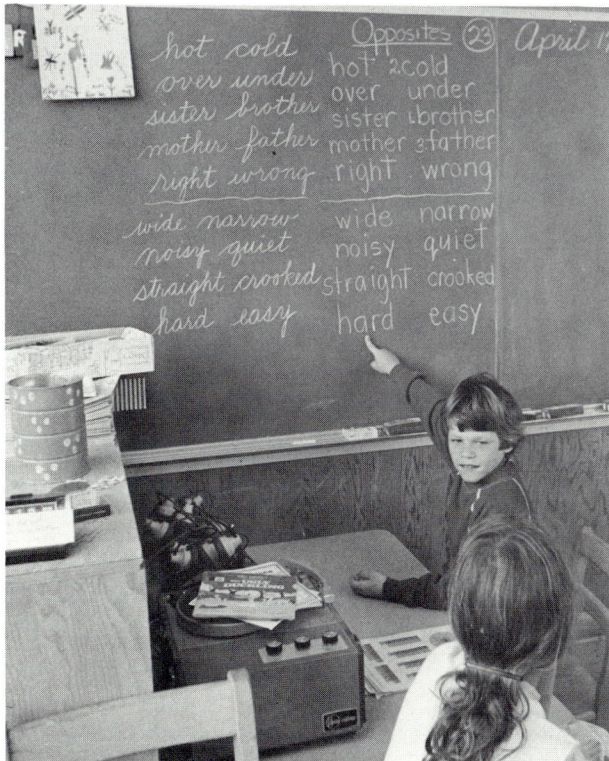

Children learn that there are two forms of writing: manuscript and cursive. The transition and relationship are shown here. Students may have some difficulty in making the transition.

sentences, paragraphs, or short stories based on an actual experience or happening.

10. Demonstrate his readiness to begin learning and using cursive writing.

CURSIVE WRITING

Like so many areas of educational research, the examination and study of handwriting, too, has resulted in some ambiguous findings. Here, also, the oft repeated conclusion is: "The findings are as yet inconclusive, and leave numerous areas to be yet researched before finality of procedure exists!" Much of the current practice, therefore, tends to be based on opinion rather than empirical evidence. Certainly this is true of the findings that relate to the optimum time for making the transition from the early learnings in manuscript writing to the more advanced experiences in cursive script. However, common practice in a great majority of American schools indicates that the opportune time for this transition learning should probably be at the very end of the second grade or during the early part of the third grade. In some instances resulting from slower development of muscular abilities, the introduction of cursive writing may be delayed even a year or two or indefinitely.[3]

Readiness for Cursive Writing

The problem of knowing the best time for beginning cursive writing has plagued teachers for years. Just what kind of evidence does the teacher need to observe before instruction actually begins? While there are numerous guidelines available from a number of sources, the following is perhaps a synthesis of the best available. They are at best a listing of guideline competencies which may serve as indicators of readiness to write via cursive script.

1. Is the child able to do his manuscript writing fluently, independently, and with correctly formed letters?
2. Does he show evidence of being muscularly mature to the extent that he can maintain a continuous motion such as is needed in cursive writing?
3. Is he able to hold his pencil or pen properly?
4. Does at least half the class demonstrate the ability to correctly and easily form manuscript letters?
5. Does the child evidence a desire to write in cursive script?
6. Is the student able to read simple sentences which have been written by the teacher in cursive style either on the chalkboard or on paper?

---

3. Gertrude Hildreth, "Simplified Handwriting for Today," *The Journal of Educational Research*, February 1963, pp. 330–333.

7. Can he write the entire alphabet from memory using manuscript writing?

If the answers to the above queries are mainly in the affirmative, it is a good indicator that the teacher should begin the introductory steps to cursive writing.

Manuscript and Cursive: Two Languages in Writing

Before beginning the actual instruction that underlies the transition from print script to cursive writing, the teacher should consider the following differences. These variances should be first discussed with the students and then demonstrated on the chalkboard. Let us consider these differences as they relate to each style of handwriting.

Manuscript writing. How does it differ from cursive?

1. In manuscript writing, each letter is made separately. The writing instrument is lifted from the paper after completing each stroke.
2. When using the manuscript style of writing, the child should remember the form is always vertical.
3. Manuscript letters closely approximate print, and therefore are easy to read.
4. When utilizing, the student should place the paper at right angles with the desk.

Cursive Writing. Note the following differences.

1. In cursive writing, all letters are joined. When writing, the child does not lift the pencil from the paper until he comes to the end of the word.
2. In cursive writing, there is a definite slanting of the letters toward the right.
3. Letters in cursive style are different from printed letters in their basic form.
4. Uppercase, capital letters, are often different from their small, or lowercase, counterparts.
5. When using cursive writing form, the child should place his paper in a slanted position on the desk.

Whereas there are basically only two distinct strokes to be used in forming the letters of the print script alphabet, the young learner will need to learn many new strokes, either singly or in combination, in forming the symbols of the cursive style of writing. Here it will not be the simple matter of combining straight lines and circles or portions of them to form written script. Indeed it will be necessary for the teacher as well as the student to be aware of the following points.

In introducing the new forms of cursive writing, the letters should be introduced singly by the teacher. She will compare and/or contrast them with their equivalent forms in print script, calling attention to their differences and likenesses. The chalkboard affords an excellent teaching media for this type of learning, and the child can often work side-by-side with the teacher or groups of peers in following the larger model furnished by the writing introducing the new learnings. The instructor should be certain that the students are familiar with the new terms used to describe the formation of cursive letters. Terms necessary for the clear understanding of the students are included in the following list.

Terms Referring to the Positioning of Letters in Relation to the Paper, Lines, and Spaces Used

1. *Base Line:* The bottom line on which letters are written in each line of work.
2. *Top Line:* The solid line above the base line that makes a space within which the student writes either capital or small letters.
3. *Half Space:* The midpoint between the base and top lines.
4. *Below Base Line:* The space beneath the base line which is used for descending letters which extend downward.

Terms Which Refer to the Actual Formation of the Lowercase Letters

1. *Cross Stroke:* The short, horizontal line used in crossing the small *t*.
2. *Oval Form:* The elliptical form used in writing such letters as small *o* and *a*. This is not a round circle, but a slanted oval. It is also modified in letters such as *c, d, g,* and *q*.
3. *The Up-Stroke:* The introductory movement used in writing such letters as the small *t, d, l,* and *p*.
4. *The Down-Stroke:* The stroke usually following the upstroke in which a downward line is formed such as in the second stroke in the small *t* and *p*.
5. *Upward Loop:* The ascending loop formation used in writing such small letters as *b, d,* and *l*.
6. *Downward Loop:* The descending loop used in forming such lowercase letters as *p, q,* and *f*.
7. *Hump Stroke:* The rounded formation used in writing parts of such letters as small *h, m,* and *n*.
8. *Terminal Connector:* The upswing ending stroke which swings to the right and forms the connecting line to the next letter.

Terms Which Are Used in Describing the Formation of Capital Letters

1. *Downward Slant:* That stroke that is used in forming the letters *B, P,* and *R*. This is a diagonal, downward line beginning near the top line and extending to the base line.
2. *Cane Beginning:* The combined loop and downstroke used by the writer in forming such letters as uppercase *H, K, M, N, U, V,* and *W*.

3. *Boat Stroke:* The ending swing stroke of such capital letters as *B, F, G, I, S,* and *T* that resembles the prow of a small sailboat.
4. *Descending Loop:* The terminal descending stroke used in writing the capital letters *J, Y,* and *Z.*

These terms, though not all-inclusive, are most applicable to the several program-systems of handwriting being taught in contemporary American schools.

INDIVIDUAL DIFFERENCES IN HANDWRITING

In teaching children to write, the teacher will immediately discover that individual students rapidly develop their own personalized style of handwriting. Although the basic letter formations are followed, they will adapt certain characteristic strokes in an attempt at distinctiveness. Realizing this, and realizing that each student is unique, the teacher will allow a certain freedom of style. This bid for individuality is normal and healthy. The basic criteria for judging handwriting efficiency and utility is after all that it be *legible.* Certainly this does not minimize that there is a certain artistic quality that may be appealing, but the prime consideration is: "Can it be read?"

How then does one assess handwriting? What are the criteria of "good" writing? Most authorities agree that there are some six basic guidelines to consider either for diagnostic purposes or for determining satisfactory progress at various levels of learning. Certainly in applying these criteria, the student should make his comparisons between his work and the model of expected handwriting done by students at his own age and grade group. Most handwriting manuals provide this scaled, progressive-type model for the student's use as well as a guide for the teacher's expectations.

Criteria for Assessing Writing Improvement

Children can be encouraged to make use of these six basic skill criteria for judging their own written materials. Some form of checklist for recording progress can be used for individual evaluation. These skills include:

- *Formation:* the correct writing of letters, their being like the model as to shape and form.
- *Uniformity:* the size and height of letters, the correct proportions and evenness.
- *Slant:* the parallel configuration of like strokes.
- *Spacing:* the consistent distance between letters within words and between words.
- *Alignment:* the uniformity of all letters resting on the base line.
- *Style:* general format of writing—its neatness, margins, and general attractiveness.

In making use of these rather general criteria for assessing writing skills, the teacher and student at this level may wish to be alerted to the more specific types of manipulative difficulties often occurring and resulting in confused legibility. These errors fall into several categories of malformation. The following examples should serve as signposts.

- *Improper Closure:* the letter *a* written as either *u*, *o*, or *ci*; *b* written as *li*, *d* as in *cl*, and *o* as *a* or *u*.
- *Closed Loops:* the *e* like an undotted *i*, the *l* as uncrossed *t*.
- *Other Errors:* *h* written as *li*, *i* written as *e*, *m* and *n* resembling *w* and *u*, and *t* like *l*.

HINTS TO THE TEACHER

Any teacher who wishes to induce and nurture good handwriting skills in children, either in manuscript or cursive styles, would do well to examine and make use of one of the many good commercially produced guides accompanying the several available writing systems. The specific helps offered in these small volumes, and the graphic models which detail the differences between varying programs, are an invaluable aid to the teacher. These accompanying manuals are usually broken down into grade level areas, and are readily available to the instructor desiring instructional guidance from the publisher and school as well. These handwriting textbooks are also designed for student use, and provide adequate exercises with illustrative models of the strokes, the actual letters, and drills for making use of new learnings. To ignore these helpful aids is folly indeed.

Summary

As a résumé of the preceding considerations, the teacher/intern is reminded that:

1. Learning the tasks of handwriting is a skill.
2. It is an important skills tool for the writer to communicate via the written language.
3. Important to writing instruction is the issue of readiness and the teacher's awareness that all children do not reach this level at the same time.
4. Manuscript is usually the child's first experience with actual writing.
5. Well-planned, sequential instruction is a vital part of success in teaching handwriting.
6. The transition to cursive writing occurs usually about the third grade level of work.
7. Cursive writing is configurationally another language.

8. Careful introduction to, and use of, this new form of handwriting needs to be cautiously nurtured using the models of manuscript writing as a basis of new learnings.
9. The teacher needs to help the student develop a "writing conscience" for self-assessment of progress.
10. Individuality of style will assert itself and needs to be allowed within limits.
11. The major issue of handwriting instruction and its evaluation is the fact of its legibility.

SECTION II ■ SPELLING, ENCODING TOOL OF WRITTEN LANGUAGE

When handwriting is first initiated, the child is involved in the recognition of printed or written words as well as their correct spelling. These interrelated tasks are hardly distinguishable one from another. Actually all of them are part of the whole area of the communication of ideas. However, spelling becomes immediately important to the writer if he is to engage in the output activity of relating his ideas and/or concepts to others.

It is safe, then, to say that the person begins with a concept, an idea, that he desires to communicate to others outside the immediate circle of his ability to talk or speak. Since oral language is not functional in this setting, he must rely on some other form of transmitting his thoughts, desires, or information to others in a meaningful, intelligible form. Hence, the necessity of correctly writing his messages, of coding his ideas, in a standard, organized manner. This, then, becomes the basis for teaching the student to spell his language correctly, or in the accepted sequence of written symbols. Unfortunately for the learner, the English language has not lent itself easily to the codification needed in spelling. There are contemporary and ancient languages where each speech sound is represented directly by one written symbol, where spelling in itself is not taught. In these phonemic languages, the task of the learner becomes that of learning his graphic symbols, his alphabet; and then assign, symbol by symbol, the written letters to the speech sound of individual words.

The exotic history of the English language reveals that the language has matrixes in several linguistic systems. We have handily borrowed from German, French, Latin, and Greek, as well as the ancient languages indigenous to the British Isles. The result, naturally, is the evolving of one of the most complex languages of the modern world. This end product is, and has been, the bane of both teachers and students in English usage schools for some generations.

As a result of this linguistic hodgepodge, there have been numerous reform movements to modernize and simplify the spelling of many common words. These phonemic alphabets, diacritical pronunciation systems, and recommended "new" spellings have rarely outlived the generator of the ideas. Thus, like it or not, the teacher and teacher-to-be are left with a language that is evaluated by some as being unteachable. Likewise, the instructor is faced with the task of teaching that language in its correct written form to students so that they can in turn use the vehicle in freezing the oral tradition.

Over the years, there certainly has been no paucity of research efforts to untangle this spaghetti language of ours. The results have been spectacularly inconclusive. The reported studies have revealed that numerous approaches, methods, and programs have been developed and used in a wide spectrum. This broad attempt has covered a complete circle of ideas from rote memory (some call it memory bank) to "felt thought." It is no wonder, therefore, that there has been a feeling of utter frustration on the part of many teachers. Indeed, numerous educators have concluded, perhaps facetiously, that the learning and use of spelling is indeed in the realm of "native talent." The authors of this text, after reviewing a body of material for the preparation of this work, have actually wondered if this latter theory may not have some merit for consideration. The end result is, of course, not to be solved here. We do not have the answer to the query: "What is *the best* way to teach spelling? How is the task to be successfully and easily completed?" Nor can the question be answered at this time on the basis of empirical evidence. The matter is still largely involved with expert opinion and practical experience.

However, since we do have this fascinating language to teach and since it is somewhat phonemic in structure, we can make use of certain generalizations and patterns for learning its correct and/or standard spelling. It must be noted, though, that many of the "rules" are nonfunctional in many spellings currently in use.[4]

LEARNING PATTERNS FOR SPELLING

Although spelling in itself is actually the converse process from the reading act —one is the encoding of language and the other is the decoding of written language —there is a certain similarity in the patterning of the learnings. As in reading, the student is involved with sensory stimuli and making use of three learning modalities, input channels. These three then become the basis for the child's learning strength and for the structure of the teacher's program.

The visual syndrome. The instructor must be aware of the visual aspects of the child's learning to spell his language. Certain learning phenomena involve the student's seeming ability to employ visual "photography;" that is, his learning by examining the written model in its configurational pattern. This gestalt experience makes use of the holistic sight memorization of words, segments, or terms. This use of visual memory can be tested and identified by the diagnostic teacher and becomes the basis for a successful program of instruction for those learners whose

---

4. Paul R. Hanna and Jean S. Hanna, "The Teaching of Spelling," *National Association of Elementary School Principals*, N.E.A., 1965. Reprinted in *Language Arts in the Elementary School: Readings*, ed. Hal D. Funk and Dewayne Triplett (Philadelphia, Pa.: J. B. Lippincott Co., 1972), pp. 429–442.

strength modality is mainly visual. In other words, it appears that some students can best learn their spelling tasks by looking at words, by visually reproducing them in their correct form.

The oral-aural aspect of spelling. A second group of learners would seem to be oriented to hearing the sequential components of the words being learned. This aural-oral input is somewhat related to the reading student who best learns via the sound-symbol approach. Thus, when a teacher discovers that particular students respond better to verbal stimuli than to visual cues, her system of teaching spelling can well be based on this more synthetic building up of whole words from individual sound representations. This approach to the subject from how words sound and how words are formed structurally, makes use of single letters and combinations of letters which record specific phonemes. In this technique, the teacher is concerned with such learnings as root words and affixes, compound words and contractions, inflectional endings, syllabication, and in some instances the sound patterns represented in written form. It has been in utilizing this type of approach that the "rules" of spelling have chiefly been employed. These deductive principles, however, have often been proven erroneous and must be introduced only as temporary aids for the student's use.

The haptic learning of spelling. A third segment of students may be discovered to be neither particularly strong in learning by means of the visual or aural modalities. These are those who are best reinformed by activities and tasks involving the use of the kinesthetic-tactile impulses. This using the input from touching, tracing, writing, and movements of muscles has been found by some to be most effective in learning to spell. This is evidenced by the learner who appears to best learn his new words by "writing" them in the air or on the desk top with his finger, or by actually writing them a certain number of times on his exercise paper.[5]

UTILIZING THE LEARNING MODALITIES OF STUDENTS

If indeed, students do learn in the three modal patterns suggested above, it then becomes important that the instructional program be developed which will make use of these input strengths. The visual learner will most easily succeed in his spelling tasks by making use of visual clues. For example, those spelling programs which suggest a particular "seeing" sequence can be classified as being focused toward the visual learner. The steps in such a system include: (1) LOOK at the word—note its shape, length, the irregularities; (2) Close your eyes and SEE the word in your mind; (3) WRITE the word as you *saw* it; (4) EXAMINE the word as you wrote it; and (5) COMPARE the word as it was written with the

5. Edna Lue Furness, "Pupils, Teachers, and Sensory Approaches to Spelling," *Education,* February-March 1968, pp. 267–273.

model provided. Note that the emphasis in such programs is on the child's ability to see and visualize written language.

It should be pointed out that in utilizing such an approach, as with any other perhaps, the child should be encouraged to make use of both systems of writing, manuscript and cursive. Certainly this infers that the models provided for a visual program be written in both writing forms. Most spelling textbooks currently being used make use of this dual script in teaching levels above the second grade.

In summary, this visually oriented spelling has sometimes been referred to by some in the field as "eye" spelling or "thought" spelling as twin functions involved in making use of the visual strength input channel.

The second type of learner, the oral-aural student, can probably best learn spelling from an approach which permits him to hear the component sounds that make up the word or term being learned. This type of spelling program has sometimes been given various names such as "ear" spelling and/or "lip" spelling. This phonetic system affords the teacher opportunities for pointing out to the learner the structure of words from graphic symbols representing each speech sound.

This is closely related to the so-called approach of language learning which says that writing and spelling are but transcriptions of the phonemes (speech sounds) of oral language into graphemes (written symbols representing phonemes). Spelling tasks within this system then become a matching of speech sounds with the proper written letters of the alphabet in use. Although it has frequently been argued that English is not a phonemic language, and that to approach spelling via this oral-aural approach is fallacious, some well-reported, recent research studies challenge this assumption. Actually it has been discovered and confirmed that about 80 percent of the words which are used in the elementary student's vocabulary can be correctly spelled from the auditory clues provided in the phonetic spelling system. Some authorities have indeed gone so far as to say that even a limited knowledge of the linguistic relationships, phonological correlates, existing between the written letters and the spoken sounds of the English language, can provide the power for spelling a sizeable majority of the words used in the child's spoken vocabulary.

It appears that, for some reason, a third group of children learns best from the haptic input. That is, they seem to learn most easily by utilizing their sense of touch and muscle in creating the words again and again. This is known by some teachers as "hand" spelling. In utilizing this technique for instructional purposes, the teacher will provide many exercises of writing words, copying words or sentences, manipulating cut out letters or blocks, or by even tracing models. This type of drill, rote learning, has often been discouraged as "old-fashioned," but because there are still those learners needing this kind of input, the aware teacher will make use of such tactile-kinesthetic activities.

Lest some take the authors to mean that unlimited writing exercises for the child's learning to spell are defensible practices, it should be pointed out that some researchers have found that only a limited number of such activities should be

Many young learners discover the importance of haptic input for learning spelling via writing their word lists. Others, however, need different modalities.

included in the viable instructional program. Actually it is questionable if the child should be directed to copy each word more than a maximum of four or five times; any further drill of this type can be safely termed a waste of time and effort.

Although each of these three types of students has been examined separately, and teaching emphases consistent with each have been identified, the seasoned educator is aware that as in other areas of language arts instruction, an eclectic combining of some facets of each—visual, aural, or haptic—input stimuli should be utilized in developing the "best" spelling program. This pragmatic system of learning to correctly spell the language will result in a balanced combination of teaching strategies, learning activities, reinforcing exercises, and sound introduction to new tasks that provide for each learner despite his strength modality.

TEACHING MATERIALS FOR THE SPELLING PROGRAM

Most school districts, and indeed some states, provide approved textbooks for the student and teacher's use in learning to spell. These texts are commercially produced by teams of experts and indeed have noticeable strengths. These favorable aspects include:

1. They are a sequentially organized series of learning experiences designed to induce an interest in and mastery of the act of correctly spelling the language.
2. They utilize a scientific basic word list which has been developed from investigations into children's use of words in oral and written language.
3. They are attractive in appearance and well designed with a modicum of eye appeal for young learners.
4. They are, by and large, created by persons from all levels of education who have a knowledge of language as well as practical experience in teaching children the skills of spelling.
5. They provide the teacher with many additional clues for expanding and enriching the spelling program.

On the other hand, however, some of these asset features have certain limitations for a successful instructional program. Some such factors should be noted by an alert teacher. They are:

1. The well-organized weekly schedule provided can easily become a sterile, programmed learning sort of exercise, if the teacher is content to follow it verbatim.
2. There will be little scope for a creative approach to spelling instruction if the teacher follows the handbook to the exclusion of spontaneous, fresh, innovative practices.
3. It should be remembered that any such system of teaching can be limited by a particular bias in emphasizing a specific, single approach to learning to spell. In other words, a single-strand modality, or a strong focus on linguistic patterning, or any other such limiting factor limits the effectiveness of the system to only those children who learn via a narrowed strategy.
4. Since most of these commercial spelling programs are often based on one specific word list which may have the advantage of scientific selection, nevertheless, it does not always meet the esoteric spelling needs of children in particular areas. Such spellings as the name of the state, county, or city involved, his address, plus various other personal spelling needs are related to his dialectic vocabulary.

5. Following such a prescribed system of spelling lends itself little to any attempt at an individualized teaching approach. Just as certain children display specific decoding difficulties and need graded materials, so in spelling, a differentiated load expectation as well as a level of difficulty needs consideration.
6. Perhaps the major limitation to a basal spelling device is that it may be viewed by some teachers as a panacea—*the* ideal spelling program—and as a result, it will fall far short of the expectation of being a cure-all program.

In summary, then, the identified advantages as well as the limiting effects of a prescribed spelling approach using textbooks and their accompanying activities are not to be viewed as all-inclusive. Rather, they are suggestive of the pros and cons applicable not only to spelling instructional materials and programs, but of any curriculum media used exclusively.

THE TYPICAL WEEKLY SPELLING PROGRAM

Reference has been made to typical commercial programs of instruction in spelling. Though these may vary greatly in areas of emphasis, basic word listings, and teaching approaches, the authors have found in their examination of a number of recent spelling manuals that there is a similarity found from a synthesis of a number of weekly scheduling suggestions. In the main, a number of programs follow a general pattern, day-by-day. The following is a typical example.

Monday: Some kind of pretest assessment of the new words which are used for the week. This is followed by an introduction of the new words making use of contextual settings: words in sentences, paragraphs, or short stories.

Tuesday: Examine and analyze the words being learned, noting unusual spellings, structural components, or any known words previously studied. Allow for time to be given for the writing of the words, the completing of the suggested activities for second day learnings, and/or for group or individual practice.

Wednesday: A dictated progress test for determining additional work needed. This test, like the pretest, should be corrected on the spot by exchanging papers or self-evaluation, or the teacher may go from desk to desk for a check of work done.

Thursday: The lesson often centers around further suggested exercises or activities using the practice book. Further work on "hard" words misspelled in the progress test or expanding the word knowledge of students by noting derivatives, or small group and individual work with students who have special needs.

Friday: A final test is administered, using either the exercise book itself or a booklet for keeping tests in succession. The teacher may wish to check the work with each individual child or correct them and return them to him as soon as possible.

EXPANDING ACTIVITIES TO STRENGTHEN THE BASIC PROGRAM

Even though many of the basic spelling programs have been assessed as being sound and provide the structure for good instruction, the authors feel that to confine teaching to this one medium, schedule, and strategy often results in a rigid, sterile, conformist spelling-teaching syndrome. Therefore, it is suggested that the intern/teacher consider the following hints for enhancing the instructional program by providing for individual student needs, varied activities, and increased interest and enrichment.

1. Make every effort to utilize the student's individual learning patterns; discover his modality for learning by giving simple auditory and visual discrimination assessments and note his use of tactile input.
2. Provide for the child's learning his own words as they are needed in written work; develop an individual dictionary for each student using word cards and filing box, a manilla envelope for keeping new words, or an exercise booklet for listing in alphabetical order new words needed and learned. These are the words he *wants* to know or that are indigenous to his area—the organic spelling approach.
3. Some children who have a talent for spelling will often get all their words correctly spelled in their pre- or progress tests and not need additional work in studying their word lists. For these learners, provide other language learning activities involving recreational reading; creative, original writing; word games; tutoring situations in which they "teach" a friend needing help; or provide an additional list of "power" words to be studied, learned, and used in meaningful activities.

Help for the Reluctant Speller

It is not unreasonable that the child who is having difficulties in reading (decoding language) will also have like difficulties in encoding (writing and spelling) his language. This difficulty will often affect his total feeling about language learning. Since spelling tasks are an integral part of this area, he may develop a severely negative feeling tone about spelling instruction. This dislike of learning and using written words will manifest itself in noticeable overt behaviors as signals to the alert teacher that here are learning problems that need systematic, careful attention. Continued nonsuccess, week after week, will affect not only his spelling performance, but all areas of his written communication skills. Immediate attempts at interesting this student, giving him tasks that afford him success, and a tailoring of the program to meet his specific learning and pacing needs are important. The following suggestions are offered to the teacher working with this reluctant learner.

1. Once his learning style and modality have been determined, utilize a program of instruction consistent with his unique patterning. Often the disabled speller

is neither particularly visually or aurally strong, and will need many activities making use of kinesthetic input. Many of these game exercises involve such things as letter tiles, textured letters, manipulative blocks, simple affixes, and root words. Meaningful tasks involving models and copying, using either print script or cursive writing, should be provided.

2. Many teachers in assessing the varying needs of students in their classes or groups become aware of the need for graduated, or differentiated, assignment expectations. The word lists presented each week for mastery are too long and difficult for some students to attempt realistically. Therefore, the assigned words need to be culled for presenting the easier ones, and a reduced number of new words be presented. Better yet, let the student make the choice of the number of words to be attempted and the particular words he can learn within the prescribed time. The number of new words then can gradually be increased as the learning ability strengthens. Some teachers have found that as few words as one or two are a sufficient task for some children. However, the ingredient of success increases the student's appetite and impetus and often activates him to improve his skill and enlarge his capacity for an enhanced attempt at spelling learning.

3. Further, it should be pointed out that some reluctant learners have been unsuccessful in learning handwriting to the extent that they have not even made the transition from manuscript to cursive writing. Hence, these students (sometimes as far-reaching as intermediate and upper grades) need to be allowed to continue their use of print script for such tasks as spelling, which requires the further skill of correctly sequencing and forming letters with ease.

4. For the reluctant speller it is even more imperative that the element of meaning be continually stressed by the competent teacher. His words should be presented to him in context so that he has the additional help of seeing and hearing the word couched in the linguistic patterning of his own speech—a meaningful cluster of words. Some teachers have used such instructional techniques as asking the student to orally define, explain, expand, or use the word in his own sentence for determining his understanding of its particular meaning.

These few suggestions are meant only to alert the teacher/intern to the presence of the slower learning child in the classroom. The emphasis here is on the student who has average ability despite his level of achievement. Certainly the child who has serious learning problems will need additional attention and specialized instruction outside the normal classroom setting.

Signposts for the Successful Teaching of Spelling

Teachers utilizing the typical commercial programs for spelling instruction will readily be aware of the need for modifying and enriching their patterning. Hence, the authors have included a list of general teaching hints which may serve as guides and/or suggestions.

1. Despite the inference by some that the commercial materials are self-teaching instruments to be utilized in an individualized approach, the opposite is indeed true. Careful teacher supervision and guidance needs to undergird the learning experiences continually.

2. As the teacher carefully observes and works with the students in spelling, she will be systematically noting weaknesses and strengths, interests and motivation, as well as the use of spelling skills throughout the entire program of written activities. Hence, continuous diagnosis, so necessary in the success of any individualized instructional program, is being carried on as a basis of further prescription and scheduling.

3. Always seek to determine the extent to which all students understand the meanings of every word used in the lists to be learned.

4. In introducing the new words from time to time, the careful teacher will not only pronounce each word accurately, but will make use of the additional visual input by writing it on the chalkboard in both print and cursive script. This

English is a codified language and follows specific patterns guided by generalizations and rules. Learners should have opportunities to interact with these guides which serve as aids in their learning to spell their language.

utilizing of both written languages will provide a double reinforcing of the form and sequence of each word being learned.

5. It is a proven technique of value for the teacher to follow a simple pattern when dictating words to be written or spelled orally as a learning activity. First, pronounce the word itself, use it in a simple sentence, and then repro-nounce the word clearly.

6. Often, spelling errors may be confused with poor handwriting performance. Hence, it is important that proper formation of letters and legibility be em-phasized concurrently with spelling instruction. Handwriting can be taught in tandem with spelling as interrelated skills to be later used in all phases of written language usage.

7. When children have completed their writing of spelling words dictated by the teacher, time should be allotted for, and consistent encouragement be given to proofreading. Such items as crossed *t*'s, dotted *i*'s, and closed letters, should be carefully examined before handing in papers for correction.

8. Immediately after finishing with spelling tasks, the correction procedure should be carried out. This instant awareness of correct work and errors made is im-portant as reinforcement of the learning process.

9. When using a commercially prepared program, or a sequential skills contin-uum designed by state, county, or district, it is important to follow the step-by-step pattern suggested by the developers. This is necessary because later skills are often dependent upon and related to earlier learned skills.

10. Some students in the normal classroom will be of superior ability and achieve-ment and need to be provided with additional challenge. Some of these addi-tional activities may indeed be enriching in nature and scope; however, some later tasks may also be introduced at earlier levels of learning. Examples of these are power lists of words to be learned and used, dictionary usage for increased language enhancement (definitions, pronunciations, derivations), and expan-sion by learning synonyms, homonyms, and antonyms.

11. Another language skill often associated with spelling instruction, although not actually spelling in itself, is that of alphabetizing extending from first letter arrangements into use of the second and third letters.

12. Despite the crowded curriculum and scheduling patterns of many modern classrooms, sufficient time *must* be allowed for students to study spelling as-signments. This can be individual work, small group work, or sometimes even the entire class working on spelling tasks involving both oral and/or written work.

13. Far too often spelling is viewed by both teachers and students as a kind of rote learning process rather than as an interesting involvement with words and lan-guage. This fascination with our language, its evolvement, change, and growth is essential to good spelling success. Foreign words (garage, patio, etc.), the inconsistencies of letter combinations (such as ough, tion, etc.), tabulations of the number of times that certain spelling "rules" are broken can help to

develop a linguistic awareness in many students. This awareness will prove to be a major element of success in learning to spell, and makes use of the interest element of the idiosyncracies of our language.

14. Each student should be encouraged to compete with himself, not with others within the class. Any reporting of progress and success should be kept as an individual charting of gains. Often class records have been conspicuously displayed, and the inabilities and failures of some students have been cause for embarrassment rather than an impetus or motivating device as intended.

While these suggestions are obviously generalizations, they should afford the teacher of spelling with certain guidelines for meeting the needs of variety and effectiveness in most of the systems of commercially produced materials and/or locally developed programs.

Spelling Skills Continuum

Reference has frequently been made in the text to a developed continuum of skills to be achieved by students at differentiated learning levels. These competencies, can by no means, be thought of as arbitrarily belonging to a clear-cut grade or age level, but should provide the teacher with suggested areas of skills thought to be commensurate with student abilities at suggested times. Note that general performance objectives are stated for broad areas of learners—The Primary Level, The Intermediate Level, and The Junior High School Level. Within each level, grade by grade, skills are then listed in a developmental skills type of sequence to provide the teacher/intern with a framework for guiding the learner progressively through the continuum of spelling skills felt to be essential to success in the elementary school.

The Primary Grades (K-3)

During the child's placement in or at the completion of his work in the primary level, he should master the following skills.

1. Articulate sounds correctly, pronounce words clearly, and utilize clusters of words correctly in order that he demonstrate readiness for spelling instruction.
2. Make use of phonetic clues, structural clues, visual clues, and aural clues in attempting spelling tasks.
3. Combine familiar, simple root words into meaningful compound words commensurate with his oral vocabulary.
4. Manipulate basic words and derivatives, discover basic words imbedded in derivatives, and form derivatives from combining basic words with affixes.
5. Utilize the apostrophe in forming contractions and possessives from base words.

6. Display the knowledge of inflectional forms of base words by adding "s" or "es" to designate plurals.
7. Demonstrate his increasing ability to spell by using correct spelling in all of his written work.
8. Follow his "spelling conscience" by correcting his errors in all written work.
9. Make use of reliable sources (dictionary, spelling word list, language glossary) for checking the spelling of words he is uncertain about.
10. Be familiar with and be able to manipulate the following spelling concepts:
    a. The vowels: a, e, i, o, and u.
    b. The consonants: all letters except the basic vowels.
    c. The long vowel sounds.
    d. The short vowel sounds.
    e. Silent letters, singly and in combination with others.
    f. Syllables in particular words.
    g. Compound words.
    h. Root words.
    i. Affixes: prefixes and suffixes.
    j. Simple contraction forms.

During his primary years, the student will demonstrate his language competencies by utilizing his general skills of listening, speaking, and reading as prerequisite skills to his learning to spell. The beginning of his spelling instruction will focus first of all by building on his abilities to say and hear whole words. Later he will listen to and repeat individual sounds which are components of the entire words in use. Thus the concept of the structuring of whole words from various sounds is built from the child's own oral language. Much of the instructional program will center in his other language vocabularies, particularly his oral speech and reading tasks.

First Grade Skills Continuum

The following suggested skills can be used by the teacher to gauge normal student progress in the development of spelling competencies.

1. Adequately achieve the requisite basic spelling skills outlined in the selected spelling text in use.
2. Employ recognition skills learned in reading and build new words from known words that are appropriate.
3. Be able to transfer oral language into written form; correctly spelling words used in speaking.
4. Use a written model for copying short passages without spelling errors.
5. Take simple dictation (short sentences) and write words without making errors in spelling.

Second Grade Skills Continuum

As the child progresses into the second grade level of work, there is evidence of a slightly more difficult and sophisticated category of spelling skill required for this work. Following are some continuing skills that have been identified.

1. Demonstrate his ability to handle the requisite skills outlined in the basic spelling program in use.
2. Indicate his continuing growth in spelling readiness by using complex sentences in both oral and written language.
3. Increasingly make use of creative writing techniques such as adjectives, adverbs, synonyms—in short, to employ more colorful, picturesque language in written work.
4. Demonstrate a higher level of achievement in written language by correctly using and spelling words with common prefixes and suffixes.
5. Utilize several basic spelling generalizations which can be applied to a growing number of words.
6. Become aware of an individualized method of learning to spell. This technique will be based particularly upon his own pattern of learning modality.

Third Grade Skills Continuum

By the time the student reaches the third level of school learnings, he increasingly utilizes basic skills to express himself in correct, legible written language. The new plateau of skills may include such competencies as those following.

1. Be able to meet the expected level of spelling tasks that are provided and specified in the basic spelling textbook or program system.
2. Demonstrate the number of generalizations he has learned by accumulating a growing number of new words consistent with the "rules" and proper spelling practices.
3. Show by the number of words he spells correctly that his own sense of spelling responsibility serves to direct his individual work.
4. Continue to utilize his own learning modality pattern.
5. Increasingly employ his new words in written work needed in other content areas of the curriculum.
6. Recognize and use variant forms of words, antonyms, synonyms, and homonyms.
7. Handle more difficult and sophisticated compound words with a growing facility.
8. Make correct use of plurals, contractions, and possessives in his written work.
9. Begin mastery of the rudimentary rules of syllabication.

10. Increasing use of affixes and roots shows a definite level of sophistication.
11. Progressively makes use of reference skills in his written work—dictionary usage, alphabetizing, abbreviations.

The Intermediate Grades (4–6)

Consistent with statements relative to the change of pace which takes place in reading purpose at the beginning of fourth grade, the teacher will be aware that much the same is true of written work. By the time the student has worked through the primary grades, he becomes proficient to the degree that less time will be spent in teaching the "how" of language skills, and more and more effort will be spent in guiding the "why" of written communication. In other words, he will be less concerned with "learning to spell and write" and more occupied with "spelling and writing to communicate ideas to others." Hence a look at performance objectives consistent with this level of learning, as well as the component skills to be taught, will be a useful tool for the teacher/intern in both instruction and assessment of learnings attempted. The competency goals listed below should be mastered during the child's placement in, or at the completion of his work in, the fourth through sixth grades.

1. Demonstrate his responsibility for correctly spelling the words he uses in his written work; work independently without outside help from teacher or peers.
2. Utilize his specific learning pattern to master his own "problem words."
3. Master the basic word list provided by the instructional program which presents the most used words in writing at the specified level.
4. Continuously make use of the dictionary for discovering correct spelling, pronunciations, and usage of needed new words.
5. Demonstrate proofreading skills as an indication of his growing spelling conscience and sensitivity to incorrect spelling.
6. Apply the basic spelling generalizations which provide phonetic and structural guides.
7. Correctly use the technical terminology which applies to spelling—stressed syllables, synonyms, derivatives.

Fourth Grade Skills Continuum

The teacher at fourth grade level may generally be responsible for the development of such skills as those listed below. These more discrete abilities reflect the ascending progression of learnings and the cognitive levels involved by the developing student.

1. Successfully maintain the level of achievement expected in the basic program of spelling at this fourth level of work.

2. Learn the more sophisticated skills of alphabetizing required by the middle-grade student.
3. Recognize and utilize *guide words* in looking for particular terms in the intermediate level dictionary.
4. Correctly pronounce words by using phonetic spellings and diacritical markings given in the dictionary.
5. Utilize learned generalizations relative to long and short vowel sounds, irregular pronunciations, digraphs, diphthongs, letter clusters, and other various letter combinations.
6. Analyze and utilize more difficult contraction forms.
7. Master more difficult tasks involving knowledge of roots, affixes, and endings.
8. Continue learning activities using syllabizing, word forms, silent letters in combination, plus other irregularities.
9. Recognize word formations indicating plurals, tense, and form.
10. Handle spelling dictation appropriate to this level and function with minimum repetition.

Fifth Grade Skills Continuum

As was indicated previously, it is often difficult to say that a particular skill "belongs" in or to a specific grade level expectancy. However, one considers slightly more discrete and difficult tasks for each succeeding grade involved. One can note that following the fifth grade continuum, there is a lessening of emphasis on skills, and an increasing emphasis on application of previous learnings. The following abilities have been included as a guide to teachers/interns for strengthening spelling performance at this more advanced level.

1. Achieve the standard of grade expectations for spelling outlined in the basic text.
2. Compile a personal list of "spelling demons" for mastery.
3. Review and strengthen skills involving the following previously introduced learnings.

    a. Compound words   e. Phonetic-structural analysis
    b. Syllabication   f. Suffixes and prefixes
    c. Common word endings   g. Forming plurals
    d. Contractions   h. Alphabetizing

4. Some additional advanced skills might be included for consideration by teacher and student at this level.

    a. Proofreading   e. Dictionary spellings
    b. Antonyms/synonyms   f. Diacritical markings
    c. Phonetic spellings   g. Continued simple dictation
    d. Tenses and numbers   h. Achievement of correct spelling

Word recognition, though often called a reading skill, can, through its visual aspects, provide children with a valuable aid in learning to spell words.

Sixth Grade Skills Continuum

Here, again, note that much of the coursework will center on refining basic skills, reviewing and strengthening previous learnings, and extending the utilitarian aspects of spelling. However, several additional areas will be specified as important components of the instructional program at this top boundary of the intermediate level of education.

1. Functioning at a level of achievement commensurate with the expectations outlined in the program of instruction in use.

2. Continued diagnosis of needs for the student needing corrective work and/or remediation work.
3. Individual assessment; self-correcting and expansion of the word lists involved.
4. Review of, and mastery of, a list of "'Spelling Errors Most Commonly Made."
5. Review of the basic skills involved in spelling as outlined in the Fifth Grade Continuum. At this further grade the student will be achieving at a new level, applying higher concepts, more difficult tasks, and extended activities.
6. Inasmuch as the student should now be reasonably aware of his individual modality of learning and his developed system of spelling mastery, he will continue to refine his style and ability.

Upper-Grade Objectives and Skills (7–8)

In some school systems, the formal teaching of spelling to all students shows a decided decline at the junior high level of instruction. Indeed, it becomes largely a program of remediation for the deficient student, and an individualized program of enrichment and extended learning for others. In some instances the instruction period is embedded in a block approach to the entire language arts area. In each of these types of learning experiences, however, there is usually a continued emphasis on increased facility in dictionary usage, the development of "spelling sense" in all forms of written work, a general strengthening of basic skills, and an awareness of the functional utility of spelling in the whole schema of written communications. If a commercial program is adopted for teaching further spelling, it often centers around a "power" type of learning for mastery at all levels of spelling usage.

SUMMARY

This examination of the contemporary skills being emphasized allows the teacher/intern to see the general pattern of learnings which have evolved from consistent practice, some research findings, and the theoretical base of learning and developmental levels. Expert opinion has largely been responsible for the teaching approach, the materials and media involved, and the sequential introduction of more advanced skills.

Again, it should be noted that in most situations, the teacher/intern will be furnished with a framework for teaching this strand of written language. Many helpful suggestions and procedures will be provided. However, these may prove inadequate or sparse, and it is hoped that the informational guidelines presented here will be used as "activators" for more than a basic instructional program.

THE DEVELOPMENT
OF LANGUAGE
THROUGH LITERATURE

CHILDREN'S LITERATURE AND THE LANGUAGE ARTS PROGRAM

13

SECTION I ■ THE SETTING FOR INSTRUCTIONAL ENRICHMENT

Children's Literature and the Listening Skills

Literature for children, in recent years, has had a rebirth. Literally thousands of new titles emerge from the publishers each year. These new titles, along with the more successful titles from years past and the classics, comprise a treasure trove for the language teacher that cannot be overlooked or ignored.

Children's literature, unlike the traditional textbook, has one major goal to achieve. Through the art of words and illustration, it brings delight and insight to the children who will interact with it. Literature should be thought of as an aesthetic experience. It provides an opportunity for an author and illustrator to meet with a child's imagination. The result of this meeting can, and should, be spectacular!

Pragmatically, however, the wise teacher can expect more from children's literature than just the important aspect of aesthetics. These books can provide valuable language learnings, and provide them in a unique and exciting way.

Certainly the teacher of the very young, in preschool or kindergarten, knows the importance of developing that first vocabulary, listening, as the foundation of all language skills to follow. How better, then, can we provide that youngster a listening environment than by reading to him from good examples of children's literature?

As a reason and a model for listening, a good piece of children's literature has few peers. The child hears words in context, words that tell a story, words that are carefully chosen to induce identification and emotional reaction, words that he can understand. These words, accompanied by lavish illustrations, offer hours of

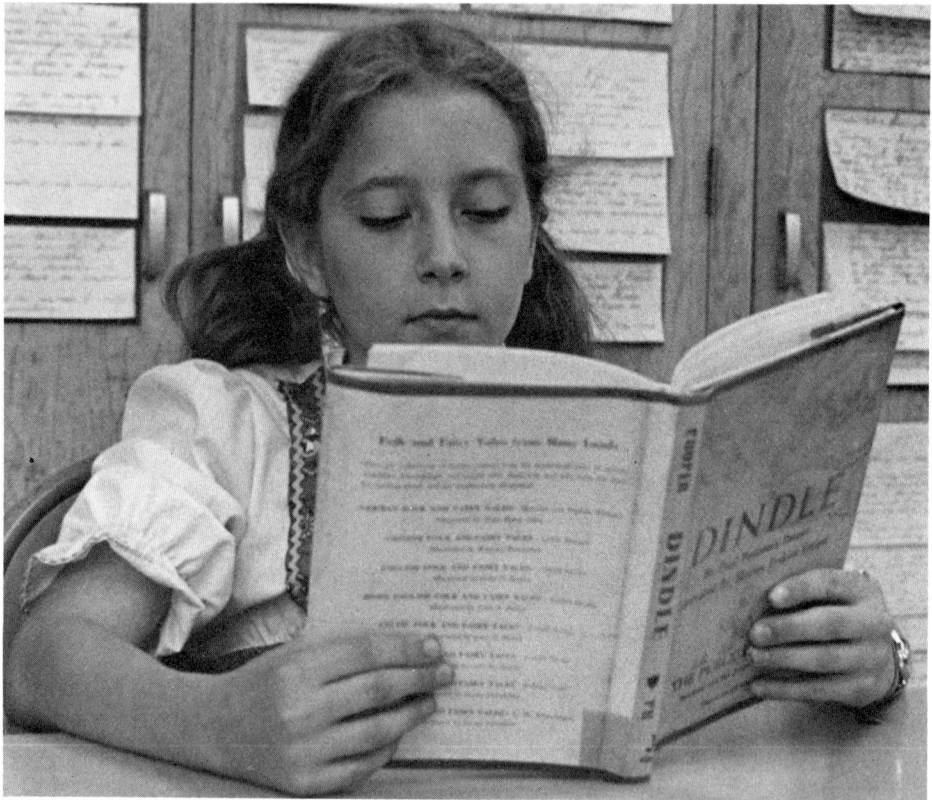

The real reason for reading is to have children interact with literature. This literature affects most language development.

thoughtful listening and looking. New words for him are couched in a contextual syndrome that offers a maximum opportunity for him to understand and add to his new listening vocabulary.

Most children's literature that is designed for very young children comes in a special format. These books are called *Picture-Story Books*. They are phenomena unique to children's literature in that they really present a twice-told tale. The picture-story book tells the story once in words and once again with illustration. The text and illustration reinforce each other very well in these books; they move together throughout, pacing each other very closely.

As a result, the teacher who reads to children from these books, needs to present both the text and the illustration to the children who listen. It is important that children see the illustrations in these fine books.

A good teaching strategy for bringing these books to children so that they will listen and look in a meaningful and gainful way is to bring the youngsters, in a group, up close to the teacher who is reading. Often a good teacher will arrange a class on the floor in a semicircle, while she sits in a chair near the center. She can then read, offer the illustrations for close scrutiny, and guide the discussions about the book in a relaxed, delightful way.

For the very young child, we need to be aware of his limited attention span. It is often difficult, if not impossible, for a preschooler or kindergarten child to remain seated for more than fifteen minutes. In choosing a book to bring to these children, one must remember that time limitation! Most good picture-story books are geared for that time span, and can be leisurely presented to children, in their entirety, within a fifteen-minute time span.

Certainly the development of listening vocabulary does not stop with the preschool/kindergarten/primary youngster! Its development needs to continue through the grades and beyond. As the youngster matures and goes into the intermediate grades and the upper grades, his need to listen to children's literature read orally to him does not diminish. Many teachers believe that need, in fact, increases. His attention span has increased, and he is able and quite willing to listen to us read up to forty-five minutes and even an hour per day, if we are willing. His need for the picture-story book (designed for young children) may have diminished, but his love for the lavishly illustrated book has not. He still enjoys and benefits from the picture book geared for the older child.

His real enjoyment comes from the junior novel, the children's book that is divided into chapters, presented one or two per day. These exciting, well-written books are, many times, above his reading level, and he finds it difficult to read them on his own. Presented to him in oral form, however, it is another matter. He will listen happily for as long as we will read. New words, new expressions, new ideas come to him through this medium. His listening vocabulary is expanding all the while. He needs, and wants, to have continuing listening experiences. These can be amply provided by a host of books ready and waiting to service this need.

The following bibliography has been compiled from books that offer rich experiences in listening. One should note, however, that this bibliography (like all others) is only a limited offering. It is designed to start the teacher off on a delightful hunt through the realm of children's literature. There are many books available here that will supplement this bibliography.

BOOKS GOOD FOR LISTENING
Preschool/Primary Levels

AESOP. *Aesop's Fables*, ill. by Alice and Martin Provensen. Golden, 1965. 4–10.

ALEXANDER, LLOYD. *The King's Fountain*, ill. by Ezra Jack Keats. Dutton, 1971. 4–8.
  Problems arise over thirst in the village if the king builds a fountain. Brilliant illustrations.

ANGLUND, JOAN WALSH. *The Brave Cowboy,* ill. by the author. Harcourt, 1959. 3–7.
>The Old West of cowboys and rustlers comes to life in a child's bedroom. Both real and make-believe join nicely in the illustrations.

ASBJØRNSEN, P. C. and MOE, J. E. *The Three Billy Goats Gruff,* ill. by Marcia Brown. Harcourt, 1957. 4–8.
>Children have been delighted with this Scandinavian tale for generations. This version, with the illustrations by Miss Brown, is bound to please several more generations.

BEMELMANS, LUDWIG. *Madeline,* ill. by author. Viking, 1939. 4–8.
>The famous story of Madeline and the appendectomy. The first of the Madeline books and certainly the best!

BERG, JOAN. *Bigger Than an Elephant,* ill. by the author. Crown, 1968. 3–6.
>Size relationships are the issue here. Each animal is pictured with a child to show relative size. Across-the-page illustrations add to the effectiveness of this book.

Book of Nursery and Mother Goose Rhymes, ill. by Marguerite deAngeli. Doubleday, 1954. 3–7.
>Favorite rhymes illustrated with gentle, unassuming illustrations.

BROWN, MARCIA. *Once a Mouse,* ill. by the author. Scribner, 1961. 5–8.
>This near classic retelling of an old Indian tale offers countless hours of listening, and listening again. A Caldecott winner.

BROWN, MARGARET WISE. *The Golden Egg Book,* ill. by Leonard Weisgard. Golden, 1946. 3–6.
>Two good friends (a duck and a rabbit) enjoy the newness of spring.

———. *Little Fur Family,* ill. by Garth Williams. Harper, 1946. 2–6.
>Delightful tale of family life around an old tree in the forest. Tiny book.

BURCH, ROBERT. *Joey's Cat,* ill. by Don Freeman. Viking, 1969. 4–7.
>A story about a mother cat who protects her kittens. Joey and his family are black Americans. A good family setting.

BURTON, VIRGINIA LEE. *Mike Mulligan and His Steam Shovel,* ill. by the author. Houghton, 1939. 4–8.
>A near classic story of the race between men and machines. Mike, and his steam shovel Mary Ann, will entrance all.

———. *The Little House,* ill. by the author. Houghton, 1942. 4–9.
>Delightful story of urban renewal, of sorts. Seasons change, night and day exchange places. A real treasure. A Caldecott winner.

CARLE, ERIC. *1.2.3. to the Zoo,* ill. by the author. World, 1968. 3–6.
>A counting book containing across-the-page illustrations showing both the number and the numeral. Colorful, well-rendered animals in a train car are part and parcel of this delightful book.

DUVOISIN, ROGER. *A for the Ark,* ill. by the author. Lothrop, 1952. 5–8.
>The sage Noah brings animals on the ark alphabetically. All previous letters are kept on the page, waiting for the new one coming up. Illustrations are a delight.

MERRILL, JEAN. *How Many Kids Are Hiding on My Block?,* ill. by Frances Gruse Scott. Whitman, 1970. 4–6.
>Multiracial hide-and-seek. Lots of fun to find the eleven children at play.

PERRAULT, CHARLES. *Puss in Boots*, ill. by Marcia Brown. Scribner, 1954. 4–8.
  This tale from the French classic has delighted children for generations. Illustrations enhance beautifully.
———. *Cinderella*, ill. by Marcia Brown. Scribner, 1954. 4–8.
  A Caldecott winner. Beautifully retold story of the deprived child who found her fairy godmother.

A good school will provide a wide selection of literature from which children may choose. Regularly planned visits to the school library are times well spent.

BOOKS GOOD FOR LISTENING
Intermediate Level

AGLE, NAN HAYDEN. *Maple Street*, ill. by Leonora E. Prince. Seabury, 1970. 8–12.
  Story of a family living on a street that is "changing" in economic structure, and a girl's attempts to get along with the new poor people moving on the street.
ATWATER, RICHARD and ATWATER, FLORENCE. *Mr. Popper's Penguins*, ill. by Robert Lawson. Little, 1938. 9–12.
  This delightful tale of Mr. Popper and his gift of penguins from Antarctica has been in demand for over thirty years. Anyone hearing it will understand why.
BAUM, BETTY. *Patricia Crosses Town*, ill. by Nancy Grossman. Knopf, 1965. 9–12.
  A black girl attends an all-white school and learns much about herself and others. Others learn as well. Integration and the problems it can cause are central theme.
BRIO, VAL. *Gumdrop and the Farmer's Friend*, ill. by the author. Follett, 1968. 6–9.
  A story about an antique car and some attempts to steal it. Lots of fun!

BURCHARDT, NELLIE. *Reggie's No-Good Bird,* ill. by Harold Berson. Watts, 1967. 8–12.

Story of a troublemaker in a city housing project who changes into a constructive young man when he tends a baby blue jay that he knocked out of a tree.

CARLSON, NATALIE SAVAGE. *The Empty Schoolhouse,* ill. by John Daufmann. Harper, 1965. 7–11.

Desegregation in a parochial school in Louisiana, and the plight of Lullah Royall, a black girl, are the central points of this story. Some fine listening in this timely book.

———. *Ann Aurelia and Dorothy,* ill. by Dale Payson. Harper, 1968. 9–12.

The story of a friendship between a black girl and a white girl. In this case, the stronger of the two, and the one with the fewest problems, is the black girl. Friendship grows naturally.

CLAYTON, BARBARA. *One Special Summer,* ill. by Jessica Zemsky. Funk & Wagnalls, 1966. 8–12.

Early adolescent boy and girl meet and find qualities in each other that they admire. A long summer and a lost Indian village bring these two friends together.

CLEARY, BEVERLY. *Henry and the Paper Route,* ill. by Louis Darling. Morrow, 1957. 8–12.

One of several of the delightful *Henry* books by Cleary. In this one Henry tries to prove his "business sense" and take over a paper route. One of the best!

———. *Ramona the Pest,* ill. by Louis Darling. Morrow, 1968. 8–10.

Just as appealing as Henry! Ramona is well worth meeting and offers lots of listening fun.

CORBETT, SCOTT. *Pippa Passes,* ill. by Judith Gwyn Brown. Holt, 1966. 8–11.

A child movie star runs away from an aunt and uncle who are using her abilities for their own profit. Lots of intrigue and some humor.

CORNISH, SAM. *Your Hand in Mine,* ill. by Carl Owens. Harcourt, 1970. 7–9.

The story of Sam, a sensitive brown boy, who lives with his own poetry, but never seems to write it down for anyone to read.

CRETAN, GLADYS YESSAYAN. *All Except Sammy,* ill. by Symeon Shimin. Little, 1966. 7–9.

Each person should value the talent he has. Sammy does. His family are musicians, and he is a talented baseball player.

DE JONG, MEINDERT. *The Singing Hill,* ill. by Maurice Sendak. Harper, 1962. 8–12.

The feeling of loneliness is explored as Ray and his family adjust to a new home. Good family feeling developed in this fine book.

DICK, TRELLA LAMSON. *Burro on the Beach,* ill. by Ted Lewin. Follett, 1967. 9–12.

An action packed summer spent on the Pacific Coast. Lots of adventure, change, and excitement. Good for oral reading.

BOOKS GOOD FOR LISTENING
Upper Level

ARMSTRONG, WILLIAM H. *Sounder,* ill. by James Barley. Harper, 1969. 12-up.

A sensitive story of a rural black family living as sharecroppers in the South, and their struggle to survive as a family. Magnificent writing. Made into an award winning film.

BALL, ZACHARY. *Bristle Face*. Holiday, 1962. 11–15.

Splendid book for boys. An orphaned boy, a dog, and a lonely man are brought together in a mountain setting.

BEAM, MAURICE. *Adventure in Survival*, ill. by Dirk Gringhuis. Putnam, 1967. 12–14.

Modern-day Robinson Crusoe theme. Very exciting listening.

BONHAM, FRANK. *Durango Street*. Dutton, 1965. 12-up.

With the help of a social worker, a ghetto hero returns from detention camp in his old environment and learns to live a more positive life. Realistic inner-city life.

BURT, KATHERINE NEWLIN. *Girl on a Broomstick*, ill. by Carolyn Cather. Funk & Wagnals, 1967. 10–14.

Pseudowitchcraft from an imaginative thirteen-year-old girl. Final result is much self-understanding.

HARRIS, MARILYN. *The Peppersalt Land*. Four Winds, 1970. 10–16.

Two girls learn about friendship, themselves, and racial prejudice. One girl is white, the other is black. Human relationships is the theme of this book.

HENTOFF, NAT. *Jazz Country*. Harper, 1965. 10–16.

Tom Curtis wants to become a jazz musician. He finds it difficult to break into the black syndrome, as he is white and finds prejudice gets in his way.

HUNT, IRENE. *Up a Road Slowly*. Follett, 1966. 12-up.

This Newbery winner is a tender study of a girl who, after the death of her family lives with a spinster aunt. During the next ten years, Julia grows up to be a talented perceptive young woman.

KONIGSBURG, E. L. *From the Mixed-Up Files of Mrs. Basil E. Frankweiler*, ill. by the author. Atheneum, 1968. 8–12.

Newbery winner in 1968. A delightful story of a brother and a sister who run away to live in the New York Metropolitan Museum of Art.

KRUMGOLD, JOSEPH. *And Now Miguel*, ill. by Jean Charlot. Crowell, 1953. 10-up.

A sensitive story of a Mexican-American boy's quest for adulthood. Set in the sheep country of New Mexico, it offers many insights into the Mexican-American culture. A Newbery winner and the genesis of several films.

NORRIS, GUNILLA B. *Take My Waking Slow*, ill. by John Gundel Finger. Atheneum, 1970. 12–16.

Richie learns that he cannot depend on his family to get things done, so he learns to rely on himself.

RODMAN, BELLA. *Lions in the Way*. Follett, 1966. 10–16.

Desegregation problems at an all-white high school is the setting for this exciting story of civil strife and human rights.

SWARTHOUT, GLENDON and SWARTHOUT, KATHRYN. *Whichaway*, ill. by Richard M. Powers. Random, 1966. 10-up.

A young cowboy learns to depend upon himself to survive. Good adventure in each chapter.

TAYLOR, THEODORE. *The Cay.* Doubleday, 1969. 8–14.

> A sensitive story of a World War II torpedoed ship and the two survivors, a black man and a white boy who is blinded. They survive on a desert island and learn much about themselves and each other.

WIER, ESTER. *The Loner,* ill. by Christine Price. McKay, 1963. 11–15.

> A boy named David has a hard time of it finding his own identity and getting along with other people. Setting is on a western sheep range.

———. *The Winners,* ill. by Ursula Koering. McKay, 1968. 11–15.

> Scrub Nolan is sent to his aunts in Florida with two greedy migrant brothers. Scrub escapes and lives in the Everglades with an Indian boy on a houseboat. Interesting sidelight is the portrayal of the poachers and the slaughter of wildlife.

STORYTELLING: A UNIQUE OPPORTUNITY FOR CREATIVE LISTENING

Literature for children comes in other forms than print. Certainly some literature has been successfully translated into film and kinescope. Much of the child's experience with literature comes from a passive viewing of this medium. Many authorities decry the excessive use of film and television as a vehicle in presenting literature. They complain that the real creativity of using the imagination in constructing one's own images has been bypassed when film is utilized. The authors tend to agree that this can be the case when film is substituted for most literary experiences. They do, however, see value in a balanced program where the film is offered as a supplement to a good literary environment.

One valuable technique of bringing literature to children in a form other than print is with the art of storytelling. Storytelling implies the ancient art of literature in the oral tradition. It was, and is, the world's oldest form of literature. In storytelling one recreates a structure of literature using one's own words to retell a story. Most folk stories were born in this oral tradition and remained in the realm of the storyteller until they met the magnificent invention of Gutenberg, the printing press. They then became "frozen in print" and became part of the new literature through the medium of print, lost to most in their original form, the oral tradition. They wait, however, in their prisons of print to spring to life through the magic of the storyteller.

Storytelling, unlike oral reading to children, does not remain static. It changes constantly with each teller and group of listeners. The storyteller keeps in mind the structure of the story; the incidents of the story; the names, places, and events of the story; but never memorizes a story for rote telling.

Dewey Chambers, in his book *Children's Literature: Storytelling and Creative Drama,*[1] outlines the melodramatic structure of most good tales for telling. He

---

1. Dewey Chambers, *Literature for Children: Storytelling and Creative Drama* (Dubuque, Iowa: Wm. C. Brown Company Publishers, 1970), p. 17.

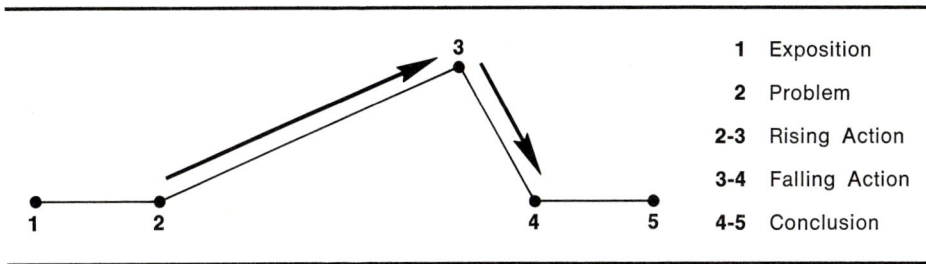

1 Exposition

2 Problem

2-3 Rising Action

3-4 Falling Action

4-5 Conclusion

divides them into the following structure. The teacher-storyteller prepares her story based upon that structure and creates with it.

Storytelling offers youngsters in any grade an opportunity for active, creative listening that is difficult to come by in this age of mass media and our dependence on the machine.

Sources for Storytellers

CALLWELL, EILEEN. *A Second Storyteller's Choice.* New York: Henry Z. Walck, Inc., 1965.

CHAMBERS, DEWEY W. *Literature for Children: Storytelling and Creative Drama.* Dubuque, Ia.: Wm. C. Brown Company Publishers, 1970.

CUNDIFF, RUBY E., and WEBB, BARBARA. *Storytelling for You: Handbook of Help for Storytellers Everywhere,* Yellow Springs, Oh.: Antioch Press, 1957.

SAWYER, RUTH. *The Way of the Storyteller.* New York: The Viking Press, Inc., 1962.

SHEDLOCK, MARIE L. *The Art of the Storyteller.* New York: Dover Publications, Inc., 1951.

TOOZE, RUTH. *Storytelling.* Englewood Cliffs, N. J.: Prentice-Hall, Inc., 1959.

CHILDREN'S LITERATURE AS A MODEL FOR SPEECH

Children's speaking vocabularies are directly related to their listening vocabularies. As was pointed out in an earlier section of this book, the latter develops from the former.

If, then, children's books offer a rich and rewarding opportunity to listen, should they not enhance the speaking vocabulary? The answer is obvious. Of course they do! Children hear words, both familiar and unfamiliar, used in new and common contexts. They are involved in an oral language milieu when they are invited into the world of literature as the teacher reads. When input occurs (listening) as the teacher reads, output (speaking) is a natural result. This logical outcome should and needs to be encouraged.

As the teacher shares a book with young children, and youngsters interact with the oral reading and the illustrations offered in the book, they want to talk about what they heard and saw. They will comment about the adventure, ask questions, guess outcomes; they will interpret ideas and concepts. All of this requires speech. They will question new words, ask about how words are used, and often stop the teacher for an explanation as to what is happening in the story. This too requires speech. New words, both heard and spoken, are part of this experience. So too are familiar words, words common to the youngster's experience; and reinforcing them, making them a more permanent tool in the child's life space.

Just as important as hearing and thus using new and familiar words, is how these words are strung together so that meaning is conveyed when they are used. Speaking, as pointed out earlier, is essentially imitating what one has heard. If one hears language used in an organized manner, with complete sentences and correct grammatical structure, the probability of recreating this syndrome is certainly greater than if the youngster has not had this experience. It must be remembered that for some children, the only standard, linguistically correct language he is likely to hear may come from his experiences in the classroom. Part of what he hears in that classroom needs to be that which comes from children's books.

As the child matures and enters the middle and upper grades, his speaking vocabulary, as it relates to his listening vocabulary, continues to expand. He is more and more able to move into the abstract, into more complicated ideas and thoughts. This requires additional fluency with language and certainly with the spoken word. He requires models of speech, models that will expand his linguistic horizons.

Certainly one vehicle to encourage and enhance his new need for an increased, more sophisticated speaking vocabulary is children's literature. As more and more opportunity is provided him to interact (both at the listening and reading levels) with this literature, that vocabulary will be strengthened and increased.

It is unfortunate, indeed, when the teacher of middle- and upper-grade children feels it unimportant to read to her class each day. That oral reading each day, perhaps a chapter at a time from one of the many fine junior novels, is a valuable (and enjoyable) experience for continued language growth.

The authors, both elementary teachers for many years, found that with intermediate- and upper-grade children, a viable time to provide this oral reading was immediately after the lunch recess. Children come in from the playground or gymnasium excited, stimulated by games and conversations; energy is running high from the physical activity that is typical of the elementary student. Attempting to get the students "in order," or quieted down so that instruction may continue is always something of a problem. By actual time check, fifteen to twenty minutes is required to get the group ready for planned classwork.

After several months of this same, seemingly endless problem and the wasting of valuable time, the authors decided that immediately after the noon recess, oral reading would be the order of the day. The first book offered (and this was the fourth grade) was Armstrong Sperry's magnificent *Call It Courage*. The teacher simply sat on a chair at the head of the class and began discussing the book to be shared with them. It was announced that the time period each day would be twenty minutes of reading, and extra time for discussion. If time was wasted getting into the classroom and order was slow in arriving, the teacher would wait, and deduct that time from the oral reading.

After several days and several chapters of the adventures of Mafutu on his Pacific island, it was delightful to find the children in the room, seated quietly, ready to listen to the oral reading in less than five minutes. After several months of this activity and several books later, somehow or other when the teacher arrived in the classroom, the current book would be placed on the chair *open* to the page that started the day's reading. The children wanted no time wasted! This was their time! Anyone, including the teacher, who dallied about getting down to the exciting job at hand was quickly reminded of the ticking clock.

Usually at these times, the children would give a synopsis of the previous plot to refresh all the listeners. At the end of one chapter (and sometimes when things got very exciting, two chapters) came the time for discussion. "What's going to happen?" "How did he feel?" "Have you had a similar experience?" "What events caused the current problem?" etc., etc., etc. The conversation flowed naturally and excitingly. There was really something to talk about! The children had shared a common experience and could now react to it with oral language. What delightful sessions these can be. What wonderful language experiences. How quickly children are able to do real literary analysis through conversation. How vastly superior these sessions are to the dreadful, traditional book report.

To speak and to develop an effective speaking vocabulary, a child needs models from which he can learn. Since speech is essentially an imitative phenomenon, that model becomes more basic to his learning universe. Listening to and discussing good children's trade books is an effective model, and a genesis for developing that important second vocabulary, speaking.

BOOKS GOOD FOR SPEECH DEVELOPMENT
Preschool/Primary Level

ANDERSEN, HANS C. *The Emperor's New Clothes,* ill. by Erik Blegvad. Harcourt, 1959. 5–10.
  Classic story of the vain king who is bilked by two clever "weavers." Children have loved it for years.

BELPRE, PURA. *Santiago,* ill. by Symeon Shimin. Warne, 1969. 5–9.
  Lots to share when a Puerto Rican boy in New York City wants his classmates to see pictures of his beautiful chickens left behind in Puerto Rico.

BEMELMANS, LUDWIG. *Parsley,* ill. by the author. Harper, 1955. 4–8.
  An old stag outwits the hunters in a beautiful Alpine setting.

BERNADETTE. *Hans the Miller Man,* ill. by the author. McGraw, 1969. 5–8.
  Hans goes into the world searching for a friend, leaving behind a caterpillar who has tried to be a friend, but was unnoticed. When Hans returns, he sees a beautiful butterfly.

BISHOP, CLAIRE H. *The Five Chinese Brothers,* ill. by Kurt Wiese. Coward, 1938. 5–9.

An old tale of five brothers who look exactly alike, but have remarkable, separate talents. Those talents save each other's lives.

BOLOGNESE, DON. *A New Day*, ill. by the author. Delacorte, 1970. 4–8.
A delightful retelling of the Nativity. The setting is the southwestern United States, and the characters are migrant workers.

BOND, JEAN CAREY. *Brown Is a Beautiful Color*, ill. by Barbara Zuber. Watts, 1969. 4–8.
Rhymed verse tells of all the things that are wonderfully brown. Brown cartoon illustrations are lots of fun.

Brian Wildsmith's Mother Goose, ill. by Brian Wildsmith. Watts, 1965. 3–6.
Familiar Mother Goose is illustrated by Wildsmith. The results are spectacular!

BROWN, MARGARET W. *Wait Till the Moon Is Full*, ill. by Garth Williams. Harper, 1948. 4–8.
A young raccoon wants to see the night, but he is told to wait until the moon is full. Poetic text and the illustrations are a sheer delight.

BROWN, MARCIA. *Felice*, ill. by the author. Scribner, 1958. 5–8.
Story set in Venice about a gondolier's son who wants a cat and gets one. He names it Felice. Illustrations are exceptional.

BYARS, BETSY. *Go and Hush the Baby*, ill. by Emily A. McCully. Viking, 1971. 3–5.

CARLE, ERIC. *The Tiny Seed*, ill. by the author. Crowell, 1970. 4–7.
Changing seasons and the life cycle of plants is beautifully told with illustrations and poetic text.

———. *Do You Want to Be My Friend?*, ill. by the author. Crowell, 1971. 4–7.
Told almost without text, it is the story of a mouse who looks for a friend. Excellent for oral retelling from the wonderful illustrations.

DOMJAN, JOSEPH. *The Little Cock*, retold by Jeanne B. Hardendorff, ill. by the author. Lippincott, 1969. 4–8.
The old folktale of the brave cock who is robbed by the greedy Turkish Sultan, and how he got his stolen halfpenny back. Art work is excellent.

EICHENBERG, FRITZ. *Dancing in the Moon*, ill. by the author. Harcourt, 1955. 4–8.
Learn to count up to twenty by enjoying the antics of unusual animals. All done in brief rhymes.

ELKIN, BENJAMIN. *Such Is the Way of the World*, ill. by Yoho Mitsuhashi. Parents, 1968. 4–8.
African-designed illustrations take this old folk tale from the commonplace into the realm of art. Lots to talk about, especially about the fine illustrations.

BOOKS GOOD FOR SPEECH DEVELOPMENT
The Intermediate Level

ADRIAN, MARY. *The Indian Horse Mystery*, ill. by Lloyd Coe. Hastings, 1966. 8-up.
Rustlers set grass fires that cause problems with cattle, as well as the ranchers. Calf thefts cause all kinds of problems.

BAWDEN, NINA. *The White Horse Gang,* ill. by Kenneth Longtems. Lippincott, 1966. 8–11.

Problems bother the "White Horse Gang." So one member can return to America, they kidnap a spoiled boy who really enjoys the whole experience. Danger lurks in the English village, however.

———. *The Witch's Daughter.* Lippincott, 1966. 8–12.

Perdita lives in Scotland on an island, with a strange foster-mother thought to be a witch. She makes friends with other children, however, and they discover a secret, precious stone.

RAYMOND, CHARLES. *Jud.* Houghton, 1968. 9–13.

Jud's family decides to move to the country. Jud is sure he will dislike country living. As Jud and parents discuss, Jud finds he will like country living.

RINKOFF, BARBARA. *A Guy Can Be Wrong,* ill. by Harold James. Crown, 1970. 8–12.

Carlos Martinez spends two weeks with a well-to-do family in the suburbs. Carlos and the son of the family have some tense times, but learn to be friends.

———. *Member of the Gang,* ill. by Harold James. Crown, 1968. 9–13.

Values change as Woodie learns that loyalty to the gang does not ease the plight of the urban slums. Setting is stark and dramatic.

ROBERTSON, KEITH. *Henry Reed's Journey,* ill. by Robert McCloskey. Viking, 1963. 9–12.

A delightful book in a series, Henry crosses the country and sees America. As he travels, he exposes the shortcomings of the adults he meets. Illustrations are lots of fun.

ROBINSON, JOAN. *Charley,* ill. by Prudence Seward. Coward, 1969. 8–12.

Charley, thinking she is unwanted, runs away to save her pride. Her ability to cope, and her vivid imagination make this story very believable.

ROBINSON, VERONICA. *David in Silence,* ill. by Victor Ambrus. Lippincott, 1965. 8–12.

A very tender story of a boy who is born deaf and is rejected by the other boys at school. A valuable book to help children understand afflictions of others.

SACHS, MARILYN. *Veronica Ganz,* ill. by Louis Glanzman. Doubleday, 1968. 8–12.

A delightfully funny story of how a tomboy learns to be a young lady. Veronica is the heroine, and she is one you will never forget.

SHEARER, JOHN. *I Wish I Had An Afro,* ill. by the author. Cowles, 1970. 8–12.

Told in the first person, a moving tale about eleven-year-old John's adventures, in and out of school. All his hopes are revealed. Black poverty is the central theme.

SHOTWELL, LOUISA R. *Adam Bookout,* ill. by W. T. Mars. Viking, 1967. 9–12.

Adam finds life in New York very different from that of his former home in Oklahoma. The new relationships he finds are the backbone of this fine book.

———. *Roosevelt Grady,* ill. by Peter Burchard. World, 1963. 9–12.

This highly recommended book tells the tale of a migrant family and their quest for a permanent home. Excellent source to start children discussing.

SNYDER, ZILPHA K. *The Egypt Game,* ill. by Alton Raible. Atheneum, 1967. 8–12.

Children engage in dramatic play about ancient Egypt. Excitement builds when a murderer comes to the neighborhood, and an oracle's word comes true.

BOOKS GOOD FOR SPEECH DEVELOPMENT
The Upper Level

BONHAM, FRANK. *Viva Chicano*. Dutton, 1970. 12-up.
A well-developed story of a teenage Mexican-American and his problems with his family, the gang, and the police.

BOVA, BEN. *Escape*. Holt, 1970. 12–14.
A boy in a reform school is guarded by a very special computer system. In the end, the hero must decide between his friendship with a black boy or making an escape.

BUTTERWORTH, WILLIAM E. *Orders to Vietnam: A Novel of Helicopter Warfare*. Little, 1968. 11–14.
A draftee learns responsibility for other's lives. Takes place in the war zone of Vietnam.

CAVANNA, BETTY. *The Country Cousin*. Morrow, 1967. 12–16.
A rural girl goes to town to work in her aunt's dress shop. While she works, she discovers she has an ability as a dress designer. Some romance.

DONOVAN, JOHN. *Wild in the World*. Harper, 1971. 12–16.
Man is a social creature, and this junior novel says it clearly. It is about the friendship between a lonely youth and a survivor. Lyrically written.

DUNNE, MARY COLLINS. *Reach Out, Ricardo*. Abelard, 1971. 10–16.
A dramatic and true to life story about what happens to a family and a whole community when grape pickers strike for recognition of a union.

FITZHUGH, LOUISE. *Harriet the Spy*, ill. by the author. Harper, 1964. 10–14.
Harriet, the resourceful sixth grader, wishes to be a famous writer and prepares for that day by observing and taking notes of everything that is of interest to her. The results are comical and at times fairly grim.

HAMILTON, VIRGINIA. *The House of Dies Drear*, ill. by Eros Keith. Macmillan, 1968. 10-up.
A suspenseful story about a black professor and his family living in an old mansion that was once a station on the underground railway.

HINTON, S. E. *The Outsiders*. Viking, 1967. 12-up.
The concerns of urban youth told in a gripping, accurate manner. An excellent example of good writing for adolescents.

JACKSON, JACQUELINE. *The Taste of Spruce Gum*. Little, 1966. 11–15.
A girl finds it difficult to accept a new father and life in a Vermont logging camp.

L'ENGLE, MADELEINE. *The Young Unicorns*. Farrar, 1968. 12-up.
A teenage gang, a mysterious blind girl, and a reformed member of the gang are those involved in a war between good and evil. Takes place in New York City.

MADDOCK, REGINALD. *The Pit*, ill. by Douglas Hall. Little, 1968. 10-up.
A boy runs to the wild moors to escape cruel schoolmates and an unforgiving father. The boy is accused of theft, but when the real thief is found, an exciting story is revealed.

MOREY, WALT. *Angry Waters*, ill. by Richard Duffari. Dutton, 1969. 10-up.
Fifteen-year-old Dan, on parole, is sent to work on a farm. He finds importance in

the work after many trying episodes. Three escaped prisoners have Dan aid their escape. Dan helps in their recapture and returns to the farm with real confidence.

NEVILLE, EMILY. *It's Like This, Cat,* ill. by Emil Weiss. Harper, 1963. 10–14.

A moving story about an adolescent growing up and accepting, as well as understanding, life. "Cat" is a stray who is defended by the boy in spite of adversities. Newbery Award winner, 1963.

RICHARD, ADRIENNE. *Pistol.* Little, 1969. 12-up.

Billy grew up in the West during the Depression. The family is forced to move to a dam site that offered a job for the father. Here, he sees his father's limitations and his need for independence. The hero helps the family move back home, and he heads for the city for independence.

CHILDREN'S LITERATURE AS A REASON TO READ

There is probably no area of the elementary school curriculum that receives more attention, causes more concern, and enjoys greater emphasis than the reading program in our schools. The American school *is* a reading school. If one is to find success in the public school system of our country, one must master the skills and controls of reading. "What can they do if they can't read?" is the question that echoes the length and breadth of the country. What indeed? The task of learning to read is certainly one of the major tasks that faces every student as he moves through the grades. Many are successful in their attempts to master the printed page. It is an unfortunate situation for those who are not successful.

The task of learning to read enjoys not only the real concern of the professionals in the field of education, but the public at large as well. The parent eagerly scans the report card certainly looking first at the teacher's evaluation of how his child is advancing with the skills of reading. How pleased the parent is if his child is advancing with those skills. How happy he is if the youngster can call words by name. He is more than delighted when the child derives meaning from the words he calls. The frustration is very immediate, however, if his child cannot cope with words in print.

We as professional educators share this concern. We are delighted with the youngsters who learn from our instruction and move successfully through the stages of learning to read. Our dilemma is very real when the student fails or does not achieve as we think he should in his attempts at learning to read.

Professional instruction on the teaching of reading echoes the concern of parents and teachers. School districts, colleges, and universities are constantly offering workshops, institutes, courses, colloquiums, and the like to aid teachers in helping children master the mysteries of the printed page. Probably no area in the curriculum, and certainly in the language arts curriculum, enjoys more attention. This attention is timely and good.

This concern is felt in the graduate schools of education across the land. Master's theses and doctoral dissertations have delved into the subject. Research has investigated all areas of reading and reading instruction. This research is continuing today. The result of this valuable research is, of course, that the student of teaching probably has more information about how children learn to read than any area in the elementary school curriculum. As valuable and as valid as it is, some children still do not make a successful adjustment to reading instruction.

Certainly publishers sense the concern of parents and teachers and are attempting to meet the apparent needs. Each year new approaches, new programs, new philosophies, even new alphabets appear under the banner of an eager publisher. If, they reason, they can meet all the many needs of the reluctant reader, the rewards will be a financial bonanza. Some of the attempts by the publishers are laudable, some are completely ridiculous! Some actually offer a panacea. "Just follow the manual," we are told, "and the rest is foolproof!" It's amazing that any professional would accept a panacea. The professional knows, and research has verified, that there is no one best way, no single panacea, for helping children learn to read.

Learning theory has told us that learning (all learning, not just learning to read) is as individual and unique as a thumb print. Attempting to teach all children with the same approach, no matter how good it is, is naïve at best, dangerous at worst.

The Reason for Reading

One major question seems to elude some teachers as they go about the task of teaching children to read. That question, so simple and so basic, when not asked is a glaring professional error. The question is: *Why are we teaching children to read?* Why are we spending so much time helping children learn to decode and encode words, to master the skills of reading? Hopefully so that they will become readers of books! Hopefully our teaching will provide more than just children who know how to read; but in practice, too often children don't read once they have learned how. Hopefully reading instruction will open up the wonderful, magical world of literature for children, so that the wonder of books and the printed page will follow them into adult life. Hopefully we are providing children with a positive attitude toward reading. An attitude that will make the acquisition of skills and controls needed for reading meaningful and worthwhile to them.

Yet, too often, how do we as teachers go about helping children become readers of books, rather than those who simply know how to read? Too often we are so busy teaching the skills and controls of reading that we forget their purpose. Often we are so tied to the basal reader or other developmental devices that we neglect the real purpose of teaching children to read!

The authors visit many classrooms during the school year. They visit as consultants and as supervisors of student teachers. So many times the following conversation is evident in classrooms.

Teacher: Sally, have you finished your reading?
Sally: Yes.
Teacher: Have you completed the workbook pages, and made
    the corrections on yesterday's assignment?
Sally: Yes.
Teacher: What about your spelling list?
Sally: I know the list.
Teacher: Your social studies, Sally? Have you completed the assignment?
Sally: Yes.
Teacher: How about your arithmetic? Have you completed the assignment?
Sally: Yes.
Teacher: Then you have completed everything?
Sally: Yes.
Teacher: Well, since you have completed all the important work,
    why don't you get a library book and read?

This mock dialogue, of course, points up one of the major concerns of good teachers of the language arts. Reading, *real* reading, is relegated to the unimportant. It is thought of as something to do after all the important work has been done. The trade book becomes a device for social control, a way of keeping children busy. It is not thought of as a viable and valuable way of bringing children and the printed page together in a meaningful way.

The teacher who relegates recreational reading or the utilization of trade books as a regular part of the classroom operation to a "sometimes thing" or "an activity to do after all the important work has been done" is really doing some very effective teaching! She is teaching children by this action, that reading, real reading, reading of books, is unimportant. The reading of books is much less important than endless pages of workbook assignments, exercises, questions at the end of the chapter, and the like. This teacher is very likely developing within her students the attitude that learning to read is more important than real reading; that books, the ultimate goal of learning to read, really have no place in a learning environment. If this is the case, that teacher is cheating the children she is attempting to teach.

Is the teacher who relegates children's literature to the "sometimes" or to the "after everything important has been finished" category, a teacher who is uninterested in the growth of her students? Probably not. In all likelihood she is a sincere, conscientious teacher who wants the best for her pupils. She probably views test scores with alarm and is of the opinion that the skills of reading need to be secure before the youngster is involved with literature.

What has research told us about the role of children's literature in reading skill development? It would take many volumes to relate it all. For our purposes, however, it may be good to list some of the generalizations concerning skill and attitude development that have come about as a result of research. The conscientious reading teacher will want to know that:

1. Preschool language (listening and speaking vocabulary) development is increased significantly if children are provided a rich experience through children's books. Oral reading to young children and much interaction with picture-story books is advised.
2. In working with disadvantaged children (in projects such as Head Start, as well as in the classroom), the opportunity to interact with children's books increases language development and thus increases their ability to successfully cope with beginning reading instruction.
3. The relationship between oral language and reading has been confirmed. Oral language can be enlarged and significantly enhanced by interaction with children's books when read aloud.
4. The slower the youngster in his academic progress (reading), the more difficult it is for him to deal with words in isolation, unrelated to a meaningful experience. Vocabulary is thus learned best in a context of emotional and intellectual meaning. The children's trade book is a good source for this kind of learning.
5. The advanced reader is better able to achieve greater growth when children's books are a part of his reading program than he may achieve from a basal program alone.
6. Because of the emotional involvement that occurs when a youngster reads a book of his choice, his use of context skills often overcomes what appears to be problems in other reading situations.
7. Because more reading is done when children's books are a part of the reading program, skills are given an opportunity to be used more often. They thus are more likely to become a part of the child's collection of permanent reading tools.
8. Because boredom is less likely to occur when a rich program of literature is evident in a reading program, attitudes toward learning to read improve significantly.
9. Research does not indicate that children learn to read best by the traditional basal reading approach. Evidence is present to indicate the opposite to be true.
10. The youngster who has failed to respond to traditional approaches in reading instruction often responds to an approach based upon the individualization of his instruction using trade books rather than textbooks as instructional material.[2]

A PRAGMATIC USE OF LITERATURE IN THE READING PROGRAM

The remarks above should not be construed to mean that there is no place in the reading program for the basal text or other instructional devices. It is not the

---

2. Dewey W. Chambers, *Children's Literature in the Curriculum* (Chicago, Ill.: Rand-McNally & Co., 1971), p. 12.

purpose here to do away with all tradition in the teaching of reading. Quite the opposite is true.

The authors, as evidenced in Part Three of this text, in no way accept a panacea for all reading needs and reading ills. Therefore they cannot replace one method or approach with another. They do ask, however, to examine some of the rationale behind any reading program.

Skills and controls of reading must be taught. These are difficult, complicated, and involved tasks. A teacher, left to her own devices, will be hard pressed to help children grasp and understand the skills necessary to cope successfully with the printed word. To the author's knowledge, no child has ever been taught to read by simply having a trade book placed in his hand and letting him teach himself. Those skills and controls needed to help the youngster interact with print in a meaningful, knowledgeable way must be taught. They must be taught in a scientific, sequential, carefully planned way. Thus the value of the basal approaches.

Most basal approaches in the teaching of reading have been prepared by some of the finest reading specialists in the country. They have spent many years investigating how best to introduce children to the skills and controls of reading successfully. They have, in most cases, organized the reading skills carefully, sequentially, and scientifically. Their work, in the form of basal reading materials, is an invaluable source for the teaching of reading. They should be used. Without the aid of these materials, most reading programs in the elementary schools would be a shambles. They, by and large, do an excellent job of helping children learn the skills of reading. But that is all they do! A successful reading program needs to be more than just a program to give children the skills and controls of knowing how to read.

The reason for reading instruction remains the same. We want our children to emerge from our teaching with more than just knowing how to read. We want them to read once they have the skills that will allow them to read. We want to instill the love of reading into their world, so that they will indeed become readers of books.

Some who share the concern of developing readers of books, rather than more students who can, but don't read, have developed a program that they feel will cure all ills. This program is called by many names, the most common of which is "Individualized Reading" or "The Self-Selection Program." There are many variations on this theme, but basically it refers to a reading program that is based upon children's literature. It is the contention of the followers of this approach that the basal text, or any basal device used to help children learn to read, is unnecessary. The same skills and controls that are found in the basals can be taught by having children interact with trade books only, they tell us.

The devotees of this approach assure us that if the Individualized Reading Program were utilized, and the basal reader were exchanged for a wealth of good children's literature, magazines, and the like, reading instruction would improve. With the individualized approach, we are told the child will:

Certain skills need to be taught in a good literature program. One such area is the use of the card catalog and the location of specific books.

- Move more rapidly with this approach than he has with the basal approach because he will not be hindered by group instruction techniques. The program will be designed for his individual needs.
- Achieve self-improvement more readily and avoid personal frustrations because he will not be compared directly with others in a reading group.
- Read more extensively and widely because he will be allowed to choose his reading material from a wide range of choices provided for him.[3]

A new panacea, it appeared, had been found. The real reason for reading had finally been included in a program for the teaching of reading. Cheers were heard in certain quarters all across the land. At last we were teaching reading so

---

3. Ibid., p. 20.

that the results would give us readers, real readers, not more of those who could read, but in fact didn't.

When this approach was subjected to research, however, it was found that like all panaceas it did indeed have its weaknesses. It made assumptions that could not be supported. It proved to be "unworkable" in some instances.

One well-known study, reported in *The Harvard Report on Reading in Elementary Schools*,[4] did indeed give us reason for caution. The study was a carefully controlled, well-documented report of reading practices in more than a thousand public schools in this country conducted by Harvard University and supported by the Carnegie Foundation of New York.

The study, which could be representative of others, told us that while this program appeared sound in its theoretical state, teachers and administrators who were asked to work with it overwhelmingly rejected it after they had used it for the prescribed period of time. Of the 407 persons polled in this study, 350 did not favor this approach at all. Twenty-four of those that worked with the experiment did like it, and 26 were not sure but thought it might work with certain modifications.[5]

What were the reasons that caused the group involved in this study to reject this approach so overwhelmingly? Why would a group of practicing educators turn down so promising a technique?

The Harvard Report itself gives us some insights into the reasons why. The following points may indicate why so many administrators and teachers avoided the Individualized Reading Program.

1. Too few teachers in the study possessed the ability or knowledge to work with this technique in an effective way. A sound knowledge of children's books plus a real understanding of teaching of reading is a prerequisite in the program.
2. There was an inadequate supply of children's trade books available to students and teachers.
3. The teachers felt that the reading skills were presented in a "haphazard" way.
4. Class size was too large to work effectively with this program.
5. If enough trade books and good, trained teachers were available, many thought they could support the program.
6. The approach was good, it was felt, for academically talented students. It was not, however, good for the average or slow student.
7. The program was a good one for "supplementary" reading, but not to replace the basal program.
8. The approach would be good after the reading skills were taught, but not before.

---

4. Mary C. Austin et al., *The First R, The Harvard Report on Reading in the Elementary Schools* (New York: The Macmillan Co., 1963), p. 88.
5. Chambers, *Children's Literature in the Curriculum*, p. 21.

It appears from this study, and others like it, that two basic problems surfaced when teachers used any of the variations found in the Individualized Reading syndrome. These were that (1) teachers felt inadequate and untrained to utilize this approach, and (2) not enough trade books were available to teachers so they could (if trained) use this approach.

Needless to say controversy followed this report and others like it concerning this approach. Some agreed and some disagreed strongly with the research. One point emerged clearly, however. Individualized Reading, and other approaches similar to it, did have weaknesses. They did not prove to be the panacea some had hoped they would. Few thinking educators ever expected that they would.

The issue remains, however, that the purpose of teaching children to read is that they will be readers of books, not just more of those who know how to read, but often don't. What, then, is the role of children's literature in the reading program? If the individualized approach is not the panacea, what direction should a teacher take?

The wise teacher will use children's literature as a regular part of the reading program along with the basal text or any other basal materials. She will arrange her class schedule so that all children will have opportunities to interact with children's trade books as they are learning the necessary skills and controls from the basal device. As the teacher works with various groups of youngsters in the reading program, she frees others for recreational reading or a modified individualized reading program. Often, for children who are reading above their grade level, three or four reading periods per week are given over to reading of children's literature. The other periods in the week for this group of advanced readers are spent with the teacher discussing the books they are reading, or in receiving basic reading instruction. Another group, which is reading at or near that grade level, will receive regular reading instruction in the basal device three or four reading periods a week and be free for recreational reading during the remaining reading periods of the week. The remedial reader, perhaps, needs more direct instruction during his reading periods. This group, then, may receive teacher-guided reading instruction from the basal device four periods a week, with one day for recreational reading.

The plans for the integration of children's literature into the reading program are as diverse as the people who plan them. They are as creative as their creators. However this integration is achieved, the fact remains that children are reading—really reading—while they are being taught to read. That is the basic issue.

Sometimes well-intended teachers will shrug off the integration of children's literature as a regular part of their reading programs. They argue that the place for recreational reading is the home. Why should a teacher provide for this kind of reading in the classroom? The classroom is a place for teaching and learning! Recreational reading should be done outside the school setting. With the elementary curriculum as crowded as it is, how can teachers afford the time for this kind of activity?

Perhaps, for these teachers, a realistic look at many of the homes from which the children come may change their attitude about children's literature as a regular part of the reading program. Will the teacher expect children to take their literature home to read if:

- The classroom is the only quiet, orderly place in the child's life? For many children this is true! The hustle and bustle of the usual household, the lure of television, the competition from brothers and sisters and the like, render many home environments inhospitable for recreational reading.
- The child has physical needs that must be met after school? Some children will choose the basketball court, the swimming pool, or other large muscle activity for his after school recreation. He has, after all, been in the classroom all day, and his large muscle activity is important. Reading has a place in the lives of children, but only a place. Certainly it should not be forced to take the place of healthy exercise and play.
- The youngster has work responsibility? Many children, even today, have work responsibilities after school. For some, it is a regular job. For others, it consists of duties around the home. Whatever the responsibility, it needs to be met, and additional work from school may, by necessity, suffer.

Time must be provided for interaction with children's literature in the classroom. That time needs to be "official" time, set aside and counted as a regular part of the day's activity, not incidental time. Most frequently that time can be most justified when it is a regular part of the reading program.

CHILDREN'S LITERATURE IN THE CONTENT AREAS

Children's literature can, for the creative teacher, enhance and improve much more of the curriculum in the elementary school than just the reading program. All the while this literature is being used to undergird other content areas, the reading abilities of the children who utilize the books are being improved.

The social studies are a favorite place to utilize literature for children. So often, the skeletal textbook leaves much to be desired in helping children learn about man and his interaction with his physical and social environment through a unit of study. So often these texts ignore the human element, how people felt and reacted to the forces around them. Many social studies texts seem overly concerned with what man has done, with events, with movements, but not often with man himself. This is where children's literature can fill a vast void.

Informational books, biographies, and historical fiction, when carefully selected to move with the social studies unit, can add flesh to the text skeleton, and bring life, real life, into a unit in the social studies. These fine books, on every reading level, can take the child on journeys, to historical times, through social movements in a delightful, accurate way. They can add drama, excitement, and identification to a social studies unit better than any medium available to children in a classroom setting.

This same truth is evident in many other areas of the elementary curriculum. Science experiments, mathematics investigations, the fine arts—all can be enhanced and made more effective with the use of children's literature as an undergirding factor.

The new teacher would be well advised to confer with the school or district librarian before the term begins. The librarian can easily gather a collection of trade books for any number of academic activities and have them delivered to your classroom ready to serve the children when they are needed. These books are a treasure trove that should not be overlooked in any program.

BOOKS TO ENHANCE THE READING PROGRAM
Preschool/Primary Level

Appley Dapply's Nursery Rhymes, ill. by Beatrix Potter. Warne, 1917. 3–6.
> This near classic book of rhymes is beautifully illustrated by the creator of *Peter Rabbit.*

BROWN, MARGARET WISE. *Where Have You Been?,* ill. by Barbara Cooney. Hastings, 1952. 3–6.
> Questions and answers about familiar animals are written in simple verse. Can easily be "reread" through illustrations.

DE REGNIERS, BEATRICE SCHENK. *The Giant Story,* ill. by Maurice Sendak. Harper, 1953. 3–6.
> Tommy pretends to be a giant. He marches about, flexes his muscles, and extends his chest. Sendak's illustrations are charming.

DE LA FONTAINE, JEAN. *The Hare and the Tortoise,* ill. by Brian Wildsmith. Watts, 1966. 4–8.
> Magnificent illustrations enhance the meaning of this old, and much loved, fable.

EICHENBERG, FRITZ. *Ape in a Cape,* ill. by the author. Harcourt, 1952. 4–6.
> An alphabet of strange animals that is bound to cause a lot of laughter. Illustrations add much.

EMBERLEY, BARBARA. *Drummer Hoff,* ill. by Ed Emberley. Prentice, 1967. 4–8.
> Vivid illustrations tell about a remarkable cannon. This book won the Caldecott Award in 1968.

ETS, MARIE HALL. *Play with Me,* ill. by the author. Viking, 1955. 3–6.
> A very small child attempts to make friends with animals, only to have them scurry away. When she sits quietly, they come to her. A very sensitive story.

———. *Gilberto and the Wind,* ill. by the author. Viking, 1963. 3–6.
> A Mexican boy's adventure with the wind. The wind becomes a playmate in this delightful book. Illustrations are very gentle and add much to the book. This story is also available in Spanish.

FEINSTEIN, JOE. *A Silly Little Kid,* ill. by John Paul Richards. Steck-Vaughn, 1969. 4–7.
> A boy who wants to be bigger than he is, finds that it is nice just to be himself.

FLACK, MARJORIE. *Angus and the Ducks,* ill. by the author. Doubleday, 1931. 4–7.
The adventures of a Scotch terrier puppy will hold the interest of any young child. His attempts to read this will be rewarded.

GAG, WANDA. *The ABC Bunny,* ill. by the author. Coward, 1933. 3–6.
A bunny carries the continuity of the text. Black-and-white illustrations with each succeeding letter of the alphabet introduced by a large capital in red.

Mother Goose, ill. by Frederick Richardson. Hubbard, 1962. 3–6.
Clearly one of the best of the *Mother Goose* books. Each rhyme is illustrated with a delightful "old-fashioned" picture that is bound to delight the young reader.

SHIVKUMAR, K. *The King's Choice,* ill. by Yoko Mitsuhashi. Parents, 1971. 4–8.
A simple tale from India, illustrated by Indian style illustrations. Story of a kind and noble king and his triumph over trickery.

TUDOR, TASHA. *A Is for Annabelle,* ill. by the author. Walck, 1954. 5–7.
A doll's adventure reveals the alphabet. Designed mainly for girls. Watercolor and pencil drawings enhance the text greatly.

WILDSMITH, BRIAN. *Brian Wildsmith's ABC,* ill. by the author. Watts, 1963. 3–5.
Brilliant illustrations of various objects and animals are the major feature of this excellent book. ABC's are focal point. A magnificent volume.

YOLEN, JANE. *The Seventh Mandarin,* ill. by Ed Young. Seabury, 1970. 5–8.
An original fable set in the ancient Orient. Beautiful illustrations enhance this fine tale.

BOOKS TO ENHANCE THE READING PROGRAM
The Intermediate Level

ESTRADA, DORIS. *Periwinkle Jones,* ill. by Jo Ann Stover. Doubleday, 1965. 8–10.
Periwinkle Jones is a delightful girl who leads her cousin on all kinds of adventures. A humorous, imaginative book.

FISHER, LAURA. *You Were Princess Last Time,* ill. by Nancy Grossman. Holt, 1965. 8–12.
Susie is a tomboy, yet she yearns to change her ways and to have lovely long hair. Her progression to her desired state is both humorous and touching.

HAYES, WILLIAM D. *Project: Scoop,* ill. by the author. Atheneum, 1966. 8–12.
Story about a disagreement between the school principal and the editor of the school paper. Lots of fun, and shows clearly the power of the "press."

HOLMAN, FELICE. *Elisabeth, the Treasure Hunter,* ill. by Erik Blegvad. Macmillan, 1964. 7–9.
A delightful sequel to *Elisabeth, the Bird Watcher,* this time we go on a treasure hunt at the beach. Lots of clever clues will delight young naturalists.

HOOKER, RUTH. *Gertrude Kloppenberg,* ill. by Gloria Kamen. Abingdon, 1970. 8–12.
Gertrude's diary for six weeks reveals a shy, unsure girl who grows into a wider and wider world.

HUSTON, ANNE. *The Cat Across the Way,* ill. by Velma Ilsley. Seabury, 1968. 8–12.
Moving from a small town into a large one upsets the heroine's life. Her friendships in the new town have their ups and downs. The heroine's cat is a central figure.

JUSTICE, MAY. *A New Home for Billy*, ill. by Joan Balfour Payne. Hastings, 1966. 7–11.

   The quest for a new home for an inner-city black family is the theme of this fine book. Realistic, believable story.

KONIGSBURG, E. L. *Jennifer, Hecate, Macbeth, William McKinley, and Me, Elizabeth*. Atheneum, 1967. 8–11.

   A delightful tale set in suburban New York City. Friendship develops between two girls as one studies witchcraft under the direction of the other.

KOOB, THEODORA. *The Tacky Little Icicle Shack*, ill. by Kurt Werth. Lippincott, 1966. 9–12.

   Children open a roadside ice-cream stand. Complications arise when their father becomes ill. Ability to adjust makes some very interesting episodes.

LADD, ELIZABETH. *Treasure on Heron's Neck*, ill. by George Porter. Morrow, 1967. 8–12.

   A ten-year-old girl living with her father in a remote part of Maine, wants a wild animal for a pet. She discovers that wild animals are best left to the wild.

LEWIS, RICHARD W. *A Summer Adventure*, ill. by the author. Harper, 1962. 8–12.

   A gentle story of a boy who acquires a zoo of his own. Much emphasis on ecology and the balance of nature.

LEXAU, JOAN M. *Striped Ice Cream*, ill. by John Wilson. Lippincott, 1968. 7–10.

   A girl's wish for chicken, spaghetti, and striped ice cream for her birthday party, reveals the warmth and tenderness of a family. The family is black.

McCLOSKEY, ROBERT. *Homer Price*, ill. by the author. Viking, 1943. 9–12.

   Delightful romp with the adventures of a Midwestern boy in a small town. Anything can happen, and usually does.

MARTIN, PATRICIA MILES. *Trina's Boxcar*, ill. by Robert Jefferson. Abingdon, 1967. 8–10.

   A recent family from Mexico arrives in the United States. They live in a boxcar and travel about the United States. The story of the heroine's quest to read and write English and to find a friend is quite moving.

MILES, MISKA. *Hoagie's Rifle-Gun*, ill. by John Schoenherr. Little, 1970. 8–10.

   A very moving, simple tale of survival, as told by two boys out on a hunt for dinner. A hope for a better tomorrow is an important theme.

NEFF, PRISCILLA HOLTON. *Tressa's Dream*, ill. by Marcia Howe. McKay, 1965. 8–11. Tressa wants to buy a neglected Shetland pony. She earns enough money to buy the pony, and he joins her other friend, a goat. A nice, warm story.

BOOKS TO ENHANCE THE READING PROGRAM
The Upper Level

ALEXANDER, LLOYD. *The High King*, Holt, 1968. 10–14.

   The last of the magnificent chronicles of Prydian makes for some of the best fantasy in our language. A real classic in the making.

ANGIER, BRADFORD and DIXON, JEANNE. *The Ghost of Spirit River*, ill. by Kenny E. Carey. Atheneum, 1968. 9–13.

Exciting chase on the Alcan Highway for wild horses that escaped from a van after a mysterious accident. Lots of adventure and change. Good reading.

BONHAM, FRANK. *Mystery of the Fat Cat*, ill. by A. Smith. Dutton, 1968. 10–14.
Ghetto locale offers the Dogtown Boys' Club a chance to inherit a huge estate being enjoyed by a huge tomcat.

BURNFORD, SHEILA. *The Incredible Journey*, ill. by Carl Burger. Little, 1961. 9-up.
A fine adventure story of three animals, a cat, a bulldog, and a Labrador retriever traveling through the Canadian wilderness to get home.

CHRISTOPHER, JOHN. *The Pool of Fire*. Macmillan, 1968. 10–14.
Science fiction at its best! The last of a trilogy set in the 21st century when our planet is conquered by tripods. Man's attempt to reconquer his planet makes for very exciting reading. First parts of this trilogy are *The White Mountain* and *The City of Gold and Lead.*

CHRISTOPHER, MATT. *The Year Mom Won the Pennant*, ill. by Foster Caddell. Little, 1968. 9–12.
When the fathers have no time to coach the Thunderballs, the mothers take on the task. It's lots of fun, with a great deal of sparkle.

CORBETT, SCOTT. *Cutlass Island*, ill. by Leonard Shortall. Little, 1962. 11–15.
Thrilling story of two teenage boys who help in the capture of narcotics smugglers. Exciting battle using old weapons to hold smugglers at bay climaxes the story.

FRIENDLICH, DICK. *Touchdown Maker*. Doubleday, 1966. 12–14.
After a serious mistake at the championship game, Russ joins the team at his new school. Inner doubts cause conflict with his new teammates. A good sports story.

HENRY, MARGUERITE. *King of the Wind*, ill. by Wesley Dennis. Rand, 1948. 10–14.
One of the best of Henry's horse books. An exciting tale of Sham, who was intended as a gift to the French King from the Sultan of Morocco, but falls on hard times until he reaches England. A Newbery Award winner.

JACKSON, C. P. *Junior High Freestyle Swimmer*, ill. by Frank Kramer. Hastings, 1965. 9–13.
A new team member finds a friend and they team up against the squad's bad guy. Success of the team brings about understanding and friendship.

KINGMAN, LEE. *The Year of the Raccoon*. Houghton, 1966. 12–14.
Joey feels lost as a member of his dynamic family until he finds a pet raccoon who helps him cope with his world.

MEIGS, CORNELIA. *Invincible Louisa*, photos. Little, 1933. 10–14.
A lively, warm biography of Louisa May Alcott, author of *Little Women.* Newbery Award, 1934.

PEASE, HOWARD. *The Black Tanker*. Doubleday, 1941. 12-up.
Master storyteller for boys, tells another mystery-adventure at sea. Danger, intrigue, and adventure mark this book as they do all the books by Howard Pease.

SALTEN, FELIX. *Bambi*, ill. by Kurt Weise. Grossett, 1931. 10–12.
A very tender nature romance about life of a deer in the forest. A great deal of symbolic value in this near classic.

SPERRY, ARMSTRONG. *Call it Courage*, ill. by the author. Macmillan, 1940. 10–12.
A very dramatic story set in the South Pacific of a boy who faces the thing he fears most and becomes a man. A distinguished book. Newbery award winner.

CHILDREN'S LITERATURE AS A GENESIS FOR WRITING

Before children begin the difficult and abstract task of composing with written words, they need much experience with language. As has been noted before in this book, they need first a listening vocabulary, then a speaking vocabulary, and finally a reading vocabulary before they attempt their first encounter with written composition. In the sections that precede this one, the relationship between children's literature and the first three vocabularies have been explored.

The relationship between children's literature and the writing vocabulary is an important and valid one as well.

As children interact with their literature, they are dealing exclusively with language in its printed form. With the exception of those times when the teacher or parent reads orally to them, the world of books is a world of print on paper. It is the world of writing. It is a world of words used in an artful, meaningful, evocative way. It is the world of the author speaking to his audience through the medium of written expression. That children can be amused, saddened, delighted, and made wiser through the remains of ink on metal placed in an orderly fashion on paper is a wonder of the creative ability of man, and the nadir of the abstract.

When we ask children to compose with written language there are several important variables that need to be considered: (1) Does he have the skills and controls of the mechanics of writing to allow him to compose? (2) Does he have something to say? Since writing is an output activity, what input has been provided him so that he can communicate with the written word? (3) What models of written expression has he been exposed to that might serve as an example for him when he begins to write?

The latter two variables can be strengthened and enhanced by the use of children's literature as a regular part of the language arts program in the elementary school. Reading and listening to oral reading from children's books is experiencing. It is a time of input. It is a time of gathering new ideas, meeting new people, visiting new and different places. It is a time of exploring new and familiar worlds. These books, therefore, provide background experiences from which the child can draw when he begins to compose. The enriching experiences a youngster gleans from interacting with literature (either read or heard) helps provide a background from which he can draw when he begins to write.

The writers recall vividly an excellent example of this phenomenon. They were visiting a fifth grade classroom to observe a particularly gifted teacher work with her class in creative writing. The group had been concerned with the westward movement of the pioneers as a social studies project. The teacher read each day several chapters of an exciting historical fiction junior novel about a boy traveling west with a wagon train in the 1840s. The children eagerly awaited each oral reading period so that they could don imaginary buckskins and travel west with their literary hero. After each oral reading session, the teacher and the students discussed the adventure and examined the syndrome of events that had happened.

The library corner likewise, was filled with books concerning the westward movement. There were picture books dealing with this period in history, biographies of famous people of the times, historical fiction of all types, and informational books of various descriptions waiting to be examined. The reading levels of these books varied from the primary level up to the junior high school level. They were, we were told by the teacher, used frequently. Indeed, many were evident on the desks of the students.

As we entered the classroom, the teacher was finishing a chapter of the book she was reading to the class. She and the children discussed the adventure, extending what the children had heard to a surprising level of sophistication.

As we watched, the teacher skillfully directed the children into a discussion of what kinds of things the hero of the book would have written into a diary had he kept one. The youngsters eagerly contributed ideas about the diary and its contents. The teacher made notes of several of the ideas on the chalkboard, as a way of summarizing the ideas of the students. She then suggested it might be interesting if the children themselves wrote three or four days of an imaginary diary, putting themselves in the place of the hero of the book. There was real interest evidenced as she passed out paper and discussed the forms one could use for writing a diary. The children very quickly got to work and were working diligently on this creative writing project when we left.

Three days later we were afforded another opportunity to visit that same classroom. When we did so, we requested to hear some of the diaries that were composed. The children were eager to share their diaries with us. One after another they read to us from their diaries. They were exciting, accurate, and remarkably well-written. When we asked the children how they got the ideas they had used for their writing, the following quotes were typical.

Jeff C.	"That's what happened to Jed (the hero) for four days."
Susan K.	"Miss O'Brien (the teacher) read to us, and this is what happened."
Craig M.	"I'm reading *Tree in the Trail*. I used that book for my diary."
Nancy S.	"I used my favorite parts of the book Miss O'Brien is reading to us. I just pretended I was there and made it up."

Input had occurred through a children's book, and output in the form of creative writing was one result.

This example can be replicated in many ways from the primary grades to the upper grades and into the junior high school. Literature does provide experiences, vicarious though they may be, and experiences are necessary for writing to occur. It simply provides children the material with which to create.

The variable of written models to serve the student as examples of written language when he begins to write can certainly be found in good children's literature. The very fact that these books are examples of excellence in written language should serve notice as to their value.

When a youngster interacts with the fine writing that is available in these books, he is interacting with a model. He sees and hears words strung together to evoke beauty, wonder, suspense, and all the human emotions. He is witnessing the art of some of the finest writing the culture has to offer him.

As he reads, or listens to a reader, he experiences many forms of written expression. Factional writing, expository writing, fanciful writing, poetry, and all the examples of how man communicates with other men through the medium of putting words on paper are available to him. For the fledgling writer this experience is invaluable!

The teacher, who often arranges for the meeting of children with literature, r eeds to make children aware of how an author uses words to create the effect he does. Discussions about style, about construction, about use of words are often very valuable for the beginning writer. These elements are brought to his attention, so that he may attempt their use when he writes. The discussions do not need to be labored or didactic in their approach. Rather they should flow from the children as they are brought to recognize certain techniques an author may use. These sessions can immediately follow a reading session and result in some attempts at recreating technique.

Literary analysis does not just belong at the university level. Elementary school students are capable, at their level, of analyzing literature to better understand how an author uses language to produce a work of art. When he begins to understand the technique of writing by examining good models of writing, the probability of his growth with that written language is certainly better than before.

BOOKS TO INDUCE WRITING
Preschool/Primary Level

And So My Garden Grows, ill. by Peter Spier. Doubleday, 1969. 4–8.
> Part of Spier's larger Mother Goose Library. Watercolor illustrations make this a very inviting book for children.

BROWN, MARGARET WISE. *Nibble Nibble*. Scott, 1944. 4–6.
> A small book of poems using many parts of nature as theme. Good model for later poetry writing for very young children.

CHUTE, MARCHETTE. *Around and About,* ill. by the author. Dutton, 1957. 4–8.
> Sixty rhymes that match delightful silhouettes.

CLIFTON, LUCILE. *Some of the Days of Everett Anderson,* ill. by Evaline Ness. Holt, 1970. 3–7.
> Nine poems telling about the many moods of a six-year-old. The six-year-old just happens to be black.

DE LA FONTAINE. *The North Wind and the Sun,* ill by Brian Wildsmith. Watts, 1964. 4–8.
> Wildsmith's vibrant illustrations take this old tale into a new dimension.

DE REGNIERS, BEATRICE SCHENK. *A Little House of Your Own,* ill. by Irene Haas. Harcourt, 1954. 4–6.
> A little house of your own can be any number of hiding places. Can start the youngster off on all kinds of adventures.

————. *May I Bring a Friend?* ill. by Beni Montresor. Atheneum, 1964. 4–6.

A boy brings many unusual friends when he visits the palace of the king and the queen. Very funny. Children may write their own.

FALLS, C. B. *ABC Book*, ill. by author. Doubleday, 1923. 4–6.

Woodcuts make this "classic" ABC book a must for beginning writers. Animals are seen throughout in four colors.

FISHER, AILEEN. *Cricket in a Thicket*, ill. by Feodor Rojankovsky. Scribner, 1963. 4–6.

Nature poems lead the children on a delightful walk in the woods. Drawings enhance every page.

FLACK, MARJORIE. *The Story About Ping*, ill. by Kurt Wiese. Viking, 1944. 4–6.

The near classic story of a little duck in the waters of the Yangtze River. Children have loved it for generations.

————. *Boats on the River*, ill. by Jay Hyde Barnum. Viking, 1964. 4–6.

An excellent informational book that tells about the many forms of transportation on the river. Experience stories can result.

FOSTER, JOANNA. *Pete's Puddle*, ill. by Beatrice Darwin. Harcourt, 1969. 3–6.

Lots of fun for rainy weather as Pete looks to a puddle for all kinds of adventure.

GAG, WANDA. *Millions of Cats*, ill. by the author. Coward, 1938. 4–6.

This famous old tale of the old man who sets out to find one cat, but returns with "hundreds of cats, thousands of cats, millions and billions and trillions of cats" has been a favorite for generations.

GOUDEY, ALICE E. *The Day We Saw the Sun Come Up*, ill. by Adrienne Adams. Scribner, 1961. 5–7.

A child's view of the world around him told in a charmingly sensitive manner.

HALE, LINDA. *The Glorious Christmas Soup Party*, ill. by the author. Viking, 1962. 4–8.

The old stone soup story served up at Christmas by some talented mice!

HEYWARD, DUBOSE. *The Country Bunny and the Little Gold Shoes,* ill. by Marjorie Flack. Houghton, 1939. 3–7.

A modern fairy tale about an ordinary bunny who is chosen to help in the delivery of Easter eggs. Appealing illustrations.

IPCAR, DAHLOV. *I Love My Anteater with an A*, ill. by the author. Knopf, 1964. 5–8.

Each letter is represented by an animal, some familiar, some strange. Lots of fun.

PETERSHAM, MAUD AND PETERSHAM, MISKA. *An American ABC,* ill. by the authors. Macmillan, 1967. 5–9.

The ABC's are presented through the history of the United States. Illustrations are quite colorful.

BOOKS TO INDUCE WRITING
The Intermediate Level

AIKEN, CONRAD. *Cats and Bats and Things with Wings*, ill. by Milton Glaser. Atheneum, 1965. 6–10.

The nature of various animals told in sixteen poems and illustrations. A good model for poetry writing.

ALEXANDER, LLOYD. *Time Cat.* Holt, 1963. 9–12.
> Delightful fantasy about a boy and a cat who are able to journey into various histori-
> cal periods. History is left alone, and the fantasy is wonderful.

————. *The Marvelous Misadventures of Sebastian.* Dutton, 1970. 8-up.
> Sebastian, a teenage fiddler, gets mixed up with some very unusual aristocrats of
> Europe and muddles his way to success and the removal of a cruel usurper to the
> throne.

BAILEY, CAROLYN S. *Miss Hickory.* Viking, 1946. 7–10.
> The famous Newbery Award-winning story of a remarkable doll. It will enchant all
> who come into contact with it.

BENET, ROSEMARY AND BENET, STEPHEN. *A Book for Americans,* ill. by Charles
Child. Holt, 1933. 7–10.
> A unique way to look at the historical figures important to all Americans. All done in
> verse.

CARLSON, BERNICE. *Act it Out,* ill. by Lazzlo Matulay. Abingdon, 1956. 8–12.
> All about puppets, pantomime, tableau, shadow plays, and so on. Can serve as a
> model for playwriting in the classroom.

CHUBB, MARY. *An Alphabet of Ancient Egypt,* ill. by Jill Wyatt. Watts, 1968. 8-up.
> An interesting, informative book about how alphabets came about. This one deals
> with the writing of the ancients in Egypt. Should create a real interest in words.

COATSWORTH, ELIZABETH. *Sparrow Bush,* ill. by Stefan Martin. Norton, 1966. 8–10.
> This book by the famous children's poet tells of the world of nature. Well worth
> hearing again and again.

HELFMAN, ELIZABETH S. *Signs and Symbols Around the World.* Lothrop, 1967.
7-up.
> An interesting look at how people all over the world and through the ages have
> communicated with alphabets, signs, numerals, symbols, trademarks, trail signs, and
> a host of other ways. Makes for very interesting reading, and attempts at writing.

HENRY, MARGUERITE. *All About Horses,* ill. by Walter D. Osborne. Random House,
1967. 8–12.
> As we all know, few people who write for children know more about horses than
> Ms. Henry. This is an informational delight, illustrated by photographs.

HOBAN, RUSSELL. *The Pedaling Man and Other Poems,* ill. by Lillian Hoban. Norton, 1968. 8-up.
> People, places, common events are observed through the eyes of a poet.

HOPKINS, LEE BENNETT. *This Street's for Me!,* ill. by Ann Grifalconi. Crown, 1970.
4–9.
> A collection of poems telling about inner-city life. All the hustle and bustle of city
> living is found in this delightful collection.

LAUBER, PATRICIA. *The Story of Dogs,* photos. Random House, 1966. 8–10.
> Easily read story of the history of dogs. Clear photos enhance this interesting book.
> Can serve as a genesis for writing about one's own dog!

McGREGOR, R. J. *The Young Detectives,* ill. by William Gimmond. Penguin, 1934.
8–up.
> This old tale still packs a lot of adventure, thrills, and some excitement. Young
> followers of mystery stories will find this a "must." The setting is delightfully English.

MILNE, A. A. *The World of Christopher Robin*, ill. by E. H. Shepard. Button, 1958. 6-up.

All those delightful poems found in *When We Were Very Young*, and *Now We Are Six* in one handsome new volume.

BOOKS TO INDUCE WRITING
The Upper Level

AIKEN, JOAN. *Nightbirds on Nantucket*, ill. by Robin Jacques. Doubleday, 1966. 10–15.

A wild and woolly fantasy set during the whaling days. Lots of fun, excellent writing, and material meant to set the imagination spinning.

ASIMOV, ISAAC. *The Egyptians*. Houghton, 1969. 12-up.

A thorough look at the ancient Egyptians by one of the finest nonfiction writers for children working today. All aspects of that ancient culture are described.

BAITY, ELIZABETH. *Americans before Columbus*, photos. Viking, 1961. 10–15.

Many fine photographs precede the actual text. The text gives a clear account of the early people living on the American continents before the Europeans came. This kind of book helps the more able research for a report.

CHUTE, MARCHETTE. *Stories from Shakespeare*. World, 1956. 12-up.

While in no way pretending to be a substitute for the plays, these retellings of the plot levels are a valuable aid in helping children learn the stories before stepping into the Bard's own language.

DANSKA, HERBERT. *The Street Kids*, ill. by the author. Knopf, 1970. 10–14.

Both tragedy and humor sparkle in this tale of an apartment house watchman and superintendent. A well-written story.

deSAINT-EXUPERY, ANTOINE. *The Little Prince*, tr. by Katherine Woods. Harcourt, 1943. 8-up.

The classic tale that goes deeply into life and philosophy. The Little Prince is stranded on a desert and teaches us a lot.

DIAS, EARL J. *New Comedies for Teenagers*. Plays, Inc., 1970. 12-up.

A good collection of plays. Most are one act plays that are royalty free. An excellent model for youngsters who would write in play form. A new experience in writing for many youngsters.

DORLIAE, PETER G. *Animals Mourn for Da Leopard*, ill. by Irein Wagboje. Bobbs, 1970. 10-up.

A delightful dish of West African folktales. Much about mores revealed in story.

FINGER, CHARLES J. *Tales from Silver Lands*. Doubleday, 1924. 10-up.

This near classic collection of folktales from Latin America provides lots of good reading and a good look at folktale technique. Young writers can use it as a model.

GREGORY, HORACE AND ZATURENSKA, MARY, comps. *The Silver Swan: Poems of Mystery and Romance*, ill. by Diana Bloomfield. Holt, 1966. 12–16.

A collection of poems for the more mature child. Excellent model for poetry writing.

JORDAN, JUNE. *Who Look at Me*, ill. with paintings. Crowell, 1969. 10-up.

Poems about the black experience in America. Illustrations are most effective. Excellent model for poetry using ethnic background as a genesis.

KOHN, BERNICE. *Secret Codes and Ciphers,* ill. by Frank Aloise. Prentice, 1968. 9–13.

> The differences between codes and ciphers is explained in a way that provides lots of fun for individuals and groups. An excellent source for studying communication. Children can make their own codes, and break the codes of their friends after reading this fine book.

McCORD, DAVID. *All Day Long: Fifty Rhymes of the Never Was and Always Is,* ill. by H. B. Kane. Little, 1966. 12–15.

> All childhood experiences are captured in this delightful collection of poetry. All contemporary and all delightful.

UCHIDA, YOSHIKO. *Samurai of Gold Hill.* Scribners, 1972. 10-up.

> A true account of the first Japanese in California. Set during the Gold Rush, these people came to the gold fields not for gold, but to raise silkworms. Well written and accurate.

SUMMARY

Children's literature is an invaluable tool in helping children develop with their language. As an aid in developing the listening skills, it is invaluable. The teacher who will read to students will find her time well spent. As an aid in developing speech, it likewise has great merit.

With the skills of reading, this literature for children finds its greatest niche. All teachers know that children who will read after they have been taught how to read is the real test of any reading program. A fine program with literature as an undergirding factor in reading is most viable.

Literature for children likewise can serve as a model for written language. Good books read orally to children, or silently by them, give children experiences with our language that can serve as a genesis for their own writing.

Selected Readings: Children's Literature

ANDERSON, VERA. *Reading and Young Children.* New York: The Macmillan Co., 1968.

ARBUTHNOT, MAY HILL, and SUTHERLAND, ZENA. *Children and Books.* 4th ed. Glenview, Ill.: Scott, Foresman and Company, 1972.

BECHTEL, LOUISE SEAMAN. *Books in Search of Children.* New York: The Macmillan Co., 1969.

CHAMBERS, DEWEY W. *Children's Literature in the Curriculum.* Chicago, Ill.: Rand-McNally & Co., 1971.

FADER, DANIEL N., and McNEIL, ELTON B. *Hooked on Books: Program and Proof.* New York: G. P. Putnam's Sons, 1968.

FRANK, FOSETTE. *Your Child's Reading Today.* Rev. ed. New York: Doubleday & Co., Inc., 1969.

HAVILAND, VIRGINIA. *Children's Literature: A Guide to Reference Sources.* Washington, D. C.: Library of Congress, 1966.

HAZARD, PAUL. *Books, Children and Men*. 4th ed. Trans. by Marguerite Mitchell. Boston: The Horn Book, Inc., 1960.

HOPKINS, LEE BENNETT. *Books Are by People*. New York: Citation Press, 1969.

HUCK, CHARLOTTE S., and KUHN, DORIS YOUNG. *Children's Literature in the Elementary School*. New York: Holt, Rinehart & Winston, Inc., 1968.

JOHNSON, EDNA et al. *Anthology of Children's Literature*. 4th ed. New York: Houghton Mifflin Co., 1970.

LAMB, POSE, ed. *Children's Literature Series*. Dubuque, Ia.: William C. Brown Company Publishers, 1970.

LANES, SELMA G. *Down the Rabbit Hole: Adventures and Misadventures in the Realm of Children's Literature*. New York: Atheneum Publishers, 1971.

LARRICK, NANCY. *A Teacher's Guide to Children's Books*. 3rd ed. Columbus, Ohio: Charles E. Merrill Publishing Co., 1960.

ROOT, SHELTON, ed. *Adventuring with Books*. New York: Citation Press, 1973.

ROBINSON, EVELYN ROSE. *Readings About Children's Literature*. New York: David McKay Co., Inc., 1966.

SMITH, JAMES STEEL. *A Critical Approach to Children's Literature*. New York: McGraw-Hill Book Company, Inc., 1967.

PART
SIX

A GLOSSARY OF
READING TERMS

Possibly no area of the curriculum of the public schools is more demanding of its instructors than the Language Arts. Specifically, the teacher of reading, the reading specialist, the consultant in reading, and/or the reading clinician is faced with a barrage of terminology which is esoteric in nature and must be specifically interpreted by the professional. This is not a static body of vocabulary, but is a continually growing entity.

It is with an awareness of the need for a glossary which covers current terms as well as the tried and proven terminology, that the authors have compiled this inclusive list for use by today's person in reading.

The terms are drawn from many sources: pure reading terms, psychological terms, neurological terms, and linguistic terms. The definitions have been kept as simple as possible to provide easy understanding and usage for the busy professional in his work in the area of reading instruction, reading remediation, and learning disabilities pertaining to reading success.

A GLOSSARY OF
READING TERMS

Ability grouping: a means of providing for the individual learning needs of children. These may be groups formed heterogeneously or homogeneously on the basis of intelligence, achievement, or reading-skills performance.

Abstract ability: the ability to identify and understand relationships. The ability to respond to abstract symbols and concepts as well as concrete objects.

Accelerator: a mechanical device which makes use of a line marker, shutter, or shadow to allow the reader to cover material at a specified rate—lines per minute, words per minute, etc. There are a number of such devices—Rateometers, Reading Pacers, Controlled Readers, Rate Controllers, Skimmers, and Reading Accelerators.

Accent: the emphasis or stress which is given to a particular syllable or syllables of a word which results in its standing out from other syllables of the word. Syllabic prominence resulting from the degree of stress or height of pitch used by the speaker.

Achievement age: a specific level of accomplishment of performance stated as an age at which such achievement is normally reached. Also referred to as *educational age*.

Achievement quotient: a term designating the ratio between accomplishment and mental maturity. This index of progress is computed by dividing the achievement age by the mental age and multiplying the quotient by one hundred. Hence, $\frac{AA}{MA} \times 100 = AQ$.

Acuity: the degree of sharpness of perception as related to vision, hearing, and/or other sensory responses.

Adaptive behavior: any response which aids the organism to meet the demands of his environment. This is accomplished by learning from past experiences and also by instigating new and more difficult situations.

Adjustment: the process by which modes of behavior are adapted to assist the individual to achieve a more satisfactory relationship within his personal or specific environment.

Adjustment inventory: an instrument for the self-assessment of an individual's identified personal and/or social maladjustments or problems.

363

Affect: the emotive quality or feeling tone; specifically, the dynamic quality of emotion.

Affix: a linguistic term designating a bound morpheme which may be found either preceding or following a base word; hence, prefixes and suffixes.

Age—developmental: the organismic age; a total of all the indices of age-equivalents which relate to functional rather than intellectual development patterns.

Age—entrance: the minimal, actual chronological age, which permits enrollment or entrance to school.

Age—mental: the age level equivalent of an individual's intellectual or mental maturity: MA.

Age—reading: a term which equates reading performance or ability to chronological years based on the scores from a standardized reading test; hence, a student reading as well as the average eight-year-old, is said to have a reading age of eight years despite what his actual chronological age might be.

Agraphia: a form of aphasia which is manifested by the individual being unable to encode his thoughts in written language symbols.

Allograph: the variant or positional forms of written symbols; a changing of the form of a letter because of its position in a word. An example is the combining of a and e as æ.

Allomorph: a differing form or variant of a morpheme (word), resulting from positional environment; hence, the forms of *be: am* with I, *are* with you, *art* with thou, and *is* with he, she, or it.

Allophone: the total members of a phoneme class. They are phonetically alike, and do not show contrasts in meaning or cause confusion in interpretation. For example, the [d] at the end of *seed* and the [d] at the end of *mind* are both allophones of the phoneme /d/. In linguistic usage, slanted lines are typically used to indicate phonemes, and brackets are used to indicate allophones.

Alphabet approach: an atomistic, or synthetic, methodology to beginning reading in which the individual letters of the alphabet are first learned with an associated sound; these are then combined with other letters, and finally words are developed. It has commonly been called "The ABC Method."

Alternate forms: equivalent forms of a particular standardized testing instrument which parallel each other so closely that comparable scores are reached by individuals or groups being measured by alternate forms of the evaluative test.

Ambilateral: the use of organs (eyes, ears, arms, legs) on either side of the body with equal facility.

Ambidexterity: the equal skill displayed by using either hand; proficiency in using both hands equally well.

Ambiocular: the ability to use both eyes independently at will and at the same time without normal fusion.

Analytic methodology: a method of teaching reading by using whole words or meaning segments; the use of a sight vocabulary approach which is holistic or global.

Anchoring—perceptual: in perceptualization, the response is determined by a frame of reference rather than by the qualities of an object itself. A somewhat indistinct item in a picture may be recognized as a particular object when perceived by the individual to have the properties of a specific entity.

Anecdotal record: an account frequently used in the school or clinic setting to record casually observed happenings and/or behavior which appears to the observer to have significance; a type of "diary" reporting of information.

Anomaly: anything that is irregular or deviates from the norm; an abnormality.

Anthology: selections from literature which have been extracted and formed into a collection which may be of a general nature or limited to a specific area; for example, humor, poetry, or a particular subject.

Antonym: a word having the opposite meaning of another. *Huge* is an antonym of *tiny*.

Anxiety: an affective condition resulting from a distressed state with a feeling of intense apprehension. This may be attached to some object or situation, or be free-floating.

Anxiety level: a term used to describe the intensity or degree of anxiety present at a given time or in a particular situation; a continuum gradient extending from very low intensity to extremely high level.

Apathy: indifference to, or lacking interest in, or emotion to, an object, person, or situation.

Aphasia: the inability or impairment of the ability to use language. It may be sensory—noncomprehensive; or it may be motor—inarticulation.

Approach tendencies: behavioral responses which show a favorable attitude—a moving toward—a learning task, an experience situation, or an object.

Aptitude: a natural or acquired ability or trait which may predict or indicate future success or achievement.

Aptitude test: a predictive instrument made up of items and tasks which have been found to correlate with scholastic achievement.

Articulation: the formation of speech sounds that involves production of words by means of the physical processes of utterance.

Articulator: any movable speech organ—the lips, tongue, jaws, throat.

Articulatory defects: various anomalies in producing speech; these may include distortions, omissions, or substitutions of phonemes which would normally be present after the maturation necessary to produce sounds.

Ascending letters: those letters such as *b, d, f, k, l* which, because they extend above the line in printing or writing, may serve as configuration clues in reading.

Aspirate: a sound requiring a certain intensity of air expulsion in order to pronounce it correctly; an unvoiced puff of air such as represented by the letter *h* and its variants.

Asemia: the lack of ability to use communication symbols such as figures, or words, whether verbal or nonverbal.

Association grouping: the formation of work or study groups on the basis of members feeling free to associate with one another by choice; a form of affiliation-need grouping.

Associative learning: a form of reintegration making use of the principle that events happening together tend to strengthen the response thus cued. It may occur between ideas, words, or stimulus and response.

Associative learning disability: a condition in which an individual exhibits difficulties in not only making associations between meanings and language representations, but also in retaining such expressions with their word forms. The condition may result from a variety of causes.

Asymbolia: a form of asemia in which the person is unable to understand or use a specific set of language symbols.

Atomistic methodology: a method of teaching reading which begins with small parts and builds toward whole words; hence, any method of decoding such as an alphabet approach, a phonic-linguistic approach. Sometimes called a synthetic method.

Attention span: a term used to describe the length of time, or the extent of the ability, a person can concentrate on a particular task. In reading, it is the limit of a reader's ability to read without distraction. Some experts prefer the term interest span.

Audience reading: an oral reading activity for which the reader has prepared to entertain, interest, and keep his audience listening as he reads with expression, intonation, and affect.

Auding: a neologism which describes a deep level of listening; it comprises not only hearing, but listening with comprehension and interpretation of spoken language.

Audiogram: the graphic record of a hearing test using the audiometer which shows auditory acuity expressed in decibels at specific frequencies of pure tone.

Auditory acuity: a term expressing the degree of hearing keenness or sensitivity; sometimes called the auditory threshold.

Auditory blending: the ability to recognize and synthesize separated sounds of a word in order to identify the word intended.

Auditory discrimination: the differentiation of speech sounds by detecting likenesses or differences in direction, rhythm, tone, or volume; the term also describes the ability to recognize not only the component sounds in a word, but to identify and reproduce their sequential order.

Auditory memory span: a term to specify the actual number of sounds, either words or digits, that a person is able to recall and repeat correctly after having heard them spoken once at a designated speed.

Augmented Roman Alphabet: a phonemic, forty-four symbol alphabet developed in England by Sir James Pitman to be used in beginning reading instruction. It makes use of all letters of the English alphabet except x and q and adds twenty new symbols. A more recent term is Intial Teaching Alphabet: i/t/a.

Auralize: to make use of the hearing sense in order to enhance the thought process or imaginative powers; a term which expresses—auralize : hearing = visualize : seeing.

Automaticity: a skill level in an area such as reading or writing in which symbols convey meaning to an optimum degree without the use of, or interference of, intermediate processes. Hence, reading at its highest level of efficiency is described as being a total visual process without the intermediary of vocalization or even auralization.

Automatization: when an act or process becomes so easily done that it is accomplished without effort, or conscious direction, it is said to be automatized, done automatically.

Automatized learning: instantaneous word recognition; learning has been accomplished at such a level that there is immediate response to the presented stimuli.

Avoidance tendencies: those behavioral responses which indicate a negative attitude—a retreating from—a learning situation, task, or an object.

Background experience: the total of experiences—ideational, linguistic, or object-based— that a person uses in approaching new learning situations. They may have been acquired either primarily or vicariously; and they may be conceptualized or remain as isolated entities.

Balanced reading program: a program of reading instruction in which all types of reading are included in the materials used—trade books, fiction and nonfiction, study materials, recreational reading, silent reading, and oral reading.

Basal age: a term used with the Binet test to designate the age level at which the testee is successful in answering all the items correctly.

Basal reader: a reading textbook which is part of a graded basic series. The program usually contains an accompanying workbook for students and a teacher's guidebook or manual and is a developmental, progressive type of instruction.

Basal reader approach: a developmental reading program making use of a series of graded reading books which are arranged in sequential order of difficulty, skills, concepts, and/or vocabulary introduction. They are often developed with a teacher's manual and student's workbook or padbook.

Basic vocabulary: a term to describe the minimum number of words and expressions necessary for a user of any language.

Basic reading vocabulary: the requisite meaning and sight vocabulary for effective reading in all subjects and areas; it is normally taught systematically throughout the basal reader used.

Basic sight vocabulary: a list of most frequently used words which is taught and recognized from memory without using analytic clues or unlocking signals.

Basic study skills: those skills necessary to success in mastering a subject area or a learning situation—note-taking, outlining, skimming, scanning, summarizing, using reference tools.

Behavior: the person's conduct, manner, demeanor, and/or reactions which result from objective stimuli as well as subjective factors.

Behavioral objectives: a teaching or instructional goal which influences the student to become different in some way from what he was before instruction took place; an educational outcome which is expected to become performable—hence, observable and measurable—after instruction takes place.

Bibliotherapy: the use of selected books or readings for improving attitudes and behavior of those who may be emotionally or mentally disturbed; the use of reading for therapy—promoting emotional and mental health.

Bilingual: being able to speak two languages with about equal facility; having learned two languages at about the same time; having two "mother tongues."

Binaural: a term describing the functioning of both ears together.

Binocular: the use of both eyes together; vision fusion at near and far points.

Blend: the fusing of letter sounds in such a way that neither identifiable letter sound is lost. The blend may be formed by two or more consonants such as *br, pl, str,* or by a combining of consonants and vowels such as *bri* in bright, or *mi* in mitt.

Bookmobile: a traveling library which is housed in some form of a bus or truck and brings its services to accessible areas; sometimes referred to as auto-library, book car.

Breve: a diacritical marking ˘ which is placed above a vowel to indicate the short sound for pronunciation.

Cadence: the flow of oral language as the voice rises and falls with louder and softer syllables; rhythm and meter are produced with accent and pause.

Caldecott Award: an annual award given to a children's picture book illustrator for excellence in artistry as judged an outstanding contribution by a panel of experts. The Award was begun in 1937 by Frederic G. Melcher in cooperation with the American Library Association.

Call numbers: the symbols, letters and numbers, appearing on the spine of a book to designate its position and category for library shelving.

Cancellation test: a technique used in many reading readiness tests; the crossing out of any unlike symbols included with others of like nature.

Card catalogue: a filing system used in libraries to catalog on individual entry cards the holdings of the collection; author, title, and subject cards are interfiled alphabetically in the index.

Card-sorting test: a task examination in which the subject is required to sort numerous cards into like groups according to the symbols, words, pictures, and such inscribed on them.

Case study: the collection of all pertinent data on a particular subject—family information, health records, educational reports—anything which may be helpful in making a proper diagnosis and prescription of a case.

Central dominance: a term describing activity control by the brain, one hemisphere being consistently dominant. If there is confusion in the control, an indication of neurological impairment or damage is present. In order to measure central dominance, the subject is given unfamiliar situations for performance assessment.

Chart stories: teacher-pupil stories developed in a language experience setting and written on sheets of large chart paper to be read and reviewed in the reading instruction. Sometimes chart stories are provided with the basal readers and provide another avenue of program to the student.

Checklist: an informal diagnostic device to list specific strengths or weaknesses of the reader; these can be checked either positively or negatively and provide a simple view of the instructional needs.

Choral reading: a recitative or oral reading activity which makes use of a total class or group in a voice choir situation. Often a poem with a repetitive refrain is used, and solo parts, dialogue responses, and a chorus are assigned. Antiphonal oral arrangements can also be used effectively in this group activity.

Chronological age: the actual life span of a person; the number of years, months, and days he has lived. This term may be contrasted with others—mental age, organismic age, carpal age. It is often written CA.

Cloze procedure: a measurement process involving the deletion of words from a selection. The blank spaces thus provided are to be filled in correctly and rated accordingly. The technique is used in determining readability level, practice work, and testing reading ability.

Code: a linguistic term to designate the symbol system for recording a language. Hence, encoding to put into the system; and decoding to interpret the system.

Coding: the process involving the translation of signals into a message; it can involve either encoding or decoding, or both; hence, reading and writing can be coding.

Cognition: the act of becoming aware of objects or knowledgeable of them; the process involves sensing and includes such components as recognizing, perceiving, evaluating, and reasoning.

Colloquial speech: expressions characteristic of, and appropriate to, informal, spoken language as contrasted to the more formal, literary language.

Communication: the manner of giving and receiving messages (information, ideas, responses, etc.), by means of words, symbols, signals, and/or signs. The transmission may be immediate, through direct contact; or it may be delayed, through the use of graphic or electronic symbolization.

Comprehension: one facet of the reading process by which correct association is made between meanings and word symbols. Passive reception of fact has been coupled with creative understanding (pondering, questioning, speculating, etc.) to give the fuller meaning to the term.

Comprehension level: the highest level of understanding at which an individual functions in response to either oral or written language; the maximum difficulty of the material to which he is able to respond.

Comprehension test: a reading test designed to measure or assess the reader's ability to gain information from passages read. The testee is usually required to answer certain questions about the material covered.

Concept: a cognitive structure in which the person is aware of an object and is able to attach meaning and significance to it as distinct from other objects or things; an interpretive act, affected by the total of the person's experiential gestalt, which results from many percepts. Hence, a concept formation entails forming generalizations of the properties of objects or ideas which may be representative of other like entities.

Concept load: a measure of the difficulty level of reading material which includes (1) the number of new concepts included in the passage, (2) the difficulty of the ideas included in the material, and (3) the complexity of the organization of the concepts themselves. It is sometimes referred to as the *concept burden.*

Concepts: the generalized meanings formed by a fabric of percepts which are represented by language symbols—names, terms, words. In the perceptualization process, raw responses are organized and assimilated by generalizing and abstracting into interpretational systems by the individual.

Configuration clues: a word recognition, or unlocking aid, which makes use of the general length and shape pattern of a written or printed word. The ascending and descending letters are also important clues in "boxing" in the word.

Confirmation: a principle of learning in which the learner having an expectation finds it fulfilled through certain behavior; when a child expects to learn to read, confirmation takes place when his efforts meet the expected goal.

Consonant: literally a speech sound which is formed when there is an obstructing of the breath expelled during speech. And graphic symbol representing a sound which is not a vowel.

Consonant blend: the combined sound produced by the fusion of two or more consonant sounds in a word. The basic sound of each letter is retained.

Consonant digraph: a combination of two consonants in which they each lose their basic sounds and a single new sound is formed—*th* as in think, or *sh* in shoe.

Consonant-vowel blend: a blend sound composed of one or more consonants and a vowel. Both sounds are fused without either being altered—*fo* as in fog.

Consultant: a reading specialist who acts in an advisory position with teachers and/or administrators in developing and arranging for special reading programs and for helping with specific reading problems.

Content analysis: an objective, quantitative, and systematic analysis of ideas or concepts in printed material; a descriptive process for examining materials for the presence or absence of the selected items of analysis.

Content word: a linguistic term which designates those morphemes which have a referential meaning and are sometimes called *full words;* words with semantic or lexical meaning as contrasted with grammatical or functional meanings. Examples: *house* or *man* vs *in* or *that.*

Context clues: an instructional aid to unlocking words—word recognition—in which the surrounding words, phrases, or the entire sentence are used to gain meaning from the material being read.

Context reader: a person who relies on the context clues in order to guess at new words because of his weakness in other areas of word-attack skills.

Controlled vocabulary: word lists composed of the listening and speaking vocabularies of children. These are introduced in a set rate and pattern in many lower-grade, basal reading programs or trade books.

Corrective reading: that program of corrective instruction so designed as to overcome reading retardation within the regular classroom.

Craig reader: a modified combination of controlled reader and tachistoscope using strip materials mounted in plastic. One of the mechanical aids used in many reading labs and/or remediation clinics.

Creative reading: a term sometimes used synonymously with "critical reading." However, the present term should be used to describe that level of reading which involves interpreting implied meanings, intuitive flashes of prediction, and varying shades of meaning; symbolic, indirectly stated.

Critical reading: a high-level comprehension skill in reading which involves the ability to determine truth from fiction, fact from fancy, authenticity from opinion, awareness of propaganda intent.

Cultural reading: that facet of reading instruction and function that purports and is designed to cultivate and improve reading interests and tastes. Reading for cultural background.

Curricular reading program: a teaching strategy developed to instruct students to read content subject matter in all areas of the academic curriculum.

Cursory reading: a rapid, scanning of reading materials in which the reader pays little or no attention to details. A gleaning of main ideas or facts.

Data sheet: a record form to be used for compiling a systematic account, or record of data pertinent to a particular case.

Decibel: a unit of measure on a logarithmic scale which measures and expresses the intensity of sound. Hence, hearing loss is described in terms of decibels.

Decoding: a popular term used in reading circles to describe an atomistic approach to the teaching of unlocking words; hence, phonic principles are a usual strategy for attacking words not known as sight vocabulary.

Defense mechanism: a descriptive term used to specify forms of behavior which are designed by an individual to protect himself by deceiving others. Some such characteristic behaviors include projection, withdrawal, rationalization, or attack.

Deficiency: lacking in quantity or quality; unable to perform because of innate abilities. A term denoting the absence of the basic mental abilities rather than a lack of standard function as in defective. The *deficient* reader is unable through inherent ability to perform satisfactorily.

Denotation: an antonym for connotation; the precise meaning of a word.

Descending letter: those letters which extend below the line in handwriting or printing. These are often noted in configuration clues in word attack.

Determiners: words whose function it is to mark nouns; that is, to signal that a noun is following. These are the Class I Forms in the Fries Classification System. Determiners may also be substituted for nouns, and the list includes such words as *a, an, any, each, either, every, neither, no, one, some, the, that, these, this, those, what, whatever, which, whichever.* Possessive pronouns are also determiners.

Developmental age: a measure combining all known age equivalents (weight, height, bone structure, maturational factors, controls) to describe development in terminology equated to age forms. Other terms used include social age, organismic age, and/or anatomical age.

Developmental reading: a descriptive term denoting reading instruction based on readiness for learning and the sequential teaching of the reading skills.

Developmental reading program: a program of reading instruction which is planned for both vertical and horizontal growth. It includes all the approaches, reading skills, and strategies that may help the individual student in progressing at his own success schedule. Such a program includes diagnosis of needs, corrective teaching, and remediation where necessary. It recognizes reading to be an integral part of, and a necessary skill for, the entire educational effort.

Dextrality: a term referring to the preference for use of the right side of the body; right-sidedness.

Diacritical mark: any of several specific symbols placed over letters of a word to guide in its pronunciation. Some decoding programs have been developed with such markings to aid the reader in word attack.

Diagnosis: in reading, diagnosis refers to the techniques by which one discovers and assesses both the strengths and weaknesses of the functioning of a person. This information is then used as a basis for more effective teaching.

Diagnosis—informal: any analysis, usually by the teacher or clinician, used to assess the performance of a reader and assess his needs, strengths, or weaknesses. Some form of checklist or anecdotal record is used to note areas for prescriptive teaching.

Diagnostic Reading Test: a form of test so designed as to aid in locating specific sources of the testee's difficulty in learning reading skills. It should give pertinent clues to direct in further guidance, instruction, and/or skills to be strengthened. Frequently the scores are converted to RGP (reading grade placement).

Dialect: the sectional, or local, modifications of a language whose distinguishing features include pronunciation, grammar, and vocabulary. Writing systems are not affected by the language variation.

Diary method: a type of observational recording which attempts to compile all the observed happenings during a specified time which relate to a particular subject; a very complete form of anecdotal record.

Dictionary skills: those functional skills necessary to successfully make use of dictionary information; spellings, word meanings, word usage, derivations, pronunciations, and/or synonyms, homonyms, and antonyms.

Digraph: the combining of two or more letters, either vowels or consonants, to form the representation of one speech sound; the *ea* in *meat* or the *gh* in *rough*.

Diphthong: two vowel sounds combined; beginning with the first and gliding smoothly into the next as in *boy* and *noise.*

Directed reading activity: a teaching strategy which is carried on at the student's instructional level of performance in order to extend and strengthen abilities. Traditionally it includes (1) purposive readiness activities, (2) silent reading, (3) some discussion or exchange to determine comprehension and vocabulary knowledge, (4) oral reading for specific information, and (5) some ongoing activities for culmination and/or evaluation.

Directional confusion: the reading disability consisting of reversals, substitutions, and regressions which result from a left-to-right disorientation.

Disability—reading: the nondevelopment or impairment of one or more skills which cause the total functioning of the student to become handicapped; hence, a disabled reader.

Disabled reader: a student so retarded in reading performance that his achievement is considerably below the level of expectancy consistent with his mental capacity.

Discrimination—auditory: the act of making distinctions between sounds; recognizing like and unlike sounds. In reading, the performing of hearing tasks, particularly as they relate to the recorded sounds represented by alphabetic letters or combinations.

Discrimination—visual: the process of detecting differences in visual symbols; likeness, differences. In learning to read, the child is frequently required to make more discrete discriminations as a prerequisite to success in decoding.

Dominance: a term referring to preference of usage whether manual, visual, or ocular, by an individual of one side of the body.

Dyslexia: a developmental dysfunction causing inability to read or recognize words; it is commonly called "word blindness."

Eclectic approach: in reading, any combination of reading approaches used in the instructional program—a basal reader plus self-selected materials or language experience.

Echolalia: a functional speech disorder in which the person involuntarily repeats a sentence or phrase of the last sentence of another speaker; also *echophrasia.*

Educational age: a term synonymous with achievement age or accomplishment age, which equates an individual's achievement score with the norm expected of his chronological age.

Encoding: translation of messages into a code; in reading, putting speech into graphic symbols—writing.

Enrichment program: a curriculum program designed to broaden and enhance learning experiences, and to extend the student's understanding of the instructional objectives. It is often developed for gifted students or accelerated programs.

Entrance age: the minimum designated age at which a student is permitted to enter a particular level of school. Often six is specified as the entrance age for first grade.

Entry word: the base words listed alphabetically in a dictionary. These are defined with pronunciation guides, and variant forms with inflectional endings provided. Synonym: root words.

Enunciate: to articulate words or word parts clearly and distinctly as a means of accurate speech.

Etiology: a term describing the origins or causal factors of a particular disorder. The etiology of reading disorders or disabilities might deal with such topics as physiological or psychological concommitments, intellectual factors, culture lag, deficient instruction.

Etymology: a branch of linguistics which deals with the origin and derivation of words. It is the history of a word from its first recorded usage, traced through its various modifications and transmissions into various languages. Thus its component parts are analyzed.

Evaluation: a process, based upon instructional objectives and student performance objectives, in which the worth and effectiveness of teaching and/or learning experiences are examined and appraised. Specific standards may also be the foundation of the assessment.

Expected placement: an assigned score, computed from combining such factors as mental age and chronological age, weighted at varying grade levels to estimate a student's anticipated achievement grade level.

Experience approach: a total, language-based, instructional program in reading in which the student(s) and teacher develop a written story from the experience of the child. This type of approach has been used with adults and has been called *organic reading*. In the school setting, it is commonly called the Language-Experience Approach.

Experience chart: a chart story developed by teacher and student in which the student(s) talk about and/or dictate a sequential report of some happening. By talking about, writing down, and then reading the story, the student is exposed to a multisensory reading experience based on his own language and interests.

Experiential background: that store of percepts and concepts derived from a person's cultural heritage, actual experience, family, environment, which give meaning to sensory stimuli. In reading, it is that fund of total experience which aids the reader to *bring meaning to* rather than *glean meaning from* the instructional media (printed symbols); the gestalt, or life space.

Experiential readiness: a term based on the premise that a certain level of experiences is necessary for the child to have an adequate store of percepts in order to be able to bring sufficient meaning to reading.

Eye dominance: a functional tendency to prefer or use one eye more than the other although the other may be capable of sight; eyedness.

Eye movement: a generic term to describe various reactions of the eye due to changes in the amount of innervation being delivered to the ocular muscles. It has been more specifically called by such terms as saccadic movement, eye pursuit, convergent action, and/or compensatory response. In reading, it deals with jerks, stops, fixations, regressions.

Eye span: in reading, the pauses or fixations that occur are effective as to the amount of material span-encompassed; the number of digits, letters, or words seen.

Families in reading: two meanings are included here. (1) Those combinations of letters which are sometimes taught as an aid in word recognition—the *en* in *men, Ben, ten,* and (2) any group of rhyming words which contain a like element—*bat, cat, fat, gat,* etc.

Far-point fusion: the ability of the eyes to function together in binocular vision so that a single perception follows. Although both eyes function and view the object slightly different so that the retinal image varies somewhat, the normal response is characterized by one clear image.

Fiction: that type of literature, usually prose, which is based on imaginative happenings and narration.

Figure-ground: a perceptive principle in which certain figures and their backgrounds are mutually indistinct; certain visual perception tests make use of this general property to evaluate ability to discriminate the unity of the figure(s) from the surrounding area.

Figures of speech: those devices which specifically make use of figurative language; apostrophe, hyperbole, metaphor, paradox, personification, and simile all make use of the device.

Final positions: when specific letters are used at the end of words, they are said to be in the terminal, or final, position.

Finger writing: a type of kinesthetic activity in which the child uses his finger instead of a pencil to make image writing on large sheets of paper or desk top, or even in the air. *Finger spelling* is sometimes used in the same fashion.

Fixations: those brief, momentary stops or pauses in saccadic movement, which are part of the reading act. That brief time when central vision occurs with the image falling upon the fovea.

Flash cards: a teaching device making use of small cards on which individual letters, clusters, words, or phrases have been printed or written. They are used for giving the student a quick exposure to which he is to respond in rapid succession as he recognizes the cue.

Flexibility: in reading, the term is used to denote an approach in which various rates and styles are introduced as they are considered appropriate to the purpose of the reading, and the degree of difficulty or nature of the material being used.

Fluency: in reading, a term used to denote an easy smoothness of speech in oral reading; it is used also to characterize the same quality in speech and writing skills.

Follow-up activity: in reading, the term refers to any activity which is intended to reinforce the skill or learning which was introduced in the directed teaching section of the lesson. The activity may be designed to provide additional practice in the skill, to clarify or enlarge the concept being examined, to supply additional experience in a content area.

Form class words: some linguists distinguish four grammatical groups. Each is denoted by characteristic markers as follows:

Group 1: (Nouns) Includes all words whose plural forms are obtained by adding the grapheme *s*.

Group 2: (Verbs) Includes all words which add such endings as *s, ed, en, ing*.

Group 3: (Adjectives) Includes those words adding *er* and *est* to form their comparatives and superlatives.

Group 4: (Adverbs) Includes those words formed by adding *ly*.

Frustration load: a reading level on which the student's abilities function with word recognition at 90 percent or below, and comprehension is 50 percent or less. The reader will frequently indicate his difficulty by such overt signals as anxiety symptoms, tension motions, and vocalization. It is an indicator to the teacher for selecting easier material for instructional reading.

Function words: those having very little or no lexical or semantic meaning, but which do carry grammatical or structural meaning. They are in closed classes in contrast to form class words. Conjunctions, modal auxiliaries, nondeterminers, and prepositions are examples of function words.

Generalization: a judgmental application of data gathered from a sample to include a whole class; hence, in reading, phonic generalizations are induced by the student after seeing several like examples from which to make the judgment.

Geographic dialect: that variety of any language which is differentiated from any and all other varieties of that same language. The differentiating is due to any unique configuration of structure, pronunciation, and basic vocabulary. When the primary domain is geographical, the pattern is called geographic dialect.

Global methodology: that strand of instructional methodology in teaching reading in which a whole word, phrase, or sentence is the base of teaching. Sometimes referred to as an analytic, or holistic, method; hence, a sight word or language-experience approach to teaching reading.

Glossary: a listing at the conclusion of a work of the basic difficult, technical, or dialectic words and terms used by the author in his subject or field. These are included with definitions and/or explanations.

Goal-directed behavior: performance or action which is prompted by or directed toward obtaining an objective.

Graded materials—reader: instructional materials, often a basal reading program, that have been developed to be used at a particular ability level. The grading is due chiefly to the controlled introduction of vocabulary and the concept level and load of the material.

Grammar—functional: designates an approach to grammar which describes the "functional part"; for example, nouns are naming words, verbs are action words. It is a pedagogical premise based on the ideology that the teaching of grammar should result in eliminating errors in language usage.

Grammar—structural: a grammar employing a consistent, analytical method for describing a sample of a specific language. Unlike traditional grammar, it is nonprescriptive; unlike transformational grammar, it is nongenerative.

Grammar—traditional: this is the grammar commonly offered in the elementary and secondary textbooks and schools of the past century. It reflects very little of the results of research studies conducted through a like amount of time. There has been an emphasis on correct language usage, but little teaching of the actual language itself. Much of the terminology and the theory of the traditional grammar is still useful and valid. Likewise, a knowledge of these is valuable in understanding the transformational-generative grammar.

Grammar—transformational-generative: grammar that provides principles for generating sentences. This grammar begins with a stipulated starting point and proceeds in a controlled grammatical order by sequentially applying various rules for expanding the sentence. By thus following this order, one is able to develop correctly formed sentences. The result is the large number of known sentences extant in any language.

Grapheme: the written symbols which record the particular sounds of a language; the letter *s* which represents /s/ a phoneme. Orthography is the writing, in proper order, of graphemes to form morphemes.

Grouping: the placing of students into various classes, categories, or grades for the purpose of improved instruction or to make better provision for individual differences.

Haptic: a generic term covering those abilities and modalities dealing with kinesthetic and tactile channels of input and learning.

Hearing comprehension: the level at which a child can understand, with 75 percent accuracy, material that is read to him. When the child's oral vocabulary is commensurate with the hearing level, the potential instructional level for reading is indicated. A term often used to express *listening vocabulary.*

Holistic methodology: based on the idea of the importance of the entire being, rather than single functions of it, such an approach involves a gestalt approach to instruction. Thus the whole child is more than the sum of his parts, and meaningful wholes will be dealt with.

Homograph: those words which, though written alike, have multiple meanings or derivations; for example, *through* not only means finished, but also a going into and beyond.

Homonym: words which are different in spelling, meaning, and/or genesis, but are identical in sound; e.g., *rain, rein,* and *reign.*

Homophone: in American English, those groups or words which have like sounds, but different meanings. They are usually spelled differently: *be, bee; sun, son; some, sum; to, too, two.*

Ideogram: in some systems of writing, objects or ideas are represented by various symbols which picture the thought involved. Characters portraying ideas such as in hieroglyphics.

Independent reading level: a level of reading, with word recognition at 99 percent accuracy and comprehension at 90 percent accuracy, at which the child can function with no teacher assistance. Sometimes referred to as the child's *recreational reading level.*

Indirect teaching: instruction which does not appear to be striving toward an immediate objective, but is nevertheless linked to it by meaningful intervening sequences; thus in reading, the goal is to read, but one may teach it indirectly in other subject areas, or in indirect steps such as dictionary usage.

Informal inventory: in keeping a case history, the teacher or clinician frequently keeps some type of checklist which records the frequency of certain types of errors in the reading performance as observed by the teacher. Also certain weaknesses or tendencies may be recorded.

Informational reading: a term used interchangeably with *functional reading,* reading to gain understanding of factual content. This is "reading to learn."

Initial consonant position: the beginning consonant, or consonant sound, of a particular word. Many reading experts believe these to be the most important clues to word recognition.

Instructional level—reading: that level of reading in which the student, making use of teacher guidance and aid, can function adequately with word recognition at a 95 percent accuracy level and comprehension at 75 percent accuracy.

Interest: an awareness that something—object or happening—has importance for an individual, that it matters to him. Hence, there is an attitude of attention resultant.

Interest inventory: a device used in assessing personality in which questions are asked that concern preferences, interests, activities, or things liked by an individual.

I.Q. (intelligence quotient): a measure of the level of mental growth or maturity which is computed by dividing the mental age of an individual by his chronological age and multiplying the quotient by 100; a measure of intellectual brightness.

ITA or **i/t/a:** sometimes referred to as the Augmented Roman Alphabet. A forty-four-symbol, phonemic alphabet developed by Sir James Pitman in England. It makes use of all of the English traditional orthographic symbols but *x* and *q* and adds twenty others in an attempt to simplify beginning reading and writing.

Joplin Plan: an administrative or scheduling program for implementing the reading program in which interclass grouping is used. Students from several grades may be grouped to form one group for reading instruction at their achievement level.

Juncture: in the flow of oral language sounds, certain pauses which indicate meaning. This may be to distinguish like words, to indicate phrases and clauses, or to specify the completion of sentences. Junctures have been described in four types by some linguists: plus juncture, single-bar juncture, double-bar juncture, and double-cross juncture. The plus (−) is open; the single bar (/), the double bar (//), and the double cross (#) are all terminal junctures.

Juvenile books: that segment of children's literature which has been specifically designed to meet the reading interests and tastes, as well as the reading ability, of adolescent youth.

Key sentence: often referred to as the topic sentence of a paragraph; the sentence giving the main thought or central idea. It may be found at the beginning, end, or within the paragraph.

Kinesthetic methodology: a tactile approach to the teaching of reading in which the student traces or forms the letters or words as a means of strengthening learning. Some clinicians use textured materials such as sandpaper to make letters which can be more clearly felt.

Kinesics: linguists use this term to designate all the nonlingual communications which accompany speech. The whole gamut of expressive actions which include bodily gestures; finger, hand, and arm signals; facial gestures such as leers, smiles, sneers, and winks; nods; nudges; and shrugs. These serve as attitudinal indicators.

Kinetic reversals: reading reversals in which the sequence of letters is reversed to form new words; for example, *saw* becomes *was* or *not* becomes *ton.*

Language arts: the branch of school learning experiences which emphasizes teaching the four communicative skills: intake—listening and reading, and output—speaking and writing. Writing covers such areas as spelling and handwriting, creative and expository writing.

Language-experience approach: an approach to the teaching of reading and writing which makes use of the child's own language and experiences. Sometimes referred to as the Organic-Reading approach.

Lateral confusion: when an individual shows a tendency to use a left-side preference for some acts and then shifts to the right for another type of activity. It is also used for shifting from side to side for the same activity.

Lateral dominance: the better performance resulting from the use of one side of the body in certain actions and thought to be based on cerebral dominance; the consistent use of either right-dominance or left-dominance. Cross-dominance and mixed-dominance also occur.

Laterality: Preferential use of the foot, hand, or eye on one side of the body; hence, sidedness. Also the awareness of, and the ability to identify, left from right.

Learning modality: those input channels by which the organism is made aware of meaningful stimuli; hence, the aural modality, the visual modality, and/or the haptic modality. All of these are made use of in a multisensory approach to learning.

Level of expectation: the attitudinal desires of a leader which result in the individual's rising to that standard of expectancy. Hence, the teacher who thinks that his students can succeed enhances their performance.

Levels of meaning: the variations signified or connoted in use of a phrase or sentence as controlled by the level of grammatical structure. When it is difficult or impossible to distinguish between the levels of meaning, ambiguity is expressed.

Lexicography: a linguistic study of the variant meanings of the terminology and words of a particular language. Lexicography commonly refers also to the art or occupation of compiling dictionaries.

Linguist: a student who has been scientifically trained to study the field of human languages. Two branches have been identified as follows: (1) the *descriptive linguist*, whose prime interest is to describe and record the significant characteristics or features of the languages of the world; and (2) the *historical linguist*, who is chiefly concerned with discovering and outlining the origins and developmental patterns of individual words, sentence structures, dialects, and languages.

Linguistics: the scientific study of human speech or language, its modifications, nature, and structures. Varied factors are included in this science. They include accent, general or philosophical grammar, morphology, phonetics, phonology, semantics, syntax, and relevant relationships between speech and writing.

Macron: a straight line placed over the vowels as a pronunciation guide to signify the long sounds they record.

Maturation: the sequence of developmental steps which take place in the normal organism when the environmental milieu is conducive to such growth changes. Some forces may modify the development or guide it into specified areas. Education and reading are two such factors.

Medial positioning: the placing of a sound or sound cluster within the word or word-group unit. The noninitial and nonterminal positioning of such sounds.

Memory span: the total number of letters, digits, pictures, or words that a person is able to correctly recall after having heard them once at a measured rate, or having them presented visually. It is measured assessment of the amount of material the individual can grasp and retain from one presentation.

Mental age: the level of intellectual development as it relates to the average attainment of children of the same chronological age.

Mental maturity: a measure of the level of intellectual growth at any given chronological age; the intelligence quotient.

Methodology: in education, the term refers to that branch of pedagogy which is concerned with the analyzing and evaluating of curriculum and teaching strategy. In reading instruction, there are two strands of methodology: global and atomistic.

Milieu: the physical or social environment of a being.

Mimetic behavior: a copying or imitating of another's behavior, or of a model.

Mirror reading: a function in which the person sees words or material in reverse order; that is, in a right to left sequence. Such reversals might be *nit* for *tin*, *pot* for *top*.

Mirror reversal: in the reading situation, that type of reversal which views single letters, portions of words, whole words, and sometimes the entire line of writing in reverse positions; hence, *b* becomes *d*, *but* becomes *tub*.

Mixed-dominance: a condition involving nonconsistent lateral dominance; it may take the form of mixed-hand dominance, mixed-eye dominance, or of cross-dominance.

Modality: in learning, the term refers to the channel of communication input; hence, the visual modality, the aural modality, or the haptic modality. The use of sense channels for response to the appropriate stimuli.

Morpheme: the minimal meaning unit of a language. It consists of some phonemes, or combinations of phonemes, and may be described as *"free"* (e.g., ear, hare) or *"bound"* (e.g., pro-, -est). It is indivisible without violating its meaning or remainders.

Motivation: activating incentives, either or both intrinsic and extrinsic, inherent or acquired, which result in the initiation and sustaining of a particular action or activity.

Multisensory approach: in reading a teaching approach making use of several sensory modalities; a combination of visual, aural, and/or haptic approaches.

Near-point fusion: the closest dimension at which both eyes can simultaneously function without double vision.

Nonliterate: referring to any society or cultural group who do not have a written form of language.

Nonreader: an individual who has had normal instruction, and is yet unable to read with sufficient skill to function adequately in his society. A reader so disabled that he will not be able to function in a normal classroom, but will require specialized instruction in corrective and/or remedial reading.

Nonsense syllables or words: contrived or artificial combinations of letters to provide pronounceable elements to be used in practicing phonics principles or word attack skills; not words in the known language of the reader.

Objective—behavioral: a measurable, observable performance which results from instruction; the performance of a student which the teacher sees as a desirable outcome from learning.

Objective—instructional or teaching: the aim or goal from any particular lesson or unit of work that the instructor sees as important in the learning sequence or developmental pattern.

Observational methodology: techniques used by the clinician (observer) to aid him in making accurate and adequate observations; these may include graphs, charts, checklists, recordings.

Oral reading: a teaching strategy which makes use of oral reading for diagnostic purposes as well as for developing speech skills dealing with expression, interpretation, and audience performance.

Organismic age: a term used to designate a developmental level which compiles the average scores of mental, physiological, and anatomical age. It is based upon the assumption that there is a systemic relationship between the function and the structure of the human organism. This concept is used by some reading specialists to arrive at or define the optimal age for reading readiness.

Paradigm: an example, frame, model, or pattern showing the total of the various forms of a word.

Percept: in reading, the term may be defined as the organism's response to a single stimulus, the primary response to what one perceived. The picture on the word card is the percept and is interpreted in the light of the experiential background.

Perception: the set of processes by which an organism is able to organize his experiences into a response; an interpretative response to sensory stimuli. Awareness, discrimination, and sensation are components of the process of perception.

Perceptual—conceptual process: reading is said to be a perceptual-conceptual process; that process by which the reader combines and organizes sensory elements into a unity based on his store of experiences as he views them.

Performance test: a measurement device for determining functional intelligence level which requires the testee to use and manipulate physical objects in order to test his manual and physical skills rather than language skills requiring oral and/or written responses.

Phoneme: the minimal unit of sound which signifies meaning, or which provides the smallest unit of contrast in paired words such as *pit* vs. *pat, put* vs. *pot.*

Phonemic language: a descriptive term referring to a language which makes use of one grapheme for each phoneme; a language having a one-to-one ratio of letters and sounds; a single letter consistently recording one sound. i/t/a can be called a phonemic alphabet.

Phonetic analysis: an instructional device for teaching word recognition which analyzes words according to the speech sounds which they contain—consonants, vowels, blends, digraphs, diphthongs.

Phonic family: a group of like-sounding, or rhyming, words which contain certain word elements which are identical; for example, *fun, bun, run, dun.* Sometimes called *word family.*

Phonogram: a single character or symbol which represents an entire word, a syllable, or phoneme; also a succession of written symbols which combine with the same phonetic value in a number of words; for example, *ice,* in nice, rice, trice.

Phrase reading: a form of reading instruction which emphasizes practice in "seeing" an entire phrase at one fixation rather than the more laborious word-by-word reading.

Pictorial test: a form of test in which pictures are substituted or used for verbal or graphic materials.

Picture arrangement test: a test situation using a set of pictures which can be arranged in sequence to tell a simple story.

Picture books: a book designed primarily for young children and composed almost completely of pictures rather than written text. It is particularly leveled for the interest and needs of early learners.

Picture clues: illustrations and pictures used in reading material which furnish the reader with clues to word meanings, story action, and word recognition.

Picture reading: in some readiness programs, the use of sequential pictures illustrating a story to aid the young "reader" in recalling events to tell a story; the use of pictures before a student has learned graphic symbols.

Power test: a testing instrument in which the content is arranged sequentially in increasingly difficult steps in order to measure the strength of performance rather than speed in responding.

Profile chart-reading: a chart representing the subject's profile of proficiencies and/or deficiencies in relation to a normal position of expectancy for several reading skills such as word recognition, vocabulary, speed.

Programmed approach-reading: a highly structured, sequential system of self-instruction in reading. The student is provided material in small increments, then frequent questions to be answered, followed by the correct answers for immediate reinforcement of the learning. The material increases in difficulty in a developmental task sort of progression.

Progress chart: a graphic recording of student progress in reading skills such as word recognition, comprehension, speed, and vocabulary learning in order to serve as an activating device, the student competing with himself.

Raw score: the original score obtained from a test before it has been treated by any statistical process, sometimes referred to as an *original* or *crude* score.

Readability: that quality of reading material that refers to its level of difficulty as based on vocabulary load, sentence structure, concept load. Numerous readability scales and formulas have been devised to measure the readability of a given selection.

Readability formula: an objective, scientific method of measuring the difficulty (or readability) of reading material. Such formulas are usually concerned with vocabulary load, structure of words, sentence length and composition.

Readability level: an expected reading level computed by using a readability formula on a particular reading material in order to indicate its level of difficulty and grade level at which it should be used.

Reading: a complex thinking process involving meaning and printed symbols. The process is multifaceted, and involves those skills and abilities necessary to bring meaning *into* the situation as well as to derive meaning *from* the act.

Reading age: a measured score of the level of reading ability of a student expressed in terms of an age. It is based on his performance on a normal reading test. If he reads as well as a typical eight-year-old, he is said to have a reading age of eight, despite his chronological age.

Reading readiness: a term pertaining to the necessary level of preparedness for formal reading instruction. Such factors as chronological age, intellectual maturity, health, vision, hearing, and experiential background are normally considered. Reading

Readiness Programs include numerous tasks thought to be helpful in developing the level deemed desirable.

Rebus story: an instructional device in which certain words are left out of a story and pictures are used in place of the words.

Recognition—word: the ability to name words; sight vocabulary and/or the ability to "read" words.

Recreational reading: reading activities specifically scheduled or designed to provide the student with entertainment, enjoyment, pleasure, or appreciation from reading.

Recreational reading level: an independent level of reading in which the student is able to read easily and fluently with no aid.

Reference books: informational books used for enrichment or expansion; additional textbooks, atlases, encyclopedias, dictionaries.

Regression: in reading, those brief right-to-left, backward movements for rereading or further examination of words or material already covered.

Remedial reading program: a prescriptive instructional program systematically followed by a trained specialist in an effort to help a disabled reader. The teaching is done individually or in small groups outside a regular classroom setting.

Remediation—reading: the individual diagnosing and prescribing instruction directed to correct specific needs and/or deficiencies. Such remedial effort is usually undertaken by specialists outside the regular classroom teaching and setting. Since the student is disabled to a degree that he is unable to function successfully in the classroom, such remediation is normally done in a reading clinic.

Reversals: reading performance in which the person reverses letters, parts of words, or words due to disorientation in the prescribed left to right progression of English. *Kinetic* reversals involve perceptual confusion in words (ton for not), and *static* reversals involve single letters (q for p).

Root word: the basic semantic vehicle for expressing a given concept or idea of a language; a meaningful morpheme from which other words are formed by adding inflectional endings, prefixes, or suffixes. Synonyms: *base word, kernel word, stem.*

Running words: a total count of all consecutive words in a reading selection, article, or book; each word or form is counted separately even though repeated, as opposed to different words which would exclude all word repetitions.

Schwa: an indistinct vowel sound occurring in an unaccented syllable and recording the approximated sound of "*uh*" as represented in phonetic script by the inverted *e*. The term itself was borrowed from Hebrew phonetics.

Self-selected reading program: an individualized reading program using self-selected reading materials.

Sentence: the grammatical arrangement of words combining a noun phrase, or subject, with a verb phrase, or predicate, to form a simple sentence. In speech, the sentence is commonly denoted by varying intonations; and in writing, the sentence is marked by conventional punctuation. The linguists avoid using a delineation which indicates that a sentence is that which conveys a complete sense unit, since this tells little of sentence structure.

Sight reading: oral reading in a spontaneous situation when the material has not been previewed or previously read.

Sight vocabulary: those words which the reader instantly recognizes without having to analyze or use unlocking clues.

Sight word: any word which must be learned without any structural or phonic clues; one recognized immediately by its configuration as a whole.

Sight vocabulary approach: an instructional approach to reading in which whole words are introduced without making use of any word analysis of letters, syllables, and such. This has often been referred to as *Look and Say Reading*.

Sinistrality: left-sided performances of the hand, foot, or eye.

Skimming: a rapid general reading of material to discover specific topics or the whole tenor of the passage.

Snellen chart: a printed card used in measuring and testing visual acuity at a distance of twenty feet; hence 20/20 vision is that which a person with normal sight should be able to distinguish at a twenty-foot distance.

Sociodrama: a type of social role-playing in which socially acceptable behavior is taught.

Sociogram: the charted responses of a group to questions which reveal their likes, dislikes, preferences. It is a device used to graphically portray the relationships existing among individuals in a group or class.

Speaking vocabulary: the total number of different words a person can correctly use in his oral speech. He may be able to get meaning from other words when listening or reading, but not be able to use them in his own speech. This often becomes the basis for vocabulary control at various levels in basal readers.

Speed reading: an instructional program designed to greatly accelerate the rate of reading, particularly among adults. Various skimming devices, accelerating devices (reading pacers, tachistoscopic machines), and techniques for covering more materials are used.

Staggered-day approach: an administrative scheduling of reading to allow half the students to arrive an hour earlier in the morning for reading instruction, and the remainder to stay an hour later in the afternoon for their reading period.

Stimulus: anything which impinges upon the sense organs of the organism; hence aural, visual, and haptic stimuli are important in reading instruction.

Stress: the degree of emphasis or prominence a syllable or sound receives. It is an important agent for meaning-bearing in speech when it is combined with *pitch*. Four levels of stress are usually specified by linguists.
1. Primary stress which is indicated with ╱.
2. Secondary stress usually indicated by ∧.
3. Tertiary stress is shown by ╲.
4. Weak stress is often indicated by the symbol ∪, but sometimes a symbol is omitted to signify this level.

Structural analysis: an instructional technique, and a word-unlocking tool, which analyzes words according to their component parts—affixes, roots, compounds, syllables.

Study skills: those essential reading skills for educational success—skimming, scanning, summarizing, note-taking, outlining, map reading, and using reference tools.

Substitution(s): a reading error in which the person uses another word in place of one not correctly recognized. Oral reading allows the instructor to detect such errors easily. Sometimes only the beginning consonant is substituted to form a word similar to the one presented—*took* for *look*.

Subvocal reading: an immature level of reading performance in which the reader moves his lips, tongue, or throat muscles slightly during silent reading activities, signifying that he is "saying" the words to himself and thus slowing down his reading rate.

Sweep: the lateral or return movement of the eyes when one line of type is finished and the eyes swing back to the beginning of the next line.

Syllabication, syllabification, or syllabizing: three interchangeable terms which describe or refer to the process of dividing words into, or forming separate syllables from, words being analyzed; identifying syllabic patterns.

Syllable: a speech unit made of a single vowel sound, or with consonant sounds; the syllable is open if ending in a vowel, closed if ending with a consonant.

Synthetic approach to reading: an atomistic methodology of teaching reading from parts to wholes; hence, an alphabetic or phonic approach.

Tactile-kinesthetic: a combination of sense stimuli from touching or tracing or writing words or symbols as an additional input modality for learning to read.

Talking-books: a book which has been recorded on magnetic tape or phonograph record and is used in a listening situation to stimulate or strengthen reading.

Terminal position: in learning consonant sounds, the student is taught the various positions in which the letter may be placed—beginning (initial), middle (medial), and end (terminal).

Topic sentence: the key sentence in a paragraph; it gives the central idea or main thought. Usually it is the beginning sentence, but it may be found embedded in the paragraph or a summary sentence at the end.

Trade books: books which are written and marketed for the general public through bookstores and/or libraries; they are to be distinguished from textbooks or specialized books.

Transfer: learning transfer occurs when the existence of a previously learned behavior affects the learning of a new or related behavior; it is the application of previous learnings to current problems.

Ungraded class: a small class of special students who need considerable individual attention within the group setting.

Unvoiced sounds: a speech sound formed by breath without vibration of the vocal cord.

VAKT: a technique for word-learning which emphasizes the visual, auditory, kinesthetic, and tactile stimuli in a multisensory instructional setting. The student *sees* a word, *hears* others pronounce it and pronounces it himself, *writes* the word, and *traces* it.

Validity: the coefficient of correlation between criterion and test scores, or the degree to which an instrument for testing actually fulfills what it purports to test; face validity. A reading test is valid if it measures reading ability.

Verbal test: any test which is composed of tasks involving language manipulation (either oral or written). Both group and individual tests of intellect and achievement use such items.

Visual acuity: sharpness and clarity of vision which measures 20/20 vision; reading at twenty feet what a normal eye can read at that same distance.

Visual discrimination: the reader's ability to see likenesses and differences, comparisons and contrasts, in visual patterns. The ability involves discriminating between gross patterns (geometric forms and pictures), and discriminating between more discrete forms (words and individual letters).

Vocabulary: the total word list of an individual. Reading people usually combine four facets to make the totality—listening, speaking, reading, and writing vocabularies.

Vocabulary load: in reading, the number of different words or meanings which are included in a particular passage; frequently the number of new words introduced.

Voiced consonants: consonant sounds produced by vibration of the vocal cords.

Vowel: speech sound which is produced with the air passing unobstructedly through the oral cavity and with vibration of the vocal cords; also the letters *a, e, i, o, u,* and *w, y,* in some usages.

Vowel cluster: a linguistic term for a vowel diphthong.

Vowel digraph: the combining of two vowels to make one speech sound—*oa* as in *coat, ea* as in *heat.*

Whole word approach: a global or analytical method of teaching reading using whole words; a sight vocabulary approach.

Word(s): any segment of speech indivisible wholly into a smaller free form. The linguist uses the terms "a simple word" to designate a word consisting of no more than two segmental morphemes, and "complex words" to describe words which are formed from two bound morphemes, a base and a superfix.

Word analysis: an unlocking device for the reader using the structural or phonetic clues to recognize words; word attack by using sound or meaning clues.

Word attack: the utilizing of all skills in order to recognize and master new words—using context clues, initial sight words, pictorial clues, phonics generalizations.

Word calling: the pronouncing of words in reading with no evidence of an associated meaning being present; also a halting word-by-word manner of reading.

Word configuration clues: use of the distinctive form or shape of words to facilitate reading—length, ascending letters, descending letters.

Word count: a frequently used process for controlling the vocabulary load of graded reading materials or basal readers; an analysis of the number of times words appear in a specified number of running words.

Word families: a group of words which contain a like element that causes them to rhyme—*ban, can, Dan, fan, man, Nan.* Some "linguistic" programs use such groups in teaching basic sight vocabulary.

Word recognition: the ability to associate printed words with the meaning and oral language sounds for which they stand; a method of word attack.

Word wheel: a teaching technique making use of a wheel which exposes parts of elements of words in an attempt to develop sight vocabulary; a repetitive device for teaching word analysis.

Write-as-you-say approach: a form of VAKT combining visual, auditory, and haptic reinforcement in learning to read; a multisensory approach to reading instruction.

Writing vocabulary: the words which an individual is able to use correctly in written expression; this involves spelling and syntax as well as knowledge of the basic words.

INDEX